Praise for *Castro's Final Hour*

"Oppenheimer's book reads like a thriller. Carefully researched, it describes the last throes of the Cuban dictatorship."

—Mario Vargas Llosa

"A wonderfully subtle and informed account."

—*Newsday*

"An extraordinarily deft, comprehensive and intimate account. . . . Oppenheimer's investigative work, delivered in wise and lucid prose, is invaluable . . ."

—*Los Angeles Times*

"In careful, readable prose laced with wit and insight, the *Miami Herald* Pulitzer Prize–winning senior foreign correspondent shows us individual, likable Cubans in full paradox . . . A very good read."

—*The Washington Post*

"Oppenheimer was exhaustive in his research . . . His reporting is solid and engrossing . . ."

—*Time*

"An important new book . . . *Castro's Final Hour* provides the most comprehensive documentation yet that the disillusionment now extends deep into Cuba's elite itself."

—*Newsweek*

"Oppenheimer gives us the most remarkable insights into the waning days of Castro."

—Tad Szulc

"A must for anyone attempting to understand the island state that continues to swim against the tide."

—*Detroit Free Press*

"Gripping . . . superb, highly recommended book."

—*San Diego Union-Tribune*

"Mr. Oppenheimer succeeded in gaining access to official sources as well as dissidents. He offers the definitive account of the 1989 Ochoa–De La Guardia show trial . . ."

—*The New York Times*

Andres Oppenheimer

>>>

A TOUCHSTONE BOOK

Published by Simon & Schuster

New York ▲ *London* ▲ *Toronto*
Sydney ▲ *Tokyo* ▲ *Singapore*

CASTRO'S FINAL HOUR

>>>>>>>>>>>>>>>>>>>>>>>>>>>>>>

The Secret Story Behind the

Coming Downfall of

Communist Cuba

TOUCHSTONE
Rockefeller Center
1230 Avenue of the Americas
New York, New York 10020

Manufactured in the United States of America

10 9 8 7 6 5 4 3 2 1

Library of Congress Cataloging-in-Publication Data
Oppenheimer, Andres, date.
Castro's final hour : the secret story behind the coming downfall
of communist Cuba | Andres Oppenheimer.—1st Touchstone ed.
p.   cm.
"A Touchstone book."
Includes bibliographical references and index.
1. Castro, Fidel, 1927– . 2. Cuba—Politics and
government—1959– . 3. Cuba—Social conditions—1959– . I. Title.
F1788.22.C3066 1993
972.9106'4—dc20   93-31433 CIP
ISBN 0-671-72873-3
ISBN 0-671-87299-0 (PBK)

For Marina and Tom

Contents

Note to the Reader

This book was completed at a time of major uncertainty in Cuba. By the time it reaches the reader, events may have shifted Cuba's political situation in any number of directions. Thus, this book does not attempt to predict how Fidel Castro will fall, or how long his final hour may stretch. It may be a matter of weeks or—like Winston Churchill's "finest hour," which lasted long beyond what everybody expected—a few years. Rather, this book intends to reveal the inside story of how Castro's Socialist revolution destroyed itself after the collapse of world communism.

From the outset, my goal was to focus on Cuba in the twilight of the Soviet bloc. I wanted to be in Cuba to record what the world already knew would be a devastating impact, and to see if the Castro revolution stood a chance of surviving without its Communist benefactors.

Most of the reporting for this book was done in Cuba. I made five trips to the island, averaging one month each, over a two-year period ending in December 1991. This, in itself, was a major accomplishment: very few mainstream U.S. journalists are allowed onto the island. When they are granted a visa, it is usually for a few days of carefully screened tours of the Castro revolution's achievements.

Thanks to the help of two Latin American friends—a former president and a well-known writer—the Cuban government authorized me to visit the country for extended periods of time and talk with top government officials.

I rented a car and moved freely throughout Cuba, and did so without visible impediments. Once or twice, I noticed I was being followed by secret police in Soviet-made Lada cars. But these were exceptional circumstances, mostly following interviews with dissidents, which did not hamper my research. I was warned by a senior official on my first reporting trip that I would not be allowed back if I was found spending time with dissidents. I saw Cuba's most prominent dissidents frequently anyway. Those interviews probably cost me a chance to spend several days traveling around the country with Fidel Castro—as sympathetic journalists are often allowed to do—but I found the trade-off worth its while. Few presidents speak more, and more often, than Fidel Castro—and few repeat their public speeches so often in private conversations.

The book is based on interviews with more than five hundred people in Cuba. Occasionally, when relating the comments of ordinary people on the street, I use only first names, to protect their identities. When I identify people who spoke out against Fidel Castro by their full names—such as Castro's daughter Alina or Che Guevara's grandson Canek—it is because they have allowed me to do so.

Most senior Cuban officials I interviewed—ministers, vice-ministers or members of the Communist Party Central Committee—are identified by their full names. Those who asked not to be identified I refer to as senior officials. My relationship with most Cuban officials was one of personal sympathy but political distrust. My accent-free Spanish—and the fact that I found some officials to be smart, well-meaning people—helped build bridges. The fact that I was not a fellow traveler, and never pretended to be one, ensured that there was distance between us.

I also traveled to Nicaragua, Panama and Mexico to research the chapters dealing with the fall of the Castro-backed regimes in Nicaragua and Panama. I talked with more than a dozen top officials in each place. In Nicaragua, I interviewed five of the nine Sandinista *comandantes*, including former President Daniel Ortega, but only four agreed to be quoted by name. The Sandinista *comandante* whom I quote without further identification is not necessarily one of the others who appear with full names.

In writing the book, I used direct quotes of conversations in closed-door meetings when at least one participant would recall what was said, or when there were official transcripts of the conversations. Only rarely, in cases where a participant at a meeting has since died, did I rely on the recollection of close associates who gained knowledge of the dialogue directly from that person. Likewise, when I say somebody "believed" or "thought" something, it is based on that person's account, unless noted otherwise. I have tried to give the source of each quote or opinion in a notes section at the back of the book.

Finally, a cautionary note. Castro's Cuba has long been the most hermetic society in the Western Hemisphere. Investigative reporting in Communist Cuba is a formidable task for a U.S. journalist, no matter how well he or she is liked. Under the Communist Party's policy of democratic centralism—the rule whereby everybody must toe the party line when talking to outsiders—history is constantly rewritten to conform to Castro's latest stand. For that reason, I have relied more heavily on personal testimonies and recorded speeches than on Cuban press reports: even Fidel's speeches were edited and often changed by the time they appeared in *Granma*, the regime's official newspaper.

In light of these limitations, this book can only begin to suggest the secret story of the demise of Castro's revolution. The definitive story will be written after Castro is gone, and his top officials feel free to speak out. I can only express my appreciation to those officials who—often with only a revealing smile, or with a telltale wave of the hand—gave me the clues to what was behind the regime's official version of events. One day, they will tell the full story.

Andres Oppenheimer

"This is the most difficult period in Cuba's history. It is not just the most difficult period of the revolution, but the most difficult in Cuba's history."

FIDEL CASTRO
DECEMBER 29, 1991

"We are enduring the greatest adversity any of us could ever have imagined. This is a catastrophe."

CARLOS ALDANA
COMMUNIST PARTY IDEOLOGY AND
FOREIGN AFFAIRS CHIEF, NOVEMBER 8, 1991

A CRACK IN THE SYSTEM

<<<<<<<<<<<<<<<<<<<<<<<<<<<<<<<<<<<<<<<<<<<<<<<<<

The Ochoa-De La Guardia Case (1986-1989)

1

The General, the Playboy and the Drug Smuggler

ᗱᗱᗱᗱᗱIt was near dawn, July 13, 1989. The six young soldiers had been roused from sleep without warning or explanation and taken to an open field on the outskirts of Havana. There, they found themselves nearly blinded by powerful floodlights. A cameraman walked nervously around them, looking for the best angle from which to record the scene.

Before them a nine-foot-high wooden pole jutted up from the earth. After waiting a while in the silence of the summer night, the men heard the rumble of a van coming in their direction. Four prisoners in handcuffs were helped out of the vehicle.

Only then did they fully realize why they were there: they were the firing squad. As their faces darkened with horror, a captain came over and handed each an AK-47 rifle. He told them some of the weapons contained empty cartridges, but would not say which. It was an old practice meant to reduce the psychological impact on the shooters. Cuba's stern-looking Justice Minister, Brig. Gen. Juan Escalona Reguera, was standing by, escorted by two military doctors.

The first handcuffed man to descend from the van was Maj. Amado Padrón Trujillo. He was a slightly overweight man in his forties, who had occupied various midlevel jobs at the Cuban Interior

Ministry over the previous twenty-seven years. Most recently, he had administered one of Cuba's many trading companies in Panama.

The second prisoner was Capt. Jorge Martinez Valdes, a man in his thirties with thick black hair and a bushy mustache. He had been trained as a radio communications technician, but had never worked as one. In recent years, he had been the aide-de-camp of one of Cuba's most important generals. Martinez Valdes was one of those obscure officers who enjoyed such coveted privileges as frequent travel abroad, thanks to their positions as assistants of top military chiefs.

But it was the remaining two prisoners whom the soldiers in the firing squad recognized immediately. Their trials, highly publicized and shown on television a few weeks earlier, had riveted the nation. Cubans had talked of little else since.

Col. Antonio "Tony" De La Guardia, fifty, was one of Cuba's top spies. A fluent English speaker and a man of refined tastes, he had been in charge of much of the Interior Ministry's intelligence apparatus until his fall from grace earlier that year. In the mid-1980s, he had been commissioned to set up a sophisticated network of Ministry-run trading firms abroad, aimed at circumventing the U.S. trade embargo on Cuba. Earlier, he had been chief of the Ministry's Special Troops, one of Cuba's elite fighting forces.

The fourth man was Div. Gen. Arnaldo Ochoa Sanchez, forty-nine, one of the most decorated—and popular—officers in Cuba. A slim, outgoing man, Ochoa had begun his career as a guerrilla in the 1959 revolution that had brought Fidel Castro to power. He had later commanded Cuban military operations in Venezuela, Ethiopia, Angola, Yemen and Nicaragua.

Only five years earlier, Ochoa had been awarded the title of Hero of the Revolution—the highest honor conferred to a military man in Castro's Cuba. What's more, Ochoa had been a close friend to Castro—one of the few people in Cuba who dared address the Comandante with the familiar Spanish *tu*.

Now, he was about to be executed on obscure charges of corruption and drug trafficking. Never in the history of the three-decade-old Marxist regime had such a high-ranking officer been brought before a firing squad.

The two lower-ranking officers were to go first. Martinez refused to move, screaming for mercy, his voice broken by sobs. Two soldiers took him by his arms and dragged him to the execution pole. They handcuffed his hands behind the post and covered his eyes with a black kerchief. Petrified, they looked on as the man was shot by their cohorts. Padrón went no more willingly. He stamped his feet and cried with desperation until his body crumpled with the gunfire.

Tony De La Guardia pulled himself together and walked to the execution place by himself. After his hands were handcuffed around the pole, he closed his eyes and held his breath. At the commanding officer's sign, he was consumed in a barrage of gunfire. His head fell sideways and his body thrashed violently in all directions before it fell.

Ochoa had decided to die with dignity. When his turn came, he walked firmly, with the resolution of a soldier who does not want his lifelong glories on the battlefield to be overshadowed by a few seconds of panic before death. First, he asked that he be allowed to give the order for his own execution, in the tradition of Cuban heroes executed by Spanish firing squads during the colonial wars. The request was denied. As he passed the firing squad, he stopped, turned to the soldiers, and told them, "Folks, do what you're asked to do. I have nothing against you. You are following orders."

He turned on his heels and walked toward the post, escorted by two officers. Like the others before him, he was offered a black kerchief to cover his eyes, but he waved it away. With clenched teeth, Ochoa stared over the heads of the firing squad as the commanding officer read the two-paragraph-long sentence from the Council of State ordering his execution.

Asked if he had anything to say, Ochoa raised his eyebrows and, his voice trembling, told his executioners: "I just wanted to let you know that I'm no traitor." He then took a deep breath, and shrugged his shoulders in a gesture of resignation, as if to say there was nothing else he could do. At the shout of *"Fuego!"* (Fire!), the AK-47s ended his life.

Castro, watching the scene in a videotape brought to him by the military doctors hours later, was jolted by the sound. An expression of grief on his face, he stared on at the monitor for a few seconds. "He died like a man," he finally commented wistfully.

<><

Ochoa's execution shook Cuba like nothing since the 1959 Communist revolution.

Rumors that Ochoa and De La Guardia had been conspiring to oust Castro swept the island. Ninety miles away in Florida, the mecca of anti-Castro Cubans, the news spread like wildfire. Hyperventilating Cuban radio broadcasters in Miami proclaimed an imminent collapse of the Castro regime. Their voices blared over Cuba's radios.

It was a key moment in world history. Communism was beginning to crumble in Eastern Europe. The newly legalized union Solidarity had just swept the first free elections in Poland on June 4. Hungary was rapidly moving toward a multiparty system, and opposition candidates were favored to win that country's first democratic local elections on July 23. Headlines from East Germany told of growing numbers of people fleeing to the West following the Hungarian government's opening of its border with Austria. There were reports of anti-government demonstrations throughout the Communist world. Even in the Soviet Union, dissidents were staging street rallies to press their demands for a Western-style democracy; more than 100,000 Siberian coal miners had just begun an unprecedented general strike, and pro-autonomy demonstrations were raging from the Baltics to Georgia.

There was widespread speculation in U.S. media that Cuba could not be far behind. The Ochoa–De La Guardia executions were seen by many Cuban experts as proof that the process of disintegration within Cuba's hermetic Marxist regime had already begun.

Castro's moves in the weeks ahead seemed to confirm speculation of deep cracks in the system. He fired Cuba's powerful interior minister, Div. Gen. José Abrantes, and dozens of top military and civilian officers, including the heads of Cuba's Customs Service and Immigration Department. He dismantled scores of government agencies that had grown increasingly independent in recent years.

Castro became more paranoid than ever. He beefed up his personal guard to such an extent that he was accompanied by two military trucks and four vans wherever he went. When he attended receptions at foreign embassies, police dogs would have to sniff the places ahead of time. Visitors at these events would see an ambulance, a van with an electric generator aboard, and a small truck with a movable radio station waiting by the curb. It was Castro's portable presidential palace: in the event of a military uprising, he could take control of the country from wherever he was.

He began to adopt an increasingly apocalyptic tone in public speeches. No matter what other Socialist countries did, Castro now proclaimed, Cuba would sink in the ocean rather than return to the corrupt capitalist world.

Three weeks after the executions, he banned distribution of the Spanish editions of *Sputnik* and *Moscow News*, two Soviet publications that were spreading the Kremlin's new Glasnost philosophy. After what had happened in Eastern Europe, he was determined not to allow a political opening in Cuba that could develop into a full-blown revolution.

Perhaps more important, the Ochoa affair would change forever the bond of trust between Castro and a sizable part of the Cuban population. For the first time, Castro's semihypnotic speaking powers failed to convince even his most ardent followers.

The maximum leader's contention that there were no political motivations behind the killing of Ochoa and De La Guardia was received with general skepticism. The Comandante was either lying or hiding the truth. There seemed to be solid evidence that Division General Ochoa was involved in shady business deals, but could he have done it without Castro's knowledge? And if he had, how come other military officers who lived much better than Ochoa were still free?

Cubans felt cheated. And the nightly broadcast of Ochoa and De La Guardia's trials, as edited by the regime, only made things worse. Ochoa's proud, self-assured stance during the proceedings had turned him into an instant popular hero, a Cuban Oliver North. Pro-Ochoa graffiti soon popped up in Havana. Visitors would not understand them at first: they read "8A." Cubans, long used to expressing their political feelings in cryptic ways to avoid charges of subversion, understood immediately. The combination of the Spanish word for number eight—*ocho*—and the letter "A" resulted in a clever symbol for Ochoa.

Cubans didn't quite know what was behind the charges against the general, but suspected he had advocated a political liberalization similar to that ongoing in other Soviet bloc countries. When the regime released an allegedly random poll of 1,027 people quoting 100 percent of them describing the defendants as "traitors, immoral, corrupt and guilty," the news left most Cubans shaking their heads in disbelief. The revolution had lost its most important asset: Castro's credibility.

<>

I would soon discover the extent of Ochoa's popularity with my own eyes, on my first trip to Cuba after the executions. Several days after my arrival in Havana, I drove by Ochoa's house on 24th Street in the middle-class neighborhood of Nuevo Vedado. It was a small, unpretentious two-story white townhouse whose front yard barely had enough space to park one car and plant a few vegetables. Even by the housing standards of revolutionary Cuba, it was a house few would have imagined belonged to a top-ranked general.

In the first months that followed Ochoa's arrest and execution, the house was surrounded by security agents to prevent journalists or foreign diplomats from talking to Maida Gonzalez de Ochoa, the general's widow. But later, as the Ochoa story was overshadowed by world events, security around the house was left to her block's revolutionary watch committee. I decided I would try to see her.

I drove past the house several days in a row, at different times, but there were always watchmen sitting on the sidewalk. Finally, one night, seeing no one there, I parked my gray Nissan rental car several blocks away, walked to the house, and knocked on her door. I found her nervous but eager to talk.

Maida Gonzalez de Ochoa is an olive-skinned woman in her late thirties, short and full-figured but attractive with her green eyes and long, black hair. She was a college professor of chemistry, married to Ochoa for seventeen years. They had met in Havana in 1970, when she was still a college student. She had been waiting for a bus on 31st Avenue when a young army officer in a military jeep spotted her and offered her a ride. They started dating two days later.

Maida and I talked late into the night. At first, she measured her words carefully, suspecting that a stranger could readily report her criticism of the government to the secret police. But if the visiting reporter was for real, she did not want to miss a chance to express her skepticism about the charges against her husband. She would become increasingly candid as the hours went by.

One thing was evident: far from being a pariah, Maida was getting almost universal support from her countrymen. At the Instituto Pedagogico, where she taught, students would often bring her presents. At the market, vendors would recognize her and give her strictly rationed foodstuffs from under the counter. Telephone repairmen insisted on installing an extra cable connection she wanted but was not entitled to. Neighbors had volunteered to do her garden's landscaping, she told me matter-of-factly and almost with a certain puzzlement.

As we talked on in her darkly lit living room, a neighbor showed up at the door, bringing a plate of food. The widow smiled, appreciating the gesture. It seemed an everyday occurrence, this show of affection for Ochoa's widow.

The story that ended with the executions of Division General Ochoa and Colonel De La Guardia had started to unfold three years earlier in Panama. It all began one muggy morning in June 1986, when a Cuban exile named Reinaldo Ruiz walked into a Cuban government office in Panama City to request an exit visa for his niece. The last thing he would have expected was for his action to set off the biggest political scandal in the history of the Cuban revolution.

Ruiz was an imposing forty-nine-year-old man—six feet, four inches tall and 270 pounds—whose bushy white beard was shot with a single streak of black. His big size, beard and authoritative voice often moved his friends to tease him about a resemblance to Fidel Castro.

A high-living hustler, Ruiz was a former administrative employee at the Colgate-Palmolive plant in Havana. He had fled Cuba to Miami in 1962, three years after the revolution. In Miami, he had held various jobs at an industrial catering service, an electrical appliance store and a catfish export business. He had gotten in trouble with the law in 1974, when he was arrested at the Los Angeles Airport for trying to smuggle 15,411 Puerto Rican lottery tickets from Mexico into the United States. He had purchased the tickets for $88,665, and hoped to resell them for nearly twice as much in California—where lottery gambling was illegal at the time. He pled guilty, and got a light sentence: two years on probation and a $500 fine.

In recent years, Ruiz had moved to Huntington Park, a suburb of Los Angeles, where he had made some money selling real estate.

He had also set up a travel agency in Panama, and—lately—had begun profiting from his new Colombian wife's cocaine deals. By the mid-1980s, Ruiz was a well-established member of California's international business community: the proud owner of two Huntington Park homes worth a total of $600,000, he was also an active fund-raiser for California's Republican Party.

In 1986, Ruiz moved to Panama. He had found a lucrative—and relatively clean—source of income: selling Panamanian visas to Cubans wanting to leave the Marxist-ruled island. It was an open secret within Miami and New York Cuban-exile communities that you could get your relatives out of Cuba by buying a visa at Ruiz's Columbia Tours and a handful of other travel agencies in Panama. Nothing in Panamanian or Cuban laws authorized such transactions, but the operation worked like a dream. In military-run Panama, much as in Cuba, you didn't much care whether something was legal—the question to ask was whether it was authorized. And the Cuban exit-visa business was known to have the blessings of the military leaders in both countries.

In an understanding between Panama's strongman Gen. Manuel A. Noriega and the Cuban regime, the Panamanian military oversaw the wholesaling of Cuban exit visas in Panama. The operation was managed by Panama's security chief Col. Nivaldo Madriñan, whose agents charged retailers—mostly travel agencies along Panama City's Via España Avenue—$1,500 per visa. The travel agencies, in turn, sold the visas to anxious relatives of Cubans wanting to leave the island; their fee was $2,500 each. Once in Panama, the newly arrived Cubans were free to go on to the Mecca of Cuba's diaspora—Miami.

The wholesale visa business was generating fabulous profits for Noriega and his cronies, as well as much needed foreign exchange for the Cuban government. And Ruiz had carved out a profitable niche in that arrangement.

Like most Cuban exiles, Ruiz had no sympathy for the Castro regime. But he had no problems doing business—even if indirectly— with the Cuban government. He had been in Cuba twice since he had left the island: in 1965, he had taken a boat to Cuba to bring his mother and sister out during the Camarioca boatlift, but he hadn't been able to get them an authorization to leave the island. He tried again in May 1980, during the Mariel boatlift, and managed to bring his mother and two cousins back to the United States.

On both occasions, he had enjoyed his stay in Cuba. The system was a disaster, but the Cubans maintained their cheerful spirit, deep sense of friendship, and close family ties—assets largely un-known to the all-business Americanos. Ruiz had felt quite at home in Cuba.

<>

But that June morning in 1986, Ruiz faced a Cuban-exit-visa problem that his travel agency in Panama could not solve. Trying to get his niece out of Cuba, he had stumbled on a major legal hurdle. Under Cuban law, the woman was barred from leaving the island because of her young age. Cuba refused exit visas to people under twenty-one, the argument being that they had yet to pay society back for the free education they had received from the Communist system.

Ruiz needed a waiver. He knew he would get it—the only ques-tion was how much the Cubans would charge. So he set off for a nearby high-rise building in downtown Panama City where the Cu-bans operated Interconsult, a semiofficial Cuban government office that dealt with, among other things, special immigration cases. Ruiz walked into the sparsely furnished room, and asked to talk with the manager.

He was told to wait. The manager, Miguel Ruiz Poo, would be with him in five minutes. The visitor's eyes widened.

"Did you say his name was Ruiz Poo?," he asked.

Minutes later, Ruiz and Ruiz Poo were chattering enthusiastically: it turned out that they were cousins. Their fathers were half-brothers who had grown up together in the Cuban province of Pinar del Río. Ruiz, thirteen years older than his Cuban cousin, even thought he remembered his newly found relative as a child. It was an unexpected, happy reunion.

The Cuban officer did little to hide his joy from his Interior Ministry colleagues. They were all part of a secret Cuban agency in Panama, whose mission was to obtain hard currency and goods that Cuba could not import because of a 1960 U.S. trade embargo. The agency was known within the Cuban secret service as the MC Department. Its Spanish initials stood for Moneda Convertible—Convertible Currency.

Unlike other Cuban officials, agents of MC were allowed to mingle with and befriend foreigners. If their relations had the potential of generating business deals, they were authorized to fraternize even with Cuban exiles, whom official propaganda depicted as the worst enemies of the Cuban revolution.

Ruiz Poo, the Cuban official, was a young, good-looking man in his mid-thirties, with the somewhat cocky personality typical of Interior Ministry officials who could travel abroad and live like capitalist businessmen. He had a law degree, and after nearly two decades at the Interior Ministry had reached the position of subdirector of Interconsult, a seemingly minor job that was actually much coveted in the gray corridors of Cuba's official bureaucracy. It was a dream assignment: total freedom to mingle with foreigners, a salary in dollars, and enough expenses paid to allow someone to save a bundle.

At lunch over a big fish stew a few days later, the tall, robust Cuban exile and his slim, younger relative hit it off immediately. The Cuban official was eager to have his cousin buy computers in the United States and to ship them to Cuba via Panama. They discussed a shipment of five IBM computers to begin with. Ruiz Poo also asked Reinaldo Ruiz for two television descrambling boxes—the sort of devices that can pull HBO, CNN or the Playboy Channel from the air without subscribing to it. The Cuban official said that one of the boxes was for Fidel's office and the other was for his brother, Defense

Minister Raúl Castro. Sure, no problem, Reinaldo Ruiz said. The goods would be delivered in Cuba a short time later.

In a matter of weeks, the two cousins had established a profitable business relationship. Reinaldo made money, and Miguel scored points with his superiors. Things were going so smoothly that it didn't take long for them to begin exploring a new, more profitable business: cocaine.

Switching from computers to drugs wasn't that big a leap for the new business partners. Cuba's MC Department had never been far from the underworld of drug trafficking that flourished in Panama and Miami. The MC, by its nature, routinely dealt with several of the drug business's players. To transport American computers and electronic goods to the island, for instance, Reinaldo Ruiz and the MC Department had to find boatmen willing to defy the U.S. trade embargo for a good fee. These boatmen, most often Cuban exiles in Miami known as *lancheros*, had to be able to travel back and forth without being detected by the U.S. Coast Guard. Only one kind of boatman could do that: the drug smuggler. No one knew the secret corridors of the Florida straits like the cocaine smugglers, and no one else would be willing to take the risk.

By the mid-1980s, dozens of MC-hired *lancheros*, many of them veteran drug smugglers, were free-lancing as carriers of U.S. goods to Cuba. They regularly would land on Cuba's Varadero beach, unload their cargos of videocassette recorders, computers and electric appliances, wander around town, and take a few days to visit their relatives in the capital. The residents of Varadero soon became accustomed to the presence of the better-dressed Cuban exile visitors: it was known they were bringing much-needed U.S. merchandise to the island.

The MC Department also needed another professional of the drug trade: the money launderer. If Cuban officials and their U.S. trading partners did not cover their tracks, American exporters could be caught for violating the trade embargo. The MC Department needed experts in disguising financial transactions and, in Panama, it had a vast supply of them. Many had learned the tricks of the trade by working for Colombian cocaine traffickers, and many were on the payroll of the Medellín drug cartel.

Occasionally, favors were needed in the other direction. The Cuban government would authorize Colombian drug smugglers to fly over Cuban airspace. On their flights back home, they carried weapons for Cuban-backed guerrillas in Colombia or Central America.

So when Reinaldo Ruiz suggested to his cousin that they ship cocaine to the United States through Cuba, the Cuban official was anything but scandalized. Nor was he surprised. The Cuban intelligence services already knew that Reinaldo Ruiz was in the drug-smuggling business, and they had passed the information on to the MC Department. Miguel Ruiz Poo knew all along it was only a matter of time before his cousin would bring up the idea of smuggling drugs.

It was a chance to make real money, far more than the nickel-and-dime computer shipments, Reinaldo said.

"You see, Ligia, my wife, is Colombian," he said. "She knows important people in the Medellín cartel. She can get cocaine. If you help me pass the merchandise through Cuba, the Cuban government could make millions."

The Cuban official reacted with cautious interest. But Ruiz Poo had little to lose. At best, his superiors at the Interior Ministry would put him in charge of the project, and his career would take a dramatic leap. At worst, his boss would reject the plan as too risky. He decided to give it a chance.

"It sounds interesting," Ruiz Poo said. "But I'll have to check it with my superiors. Give me a couple of days. I should have an answer soon."

<>

Ruiz Poo's boss, Interior Ministry Major Padrón Trujillo, arrived in Panama on a routine visit a few days later. When Ruiz Poo brought up the drug proposal, the visiting official raised his eyebrows, but agreed to meet with Reinaldo Ruiz and hear from him how it could be done.

The three men met for lunch at an Italian restaurant in downtown Panama, and Reinaldo Ruiz offered details about his plan. His wife Ligia had an excellent contact with Gustavo Gaviria, the cousin and chief financial officer of Medellín cartel boss Pablo Escobar Gaviria. He would provide the cocaine. Ruiz's two planes—a Cessna 401 and a Seneca 2 twin-engine Piper aircraft—would transport it from Colombia to Cuba. Ruiz also had a pilot he could trust: his own son Rubén, twenty-two, who had just obtained his flying license. Once in Cuba, the cargo would be placed in boats, and immediately shipped to Florida by his boaters. All he needed from the Cubans was permission to land in Cuba and keep the merchandise for a few hours, until his boats picked it up.

Padrón hesitated. This was too big for him, he said. There was an understanding within the Cuban hierarchy that it was okay to authorize drug flights over Cuban airspace. Fidel himself had okayed the Colombian cocaine flights over Cuban airspace in exchange for having the drug traffickers carry weapons to guerrillas on their way home. But stopping on Cuban territory was a different story. Padrón did not know whether it would be authorized. They would have to consult higher officials.

"We'll be chopped meat if we make a decision here," Padrón said to Ruiz Poo. "We have to discuss it with our superiors in Havana."

Then, turning to Reinaldo Ruiz, he added: "Come to Havana. We'll arrange a meeting with the right people at the Ministry."

<>

Within two weeks, the Ruiz cousins had taken a regular Cubana de Aviación flight from Panama City to Cuba. They were welcomed at Havana's José Martí airport by Major Padrón, who was waiting for them by the immigration booth marked "diplomats and journalists."

He expedited their passage through immigration and customs, and ordered the driver of his Lada to take the group to the seaside Comodoro Hotel. The four-story hotel and its adjacent bungalows were a favorite place of the Interior Ministry. A relatively small hotel of only 124 rooms, it was about five miles west of downtown Havana, a perfect place to house undercover contacts. Chances of running into Western diplomats or journalists were much smaller there than at the giant downtown Havana Libre or Riviera hotels. As soon as the Cuban officials dropped him off at the Comodoro, Ruiz left his bags, and headed for his sister's house. It was a happy reunion: he had not seen her in several years.

The next morning, Ruiz Poo showed up early at Ruiz's hotel. They were going to meet a top Interior Ministry official to discuss his plan, he told his cousin. The man turned out to be Colonel De La Guardia, head of the MC Department. His office at 7007 66th Street, in the elegant western Havana section of Miramar, was a two-story mansion that had obviously belonged to an oligarch in the days before the revolution.

De La Guardia, a dandy who sported designer jeans and a Rolex watch, was waiting for them at his desk. They shook hands, and went straight to business. First they talked about ways to ship Cuban cigars to the United States circumventing the U.S. trade embargo. Minutes later, they plunged into the issue that interested them most: cocaine trafficking.

De La Guardia didn't seem the least nervous about discussing a drug deal: he talked about it matter-of-factly, pointing to potential technical troubles that had to be overcome in the delivery, storage and trans-shipment stages. The man was a pro. The Cuban exile didn't ask De La Guardia on that occasion if the operation needed to be approved at a higher level. After all, he was a full colonel, and they were talking in his ministry office.

From then on, the Cubans gave Ruiz semiroyal treatment. He was wined and dined by Interior Ministry officials at Havana's best restaurants. De La Guardia, Padrón and Ruiz had a special table reserved for them at the candlelit Tocoloro restaurant, and Ruiz was given a front table at the Tropicana Club, where he enjoyed Cuba's best-known variety show.

On the weekend, De La Guardia invited Ruiz for an outing in his boat, the two-engine, thirty-foot fishing vessel *El Tomeguin*. It was a beautiful Sunday afternoon, with clear tropical skies and just enough wind to sit in the sun without getting too hot. De La Guardia, Ruiz Poo and Ruiz sipped sodas, their feet stretched on the deck's seats as they enjoyed the sight of the Havana coastline bobbing in the distance. The host kidded with his new friends about what they would do with the profits of the cocaine operation. Instead of turning the money over to the government, he joked, they should rent their favorite strip-tease joint, Panama City's Pigalle night club, and lock themselves up for a week with the club's sexy Colombian dancers. The men were having fun.

"Tony," Ruiz asked at one point, when all the laughter had died down. "El señor knows about this situation?"

"Of course, Chico," responded the colonel, eager to reassure his guest that they were on safe ground.

It was the only time the Cuban exile asked De La Guardia point blank whether Fidel Castro was aware of the cocaine-smuggling plan. There was no need to mention Fidel by name. In the street language of Cubans on both sides of the Caribbean, there was no mistaking who "el señor" was in Cuba.*

---

* *It is unclear whether Tony De La Guardia had personally discussed his cocaine-trafficking plans with Castro. The Comandante, with his instinctive revulsion for money matters, seldom got involved in dirty business deals. That was Interior Minister Abrantes's job. Tony De La Guardia had Abrantes's green light to do anything to obtain dollars—including the occasional drug deal. De La Guardia's statement to Reinaldo Ruiz may have reflected the colonel's assumption that Abrantes never would have okayed something as hot as a drug operation without Fidel's blessing.*

Ruiz made two other trips from Panama to Havana on Cubana de Aviación in preparation for his first cocaine shipment through the island. On one of his exploratory trips, he brought along his son Rubén, the pilot, a loudmouthed young man with a round face and a thin black beard. He was there to check out a small landing strip on the outskirts of Varadero.

The group—Ruiz, his son Rubén, Ruiz Poo and Padrón—drove to Santa Clara and was welcomed there by other Interior Ministry officials. They examined the airstrip, and found it okay. Rubén Ruiz was concerned, however, about its location: it was at the center of Cuba, and required flying over military installations in Pinar del Río, Havana, and much of the rest of the island. Wouldn't the Cuban air force's radars detect the small plane and intercept it? he asked.

"Don't worry," one of the Interior Ministry officials said. "You have the Revolutionary Air Force at your disposal."

The pilot smiled, satisfied by the assurances. A few days later, Ruiz and his son made their first full-fledged rehearsal trip on their Cessna 401, flying from Mexico to the Varadero airstrip. They carried no drugs, just the two television descrambling boxes supposedly for the Castro brothers. Sure enough, the plane was allowed to enter Cuban airspace, unencumbered, without being asked for explanations.

Father and son shook their heads in disbelief as they flew over the heart of Cuba. Drug smuggling through Cuba! They had struck gold!

If there was one privileged man in Fidel Castro's Cuba, it was Col. Tony De La Guardia, the man who would become Reinaldo Ruiz's top-ranking contact in the Cuban government.

At fifty, De La Guardia was typical of the cosmopolitan, free-spending Interior Ministry elite that had gained power in Cuba during the eighties. As head of MC, De La Guardia had carte blanche to travel wherever he wanted at a moment's notice, to set up front companies all over the world, and enjoy the kind of comforts that dealings with Western businessmen required.

Not subject to the rigid discipline endured by his counterparts in Raúl Castro's Armed Forces, De La Guardia enjoyed a life-style in Cuba that was comparable only to that of foreign diplomats. Although a full colonel, he rarely used his uniform. His trademark attire included his Rolex watch, Calvin Klein jeans, and preppy shirts. He drove a brand new dark blue Lada 2107 with three antennas—the ultimate status symbol in Cuba.

He lived in Siboney, a western Havana suburb of palm-tree-lined streets that had been one of the wealthiest neighborhoods before the revolution. His one-story, two-car-garage home at 20600 17th Street was the kind of residence reserved for foreigners. A stately house, it sat behind a carefully landscaped front yard, with two palm trees on either side of its double wooden front door. The door itself was a work of art: a star had been carved into the wood by hand. A big hall led to the living room, whose walls were covered with oil paintings—many of them naive landscapes that the colonel himself had painted.

Proud of his artistic talent, De La Guardia had told friends he planned to become a full-time painter once he retired. Painting was his favorite diversion. On a canvas dedicated to a good friend, he had playfully written: "To Natalia, with deep appreciation for having recognized the world's greatest painter—Me."

At home, his brightly colored paintings were carefully set against a backdrop of modern white furniture and glass tables, where they dominated the scene. Also on display were a brand new videocassette recorder, a huge color TV set, and a high-quality stereo system—all luxuries that only a handful of Cuban officials could own without fear of punishment.

As a top secret agent, Tony De La Guardia spent much of his time abroad: setting up trading firms in Panama; making deals in Mexico to ship disguised Cuban cigars to the United States, or touring Western Europe to acquire weapons for various guerrilla wars Cuba was supporting around the world. Along the way, he enjoyed life.

De La Guardia's womanizing was well known on the island—a habit no doubt facilitated by his access to Western goods. He had married three times and had four children, but he was known to maintain a virtual harem of girlfriends. Late at night, his three-antenna Lada could often be seen parked outside the Tropicana or the Riviera Hotel. The colonel and his friends would slip into the car after the cabaret show was over, often with one or more women dancers in tow.

One of his longest extramarital affairs was with one of the flashiest women in Cuba. She was Iris, a twenty-six-year-old blonde aerobics instructor at La Maison, Cuba's tourism-oriented fashion center. Tony De La Guardia set Iris up in a second-floor corner apartment on 19th Street, and she decorated their love nest with batiks and Latin American crafts that the colonel would bring from various trips abroad. There was nothing secret about their affair.

Sex was the biggest perk Cuban officers enjoyed in the otherwise grim atmosphere of the Cuban revolution. And being the lover of an important officer like Tony De La Guardia was a badge of honor. Iris would tell anybody who cared to listen that she was "*la amiga*" of Col. Tony De La Guardia. It was a status that drew more deference than most revolutionary titles.

One of the countries De La Guardia visited often—one which fascinated him—was the United States. In 1977, De La Guardia had been Castro's point man to negotiate a normalization of relations with Cuban exiles in Miami. In several nonpublicized trips to Miami, he made friends with a few Cuban exile businessmen who—defying the hard-line no-dialogue stance of Miami's exile leadership—agreed to talk with the Cuban government in order to obtain the release of thousands of political prisoners.

De La Guardia had also developed a good working relationship with the FBI, which was assigned to guarantee the Cuban emissaries' security during their visits to the United States and to keep a close eye on them. FBI agents invited Tony De La Guardia and his aide, José Luis Padrón, to dinner at the luxurious Fontainebleau Hotel in Miami Beach. The Cubans were also invited to spend a weekend at the high-society Boca Raton Hotel and Club, all expenses paid. The visitors were dazzled.

Between smiles, jokes and serious talk, the Cuban officer would not avoid expressing his personal views. He once made a daring admission to Bernardo Benes, a Cuban-American banker who acted as his informal host in Miami.

"Chico, I'm not a Marxist," De La Guardia said. "But if somebody were to kill Fidel, he would have to kill me first."

De La Guardia's hosts in Miami were charmed by the Cuban's candor. They had expected a Communist bureaucrat with a hostile disposition and no sense of humor. Instead, they found a frank, jovial public servant with a knack for self-deprecation.

On one of his first visits to Miami, De La Guardia and his aide Padrón were being toured around the city by Benes and another Cuban exile when the discussion turned to the sorry state of the Cuban economy.

They were driving along U.S. 1, one of Miami's major north-south routes, parallel to the brand new Metrorail, the pride of the city. Huge palm trees had just been planted on both sides of the elevated rail platform, blending a touch of tropical green into its futuristic architecture.

"What do you think?" Benes asked triumphantly from the driving seat, pointing at the Metrorail.

De La Guardia turned toward his aide Padrón, who was sitting next to him in the back seat, and replied:

"Listen, José Luis, haven't these people heard about the new Metrorail we're going to build in Cuba, from Havana to Guanabacoa?"

"What are you going to build it with?" came the intrigued question from the front seat.

"*Con mierda, chico!*" answered De La Guardia, bursting into laughter. "With shit, man!"

Colonel De La Guardia did not try to hide his fondness for American music, food and consumer goods. Once, when Benes drove him and his aide to the Fort Lauderdale airport to take a rented Lear jet back to Cuba, the colonel asked to make a quick stop at a Burdines department store in north Miami.

They were only half an hour short of the plane's departure time. Benes pulled up his car at the store's parking lot, and watched—amazed—as the revolution's representatives went into a shopping frenzy. In a matter of minutes, they had bought more than four thousand dollars worth of electronic equipment and clothes.

"I had to help them, because they didn't have enough hands to carry the stuff," Benes recalled years later. "They were thrilled."

But Col. Tony De La Guardia wasn't just Cuba's premier special agent. He was also Fidel Castro's protégé.

Castro had discovered Tony De La Guardia in 1961, two years after the revolution, in an unlikely setting: at the annual boating race of the plush Varadero beach resort. Castro, then thirty-five and at the peak of his world fame, was there to preside over the opening ceremony of Cuba's foremost annual regatta.

Tony De La Guardia and his identical twin, Patricio, were lead rowers in the University of Havana's *Caribe* canoe, one of the two favorites to win the race. The brothers were twenty-one, young men from Havana's elegant Miramar neighborhood with little interest in studies and a fascination with fast cars, fancy clothes and beautiful women.

New acquaintances found it almost impossible to distinguish the twins: the only physical difference between them was a birthmark on Patricio's right elbow. Close friends could tell them apart by their demeanor: Tony was loud, extroverted; Patricio, subdued, and a follower.

The twins—or *jimaguas*, as they were called in Cuba—had grown up in a house next door to the Miramar Yacht Club, and could be found day and night on the club's premises. As kids, they would roam the tennis courts in dirty, worn-out designer clothes. As teenagers, they were enfants terribles: boisterous adolescents milling around the club's social quarters, often playing pranks on employees or making fun of newcomers.

The boys were expelled from at least one high school, and did so poorly in others that they were encouraged to leave. Their father, in an effort to discipline them, enrolled them at the Havana Military School, a boarding school that prided itself on reining in even the most indomitable troublemakers. The twins made the grades, but would not abandon their unruly ways. Among other things, they organized a class outing to a local whorehouse, the Tulipan House, escaping from the school dormitory at night when the guards were sound asleep.

On another occasion, the De La Guardia twins were riding in the countryside with classmates Ignacio Elso and Franz Arango, when Tony—who was in the front seat—saw the figure of a skinny bicyclist laboriously pedaling his way up a hilly road ahead of them.

"Slow down," Tony told Arango, who was driving, "I'll give him a little push."

When the car caught up with the bicyclist, Tony De La Guardia stretched himself out of the window, caught the man by the neck, and dragged him in that position for more than a hundred yards. The bicyclist was screaming, pleading to be released. The youngsters in the car roared with laughter, banging their feet against the floor.

When the poor bicyclist seemed about to lose control of his vehicle, Tony De La Guardia released him with a push. The man landed on the side of the road and remained there momentarily, an incredulous look on his face. The students applauded wildly as their car pulled away.

By the time they enrolled at the University of Havana in the late fifties, the twins had developed new interests. They had taken seriously to rowing—a chic sport in prerevolutionary Cuba, and one that seemed to make an impression on the upper-class girls they courted. The De La Guardia twins had also become interested in art, and began cultivating relationships with painters and writers. Soon, they were taking painting lessons. Only their styles differed: Tony painted naive landscapes. Patricio's work was more abstract, if equally colorful.

Through Gustavo "Tavo" Machin, a neighbor from a well-to-do family who was the twins' best friend at the time, the *jimaguas* developed a sympathy for the revolutionary cause. Castro's guerrillas had failed in their attack on the Moncada military barracks in 1953, but the bearded guerrillas were back in the mountains increasingly gaining the hearts and minds of young people in the cities. Nationwide opposition to President Fulgencio Batista's dictatorship was growing daily, especially among upper-middle-class students.

Unlike Machin, who took politics seriously enough to memorize passages of speeches by revolutionary leaders, the De La Guardia twins were largely passive supporters of the cause. They sympathized with the rebels, who wanted a major social shakeup in Cuba, but were somewhat bored by the never-ending meetings and the ideological repartee that came with political activism.*

In 1957, the De La Guardia twins left Cuba for the United States. Like many kids from upper-middle class Cuban families, they were dispatched to American colleges. Their father was worried about the growing uprising against the Batista regime and wanted to keep his boys out of trouble.

The brothers landed at Florida Southern College, a small school in Lakeland, Florida. But their minds were still in Cuba. As the revolutionary movement gained momentum at home, it wasn't long before the *jimaguas* became active in support groups. They joined the Students' Revolutionary Directorate, an anti-Batista coalition with chapters on various U.S. campuses.

Several months after their arrival in Lakeland, the twins were arrested for illegal possession of weapons. A Florida highway policeman, attracted by the sound of gunfire, found them and other Cuban students trying out M-1 and M-2 rifles in an improvised shooting range near their college. The youths had purchased the guns at the

---

* In the mid-sixties, Machin joined Ernesto "Che" Guevara's guerrilla column in Bolivia, becoming the third-ranked officer of the fifteen Cubans on the expedition. Shortly after his arrival in that South American country, "Tavo" was killed in an army ambush.

Directorate's request for Cuban guerrillas at Sierra Maestra. The police seized the rifles, and threatened to file charges that could have led to the students' deportation, but within hours, and after the police elicited promises that they would stay away from weapons thenceforward, the twins were released.

Despite the scare, the *jimaguas* continued to remain active in revolutionary groups. As soon as Fidel Castro's victorious guerrillas marched into Havana on January 1, 1959, they dropped out of Florida Southern College and rushed back to Cuba. Their chance meeting with Fidel Castro two years later at the Varadero regatta would mark their future.

It was in 1961, and the De La Guardia brothers were at the University of Havana, once again mediocre students but keen members of the school's rowing team. Rolando Cubela, a student leader close to Castro and captain of the school's rowing team, had picked the twins as part of his crew for the regatta. Patricio would be the front rower. Tony would occupy the back seat. Cubela would be number three.

The cocktail party on the eve of the boating race at the Varadero Nautical Club was an awkward affair. Castro was clearly uncomfortable about his role. In the old days, Castro's bourgeois predecessors had presided over the regatta's opening ceremony, and they had turned the occasion into a major social event for Cuba's oligarchy.

Castro, an enthusiastic sports fan, wanted to continue the tradition of the race, but was determined to do away with its high-society atmosphere. He showed up in working fatigues instead of the gala military uniform he used for special occasions, and at his side were a small group of workers and students.

Most of the guests were well-to-do members of the Nautical Club. They were also uncomfortable, not knowing quite how to act before a leader many of them were seeing in person for the first time. In previous years, most had attended the traditional party clad in dinner-jacket dress: tuxedo slacks with a white jacket.

Now, two years after the revolution, the guests were unsure about the new revolutionary etiquette. Most had come in white guayaberas. A few still wore their white jackets, but dropped their ties and kept the first button of their shirts open in deference to the new political reality.

Waiters served scotch and rum to the standing crowd. Castro chatted with those around him about the next day's competition, keeping the conversation to the subject of rowing. Only half jokingly, he said he was willing to bet that the "proletarian" canoe manned by the Varadero fishermen would win the race. Castro insisted that the fishermen—"workers of the sea," he called them—were stronger, better-trained rowers.

The University of Havana boat, on the other hand, was manned by *"pepillos"*—spoiled, undisciplined city kids, a vestige of the pre-revolutionary bourgeoisie. They had no chance to win, he argued, his agitated hand gestures dancing in air.

On the following morning, Castro, his hand-picked President Osvaldo Dorticós and several cabinet ministers officially opened the race with a short ceremony at the starting line. It was a bright, sunny day—an unusually joyous occasion in a revolution that was feeling the tensions of escalating confrontation with the United States.

After the bang that signaled the start of the regatta, Castro jumped into a motorboat and followed the competitors. Holding a loudspeaker in his hand, he cheered for the fishermen's canoe with shouts of *"Vamos! Vamos!"* (Go! Go!) and *"Adelante, compañeros!"* (C'mon, comrades!).

But to the Cuban leader's surprise, it was the University of Havana's *Caribe* canoe that won the race. A smiling but slightly humiliated Castro, a man who has always conceded he hates to lose even the most meaningless games, was soon waving the crew of the *Caribe* over to an improvised podium a few yards from the water, in order to present them with their trophy.

The Cuban leader raised his eyebrows and smiled when he noticed the two identical-looking young men who climbed the stairs of the stage. After the ceremony, a cheerful Castro took their arms and asked them how he could tell them apart in the future. Tony De La Guardia told him it was easy: he was "the good-looking one." The three men laughed.

In the months that followed, the De La Guardia twins would grow closer to Castro and more distant from Cubela. It was a clear political move. Cubela, who had led the Students' Revolutionary Directorate during the war against Batista, was becoming increasingly angry about the revolution's Marxist bent.

At twenty-six, Cubela was a charismatic student leader with political possibilities in a revolution that was still charting its course. After the revolution's triumph, he had taken several young people under his wing. Many of them, like the De La Guardia twins, were non-Communist nationalists from upper-middle-class homes who had opposed the Batista regime. But once the De La Guardia brothers met Castro, they quickly forged their own ties to the Cuban leader.

A few months later, Cubela ran into the De La Guardias at Castro's house in Varadero. The Cuban leader spent much of his time there in the early days of the revolution, alternating the business of government with fishing and snorkeling in the dark blue Caribbean waters. Hearing that Cubela was in town, Castro invited the student leader to his house for lunch. When Cubela showed up, he was surprised to see the De La Guardia twins sitting at either side of the Cuban leader. Castro proudly introduced them as brand new Interior Ministry officials.

"They are no longer in your canoe," Castro proudly told Cubela. "Now, they are on my boat."

Recalling the incident nearly thirty years later, Cubela could not help pointing out the ironies of their eventual fates. Cubela, who had become increasingly disillusioned with the revolution, was recruited by the CIA in 1963 to kill Castro. But the Cuban secret service learned of the plot and arrested him. At his trial, Cubela conceded that he had planned to first "shoot Premier Castro with a high-powered telescopic rifle," then set up a counterrevolutionary government. Under Cuban revolutionary standards such a crime carried the death sentence. But Castro took pity on his old friend, and Cubela was sentenced to only fifteen years in prison. He was later allowed to leave Cuba, and went into exile in Spain. Tony De La Guardia, who would remain at the Cuban leader's side for the next twenty-six years and be closer to him than Cubela ever was, had no such luck.

Shortly after winning Castro's favor in 1961, the *jimaguas* joined the Interior Ministry's troops who were fighting counterrevolutionary guerrillas in central Cuba's Escambray mountains. They soon became captains in the so-called LCB—Lucha Contra los Bandidos (Fight Against The Bandits)—war, and developed a reputation for boldness in the battlefield. The two brothers were now sporting beards—à la Fidel—and olive-green uniforms, which made it even more difficult to tell them apart.

Tony, the more adventurous, was a bigger version of the bully he had been as a teenager. He still seemed to thrive on scandalizing people around him. As instructor at a survival training camp in Escambray, he once took a live scorpion in his hand, brought it to his mouth, bit it, and ate it. The soldiers attending his class watched the scene jaws agape.

During the 1962 U.S.-Soviet missile crisis, Castro sent Tony De La Guardia on a special mission to New York. The young officer made the trip as part of an official delegation accompanying Cuban foreign minister Raúl Roa to the United Nations. But according to Brig. Gen. Rafael del Pino, who defected to the United States in 1987, De La Guardia was on a secret mission to set off 500 kilos of dynamite at the United Nations building if the United States invaded Cuba. Other versions of the story said the target was the Brooklyn Bridge. One of De La Guardia's closest associates told me in Havana that Tony had indeed bragged about that mission to a number of friends. Castro never confirmed the story.

In the early seventies, as a ranking officer with the Interior Ministry's elite Special Troops, Tony De La Guardia went from one covert operation to another. In 1971, following the election of leftist President Salvador Allende in Chile, he headed the first Cuban Special Troops contingent to provide military advice and support for Chile's Unidad Popular government. In 1973, he led a secret mission to Spain to study the possible kidnapping of former Cuban dictator Batista (the mission was canceled immediately—Batista died of natural causes the night Tony arrived in Madrid).

In 1975, Tony De La Guardia was in Switzerland laundering $60 million that Argentina's Montonero guerrillas had obtained in the sensational kidnapping of industrialists Jorge and Juan Born. Shortly thereafter, the Cuban secret agent was transporting millions in precious stones and gold from Lebanon to Czechoslovakia—the take from a series of bank robberies by the Palestinian Popular Democratic Front. In 1976, he was stationed in Jamaica, as head of the Cuban Special Troops contingent that provided military support to leftist Prime Minister Michael Manley.

In 1978, De La Guardia led the first contingent of the Cuban military advisers that became involved in the Nicaraguan war. After his arrival in Costa Rica to help funnel weapons for the Nicaraguan rebel Southern Front led by Eden Pastora, De La Guardia commuted regularly between Havana and Costa Rica to help the Sandinista war effort. He participated in the 1978 attack on the Nicaraguan border post of Peñas Blancas, and a year later became the first Cuban soldier to reach Managua with the Sandinista rebels; he helped take President Anastasio Somoza's presidential palace.

In 1979, partly because of his near-fluency in English, De La

Guardia was put in charge of relations with Cuba's exile community in the United States. He began spending much of his time with Castro. In fact, when Miami banker Benes visited Castro in 1979 to discuss the release of Cuban prisoners, Tony De La Guardia always was present at the talks. He looked relaxed, almost at home in Castro's office.

Once, when Castro welcomed the Miami banker into his office well after midnight, as was his habit, Tony De La Guardia began to yawn despite clear indications that the meeting was just beginning and would most likely last until daylight. At about 1:30 A.M., Benes recalls, Tony stood up and excused himself.

"I'm dead. I've got to get some sleep," he said, wishing everybody a good night.

Only a handful of men could take such liberties in Cuba. And Tony De La Guardia was one of them.

<>

In 1986, De La Guardia was assigned to CIMEX, a Cuban government corporation that specialized in import-export transactions. It was a difficult time in Cuba. The Reagan Administration had tightened the embargo and blocked all political contacts with the island. Cuba desperately needed to increase its exports and to import more technology from the West.

CIMEX was ordered to set up a network of well-disguised trading companies abroad, which would conduct transactions without anybody in the outside world knowing that the Cuban government was behind them. Tony De La Guardia was picked to carry out the mission.

Within months of his new assignment, he was heading the MC Department, which was headquartered in Havana. Increasingly, his job took him to Panama, to MC's several subsidiaries there. He soon made excellent contacts in the underworld of Panama's banking and trading industries. And one way or another, most of De La Guardia's business partners had connections to the drug trade.

Occasionally, Tony De La Guardia would even authorize a Colombian drug plane to fly over Cuban airspace in exchange for a specific favor. So, much like Ruiz Poo before him, De La Guardia was anything but shocked when a Cuban-exile businessman named Reinaldo Ruiz entered his life in late 1986 with a request for assistance in smuggling cocaine.

<>

Senior Cuban officials had been involved in drug trafficking before, and nothing had ever happened to them.

In November 1982, a U.S. district attorney in Miami had indicted four top Cuban officials on charges of smuggling cocaine through Cuba to the United States. The operation was almost identical to that proposed to Col. Tony De La Guardia by Reinaldo Ruiz years later.

Jaime Guillot-Lara, a Colombian drug lord, had shipped drugs to Cuba at the time, and had south Florida boaters pick up the cargo midsea. Between 1977 and 1981, Guillot-Lara shipped at least 2.5 million pounds of marijuana, 25 million methaqualone tablets and 80 pounds of cocaine, much of it through Cuba.

Witnesses at the Miami trial testified that the Cuban ambassador to Colombia, Fernando Ravelo Renedo, had requested—and obtained—Havana's official green light for every shipment to Cuba. The Colombian smuggler's boats had used the code word *Viviana* to alert the Cuban navy that the cocaine-laden boats should be allowed to cross Cuban waters.

In addition to Ambassador Ravelo, the indictment named Cuban navy Vice-Admiral Aldo Santamaría Cuadrado, who was charged with supervising the protection and resupplying of the drug ships from Colombia, and Rene Rodriguez Cruz, a Cuban Directorate General of Intelligence (DGI) official. None of them was ever prosecuted in Cuba. Castro had maintained that the U.S. charges were nothing but imperialist lies. Within Cuba, the U.S. indictment produced only a temporary scare, and a warning to Cuban officials not to allow drugs onto Cuban soil.

Fidel Castro and Colombia's drug barons had a long association, largely based on political convenience. The Cuban leader had first ordered his intelligence services to penetrate the Colombian drug-trafficking rings in the 1970s, to have a hand in what was rapidly becoming one of Latin America's most powerful economic and political forces.

It was a card he would later decide how to play. The American government was increasingly interested in fighting drugs at the time, and Cuba's intelligence on the cartels might have proven useful as a lure to entice U.S. officials to normalize relations with Cuba. In fact, when the Carter Administration launched an exploratory dialogue with the Castro regime in the late 1970s, one of the things the Cubans offered was to help stop drug smuggling through the Caribbean. The proposal died when normalization talks collapsed.

In the early 1980s, Castro had used his Medellín cartel contacts to fly weapons to Colombia's M-19 guerrillas. The planes would fly over

Cuban airspace with no questions asked, and pick up the weapons on improvised runways in various Caribbean islands, and occasionally in Cuba itself. Carlos Lehder, one of the Medellín cartel's top leaders, would testify years later in a U.S. court that he had met twice with Raúl Castro in Cuba to clear these flights.

The Cuban regime had used its ties with the Colombian drug traffickers to help solve a $4.6 million dispute between Panama's military chief General Noriega and the Medellín cartel in 1984. When the Medellín cartel threatened to kill Noriega unless he returned the money they had paid for protection of a huge Western Panama cocaine laboratory that had been destroyed in a DEA-led raid, Cuba persuaded the Panamanians to come to terms with the Colombians.

Meeting in Havana, Noriega and Castro spent several hours together. Two of Noriega's top aides, José Blandón and Maj. Felipe Camargo, had held preliminary talks with Fidel's senior advisers.

"They are dangerous people," the powerful head of the Cuban Communist Party Americas' Department, Manuel Piñeiro, told Camargo, referring to the Colombian traffickers. "You don't want to mess around with them."

The Panamanians heeded Cuba's advice. They returned the money to the Colombian drug barons, and released the Colombians who had been arrested at the raid. The dispute was settled.

After more than a decade of regular dealings with drug smugglers, the lines of what was permissible for Cuban officials had become blurred. Col. Tony De La Guardia felt confident he would not get in trouble for agreeing to have cocaine smuggled through Cuban territory.

<><>

On April 10, 1987, Reinaldo Ruiz launched his first cocaine-smuggling operation through Cuba, with the authorization and support of the Interior Ministry's Col. Tony De La Guardia. But things went wrong from the very beginning.

Conceptually, the plan was almost perfect. Ruiz Jr., the pilot, and an American copilot, Richard Zzie, were to fly 300 kilos of Colombian cocaine into the beach resort of Varadero. The cargo, packaged in Marlboro cigarette boxes, was to be picked up there by the elder Ruiz's boatmen, and transshipped in speedboats to Miami. The Cessna plane would return, empty and clean, to the Fort Lauderdale–Hollywood International Airport in south Florida.

The Ruiz team had arranged an alibi with the Cuban Interior

Ministry officials in case the landing raised suspicions in other Cuban government agencies or in the United States. To prevent leaks, the operation was to be highly compartmentalized. If anybody asked about it in Cuba, Tony De La Guardia would say the plane had been authorized by the MC Department to bring in a cargo of computers. If U.S. authorities questioned the pilots on their return to South Florida why they had stopped in Cuba, they would say they had been forced to do an emergency landing. Cuban officials would contact FAA authorities in Miami ahead of time, and tell them that Ruiz's plane had developed technical problems.

The operation started on track, but when the smugglers entered Cuban airspace using their prearranged codes, they heard a strong interference on their radio. It soon became clear that a Cuban MIG fighter plane had come to meet them. For a moment, young Rubén Ruiz's heart almost stopped. But the MIG plane turned out to be friendly: it radioed an offer to escort the Cessna to Varadero. The pilot sighed in relief. The Cubans were delivering on their promises.

Ruiz Jr. and his copilot Zzie landed in Varadero. A group of Interior Ministry agents was waiting for them. They unloaded the cocaine boxes and took them to a nearby Cuban Coast Guard tourism complex. It was a small development of white apartment houses for foreign tourists, which was occasionally used by armed forces officials. At the time, the development was virtually empty. There was only a construction crew, working on several bungalows. The cocaine was left there overnight, ready to be picked up on the following morning by the Miami boatmen. The *lancheros* arrived shortly after dawn in a speedboat named *Flerida*, and began loading the cargo. By that time, Ruiz Jr. and Zzie were already flying their Cessna back to the United States.

The *lancheros*, however, ruined everything. The captain of the *Flerida*, Victor Caballero, was supposed to meet another boat at high seas, which would lead him into a safe docking place on the Florida coast. Olegario "El Guajiro" Gonzalez, a veteran dope smuggler who was an expert in eluding U.S. Coast Guard patrol boats, was the man in charge of leading the cocaine-laden *Flerida* to its destination.

But the two boats never met. Rough seas delayed Gonzalez, who arrived at the meeting place several hours late. The *Flerida* crew had waited for two hours, and—nervous about sitting in the middle of the sea with 300 kilos of cocaine aboard—decided to continue the trip to Florida on its own. Caballero raised anchors, turned the *Flerida* north, and headed off at full speed.

A few hours later, a U.S. Coast Guard patrol boat spotted the *Flerida* near Alligator Reef by the Florida Keys. The U.S. boat radioed the *Flerida* to stop for an inspection. When the suspicious boat ignored the patrol's order, a full-engine chase ensued. The three men on the *Flerida* began frantically throwing the cocaine bags into the sea, leaving a trail of white bubbles in the wake of the gurgling Marlboro boxes. By the time the U.S. patrol boat reached the *Flerida*, the smugglers had dropped 206 one-kilo cocaine bags into the sea. Caballero and his crewmen were detained with 94 kilos of cocaine still aboard. The operation had collapsed.

Meanwhile, a stupid mistake by Ruiz Jr. and his copilot marred their landing in the United States as well. After radioing the U.S. air controllers that they had stopped in Cuba because of engine trouble, the pilots had flown to the Fort Lauderdale–Hollywood airport, the plane's original point of departure. Immediately, U.S. Customs officials sensed something was up: American pilots normally know—or are informed in Cuba—that aircraft coming from Cuba can only land at the Miami International Airport, where they must undergo security checks. Ruiz Jr., who had only flown to Colombia and Panama, was not aware of the special regulations applying to Cuba.

Customs agents waited for the plane at the Fort Lauderdale airport, and checked it out thoroughly. A seemingly surprised but nervous Ruiz Jr. told his engine-trouble story.

"We didn't believe a word," one U.S. Customs agent would recall later, "but the plane was clean." Ruiz Jr. and his father's Cessna would begin to be watched more carefully by Customs and DEA officials from then on.

<>

Reinaldo Ruiz, undeterred by the failure of his first try to smuggle cocaine through Cuba, did not waste a minute in planning a new operation. His team had made bad mistakes, but they could learn from them. The most important thing was that Colonel De La Guardia's Interior Ministry agents had carried out their part of the plan, and that—as far as he knew—they were still willing to go on cooperating.

Planning the second operation was somewhat more complicated, however. Ligia's Colombian suppliers had backed off from providing the group with a new cocaine shipment. They had lost their previous load because of the clumsiness of Ruiz's men, and were not ready to trust these amateurs with a new shipment.

After a few weeks of searching, Ruiz Sr. managed to put together a new group of Colombian suppliers, made up of a few remaining loyalists from the first load and several smaller investors. Then, Ruiz Sr. began lobbying with the Cubans to be given a second chance. He went to see his cousin at the Interconsult office in Panama where they had first met, and asked him to contact his superiors for authorization to try it all once more. The okay from Havana came about two weeks later. Ruiz Sr. rapidly set out to recruit a new team of pilots and *lancheros* in Miami.

Zzie, the copilot in the first trip, refused to continue working for Ruiz Sr. after he was never paid for the ill-fated shipment. No dope, no money, Ruiz Sr. had argued.

Unable to go back to Zzie, Ruiz Sr. hired a former Nationalist Chinese Air Force fighter pilot named Hu Chang. He was a tall, slim Taiwanese in his late fifties who was running Del Chang International, a small air-taxi company operating from Miami International Airport. What Ruiz didn't know was that Chang was a DEA informant.

Chang was a living legend among those who knew his past. He had been a soldier of fortune in virtually every war in Southeast Asia. A CIA contract pilot in Vietnam, he boasted that he had flown the last U.S. plane out of Saigon at the end of the war. In the 1970s, he had been the commander of an elite Taiwanese Air Force squadron, until a family reunion changed his life.

He had sneaked into mainland China for three weeks in 1978 to see his mother, whom he had not seen in thirty-two years. The Taiwanese found out, and sentenced him to death in absentia. Suddenly a man without a country, Chang went to Thailand, and from there to the United States.

Shortly after arriving penniless in the United States that year, Chang got in trouble with the law. He was arrested for piloting a Lockheed Lodestar plane full of marijuana and Quaaludes into North Carolina in 1979. The judge gave him a five-year sentence and ordered him deported.

Two and a half years later, when he was released, Chang asked for political asylum in the United States. He claimed that if he was deported, the Taiwanese would try him as a Chinese Communist spy for having traveled to mainland China. After lengthy negotiations with the U.S. Immigration and Naturalization Service, Chang found a way out: he agreed to become a U.S. government informant. He signed an agreement with the INS and the DEA to cooperate with them whenever he was needed.

Chang's deal with the two agencies left him pretty much at their mercy. As a convicted felon, he could not apply for permanent residence. He was given only a temporary U.S. residency permit, which had to be renewed every six months.

But Chang had found a receptive ear at the DEA: Gene Francar, an overweight, sloppily dressed agent with thick glasses who looked more like an absentminded professor than a secret agent. Chang enjoyed dealing with Francar: unlike most DEA agents, who seemed to model themselves after the dazzling, hyperactive drug cops of Hollywood movies, Francar was an intellectual type and spent hours listening with fascination to Chang's war stories. A biologist by training, the DEA agent had begun his career working for the Food and Drug Administration as an inspector of pesticides.

When Chang was approached to pilot the drug shipment through Cuba, he undertook the mission with unusual zeal. A fervent anti-Communist, he saw the planned trip to Cuba as a chance to expose Castro's regime. The veteran pilot could not shy away from this war, and he immediately called Francar to tell him so.

The DEA at first accepted Chang's offer to infiltrate Ruiz Sr.'s organization, but with the understanding that he would not actually fly to Cuba. The DEA plan was for Chang to go along with the smugglers' preparations until the day of the flight. Then, Ruiz and his coconspirators would be arrested on the Miami airport's tarmac on charges of conspiracy to smuggle cocaine.

It didn't work out that way. Chang and Ruiz Jr. had turned on the engines and driven the plane onto the tarmac, but discovered a mechanical problem and decided to delay the trip. Francar, who was in a van on one side of the runway with a team of heavily armed DEA agents ready to intercept the plane, saw the aircraft return to the hangar. After waiting for a while under the scorching Florida sun, Francar decided to call off the operation and go home, convinced that the smugglers would postpone the trip for at least another day.

But Ruiz Jr. insisted that the plane be repaired immediately, and within a few hours, the pilots were on the tarmac again. Chang expected the DEA to stop the aircraft about 200 yards out of the hangar, and kept looking in both directions, but no one was there. Moments later, Chang found himself in the air flying to Colombia to pick up the cocaine load, his heart in his mouth. He couldn't figure out whether the DEA had suddenly changed its plans, or the agents had just bungled it.

Chang and Ruiz Jr. picked up 400 kilos of cocaine and flew it safely to Cuba. They landed in Varadero on May 9, a sunny Saturday afternoon. As in the previous operation, the cocaine was unloaded, taken to the Cuban Coast Guard safehouse, and loaded onto the Miami speedboats that were docked and waiting. This time, everything worked smoothly. The cargo arrived in Miami two days later, as planned.

At the end of his mission, Chang was debriefed by the DEA, but the agents found themselves empty-handed: Chang had lost track of Reinaldo Ruiz. The Cuban-American owed him $100,000 for the Colombia-Cuba trip, but had failed to show up at Chang's office to make the payment. As days and weeks went by, the DEA agents began to think that Ruiz had "stiffed" the Chinese pilot. It was looking like a one-time, take-the-money-and-run operation.

But Ruiz did show up one morning at Chang's office, carrying a bag loaded down with $100,000 in cash. He was smiling, and seemed to be unaware of Chang's anxiety over his delay. Ruiz dropped the money on Chang's desk, and proposed that the Chinese pilot ready himself for a new trip to Colombia in coming weeks. Chang nodded. "You got it," the pilot said.

On hearing this, DEA's Francar and his aides came to Chang's office within minutes and seized the $100,000. Chang angrily protested.

"I risked my life doing this trip," the Chinese pilot complained. "You should let me keep at least part of it."

Now that Ruiz was once again in the game, the DEA investigation developed quickly. As Chang discussed new drug flights with the Ruizes, Francar and his agents installed a hidden video camera behind the frame of a huge world map hanging near Chang's desk. By pushing one of the buttons in his telephone—the one beside the buzzer for his secretary—Chang could activate the camera and a tape recorder. From now on, Ruiz's visits to the Del Chang International office would be a matter of record. At long last, there would be evidence to be used against the drug smuggler.

What the camera showed in fifty hours of tapes made in Chang's office over the next few months astounded the DEA agents. In discussing new cocaine shipments through Cuba, Ruiz and his twenty-two-year-old son repeatedly boasted that they had the protection of high-ranking officials in the Castro regime. Although Cuban officials had been accused of playing a role in drug trafficking in the past, Cuba had always denied the charges. The U.S. media had not paid much attention to the issue, in part because the charges had always come from convicted felons or other questionable sources. This time, however, the DEA agents had found something solid. Chang's tapes were a potential bombshell.

One of the tapes showed Rubén Ruiz bragging about his first flight carrying cocaine to Cuba. Ruiz Jr. was sitting next to a file cabinet across Chang's desk, right under the camera. Laughing and accompanying his words with enthusiastic hand gestures, Ruiz Jr. was trying to persuade a seemingly nervous pilot to make a new trip to Cuba.

Chang pretended to be worried, and the strategy worked: his partner talked even more. In street language, the Cuban-American replied that there wasn't a safer place than Cuba to smuggle drugs. He had done it many times.

"You know something? We did the slyest fucking move you could ever think of doing in your life," Ruiz Jr. said, talking about his first trip with Zzie. "We flew from Panama to Miami. . . . We put down a slow speed . . . as if you were having engine problems. . . . We went to Colombia, and straight on to Cuba. We landed in Cuba. We reported to the military. They reported to the States that the plane had to make a technical stop because it had fuel leakage problems. . . .

"We came with the receipts for the repairs they did over there. We came with everything. I'm serious, we got all these things. We flew to Hollywood International. . . . We got there. We landed. Everything went real casual. We went through Customs. They said, 'What were you guys doing in Cuba?' We said, 'Well, we had problems . . .' Okay, they checked everything out. They let us go. What the fuck could they do? Everything was legal."

Ruiz Jr. went on, as the hidden camera continued to roll, talking with growing glee about the assistance the Cubans had provided: "They had sent orders through the military, through Havana, to the States, that 333 Fox had to stop there because of fuel problems. This is through the channels . . . the toppest channels in Havana. You cannot tell me this was not the cleanest fucking move you've ever seen. . . ."

As Chang looked on, Ruiz Jr. continued: "If you have an agreement and you have it with you, they will not stop you. I have a contact over there who is the chief fighter pilot in Cuba. I'm not exaggerating . . . the chief fighter pilot in the air force over there. . . ."

Rubén recalled the time when he was contacted by a Soviet-made Cuban air force MIG fighter as he was flying a cocaine load to the island.

"They were out there. They asked me if we needed an escort . . .

I swear! Can you imagine? Forget it, man: in there, I feel relaxed. In there, we are covered, man."

Every visit by Ruiz Jr. to the veteran Chinese pilot would result in new evidence of Cuban government complicity in the drug-smuggling ring's operations.

"You know something? You know another thing we've got?" Ruiz Jr. told Chang on one of his visits. "Would you believe me if I tell you something? You know the big military boats, the ones equipped with all the radars and everything? We've got two torpedo boats! . . . And they clear, they can scan the whole fucking [U.S.] coast! And they tell you: go this way, go that way."

The young man was biting his nails as he spoke, full of excitement. He hadn't worked with the Cuban torpedo boats yet, but he had heard it was great, he said. They had to try it next time.

"Let me tell you something," Ruiz Jr. said in another tape. "I'm not lying to you. I've flown to places in Cuba that nobody has. I'm talking about military runways. I'm talking camouflaged Mig-20s, Mig-23s. Okay? I'm not exaggerating."

Every time he and his father went to Cuba, they received the red-carpet treatment from the government, Ruiz Jr. boasted. They were given the best food, in the very best places.

"You get big pork legs like this," he said, spreading his hands wide open to emphasize his words. "You get steaks this big. . . . I mean, nobody eats like that over there. We ate like fucking kings. We ate oysters. . . ."

Ruiz Sr., an old hand in shady businesses, was much more composed in his conversations with Chang. But he left no doubts that he was getting assistance from top Cuban officials.

One tape showed Ruiz Sr. sitting in the same chair his son had occupied, resting his arm on the file cabinet. He was wearing his usual white guayabera shirt, and dark slacks. Next to him, in an empty chair, was a travel bag from which he extracted Cuban-made Cohiba cigars, which he offered to everybody in the room. They were discussing hiring a new, reliable boatman to pick up the cargo Chang would drop in Cuba on the next scheduled trip.

"Does it have to go inside Cuban waters?" Chang asked, in case the boatman he was proposing to hire raised objections about the plan.

"You have to, of course, because it is protection," responded Ruiz Sr., in his slow, heavily accented English. "He can work freely over there. . . ."

Was Fidel Castro aware of his top military officers cocaine smuggling? Ruiz Sr. and his son didn't seem to have many doubts about it.

The younger Ruiz, as usual the most talkative, appeared in the videotapes telling Chang that Fidel Castro was "not seeing the drugs," but surely knew of the whole operation. And if somebody accused him of drug trafficking, how could it be proven?

"Think about it," Ruiz Jr. insisted. "You can accuse Cuba all you want, but if they don't admit to it, what the fuck do they got? Can you prove it?"

"You can't prove shit," Chang answered.

"He is doing millions in fucking profits . . . ," Ruiz Jr. said, smiling from ear to ear. "Castro gets around, man! He don't fuck around. . . . You know, if the money is right . . . For one thing, he lives beautifully."

Ruiz Sr. startled the DEA agents with an unexpected claim. Speaking slowly while puffing intermittently from his Cohiba cigar, he said:

"The money that was paid to Fidel is in the drawer."

"In Fidel's drawer!" Chang exclaimed, encouraging further explanation.

Ruiz Sr., an old fox proud of his many secrets, remained silent, puffing his cigar with a knowing, self-congratulatory smile.

<>

On February 28, 1988, Reinaldo Ruiz arrived at Panama's Omar Torrijos airport, traveling from Mexico City. He was with his new wife, Colette, a tall, striking, sexy brunette aged nineteen, thirty-one years his junior. She was one of the many attractive young women who moved in Cuba's official circles, particularly in Col. Tony De La Guardia's MC Department.

She had been dazzled by Ruiz from the very first day they had met in Havana. He would invite her to the best restaurants, tell her fascinating stories from his trips around the world, and bring her expensive jewelry from Panama. She saw him as a sophisticated, caring man—a far cry from the vulgar macho types who were courting her. Ruiz had dropped Ligia, his Colombian wife, who had given him his first contacts with Medellín cartel cocaine suppliers, and had taken Colette out of Cuba with him.

The Cuban exile had already cleared the Panamanian airport's immigration and customs checks when, as he was about to cross the door into the airport's lobby, he was approached by a Panamanian

Defense Force second lieutenant. The officer informed Ruiz there was an arrest warrant against him on drug charges. He asked Ruiz to please accompany him to the offices of the DENI, the Noriega regime's secret police.

Ruiz did not put up resistance, nor did he try to bribe his way out. The DENI was headed by Col. Nivaldo Madriñan—Ruiz's friend and partner in the Cuban exit-visa business. Ruiz was confident that everything would be cleared up as soon as Madriñan heard of his arrest.

It wasn't. On arrival to the DENI offices, Ruiz was photographed and fingerprinted like any other criminal. His demands to see Madriñan went unanswered. Furious, he asked Colette to call Col. Tony De La Guardia in Havana. The Cubans would get him out of this mess.

But it was a Sunday night, and nobody was at the MC Department's office. Neither was Colonel De La Guardia at home. Had it been Monday, or had De La Guardia been reached, Cuba's biggest scandal in recent history might never have come out in the open. But early the next morning, Ruiz was taken to Panama's International airport, where a DEA agent was waiting for him. Madriñan was nowhere in sight.

It was just three weeks after Noriega's indictment by a Miami grand jury on cocaine-smuggling charges had made headlines around the world. The Panamanian regime was eager to clean its image, and had sacrificed Ruiz, who was not part of any Panamanian drug-trafficking ring and could therefore pose no harm to Noriega. By 9 A.M., Ruiz and his DEA custodians were on a Pan American flight to Miami.

Ruiz, his son Rubén, and fifteen others were indicted on February 23 for smuggling cocaine through Cuba, Haiti and Turks and Caicos Islands. Castro learned about it three days later, when the sealed indictments were opened in Miami. The U.S. prosecutors charged that Cuban "government facilities" had been used to smuggle cocaine, and that the Ruizes' drug plane had at least once landed at a military base in Varadero.

Tony De La Guardia was worried. Castro had authorized overflight operations and contacts with the Medellín cartel to smuggle cocaine through third countries, but he had always discouraged Cuban officials from letting the cocaine touch Cuban soil. De La Guardia did not know whether Fidel was familiar with the full extent of MC's drug-smuggling activities in Cuban territory. What he knew was that he would be in deep trouble if the operation came out in the open, if for no other reason, for not taking greater precautions. He could only hope that Ruiz would not drop his name.

Upon receiving the first reports about Ruiz's indictment, Castro reacted with the same outrage he had shown in similar occasions in the past. In an interview with NBC hours after the indictment was unsealed in Miami, the Cuban leader called allegations about Cuba's involvement in drug trafficking "lies from top to bottom." He didn't know that more trouble was about to rear its head.

2

The Boys Are in Trouble

◄◄◄◄◄Within days after the Reinaldo Ruiz indictment, the Cuban regime was getting disturbing reports about potentially explosive evidence linking it to drug smuggling. A six-paragraph story buried in the *Miami Herald*'s local section March 10, 1988, disclosed the existence of a tape in which Ruiz claimed the proceeds of his drug deals had gone "into Fidel's drawer." It didn't take long for Cuba's intelligence service to find out that U.S. prosecutors had many more tapes in their hands.

For a while, however, nobody in the American press pursued the story. It began to look as if the new charges against Cuba would not be taken seriously. Castro had successfully battled drug-smuggling charges in the past. The U.S. government had already tried to discredit the Cuban regime internationally for its alleged drug connections in 1982, but the charges were buried under a myriad of other Reagan Administration tirades against the Cuban regime, and were quickly dismissed as politically motivated.

Cuba had emerged virtually unscathed from the 1982 Guillot-Lara drug case. The problem for U.S. authorities at the time was that, aside from a few minor players, none of the main characters in the Colombian-Cuban drug connection were ever caught. The U.S. government had no star witnesses in the case. Castro could shrug off the whole affair as another propaganda plot by right-wing zealots in the Reagan Administration.*

But now, the U.S. government had a star witness in its hands—and on tape. Colonel De La Guardia and his men could only hope the issue would go away as it had a few years earlier.

It didn't. As often happens in tales of international intrigue, it was an unforeseen event—in this case, the desperation of a homesick nineteen-year-old woman—that triggered new alarm bells within the Interior Ministry.

It was February 1989. Colette Ruiz was nearly hysterical and making almost daily telephone calls from Miami to Col. Tony De La Guardia's MC Department in Havana. She was homesick and heartbroken. She wanted to go back to Cuba. She was threatening to divulge embarrassing information about the MC Department's involvement in drug trafficking unless she was allowed to return to her homeland. And she was doing all of this on an open line—almost sure to be monitored by U.S. intelligence services—from her tiny apartment in Miami's West Kendall neighborhood.

Colette had moved to Miami to be closer to her imprisoned husband. Realizing that Ruiz would be spending many years in jail, she was growing increasingly impatient. Within a year of Ruiz's arrest, she found herself spending her days watching soap operas on Spanish-language television. She didn't speak a word of English. She didn't know anybody in the city. She became desperate to see her family in Cuba again.

She spent hours at a time on the telephone trying to get through to Cuba. Telephone lines between the United States and Cuba had not been upgraded in more than thirty years. It took an average of eight hours of constant dialing, and a measure of luck, to get a call through. Colette had the time, and the will.†

Lonely and angry, she had requested permission to return to Cuba. De La Guardia was not taking her calls. His top aide, Major

---

* *Guillot-Lara was still at large. He had commuted between Panama and Cuba for several years, and had settled in Cuba permanently in the late 1980s. The three Cuban officials named in the indictment lived in Cuba, and were thus off-limits to American law enforcement agencies. There was no smoking gun to prove that the indictment was serious.*
† *When I examined her Southern Bell telephone bills a few months later, they showed nearly daily calls to Havana, often surpassing forty minutes each. Several short ones were to 228486—the MC Department's offices on Havana's 66th Street.*

Padrón, had turned down her entry visa request, saying she was now persona non grata in Cuba. She was the wife of a drug smuggler who had implicated Cuban authorities in his operations. Ruiz Poo, one of her perennial suitors, was nice, but noncommittal. As weeks went by, Colette's desperation grew.

"You're a bunch of bastards," she yelled at Ruiz Poo in one of her last phone calls to the MC Department's office in Havana, after being told once again she could not return to Cuba. "You better let me in, or I'll start talking. I'm serious, Miguel, I'll start talking."

Ruiz Poo and his boss, Tony De La Guardia, soon got more ominous news. In Miami, Ruiz was rumored to be ready to plead guilty to his twenty-seven-count indictment. In exchange for a reduced sentence, he was about to cooperate with U.S. authorities. He was about to publicly testify about the Cuban Interior Ministry's role in the drug-trafficking business.

The Cubans had to move fast. Through Colette's telephone calls, Ruiz Poo sent a series of veiled threats to his cousin at Miami's Correctional Center. The Cuban official's message was short and to the point: "Don't talk against Cuba, or against anyone."

<>

A stream of nervous messages between the Miami jail and the MC Department in Havana ensued. Ruiz had sent an emissary to Cuba in early 1989 in an effort to collect $100,000 Colonel De La Guardia's group owed him. Ruiz desperately needed the money to pay for his legal defense.

The prisoner had cleared his emissary's trips with American authorities. He told the FBI he would try to encourage Ruiz Poo and De La Guardia to defect to the United States before the case exploded in their faces. U.S. officials authorized the trip. They had nothing to lose.

The messenger was Felix, a fifty-six-year-old Honduran leftist who had worked as a part-time journalist in his home country. Ruiz had met Felix through a cellmate, who had talked about the Honduran's frequent travels to Cuba. After they negotiated a fee, Felix made four trips to Cuba on behalf of Ruiz, carrying a series of messages back and forth.

On returning from his first trip, Felix brought a long memo from Ruiz Poo. The Cuban official was careful not to have anything traceable to him. He always dictated his letters to Felix at the visitors' room in Havana's Triton Hotel. The papers would only carry Felix's handwriting, but their content made it clear to Ruiz they were coming from his cousin. The first letter carried a warm, friendly message, but one that revealed a growing nervousness on the Cuban side.

Ruiz Poo reiterated his plea for silence, asking his cousin not to disclose the names of the officials he had dealt with. Ruiz Poo had also enclosed $40,000 in cash to help pay his cousin's legal expenses. He promised to send him the remaining $60,000 as soon as he could get it.

The prisoner accepted the money, and speeded up his plan to get at least one of his former Cuban business partners to defect. Ruiz knew that Tony De La Guardia, one of Cuba's top secret agents, would be priceless booty for the United States. He further knew that if he pulled that coup, he would be rewarded with a big cut in his sentence. There was little time to maneuver. His lawyers were pressing him to plead guilty as soon as possible, and his testimony would be made public shortly thereafter. Felix had to leave for Cuba right away.

Felix flew to Cuba in May 1989, a month before Colonel De La Guardia and Division General Ochoa were arrested. The visitor checked in at the Triton Hotel, and rang up Ruiz Poo to tell him he was bringing a letter from his cousin.

The Cuban official read the letter with his heart pounding. It openly asked him to defect, promising him protection and help if he fled to the United States.

"Blood is thicker than water," Ruiz had written, reminding his cousin that he would have a family to take care of him if he made the move. "We are waiting for you."

Felix returned to Miami a week later with encouraging news. Ruiz Poo had told him he was about to be transferred to Panama once again, and that he would defect as soon as he arrived in that country.

In a message dictated to Felix, Ruiz Poo said he expected his transfer to take place in August. He would contact U.S. officials in Panama, and "you should take care of the rest," he said. He then reminded Ruiz of his own words: "Remember that blood is thicker than water. Remember that, now, it is I who need your help."

The FBI agents who interviewed Felix on his return from Cuba got even more sensational news. Felix told them there was a possibility Col. Tony De La Guardia himself would defect.

The Honduran messenger had extended to De La Guardia a similar invitation to defect, and he had not received a negative response. The three of them—Felix, Ruiz Poo and De La Guardia—had discussed the issue at a meeting in the cafeteria of the Comodoro

Hotel, next to a window facing the sea. De La Guardia, visibly tense and fidgety, had remained silent. Hours later, after the two Cubans met alone, Ruiz Poo told Felix that his boss would consider the proposal.

De La Guardia, one of Fidel Castro's golden boys, was not as ready to defect as Ruiz Poo, Felix told the FBI. But the colonel was nervous, fearful of what would happen to him if the whole story came to light. Tony wanted to keep his options open. He would not rule out defection if all else failed.

"They are scared shitless," Felix told the FBI. "They feel the whole world is crumbling on them."

The news of Colonel De La Guardia's possible defection spread like wildfire among the U.S. intelligence community. It coincided with reports from another FBI informant, New York–based Cuban defector José Luis Llovio Menéndez, that a top Interior Ministry official was about to defect.

Llovio had called an FBI agent to tell a story that at first seemed farfetched. He claimed that one of Cuba's top Interior Ministry officials had called him asking for help. Llovio did not identify Colonel De La Guardia—"He asked me not to reveal his name for the time being," he said—but his description of the man left little doubt that it was one of Cuba's senior secret agents.

According to Llovio's story, the caller had contacted him several times, possibly from Panama, using a secret code they had previously agreed upon. Whenever the Cuban official wanted to talk to Llovio, he would call him at his New York apartment, tap the receiver several times, then hang up.

Upon receiving that signal, Llovio would go to a public telephone on a corner of New York's Upper West Side, and wait for a second call at 6 P.M. that day. In his last call, the Cuban officer had sounded confused and highly agitated. He jumped from one thought to the next, at times almost totally incoherent.

"Things are very different now from the time when you left," the potential defector said. "Everybody in Cuba agrees now that he [Fidel Castro] is responsible for what's going on. . . . There is an underground feeling among the leadership, including in the Ministry of Interior, that if he doesn't change, something will happen. . . . People want more freedom, and things to buy. . . . This guy has gone crazy."

The Cuban official then hinted he was in trouble, and that he was about to be sacrificed by the Cuban regime in a drug-trafficking scandal. Did Llovio think he would be welcome in the United States? Could he help?

Llovio's story left the FBI agents scratching their heads. Would a top Interior Ministry official say these things in an open call to New York? It was hard to believe, but possible.

<**>

When Felix visited Ruiz at the Miami Correctional Center and delivered the news of his cousin's imminent defection, the prisoner was delighted. *Fantástico!* he exclaimed. His plan was working out.

But hours later, his Honduran messenger made a mistake that would compromise the whole project, and perhaps contribute more than anything else to sending Colonel De La Guardia to his death. He knocked on his neighbor's door, anxious to tell her of his success in Cuba.

His neighbor was Colette Ruiz. From his prison cell, Ruiz had rented apartments for the two at 9886 North Kendall Drive, a condominium in the western, heavily Latin part of Miami. They didn't get along particularly. Felix saw Colette as a vamp, interested only in squeezing the old man out of his money. She saw him as a hypocrite, a man who could profess to being a Communist while cooperating with the FBI and DEA. But Colette was dying to hear the latest news from home.

When she heard that Ruiz Poo was asking for help to defect, she flew into a rage.

"What kind of a man is he?" she screamed. "He tells me I can't go back to Cuba because I'm married to a traitor to the revolution, and then he turns around and asks for help to jump ship?"

Hours later and without telling anybody, Colette called the Cuban Interests Section at the Czechoslovakian embassy in Washington. She was ready to leak them the news of Miguel's impending defection, if only to demonstrate that she was not a traitor and deserved to be allowed back into Cuba. She couldn't have cared less if her call landed Ruiz Poo in a Cuban jail.

She identified herself as the wife of Reinaldo Ruiz, and asked to talk with the chargé d'affaires.

"I'm calling to tell you that Miguel Ruiz will defect," Colette told the voice on the other end of the line.

"Señorita, I don't know who you are talking about. Reinaldo Ruiz? Miguel Ruiz? I've no idea who these gentlemen are."

The conversation got nastier, and the Cuban official was preparing to hang up. Before he did, Colette threw her last tirade.

"No coma tanta mierda!" (Don't be a shit-eater!) she shouted into the phone. "Call Havana immediately and tell them what I just told you, because if Miguel defects, your ass will be on the line for not telling them in advance."

The phone call took place in the last week of May. Fidel Castro had just read the news of Ruiz's guilty plea. The conservative *Washington Times* had obtained a copy of the DEA's secret tapes of Ruiz and his son, and was having a media feast on its revelations. The charges of Cuba's role in cocaine trafficking were coming back with a vengeance, this time apparently backed by solid evidence. It was becoming increasingly clear that Castro would have to do something to head off the impending crisis.

<>

There was one person Colonel De La Guardia especially feared when word spread within the Cuban regime that several internal investigations would look into the U.S. drug smuggling charges. Fidel's brother, Raúl Castro, the defense minister and head of the Revolutionary Armed Forces, made it known that he was launching his own investigation into the Ruiz drug connection, and he was pursuing it with uncharacteristic zeal.

Raúl Castro had long been looking for an excuse to get even with the heads of the Interior Ministry. The Ministry of the Revolutionary Armed Forces (MINFAR) and the Interior Ministry (MININT) were known to be rival services, whose functions often overlapped, and whose officers were deeply suspicious of one another.

Over the years, Raúl Castro had come to resent the MININT's growing powers. He had long argued to Fidel that the Interior Ministry had grown too big, too powerful, too corrupt—and too infiltrated by U.S. intelligence services. He had pleaded with Fidel to put the MININT in its place.

By early 1989, the tension between the military and MININT had risen to the danger level. The military openly complained about privileges Interior Ministry officials were enjoying—and flaunting shamelessly. Charges of corruption and ineffectiveness were flying in both directions.

On paper, the two organizations had clearly defined roles. Raúl Castro's 300,000-member MINFAR—which totalled 1.7 million men and women if one added the civilian militias—was in charge of the army, navy, and air force. The 83,000-member MININT, headed by

Div. Gen. José Abrantes, was in charge of the National Police, the Department of State Security, Special Forces, Border Guards and Firefighters. The armed forces were responsible for defending the country from foreign threats; the Interior Ministry was in charge of domestic law enforcement and counterintelligence.

But over the years, the MININT's police and intelligence branches had grown into a parallel army, with vast numbers of overseas agents involved in espionage and commercial activities. Because of their secret nature and overseas connections, MININT agencies were awash in dollars. Their officers were the revolution's most frequent world travelers.

Unlike their austere counterparts in the army, who had no access to foreign trips or hard currency, MININT officials could get unlimited products from the West. It was said that you could tell a Cuban officer by the uniform: if it was the olive-green guerrilla outfit Fidel had instituted during the revolution, it was a MINFAR officer; if it was a Rolex watch and Ray Ban sunglasses, it was a MININT officer. It was also said that a MININT major had privileges equivalent to those of a MINFAR general.

And within the MININT, the MC Department enjoyed the greatest autonomy. Because of its ultrasecret nature, it was subject to no internal or external auditing. On the books, it operated on a budget of only $70,000 a year. But everybody knew that was just a fig leaf: the agency, with several offices in Panama and Cuba, had expenses several times that of its official budget, and generated millions in foreign currency. Its success was turning the Interior Ministry into a growing power within the Cuban system.

Raúl Castro could not match Division General Abrantes's largesse with his people, and he became increasingly bitter over that. In March 1989, he went directly to his brother with his latest complaint: Hundreds of Interior Ministry officers and personal friends of Abrantes were driving around Havana in brand-new cars. Who had paid for that? The Defense Minister wanted to know.

Division General Abrantes had just spent $4 million to import 1,300 Lada cars from Panama, and had distributed them among his most trusted personnel. In Cuba, where only the privileged few owned a car, this was a source of tremendous power. It created dangerous personal loyalties to the interior minister, Raúl Castro argued, and that would only help widen internal divisions within the regime.

At the risk of exhibiting his paranoia, Raúl Castro also began to wonder aloud whether the Interior Ministry wasn't putting out damaging stories about him. The rumor around Havana was that Raúl Castro was a homosexual. There were stories that Raúl Castro had been seen with several young men, habitués of the Casa de las Infusiones—a corner café on 23rd Street and G, and a well-known hangout for gay men. The defense minister's frequent fits of hysteria didn't help dispel the rumors. Where were these stories coming from? Could it be that the MININT was spreading them to discredit the defense minister in the eyes of his brother?

The time for a showdown was drawing near. Raúl Castro put his military intelligence services to work around the clock on the drug-smuggling investigation, to see if the MININT had—as he suspected—stepped out of bounds. He needed a smoking gun. He was determined to prove that the Interior Ministry was responsible for the sloppy, amateurish cocaine-smuggling operation that had caused the Cuban revolution great embarrassment abroad.

<>

On March 23, 1989, Division General Abrantes made a speech that further infuriated Raúl Castro. On the occasion of the thirtieth anniversary of Cuba's Revolutionary Security Services, the interior minister addressed a group of writers, artists and intellectuals from the Union of Cuban Writers and Artists (UNEAC). In a friendly gesture that surprised UNEAC's largely liberal leaders, Abrantes welcomed them with a cocktail party at his office and then proceeded to read a surprisingly broadminded speech. Raúl Castro thought the content of the speech—and the nature of the audience—was clearly beyond the Interior Ministry's jurisdiction. What business of Abrantes was it to set the ground rules for the role of intellectuals in the revolution?

In his speech, the interior minister, perhaps touched by the new winds of openness in the Soviet bloc, offered the intellectuals a greater flexibility to express themselves without fear of being persecuted by Cuba's security services.

"We don't want an official culture, nor a tamed culture, nor a passive nor rigid culture, because that would be a dead culture, incapable of offering solutions to problems," Abrantes said. "That could be the ideal of a bureaucrat, but never that of a revolutionary."

He called for "free, authentic creativity" that should be engaged with the revolution, but that could include artists outside the party apparatus. "I'm not just talking exclusively about those whose thinking is closest to us, but also about those who have different ideas," he said. When Raúl Castro read the interior minister's remarks in the next morning's papers, he was fuming.

In addition to Raúl Castro's investigation into the Ruiz drug-smuggling connection, Fidel Castro asked Division General Abrantes to conduct his own investigation into the case. Abrantes was, after all, responsible for Tony De La Guardia's MC group. The interior minister had long been singled out by American drug-enforcement officials as the man behind the Cuban government's drug-smuggling operations, but he was not supposed to carry out drug operations without the Castro brothers' approval. There would be no MININT coverup: Fidel would personally oversee the investigation into the ministry's unauthorized drug operations.

By May 1989, both the MINFAR and MININT counterintelligence services were finding traces of Colonel De La Guardia's complicity all over the place.

A report by the MININT radio counterintelligence unit said it had detected suspicious radio signals—almost certain to come from cocaine traffickers in Cuba—as early as in mid-March that year. The radio communications used the code word *Gordo* (Fat Man), which Cuban officials knew was often used by drug smugglers operating between Colombia and Miami. The signals originated from somewhere in the northwestern section of Havana, near the coast, the report said.

A few days later, shortly after the Abrantes speech to the intellectuals, the radio counterintelligence detected a new radio message: this time, the Cuban side was telling its Miami contact to suspend all operations until April 5. The alarm sounded throughout the Cuban drug-trafficking network. The radio monitor also detected that the drug traffickers had changed their code word from Fat Man to *Trece* (Thirteen). And they began to move within Havana.

The radio contacts were now originating from at least four locations on the western side of Havana, investigators reported. Two such communications had been traced to the Miramar neighborhood. One seemed to originate from near Seventh Avenue and 66th Street, where the MC Department was located. Another one seemed to come from around Fifth Avenue and 20th Street in Miramar. A third one seemed to originate from the plush Barlovento yacht club, a country club used mainly for Western business people and diplomats visiting Cuba.

On April 25, 1989, Abrantes received a full dossier from his counterintelligence service. "Based on information gathered from radio contacts," it said, "it is evident that the activities of Fat Man and other code words are related to drug trafficking, and that the supply operations take place in Cuban territory or Cuban territorial waters."

Raúl Castro, pressing ahead with his campaign to discredit his MININT rivals, convinced his brother to form a joint MINFAR-MININT task force to oversee the drug investigation. The Cuban regime had more than half a dozen major counterintelligence services spying on its own officials. All were put to work on the MININT drug-smuggling case.

When Col. Tony De La Guardia, who was still at his office, received the MININT counterintelligence reports on the investigation's progress, he ordered his men to stop all drug-trafficking operations immediately. Some of the *lancheros* had taken over the business from Ruiz, and were still making sporadic transshipments through Cuba.

De La Guardia located Major Padrón and Captain Ruiz Poo in Varadero, and told them to confiscate the boatmen's radios, so that there would be no more radio intercepts. He also asked them to expel all *lancheros* from Cuba, tell them not to come back, and to destroy all evidence of their cocaine shipments.

Padrón immediately put eight *lancheros* on a boat, and escorted them out of Cuba through a little-known passage, to avoid a U.S. Coast Guard ship that was patrolling the waters in front of Varadero. The Americans were already anticipating a possible exodus of drug traffickers from Cuba.

De La Guardia was soon put on notice by Abrantes that he would be transferred to a new job. If the MC Department was to emerge soon as the culprit in the bungled drug-smuggling operation, it was better to have Tony out before the discovery.

The colonel spent his last days on the job rushing to erase all traces of his agency's drug operations. His most urgent priority was to clean the MC's financial books. The cocaine traffickers owed Cuba about $1 million, and were about to make the payment. The funds had to be collected and laundered as soon as possible, or mysterious checks would be landing on the desks of unsuspecting Cuban officials in the near future, raising new questions about the outgoing MC Department's authorities.

De La Guardia sent urgent messages to a former Ruiz assistant who had taken charge of the smuggling ring's Cuban connection, asking him to transfer $500,000 to Spain. From there, the money was to be sent in two installments to Cuba. Soon, the first $250,000 arrived—in cash.

De La Guardia began frantically distributing the money among his men. He went from house to house with bags full of dollars. He asked them to gradually turn the money in to the MC treasurer, a woman who had helped the agency launder drug-trafficking profits before.

Using phony receipts, the treasurer arranged for the first installment to appear in the books as alleged profits from coffee sales in Western Europe. The next installments would be explained, respectively, as profits from sales of furniture or pesticides. If the MININT-MINFAR investigating team raided the MC office in search of a paper trail, they wouldn't find a thing.

On April 27th, the joint MININT-MINFAR investigating committee held its first high-level meeting. Division General Colomé Ibarra and Abrantes presided over the gathering at the interior minister's office. Among the participants was Tony De La Guardia, who listened stone-faced as a MININT counterintelligence officer described the intercepted radio signals that proved somebody was carelessly conducting drug-trafficking operations from Cuban soil.

The elite MC Department was now in a panic. Raúl Castro was out to get them.

Ruiz Poo, the man who had initiated the contact with Ruiz, begged his boss to talk with Div. Gen. Abelardo Colomé Ibarra outside the joint MININT-MINFAR meetings. He pleaded with De La Guardia to explain the whole operation to Colomé Ibarra, and to offer him all the cocaine-business profits in return for calling off the investigation.

"Tony, please, turn in everything, down to the last cent we've made," a desperate Ruiz Poo said.

"Relax, relax, there's no crisis," responded De La Guardia.

A few days later, Ruiz Poo was standing at the intersection of 10th Street and Calzada, where his wife's car had run out of gas. He was pouring gas into the car's empty tank, when De La Guardia's Lada 2107 pulled up beside him. De La Guardia looked tense, but seemed to be in control. He had called Div. Gen. Colomé Ibarra, he said, and had received a reassuring response. The money would be turned in to the task force, and the whole thing would be quickly forgotten.

"Everything's all right," De La Guardia said. "Things will work out. Just stay calm."

By then, Raúl Castro had become convinced that the MININT's drug operations had run out of control, and were a serious security risk to the revolution. If members of Cuba's security services had been identified as big-league drug smugglers, the CIA would surely use the opportunity to infiltrate them. After all, most of the *lancheros* were Miami Cuban exiles. Perhaps no other ethnic group in the United States had such close associations to U.S. intelligence as the anti-Castro exiles in Miami.

Raúl Castro was particularly worried that drug money in the hands of the MININT secret police could fund a conspiracy. Nobody knew the extent of the population's discontent in Cuba as well as the country's secret services. Nobody had as much access to information about the collapse of the country's economy. The senior officials of Cuba's intelligence services might be among the first to support change in Cuba, as the Abrantes speech to the intellectuals had possibly indicated. The MININT secret police could be a time bomb ready to explode.

On Saturday, May 27, Raúl Castro ordered a surveillance team to wiretap Transportation Minister Diocles Torralba's house. A graduate of military academies in the Soviet Union, Torralba was a former head of the MINFAR's air defense forces and retained good contacts within the army. He was also close to key MININT officers: his daughter Maria Elena was married to Col. Tony De La Guardia.

Raúl Castro had gotten word that Torralba had invited a small group of military and Interior Ministry officers for Sunday dinner. He had a counterintelligence team place three hidden microphones inside the house, and two others in trees around the building.

Among the scheduled guests: MINFAR Division General Ochoa, who had just returned from Angola and was known to be irritated over the lack of financial aid for his returning troops; MININT Col. Tony De La Guardia, the Rolex-sporting head of the ministry's secret trading organization abroad; his identical twin brother Brig. Gen. Patricio De La Guardia, who was also just back from the Angola war; and Major Padrón, an MC Department employee long suspected of corruption.

The May 28 dinner turned out to be subdued. There were lots of drinks, and much small talk about the roast pork Torralba had cooked for his friends. Nobody criticized Fidel Castro directly, but the general tone of the conversations reflected a growing skepticism about Cuba's state of affairs.

At one point, the names of Maj. Florentino Azpillaga and Air Force Gen. Rafael del Pino—two recent military defectors to the United States—came up. It was in a conversation on the patio between Torralba and Col. Tony De La Guardia. One of them had muttered that perhaps defecting was the best thing they could have done. The two had been given a red-carpet reception by the gringos. They had no problems.

Ochoa was silent most of the evening, but joined in the generalized criticism of the country's state of affairs. He was most irritated by the lack of financial aid for Angolan veterans, who he said were being "bumped from place to place" like a bunch of basketballs.

When Raúl Castro read the transcripts of the conversations, he saw them as another major breach of military discipline. The top officers of the Cuban revolution could not be allowed to criticize the regime. These officers were supposed to be the eyes and ears of the revolution—not its critics. Their sympathetic talk about military defectors made them a potential security risk.

But there was something more serious in evidence here: this group of disgruntled officers could easily be penetrated by U.S. intelligence services and encouraged to move from general frustration to open rebellion. Harsh disciplinary action was required.

Raúl Castro's suspicion that Cuba's security services were being dangerously infiltrated by several U.S. agencies was not unwarranted. In addition to DEA informant Chang, the former Taiwanese air force pilot, the American government had several other collaborators who had penetrated the Cuban military's hierarchy through the drug business.

By mid-1989, the U.S. law enforcement agencies were obtaining such good intelligence on the Cuban regime's drug links that they were preparing a spectacular move: the kidnapping of Cuban Interior Minister Division General Abrantes.

The U.S. Customs Service, with assistance from the Defense Intelligence Agency (DIA), had drafted an elaborate scheme to draw Abrantes into a meeting with drug dealers in international waters. The meeting would take place near Cay Sal Bank, a stretch of shallow waters between Cuba and the Bahamas. Once there, Abrantes would be kidnapped by U.S. agents and taken to the United States to face drug-trafficking charges there. The plan was code-named Operation Greyhound.

U.S. Customs Commissioner William Von Raab, a vociferous ultraconservative and one of the last hangers-on from the Reagan Administration, was anxious to carry out the operation. Even if he could only get Abrantes on videotape in a computers-for-dope operation, it would be the Customs Service's biggest coup ever. It would also have been a major propaganda victory for the newly elected Bush Administration, which was vowing to fight an all-out war on drugs.

According to a twenty-five-page classified U.S. Customs report, Operation Greyhound would seek to "infiltrate, penetrate and prosecute members of the [Cuban] drug-smuggling organization." It said "final negotiations" between Abrantes and U.S. undercover agents were to take place in Cay Sal Bank, where Abrantes would be "apprehended."

The operation was planned jointly by the U.S. Attorney's Office in South Florida, the Customs Service, the DEA, and the DIA. The U.S. Attorney's Office coordinated the task force. Customs was in charge of the covert action. The DIA was to provide intelligence, and would coordinate with the navy and air force in case the operation sparked a battle at sea with the Cuban warships escorting Abrantes. An elite SEAL team, a squadron of F-16 Fighting Falcons, an E-3 AWACs aircraft, a Spruance-class destroyer and a U.S. Navy submarine would be ready for action. The State Department was not informed about Operation Greyhound "because they would have probably tried to stop it," Von Raab told me.

The man who was to lure Abrantes to the meeting was convicted drug smuggler Gustavo "Papito" Fernandez, a fifty-six-year-old former CIA collaborator serving a fifty-year sentence on drug-trafficking charges. Fernandez had imported 300 tons of marijuana between 1977 and 1981, part of it through Cuba. He had since cooperated with the DEA on various cases in a bid to reduce his sentence.

A Cuban exile like Ruiz, Fernandez claimed to maintain good relations with his former Cuban smuggling partners—many of them close to senior officials of the Castro regime. He wasn't bluffing. After his release from Florida's Okeechobee prison on May 23, 1989, the day Operation Greyhound was set in motion, Fernandez was wired with hidden microphones and sent to talk with his underworld contacts. It soon became clear that Fernandez's friends were in contact with top Cuban military officers.

"We were getting dynamite conversations on tape," recalls Patrick O'Brien, the U.S. Customs Service special-agent-in-charge in South Florida. "We identified at least eight men in the Cuban government who were smuggling dope. One name then kept coming up as the guy who was behind it all: Gen. José Abrantes."

Fernandez was staying in a safehouse on the Florida keys. He was allowed to leave the institution every day between 8 A.M. and 5 P.M., but only with U.S. Customs agents at his side, or watching him. As time went by, "Papito" Fernandez told his custodians he needed more freedom: he couldn't very well be a credible drug smuggler on a nine-to-five routine.

He was allowed to move into a trailer park in Key Largo. Customs Service agents moved in with him. To make him a convincing underworld figure, Fernandez was given a brand new Lincoln Continental car with a phone, a big speedboat, more than $4,000 of government "flash money" and an empty .45 caliber handgun.

Fernandez was to offer the Cuban government U.S. military secrets. A U.S. agent had given him a one-page document on Department of Defense letterhead, with some information about U.S. satellites over Cuba with infrared capability that could penetrate jungle foliage.

"It was legitimate information, but not very detailed," David Urso, the U.S. Customs agent who drafted the paper, told me. "Just enough to whet their appetite."

In exchange, Cuba would allow Fernandez to land an aircraft with 2,000 pounds of cocaine coming from Colombia. The cargo would be delivered to Fernandez on international waters. Citing worries about his own security, Fernandez would demand that Abrantes himself be present at the intelligence-for-dope exchange, or that he at least be there to receive the computers and arrange for the immediate pickup of the cocaine cargo.

Then and there, the Cuban interior minister would be arrested by American agents, supported by the U.S. fighter aircraft from the Homestead air force base in south Florida and the navy ships.

Within the Customs Service and DEA offices in south Florida, many agents were skeptical about Operation Greyhound. The idea had been first sold to the Customs Service's higher-ups by Urso—a young, action-hungry Customs agent who was not taken very seriously by veteran officers.

As to the operation itself, its shortcomings were obvious: not even the most imaginative Hollywood scriptwriter would have had Cuba's interior minister personally overseeing a drug-trafficking operation. And "Papito's" cover was weak: He was operating from his Florida home base, where it was hardly a secret that he was serving a fifty-year prison sentence. Did Von Raab seriously think that Abrantes would fall into the trap? "I didn't know, but I hoped that he would," he would tell me later.

But "Papito" Fernandez outsmarted everybody. He escaped from his watchmen on June 12, 1989—the same day Division General Ochoa and Col. Tony De La Guardia were arrested in Cuba. Fernandez was last seen comfortably eating breakfast and reading a newspaper on the steps of his trailer home. One of his Customs Service escorts was inside; he heard somebody come up to the trailer and engage Fernandez in a conversation in Spanish. The Customs agent didn't speak Spanish. He stayed inside, so as to not raise suspicions from the visitor. But hearing only silence seconds later, the agent peeked outside. "Papito" was gone. So was the Lincoln Continental, the .45 caliber revolver, and the money.

Nobody ever heard from "Papito" Fernandez again. U.S. officials speculated afterward that he somehow got in touch with the Cubans, and disclosed the whole plan in exchange for permanent refuge on the island. He escaped his custodians on the morning of June 12. Ochoa and the De La Guardia brothers were arrested late that night.

Some U.S. law enforcement officers who had expressed doubts about Operation Greyhound from the outset were delighted to find out a few weeks later that Urso, the U.S. Customs agent who had originally drafted the plan and was the top Fernandez caseworker, had been fired. Urso was arrested in Miami shortly thereafter; an August 17, 1989, indictment in Colorado had charged him with lying in his 1986 job application to the Customs Service. A Customs internal affairs investigation had run into the incriminating evidence while looking into Fernandez's escape. There were initial suspicions—later dismissed—that Urso had allowed Fernandez to flee. The Denver indictment said the thirty-five-year-old Colorado native had failed to disclose that he himself had been named in a 1984 cocaine case in Denver. Following the indictment, Urso was released on bond after two days in jail, and was "retired" from the Customs Service.

The U.S. government put a lid on Operation Greyhound, a major embarrassment. Customs Commissioner Von Raab obliquely referred to it in his testimony before a U.S. Senate Committee on the Ochoa–De La Guardia affair, but he didn't disclose the plan to kidnap Abrantes. All information on the case was immediately classified.

"Papito" Fernandez's escape couldn't have come at a more critical time. Ruiz had already pleaded guilty to drug-trafficking charges, and his testimony about Cuban involvement in cocaine smuggling was now a matter of public record. His wife, Colette, was threatening to make her own revelations about the high-ranking Cuban officers she had seen making cocaine-trafficking deals with her husband.

Fidel Castro and his brother, Raúl, in turn, were well into their own investigation of the bungled cocaine operation. They already had the MININT's radio counterintelligence reports in their hands, showing that somebody was using Cuban territory without proper authorization as a cocaine transshipment point. They also had reports of the Torralba dinner party, at which Division General Ochoa and Col. Tony De La Guardia had made scandalous remarks about Cuba's overall situation.

On top of it all, Raúl Castro was confronted with a difficult decision. He was scheduled to appoint Division General Ochoa as commander of the powerful Western Army by June 24, 1989. Ochoa had asked that he also be given the command of the Western region's navy and air force. A disgruntled general was on his way to becoming Cuba's most powerful troop commander.

Raúl Castro had long wondered whether to go ahead with Ochoa's promotion. The commander of Cuba's troops in Angola had grown cocky. Maybe he had been influenced by the Perestroika-brainwashed Soviet officers he had hung out with in Angola, or by his former teachers at the Frunze military academy in the Soviet Union. Or, perhaps, the title of Hero of the Cuban Republic had gone to his head.

At any rate, Ochoa was a potential threat, a man of great influence: more than 300,000 men had passed under his command in various international missions, and he was very popular with his troops. He had to be stopped, or his political skepticism would surely corrode the revolutionary zeal of Cuba's armed forces.

Division General Ochoa was everything Raúl Castro was not. An imposing 6-foot-2-inch-tall man with a deep voice and a ready smile, Ochoa was a combat hero who had risen through the armed forces' ranks with almost universal respect from his peers.

Unlike Raúl Castro, a paranoid desk officer who owed his position to his brother, Ochoa owed none of his success to family or political connections. He was a self-confident man, whose biggest source of pride was having risen from a peasant upbringing to the top echelons of the Revolutionary Army without losing his folksy, back-slapping ways.

Ochoa had only completed sixth grade when he joined Fidel Castro's rebel army in the Sierra Maestra. He was eighteen at the time, one of seven children of a peasant family from Cauto Cristo, a small village in eastern Cuba's Holguín province. Most of the Ochoa brothers had joined the guerrillas in 1958, fighting in the ranks of commander Camilo Cienfuegos.

Arnaldo Ochoa was one of the rebel fighters that took the city of Santa Clara in Central Cuba, and participated in virtually all major battles that led to the January 1, 1959, victory of the revolutionary forces. Once Fidel Castro took power, Ochoa became a captain in the new revolutionary army. He fought against the CIA-backed Cuban exile forces at the Bay of Pigs in 1961, and, over the next few years, he helped rout the counterrevolutionary guerrillas hiding out in the Escambray mountains.

Once the insurgents were defeated, Ochoa began a series of internationalist missions that, over the next three decades, would turn him into the most experienced field officer in Cuba's armed forces.

His resumé read like a catalogue of Cuba's military interventions abroad: in the early 1960s, at the time when Ernesto "Che" Guevara was heading a Cuban-led revolutionary campaign in Bolivia, Ochoa was heading a Cuban guerrilla cell in Venezuela. From there, he was sent to Brazzaville, in the Congo, where he led about one thousand Cuban troops that helped defend the country's leftist regime, and trained Marxist guerrillas from Namibia, Mozambique and South Africa.

After a brief stint as commander of the army in Havana in 1971, Ochoa was reassigned abroad. By 1972, he was heading a 500-man Cuban contingent training the army of Sierra Leone. During the 1973 Arab-Israeli war, he trained Syrian forces in the Golan Heights. In 1975, he led 37,000 Cuban troops in Zaire. By 1976, he was a senior commander of the Cuban forces in Angola. That year, he organized a popular militia in Addis Ababa, and led 9,000 Cuban troops in the Ethiopian fight against Somalia during the Ogaden war.

Throughout his military campaigns, Ochoa had always been a frontline soldier, and a commander ready to die for his troops. He would spend much of his time sitting with soldiers, asking about the quality of the food, commiserating about their living conditions. At his commander's office, he would always keep extra sets of Parker pens or Seiko watches, which he would use to reward officers and soldiers. A watch from Ochoa was a major status symbol within the army.

Ochoa would also make a point to cultivate good personal relations with the generals of his host countries. To avoid perpetuating the stereotype that Cuban military advisers were arrogant and pushy, Ochoa would often go out of his way to adapt to local customs. One of the campaign pictures he kept in his home in Havana shows him clad in an Arab general's uniform. He is standing, looking at the camera, decked out in a white military suit with yellow ropes hanging from his shoulders, with a Moorish hat on his head. He is not smiling.

By December 1977, Ochoa was a division general, and a top commander of the joint Ethiopian, Cuban, Soviet, Polish, Hungarian and East German troops in Angola. Over the next few years, he would set up the armed forces of Grenada for Prime Minister Maurice Bishop, and would provide military training to the armies of South Yemen, Syria, Vietnam, Libya, Afghanistan, Iraq, and Laos. In 1983, he was dispatched to Nicaragua for a two-year assignment as the top military adviser to the Sandinista regime, which was seeking urgent Cuban help to repel the U.S.-financed counterrevolutionary contra guerrillas.

By then, Ochoa was already a well-known figure within the Soviet bloc's military apparatus, and a real-life hero within the Cuban armed forces. Among Cuban civilians, he was hardly known. The Castro regime revered dozens of military officers to the point of elevating them to a status of quasi-sainthood, but they all had something in common: they were dead.

The names of Cuba's top generals were almost unknown to most people on the island. The government-run media would only mention them sporadically in brief reports on routine command rotations. In bigger stories about Cuba's wars abroad, there was only one military genius who was the guiding hand behind all of Cuba's victories: Castro himself.

In a rare exception to the rule, the Cuban regime in 1984 had awarded Ochoa and fellow division general Colomé Ibarra the highest honorary titles the Cuban military had ever granted: the orders of Hero of the Cuban Republic and Máximo Gomez Order, First Degree.

Decrees 250 and 251 of January 1984, published in *Granma*, stated that "the life of comrade Ochoa Sanchez is a living example of the qualities and merits of those men of the most humble origins who . . . cultivate the authentic traits of modesty and sincerity and who enjoy the admiration and the respect of the masses."

Ochoa's career, it said, served as a "stimulus to all fighters." The award would help recognize the "virtues of honesty, humility and a capacity for sacrifice" embodied by Ochoa, it added.

<>

Indeed, Ochoa lived a frugal life. In 1989, he still lived in the same town house on 24th Street in the Nuevo Vedado section where he had moved with his second wife, Maida, fifteen years earlier. It was a far cry from Interior Ministry's Colonel De La Guardia's spacious residence in the suburbs.

The front yard was so small that it could barely accommodate his three rows of sugar beets. At sunset, when he was in town, his neighbors would often see him sitting on the front steps, barefoot, dressed only in shorts and eating a mango.

When I visited his house a few months after his execution, I was surprised by the austerity of the place. This was not the typical Latin American general's home. It was sparsely furnished: no rugs, draperies, nor valuable works of art. The front door led into a hall with an old couch. Ahead was a TV room with four rocking chairs and two three-foot-high wooden ashtrays, which the Ochoas had brought with them from Nicaragua. It was cheap furniture. On the room's wall was an oriental tapestry with a fishing scene. A basket on the floor contained old records of the general's favorite music: instrumental arrangements by Frank Purcell, Paul Mauriat, and Michel Legrand.

The only valuables in the room were a Sony color television set and a Sony Betamax videocassette recorder—presents of Defense Minister Raúl Castro the day Ochoa was awarded with the title of Hero of the Cuban Republic. Ochoa would make fun of the complicated recorder. "Listen, chico, who on earth understands how this damn thing works," he would tell visitors whenever he pointed out the machine.

In the living room, there was a set of green plastic seats, and a table with small wooden African figurines, mostly souvenirs bought in African airports. Two of them, both portraying Rodin-like thinking women, were presents from Div. Gen. Leopoldo "Polo" Cintra Frias, Ochoa's top aide in Angola. On the living room's wall were two crossed

African spears and a shield—a gift from a former Angolan defense minister.

There was a small office facing the street, next to the entrance to the house. It looked more like a teenager's study than the workspace of a general of one of Latin America's largest armies. There were three bookshelves full of World War II history books. There were other books, mostly illustrated biographies of military men, as well as biographies of Richard Nixon and Marco Polo.

There were also U.S. car magazines, which Cubana de Aviación pilots used to bring him regularly when he was stationed in Havana.

Ochoa would almost never wear Western clothes, which he could easily buy on his trips abroad. A proud *guajiro* (peasant) at heart, he preferred his military uniform, or a pair of Cuban slacks with a guayabera. His commendation's references to his "modesty" and "unselfishness" were not empty formulas of revolutionary rhetoric: he seemed truly unimpressed by material possessions.

Like many officers of his background, he would wear a watch for two or three months, then pass it on to a good friend. In Castro's Cuba, watches changed hands constantly among members of the *nomenklatura*. They were not sold, but given away or exchanged as proofs of friendship—a symbolic gesture that the participants in the transaction were *socios*, or best buddies.

A watch revealed one's political connections, one's place in society. In a closed society in which one could fall in disgrace at any moment for the most innocent remark, a well-placed *socio* was also the best insurance against bad times. Many Cubans wryly described their political system as *sociolismo*, a witty play on Cuba's much-touted *socialismo*.

Ochoa was constantly begged by friends and assistants for his watches. But, unlike other practitioners of the watch-changing ritual, he was not interested in bragging about the sources of his own watches.

He had given away the two-time-zone Soviet digital watch that Raúl Castro had given him to keep track of the time in Cuba and Angola. He had also given away the metallic Seiko with the initials AOS in its back that Fidel Castro had given him when he was promoted to general.

Two months before his death, Ochoa had begun using a Rolex, the most common watch among top-ranked Cuban officers. He had noticed it on the wrist of Norberto Fuentes, a journalist specializing in military affairs who was writing a book on Angola. Ochoa had made an admiring remark about the watch, and it was his in a matter of seconds.

He drove around in a five-year-old red Lada 1500 with a white telephone, an old model compared with the Ladas driven by most Interior Ministry officials. The general had acquired it in exchange for an older model shortly after his proclamation as Hero of the Cuban Republic.

Ochoa loved fancy cars, but could not bring himself to drive one amid Cuba's poverty. He owned a golden Mercedes-Benz 500 SL sports car. It was one of three Mercedes that Ethiopian President Mengistu Haile Mariam had given to top Cuban officials for their assistance during the Ogaden war. The other two went respectively to Raúl Castro and former Interior Minister Ramiro Valdes.

But Ochoa almost never used his. The car spent years gathering dust in his driveway. The first time he got it out, the whole neighborhood came out to watch. He had hated the feeling.

Weeks later, on a sunny Sunday morning, the Ochoas decided to take the car on a one-day excursion to the southern city of Cienfuegos. Motorists on the Autopista Central highway turned around to get a good look at the fancy car. The Ochoas decided to get rid of it as soon as possible.

The opportunity arose in 1984, when Ochoa was based in Nicaragua. He had thrown a dinner party for the top Sandinista army officers and, as the evening wore on, the conversation moved to cars. The Sandinistas were big Toyota fans. Ochoa told his guests about the wonders of his Mercedes. He lamented it was languishing in his driveway back in Cuba.

Sandinista Army Maj. Gen. Joaquin Cuadra, the chief of staff of Nicaragua's army, jumped from his seat. *"Te lo compro!"* (I'll buy it from you!) he said. Ochoa had the Mercedes shipped to Nicaragua a few weeks later. He exchanged it for Cuadra's white Toyota, which he took with him on his return to Cuba.*

---

* *Sandinista Major General Cuadra says he inherited Ochoa's Mercedes 500 against his will. According to Cuadra, the two had not discussed a possible trade. After Ochoa had left Nicaragua for good, a Cuban officer knocked on Cuadra's door to tell him there was a surprise waiting for him at the airport. When Cuadra got there, he found the Mercedes. According to the Nicaraguan general, Ochoa had taken his Nicaraguan army–owned Toyota with him and had shipped the Mercedes as a present. Cuadra sold the Mercedes shortly thereafter to a relative.*

Ochoa didn't enjoy any kind of public attention. In his mind, it meant only trouble. He seldom attended parties when he was in Cuba, and he kept any socializing with his bosses to a minimum. Raúl Castro would periodically drop by Ochoa's house on 24th Street, bringing an invitation for a cocktail party or a power lunch. But Ochoa would rarely go.

Once, the defense minister invited the Ochoas to a gathering at his home. The general and his wife said they would be delighted, but they had a problem: they had promised Ochoa's parents they would visit with them that same night. Raúl Castro frowned. Shaking his head in friendly exasperation, he told Ochoa's wife, Maida, as he was leaving the house:

"I'm not inviting this dude anymore. He never shows up."

Ochoa and Maida laughed as they accompanied the defense minister to the sidewalk.

Ochoa's idea of a good time was getting out of Havana. He loved horseback-riding or hunting ducks in Pinar del Río. He would often go hunting for a long weekend with Chacón, his driver. In the closely knit world of Cuba's top-ranked military officers, a driver was generally one's *persona de confianza*—a person trusted to handle one's personal affairs at home as well as at the office. Chacón had become especially handy in recent years. During his stint in Nicaragua, Ochoa had fallen in love with a young Nicaraguan woman named Michelle, whom he had brought back with him on his return to Cuba. The general had installed Michelle in a comfortable house in Miramar, complete with the ultimate luxury in modern Cuba—a working telephone. Chacón took care of the furniture, the food and the bills. Ochoa spent several nights a week at his other house. To Maida, he would simply say he was sleeping at the barracks.

In addition to his medals, there was another powerful reason for the special respect Ochoa commanded within Cuba's military. He was one of the few Cubans who addressed Fidel Castro with the Spanish language's familiar *tu*. In Castro's Cuba, that could mean more than rank in the regime's hierarchy.

Ochoa and Castro had come to know one another well during Fidel's frequent trips abroad, and shared a collection of fond memories. The Cuban leader, who was usually surrounded by mediocre functionaries who accepted whatever he said with dead-serious admiration, enjoyed Ochoa's cheerful insolence.

Ochoa could use his *guajiro* humor without being disrespectful. He addressed Fidel as *"Jefe,"* but talked to the Comandante as if he were an old buddy. *"El Negro Ochoa,"* as Fidel Castro called him when he wasn't using his first name, was one of the few Cubans who could make fun of Castro and get a laugh from the Comandante.

Nobody else in Castro's entourage, for instance, would dare make jokes about the maximum leader's underwear. Ochoa had done that during a boating excursion off the coast of Chile in November 1971, when Castro made a three-week visit to that South American country following the election of Socialist President Salvador Allende.

During the boat trip, the Cubans decided to take a dip in the Pacific Ocean. The men searched their bags for bathing suits, and descended to the cabin to change clothes. When Fidel emerged in knee-long underwear, Ochoa could not help poking fun at his boss.

"Jefe, you really look sexy in that underwear!" the general said approvingly.

For many years, Ochoa would ask Castro whether he was still wearing those drawers.

On another occasion in the mid-1980s, Ochoa saw Fidel desperately looking for his half-smoked cigars in various rooms of his Havana offices.

Castro, who was trying to cut down on his smoking, had begun extinguishing his cigars halfway through, leaving them in ashtrays all over his office. His guards had acquired the habit of throwing the butts away. Once, when Fidel began to roam his office looking for leftover cigars in the middle of a discussion, Ochoa burst into laughter:

"Jefe, have you gone senile? What are you doing? Are you playing blind man's bluff?"

Fidel laughed back, suspiciously.

"Hey, you hid it, didn't you? Come on, Negro, you threw it away, didn't you?"

<>

But, over the years, Ochoa's rapport with Fidel Castro would prove to have its pitfalls. Although a committed revolutionary, the Hero of the Cuban Republic became too confident, too independent-minded. Ochoa would soon commit the ultimate sin in Castro's Cuba: he would begin acting on his own.

He was certainly in a position to do so. Like other commanders of Cuban troops in Africa before him, Ochoa had long conducted off-the-books trade transactions to help finance his war campaigns and improve the living conditions of his troops. It was standard practice for top-ranked Cuban military officers to do business deals to purchase additional clothes or better food for their soldiers. In the service of socialism, they had become enterprising capitalists.

Cuban field commanders had little choice but to engage in these transactions. If they didn't generate their own resources, they could be charged by Fidel Castro—who had little patience for budgetary explanations—with neglecting their troops. On the other hand, if they went too far in their business deals, or kept any money for themselves, they faced equally harsh punishment. In this balance between survival and acceptable socialism, the top Cuban generals were not exempt from the fears plaguing most of their countrymen.

Ochoa's predecessors in Angola had supplemented their armies' budget with exports of diamonds, ivory, quartz and other materials to Western Europe. Upon taking his command post, Ochoa had continued these shipments, and added others. He needed to generate big amounts of cash to build an airport in southern Angola. Cuba was not coming forth with the money, and the airport played a key role in his plans to win the war.

He set out to use his worldwide military contacts to broker lucrative arms deals. In 1987, he brokered a $161,000 deal with Nicaragua's Sandinista army to purchase 100 German-made M-79 grenade launchers and 12,000 projectiles. The order was placed by his good friend, Sandinista Major General Cuadra Lacayo, the proud new owner of Ochoa's Mercedes.

Ochoa was asked by the Angolan regime in early 1988 to use his connections in the international arms market to buy 100 military radios for the Angolan army. The Cuban commander was given $595,000 for the purchase. He immediately sent his aide-de-camp Captain Martinez Valdes to Panama.

Martinez Valdes soon called with good news: he had found a way to buy the equipment directly from the manufacturer, for $545,000. The Cuban mission in Angola made a $50,000 profit from the transaction, which Martinez Valdes was ordered to deposit in a numbered account of the Bank of Bilbao in Panama.

In Luanda, the Angolan capital, Ochoa generated funds by exchanging Cuban sugar, cement and other goods in the country's huge black market, known as Candonga. Cuban air force transport planes were delivering generous shipments of sugar to the Cuban army in Angola. It was one of the few products the Cubans had in excess. Ochoa instructed one of his aides, Capt. José Llicas, to sell the sugar on the Candonga. Llicas sold nearly 500 sugar sacks a month this way, and produced an average monthly income of $17,000. Because the sugar was paid in Kwanzas, the Angolan currency, the Cuban mission used the proceeds to buy African ivory, diamonds, and other goods that could be sold easily in Panama. The Cubans had developed the right connections, including a regular air shuttle, to place Angolan products in the world market.

In late 1988, toward the end of his tour in Angola, Ochoa was considering new ventures: exports of ivory, tobacco, works of art, even fighting cocks.

But Ochoa, the *guajiro* warrior, needed to expand his nonmilitary contacts in the Western business world in order to sell his rapidly expanding assortment of African products. On advice of his closest friend, Brig. Gen. Patricio De La Guardia, he approached the man who was in the best position to sell his goods abroad: De La Guardia's twin brother, Col. Tony De La Guardia, head of Cuba's network of trading firms in Panama.

De La Guardia was delighted to help Ochoa. The MINFAR general was not only his brother's best friend, he was also a close buddy of his own father-in-law, Transportation Minister Diocles Torralba. Ochoa was practically part of the family.

One of Ochoa's first requests to Tony De La Guardia was to find out what kind of prices he could get for Angolan diamonds in Panama. Captain Llicas was being offered diamonds on the Candonga market in exchange for Cuban sugar. Tony De La Guardia asked for samples, had them examined in Panama and Western Europe, and sent a message to Ochoa a few weeks later to go ahead with the sugar-for-diamonds plan.

Ochoa sent Llicas to Cuba to learn more about the diamond business. Tony De La Guardia had a driver pick him up at Havana's military airport, and then he and Llicas drove to the MININT building together. While Llicas waited in the lobby, De La Guardia went off only to return a few minutes later with a small package in his hands. Inside was a machine to verify whether diamonds were authentic. It had a scanner, and a scale on its side. If the diamond was good, a panel on the base of the scale turned bright green. The gadget would be useful; Patricio De La Guardia had just purchased four diamonds in Angola, and two of them had turned out to be fake.

It went without saying in De La Guardia's business dealings with Ochoa that they would disguise the profits of their planned ventures. It was better to keep Fidel Castro and his brother Raúl from finding out where the money had come from—just in case.

Fidel, with his almost religious disdain for money matters, would never understand his underlings' urgent need to generate hard currency. And Raúl Castro, with his paranoias and hidden agendas against the MININT, would use any transgression to make a case against his political enemies. The diamond sales would be represented as coffee exports, and nobody would ever notice.

Like anything else in the bureaucratic culture of revolutionary Cuba, it didn't matter what you did as long as there was no paper trail to cause trouble. So Ochoa continued, with the help of Tony De La Guardia, happily increasing his army's budgets and accumulating growing economic power.

By early 1989, Ochoa had $200,000 in a numbered account at the Bank of Bilbao in Panama—a huge fortune by Cuban standards. Ochoa didn't withdraw any of it for himself. The funds were to be used for the Western Army, once Ochoa was made its commander later that year.

<>

In their exploratory missions abroad to broker arms deals or sell African diamonds, Division General Ochoa's assistants soon stumbled into merchants linked to Colombia's cocaine barons.

Captain Martinez Valdes and Captain Llicas were encountering Panama's underworld of drug-connected businessmen, bankers and lawyers who could handle almost any deal with speed and absolute secrecy. They were the same type of people with whom Col. Tony De La Guardia had long been dealing in his efforts to increase Cuban exports and imports circumventing the U.S. trade embargo.

One of them was a Colombian named Fabel Pareja. He was a wheeler-dealer in Panama who had been known to help the Cubans transport the weapons they purchased in the international arms market. In 1988, Pareja suggested to Martinez Valdes that they meet with some of his friends who worked for Medellín cartel boss Pablo Escobar.

By then, Martinez Valdes was working more closely with De La Guardia than with his own boss. Ochoa was far away, in Angola, and had ordered his assistant to coordinate his activities with the MININT colonel, who was in Panama and knew the business world better than anyone. Martinez Valdes periodically called Ochoa in Luanda to inform him of his moves, but would not bother his boss with every long-shot business venture that landed on his desk. So when Pareja offered a conduit to the Colombian drug traffickers, he suggested a meeting with De La Guardia's people in Havana.

The first meeting took place in April 1988, at a house in the Marina Hemingway, a residential neighborhood largely reserved for foreign diplomats and VIP's on the outskirts of Havana. The gathering was presided over by De La Guardia's top aide, Major Padrón. Four Colombians were on the other side of the table. One of them, who had identified himself as Fernando, did most of the talking.

The Colombians proposed setting up a cocaine-processing plant in Cuba. They also brought up the idea of mass printing counterfeit U.S. dollars. They said they owned an up-to-date machine that could print the American money. All they needed was good-quality paper, and a secure place to operate it.

"That's unthinkable," responded Padrón. "It can't be done in Cuba."

But perhaps it could be done somewhere else, Padrón said. Turning to Martinez Valdes, he asked him whether his boss would be interested in doing something in Angola. Martinez Valdes said he would call Ochoa and ask. He never did. He knew the idea wouldn't fly.

At a second meeting a few days later, the Colombians were joined by a Mexican. The discussion turned to money laundering, and to a possible cocaine shipment through international waters outside Cuba. Padrón and Martinez Valdes listened with interest. Both operations could be done with little risk for the Cubans, the foreign businessmen asserted.

This time, Martinez Valdes called his boss in Luanda, and asked for permission to travel to Colombia as an emissary for De La Guardia to discuss the Colombians' proposals. He would meet directly with Pablo Escobar. De La Guardia was too high-ranking—and too well-known—to participate in such a meeting himself.

Ochoa gave his okay. His only recommendation was not to accept any drug operation on Cuban—or, for that matter, Angolan—soil. Instead, Martinez Valdes should try to convince the Colombians to hide their profits by investing them in Cuba's tourism industry.

Martinez Valdes flew to Medellín a few weeks later. He entered Colombia with a forged Colombian passport, provided by one of his business partners. A Cuban passport would have raised suspicion in Bogotá's International Airport. Because of the close collaboration between Colombian and American law enforcement agencies, a mysterious entry by a Cuban official would have been reported immediately to U.S. intelligence services.

The Cuban visitor was taken to a ranch in the hilly outskirts of

Medellín. Escobar, a man in his mid-thirties who was already the world's best-known drug lord, was waiting for him.

The Colombian cocaine baron was not interested in the money-laundering proposal. He had other plans. He wanted to pursue the possibility of shipping cocaine to the United States through Cuban waters. Escobar also wanted the Cubans' help in protecting himself from a growing offensive by Colombian government forces.

Specifically, Escobar wanted the Cubans to purchase ten surface-to-air missiles, which he planned to use if his ranch was attacked from the air. He also wanted the Cubans to allow him to station an aircraft in Cuba, ready to fly to Colombia and pick him up at any time if he was in trouble.

None of the transactions ever materialized. Preparations to smuggle cocaine through Cuba were delayed for several months due to disagreements on the drop-off point for the drugs coming from Colombia. Ochoa remained firm in his demand that the cargo be trans-shipped via international waters outside Cuba, while the Colombians wanted it done on Cuban territory.

The plan, like the negotiations to purchase surface-to-air missiles, collapsed with the arrests of Ochoa and De La Guardia in June 1989. Unlike Tony De La Guardia, the general had never gotten to carry out a cocaine-smuggling operation. But his aide-de-camp's close ties to De La Guardia's drug-smuggling ring—and Ochoa's consent for his aide's trip to Medellín—would be used by Fidel Castro a few weeks later to build a spectacular case against the Hero of the Cuban Republic.

<>

Division General Ochoa's troubles with Fidel had begun to surface during the Angolan war. Initially, they were not over money, but over the general's determination to pursue his own tactics in the battlefield.

One of the first known clashes between Fidel Castro and Ochoa took place in November 1987. At the time, Ochoa was the acting military chief of the Cuban, Soviet and Angolan forces fighting the South African–backed UNITA guerrillas in Angola.

The Cubans had taken over the command of the joint army following a disastrous offensive waged a month earlier by Soviet Gen. Konstantin Shagnovitch. The Soviet-led attack, which had been in the planning for two years, had turned into an embarrassing defeat. Angolan troops, in disarray, had retreated into the Central Angola town of Cuito Cuanavale. UNITA chief Jonas Savimbi had led thirty-five thousand of his guerrillas and some nine thousand South African troops to the outskirts of the town, and were about to take it.

Then Angolan head of state José Eduardo Dos Santos turned to Castro for urgent help. The Cuban leader agreed, but under one condition: from that point on, the Cubans—not the Soviets—would take command of all military operations in southern Angola. Dos Santos agreed. In a matter of days, Cuba's best general—Arnaldo Ochoa—was dispatched to Angola to take charge of the combined Angolan forces. With him went new Cuban reinforcement troops, artillery and combat aircraft. Within weeks, Ochoa commanded a fifty-thousand-strong Cuban contingent.

For the next twelve months, the defense of Cuito Cuanavale became Fidel Castro's biggest obsession. He had committed the best of his army to defending the city. By his own admission, the Cuban leader was spending 80 percent of his time planning each move of Ochoa's forces half a world away. At the Cuban Defense Ministry situation room, Fidel Castro spent entire days moving pins of different colors on huge maps of Angola hanging from the walls. With a child's enthusiasm, he experimented moving one Cuban battalion toward the east, or a column of tanks to the west.

"The fate of the revolution was at stake in this battle, so one couldn't even take care of government affairs at the time," Castro would recall later. "At least I didn't take care of them. . . . We dedicated all our time to this struggle, to this war."

Nothing would be left to chance. Fidel Castro took an interest in every aspect of the Angola campaign, from military operations to the supply of clothes for his troops.

"For the soldiers, even candy . . . ," Castro would recall two years later. "There wasn't a day when I wouldn't ask at the High Command how many tons of candy, cookies, chocolate had been dispatched to our troops; how they were doing, what bags they had, how they slept, what they ate."

Like everyone else in the Cuban camp in Angola, Division General Ochoa raised his eyebrows with exasperation every time a new order came from Havana. What could Fidel Castro know about conditions in Angola from his air-conditioned offices six thousand miles away?

But being a disciplined soldier, Ochoa did not contradict his commander in chief. He simply ignored the most absurd orders, and interpreted others his own way.

On December 2, 1987, only two weeks after Ochoa's arrival in Angola, Fidel Castro admonished Ochoa for the first time about his apparent disdain for orders coming from Havana.

"I asked if you had sent some information about the instructions of November 30, and I'm told that nothing has arrived here, that you usually send little information," Fidel wrote in a secret cable to Ochoa. "I hope that this habit will not prevail in this situation."

Tensions between Castro and Ochoa mounted over the next few weeks.

Castro had instructed Ochoa to beef up his troops in Cuito Cuanavale, which he saw as increasingly vulnerable to a UNITA attack. Ochoa didn't think so. He had reached the conclusion that he could repel an attack on Cuito Cuanavale with his Mig-23 jets based in the city of Menongue, 125 miles to the west, and by mining the fields surrounding Cuito Cuanavale. Under Ochoa's plan, that would free Cuban troops to open a new front in southern Angola, attack the enemy there and regain the momentum.

On December 20, 1987, Fidel learned that Ochoa had failed to move reinforcements into Cuito Cuanavale. Furious, he sent a new coded message to his general.

"We have been very displeased with the unexpected ideas (from the Cuban command in Angola), which we find inexplicable," Castro said. The Cuban leader once again pressed for new tank and artillery reinforcements for Cuito Cuanavale.

<>

At one of the year-end dinner parties at Ochoa's House No. 1 in the Cuban military headquarters in Luanda, the general confided to his closest friends what he thought of Fidel's military orders. Sitting around the table with Ochoa and his wife, Maida, were Brig. Gen. Patricio De La Guardia, his wife, Maria Isabel, who was known by her nickname "Cucusa," and two other senior officers with their wives.

"Fidel has gone crazy," Ochoa said, commenting on the Comandante's orders to move a brigade into Cuito Cuanavale. "He's completely gaga."

The guests looked up from their plates, amazed.

"Arnaldo, you're nuts," Cucusa recalls having responded with a chuckle. "How can you talk like that?! . . . You're out of your mind!"

If one thing was taboo among Cuban officials, that was criticizing Fidel Castro. For a top army general to do it, even in a light remark to a small group of friends, was a startling departure from the norm.

Ochoa and Patricio De La Guardia had been increasingly outspoken in their criticism of Castro during their stint in Angola. At first, it had been private talk between best friends. Now, they were beginning to make the disparaging remarks in front of others.

<&>

On January 26, 1988, Castro sent a new—and even stronger—secret cable to Ochoa. "I don't understand the things being done in Cuito," the Comandante complained. "Who has the top responsibility in Cuito? You often don't even bother to explain to us why things are being done, despite the fact that we are not inflexible and we are always ready to listen to your criteria."

By the end of January, when Ochoa had still not moved new troops into Cuito Cuanavale, Fidel Castro summoned the general to Havana. Ochoa arrived in the Cuban capital January 31, 1988, and spent the next four days holed up with the high command. He left February 5, for Angola with detailed instructions and a specific schedule for building up his defenses around Cuito Cuanavale.

The much-awaited UNITA guerrilla attack on the city came on February 14. The South African–supported rebels launched more than a hundred armored vehicles into the outskirts of the town, breaking its first defense lines and penetrating three miles into the loyalist forces' territory. The attack was so fierce that three Angolan brigades fled in disarray, leaving behind six of the seven tanks they had brought to one key cross point. Fourteen Cubans died in the attack.

Fidel Castro felt vindicated. He sent a coded message to Ochoa reprimanding him for the "mistakes that were made and the time that was lost" in building up the town's defenses. He said Ochoa had "consistently underestimated" the enemy's offensive capabilities.

"I can't hide from you that we feel very bitter about these events, which we anticipated and against which we repeatedly warned," Castro said in a confidential message to Ochoa on February 15.

But as the days went by, Ochoa's assessment that the UNITA forces lacked strength to penetrate further into the Cuito Cuanavale area proved right. The guerrillas had moved too far away from their supply lines, and were finding themselves in front of a stretch of mined fields. Each time they tried to break up the new Angolan defense lines, they would be hit mercilessly by the Cuban Mig-23 combat planes based in Menongue. The rebel offensive was beginning to wind down.

Ochoa was implementing his own battle plans. Instead of concentrating his forces in Cuito Cuanavale for an all-out battle there, he moved two brigades south to the border with Namibia. His idea was to open a new battlefront on the very doorstep of the South African stronghold.

The Angolan-Cuban-Soviet forces were now on the attack. UNITA rebels had to split their forces to contain the new Angolan offensive. By April, the Cubans had opened a 280-mile-long front in south-central Angola, about 125 miles further south than their original positions in Cuito Cuanavale.

<>

Division General Ochoa's differences with Fidel Castro on Angola went beyond tactics: Ochoa was convinced the war could not be won. The Angolans were not motivated. The corrupt Marxist regime the Cubans were aiding had little popular support. The Cubans were doing most of the fighting. Many Angolans saw the Cubans as an obstacle to peace, rather than a friendly army come to their assistance. A joke making the rounds in Cuban camps in Angola at the time had it that Cuban, Soviet and Angolan forces had clearly defined their jurisdictions in the joint war effort: The Cubans were doing the fighting, and the Soviets were doing the war matériel. And the Angolans? somebody would ask. Doing fine, thank you.

The Soviets had long wanted a political settlement in Angola. Soviet-American relations were warming up following Gorbachev's visit to Washington in December 1987. The two superpowers were eager for a deal that would get the Cuban-Soviet forces out of Angola and South African troops out of Namibia.

Ochoa's strategy was based on the assumption that Cuba wanted to place its forces in the best situation to negotiate from a position of strength. With this in mind, he charged ahead with another ambitious project. In early 1988, he began construction of a military airport in Cahama, on the newly opened southern Angola front. From the new airport, the Cubans would be able to launch air attacks deep into UNITA's bases in Namibia.

But Fidel Castro was not that enthusiastic about a political solution to the Angolan war. In his mind, a military victory would be a much greater prize for Cuba than a negotiated settlement, in which the Soviets and the Americans would pretty much dictate the terms.

In the end, Castro was forced to accept a political settlement.

Negotiations between the United States, the Soviet Union, Cuba and South Africa ended with the signing of an agreement on Angola in New York on December 22nd, 1988. The agreement resulted in the independence of Namibia, which would be accompanied by the departure of South African troops from the newly independent country and the departure of Cuban troops from Angola.

The signing ceremony provided the first evidence of Ochoa's fall from grace. Castro sent nine Cuban generals to the signing ceremony at the United Nations. Among them were Division Generals Colomé Ibarra and "Polo" Cintra Frias, Ochoa's aide in Angola. The nine "contributed in a decisive and exemplary manner to South Africa's joining the negotiating table after it hastily abandoned the battlefield," *Granma* said in its account of the ceremony.

Only one Cuban general was missing: Ochoa. Castro had denied the commander of Cuban troops in Angola a recognition of his contribution to the war effort.

On January 9, 1989, Ochoa learned he was being reassigned to Havana. Division General Colomé Ibarra had come to the Angolan capital bearing a letter from Raúl Castro. In it, the defense minister told Ochoa of his transfer, and announced the appointment of Division General Cintra Frias as his successor.

Officially, Ochoa was to prepare for taking over the Western Army—Cuba's largest—in June. But it was an open secret that Ochoa was in trouble with the Castro brothers. There were serious questions as to whether his promotion would go through.

Reassigned to Havana, Division General Ochoa took a few weeks' vacation. Upon his return he was to go into training for his new job at the Western Army, scheduled to begin on June 24, 1989.

He was at a crossroads. After nearly two decades of a globetrotting life filled with adventure, he was facing the prospect of a prolonged bureaucratic job at home. The world was changing. He knew that the Soviet Union would no longer support Cuba's wars abroad, and intellectually he even agreed with that. The days of fighting other peoples' wars were over.

But Ochoa didn't quite see himself in the new setting. He functioned well in the battlefield, where he could call the shots. He sensed he would not do as well in Havana's rigid military bureaucracy, he told his wife. He was not a political animal. Interoffice wars were not his terrain. And after spending most of his military career as a field commander abroad, he did not relish returning to the playground atmosphere of the Castro brothers' army.

He was also becoming increasingly irritated with Cuba's treatment of the returning flood of Angola war veterans.

Large groups of soldiers were pouring back into Cuba from Angola. After a pompous ceremony at the monument to independence hero Antonio Maceo on the highway to Havana, the veterans were left to fend for themselves. Most had no jobs, nor hopes for finding any. After years of fighting in Africa, all they had in hand was a certificate and a medal. These were good for establishing one's revolutionary credentials in case of trouble with the secret police, but in fact they had little practical value.

Many returning soldiers, men in their early twenties from the countryside who didn't have any connections in Havana, knocked on the door of Ochoa's house on 24th Street. They asked for letters of recommendation, for clothing, or for some money to help out their families. Ochoa would invite them in, and occasionally help them out. If he could not direct them where to find a job, he would at least give them a small gift—the standard Parker pen, or a cheap plastic watch.

Ochoa sympathized with the unhappy veterans, and began to openly complain to his boss about their treatment. His insistence was beginning to wear on Raúl Castro. The defense minister was also miffed by Ochoa's gift-giving. Why was Ochoa giving all those veterans imported pens? Was he trying to win a popularity contest? Who did he think he was?

By late May 1989, less than a month before Division General Ochoa's scheduled takeover of Cuba's Western Army, Raúl Castro was avidly looking for an excuse to cancel the promotion. A Perestroika-influenced general who had systematically ignored Fidel's orders in Angola and was constantly nagging about the veterans' treatment at home was not fit to be entrusted with Cuba's most powerful army.

Blocking Ochoa's nomination would not be easy, however: it had already been approved by the Central Commission of Army Cadres, the Central Committee of the Communist Party and Fidel Castro himself. But a juicy intelligence report that landed at Raúl Castro's desk at the time would provide the defense minister with a great opportunity to build a solid case against Ochoa's promotion.

A young woman, the daughter of a well-known Cuban actor, had just returned from Angola, and had wild stories to tell about Ochoa. She was telling her friends she had been sexually abused by the general and forced to have group sex with him and his top aides.

The young woman, Patricia De La Cruz, had traveled to Angola in September of 1988 as the companion of an aide to Brig. Gen. Patricio De La Guardia. In reality, she was going as De La Guardia's protégée.

She was a nineteen-year-old bombshell: tall, blond, seductive and extremely provocative. In her tight jeans and loose T-shirt in an African town where women walked around in shabby, formless robes, Patricia raised male eyebrows from the minute she arrived.

In the ultra-libertine atmosphere reigning in Cuba in the late 1980s, where sex was the only fun Cubans could afford to have, it was not unusual for senior officers to take female companions to Angola by disguising them as "internationalist workers." The women would get their medals and diplomas like everybody else, and a chance to escape the boredom of life in Cuba, at least for a little while.

Many women hoped to use their internationalist credentials back home to win points toward acquiring home appliances. In Cuba, you bought a television set or a refrigerator at your workplace, and there was often competition for a limited number of appliances. If there were two workers with equal merits applying for a television set, the Angola experience could be a determining factor.

From the minute Patricia De La Cruz arrived at the Luanda airport, she became the talk of the Cuban officers, and an object of scorn for their wives. Ochoa's wife, Maida, who accompanied her husband to the airport to welcome Patricio De La Guardia, could not help exploding into laughter when she saw the young vamp come out of the air force airplane with her boyfriend, only steps behind the brigadier general. Patricia was sporting her tight jeans and a half-cut T-shirt that virtually exposed the bottoms of her bare breasts.

Patricia would only last a few weeks in Angola. She split up with the De La Guardia aide who had brought her after three weeks. Consigned to the Cuban Interior Ministry building in downtown Luanda, a crime-ridden area where one could hardly venture into the streets after dark, she was miserable. The top officers Patricia enjoyed hanging out with, such as Ochoa and De La Guardia, lived in a compound on the outskirts of the city. She would see them only occasionally, whenever they felt like visiting the MININT building.

The young woman resented the constant water shortages, the near-daily power blackouts, and the virtual confinement Cubans were subjected to because of security risks. She felt like a prisoner. She would spend her days watching the Portuguese-language soap operas on television, and try to fight boredom by going out at night.

From the first day, the Cuban officers' wives gave her the cold shoulder, and were often openly rude to her. Behind her back, they criticized her for not working at any of the various offices of the Cuban military mission, as most Cuban military wives did. They ridiculed her for continuing to walk around in designer jeans, when virtually all other Cuban women there dressed in Angolan army uniforms.

Only a month after Patricia's arrival in Luanda, Patricio De La Guardia suggested that she return home. She was a nervous wreck, he said, and needed medical care. Besides, since she had split up with her boyfriend, there was no justification for her to remain in Angola.

Once she returned to Havana, Patricia contacted Tony De La Guardia in hopes of getting a job at CIMEX. He turned her down. She ended up testifying against Ochoa and Patricio De La Guardia shortly thereafter. Patricia is said to have told her worried mother—a pianist at the Tropicana nightclub—that she returned to Cuba ahead of time because she had been forced by Ochoa and De La Guardia to have group sex with them, and to perform acts of lesbianism in front of various other officers. Her mother, furious that she had been abused and left without a job, told the story to neighbors. Soon, the story was all over town, and made it to Raúl Castro's ears.

Raúl Castro summoned Ochoa to his office on May 29, 1989. There were three folders on his desk with the name "Div. Gen. Arnaldo Ochoa" on their covers. One was a dossier on the Patricia De La Cruz affair. Another held a series of papers related to Ochoa's business transactions while in Angola. The third contained the transcripts of the secretly taped conversations of the party at Diocles Torralba's house.

Minutes before the meeting, the defense minister had paced his office floor, reading the material in a state of near hysteria. Clearly, he had to communicate to Ochoa that he had serious reservations about promoting him to head up the western division. He decided to call in division generals Colomé Ibarra and Ulises Rosales del Toro to sit at his side and witness the meeting. Remembering the scene a few weeks later, Raúl Castro said he was beside himself, but eventually "I calmed down. I drank a cup of tea and I waited for him."

Ochoa sat in one of the chairs facing Raúl Castro's desk, and let his boss do the talking. The defense minister started by berating Ochoa for his loose talk at the Torralba party. This was no way for a MINFAR general to talk, he said.

Raúl Castro then confronted Ochoa with various allegations of misconduct. Ochoa denied any wrongdoing, saying he had never compromised Cuba's security or enriched himself from business transactions.

"You are trying to build a corruption case to divert attention from the real issue, which is the fact that there are fundamental doubts within the high command over the future of the revolution," Ochoa said.

"It is you, only you, who has fundamental doubts," Castro shot back. "You have become spoiled. The titles have gone to your head."

"The world is changing, we can't keep isolating ourselves more and more. We need to open up to the market economies, encourage tourism, seek new sources of hard currency," Ochoa went on, oblivious to his boss. "The Soviet Union is doing it, Poland is doing it, everybody is doing it. We are doing like the ostriches, hiding our heads in the sand."

Raúl Castro flew into a rage. Screaming, he called Ochoa a prima donna, a spoiled brat of the revolution. What Ochoa was saying was nothing short of treason.

"Look, Fidel is our father," Raúl Castro said, pounding on the desk with his hand. "If Fidel Castro had not been born, neither you nor I would be sitting here."

The two other generals witnessing the discussion sat paralyzed, not daring to open their mouths. At the end of three hours, Raúl Castro concluded that it didn't make sense to continue the meeting. He told Ochoa that, with so many questions about him, it would be impossible to go ahead with the appointment.

When Ochoa left the room, Raúl Castro asked the generals for their opinions on what should be done with Ochoa. One of them proposed to make Ochoa a senior adviser to the Defense Ministry. That would keep him on the sidelines for a while. The three agreed, and left it at that.

Raúl Castro didn't share his innermost thoughts with the two generals, but he was seriously concerned that Ochoa would defect. Ochoa was angry. He had just been told he would not be appointed to the Western Army. He had been denied recognition for his role in the Angolan war at a treaty-signing ceremony in New York. He was irked about the rumors that his boss would make a fuss about the

Patricia De La Cruz story. There and then Raúl Castro ordered an around-the-clock surveillance of Ochoa.

A few days later, Ochoa asked to talk with Raúl Castro alone. He wanted a second, more informal chance to appease his boss. The defense minister set the appointment for Friday morning, June 2. This time, Ochoa stayed away from any political discussion. He was determined to prove his innocence in the allegations Raúl Castro had made, and to keep from giving his boss new ammunition against him.

Ochoa offered Raúl Castro a detailed report on his business deals in Angola. Drawing arrows on a piece of paper, he specified where the profit of each transaction had gone. Most of the money from the Candonga black-market deals in Luanda had gone to build the Cahama airport in southern Angola. Not one cent had gone into his pocket.

The defense minister stood up, went around his desk, embraced Ochoa, and thanked him for being so forthcoming.

"No matter what happens, today, tomorrow and always, we will be brothers," Raúl Castro said.

Ochoa was moved. He left the room thinking the meeting had been worthwhile.

It wasn't. Division General Ochoa soon noticed that he was being followed wherever he went. Through the grapevine he also heard that there was a growing investigation into his business deals in Angola. Fidel Castro himself had ordered Div. Gen. "Polo" Cintra Frias, Ochoa's good friend and successor in Angola, to return immediately to Havana for questioning.

Immediately upon his arrival, Cintra Frias was summoned to the defense minister's office, and remained there for several hours. On Friday morning, June 9, Raúl Castro presided over a meeting of the MINFAR's top generals. At the close of the meeting, he announced that he would probably order Ochoa's arrest in coming days. That day, Fidel was hosting an official Panamanian delegation to coordinate Cuban assistance in the event the United States invaded Panama. As Fidel conferred with Panama's figurehead President Manuel Solis Palma, he was interrupted to receive word on the simultaneous MIN-FAR meeting on Ochoa.

Ochoa was told to report to Raúl Castro's office that same night at 6 P.M. He told Maida, his wife, that the meeting would be decisive:

either he would return having reached a working agreement with his boss, or he would be out of the MINFAR that evening.

He spent the morning killing time around the house, cleaning the weeds out of the sugar cane plants he had grown in the front yard, watching television. At a quarter to six, he called to his driver, who was sitting on the sidewalk. He kissed Maida good-bye. "See you, Negra," he said. It was the last time she saw him before his arrest.

The meeting was more volatile than the one before. As in the first shouting match, Ochoa sat across from Raúl Castro's desk. About half a dozen other generals sat at a nearby conference table. Ochoa exploded when the defense minister accused him of treason.

"How do you dare call me a traitor?" Ochoa asked. "Since the days of the Sierra Maestra, I have put my life on the line more often than anybody else in this room!"

In the heat of the argument, he took a direct shot at his boss.

"You haven't fought since 1959. I haven't done anything but fight since then."

How could the defense minister accuse him—the most ascetic of all the generals—of corruption? All the MINFAR generals had been at Ochoa's house, and knew very well how modestly he lived. Who could say he was personally profiting from his business deals? Who could say these transactions were not standard procedure?

"If you want to charge me with corruption, you have to clean up the entire army first, including yourself," Ochoa said.

That was the last straw for Raúl Castro. Ochoa had broken the rules, the defense minister shouted. No army could survive a foreign aggression with its generals going their own ways, bad-mouthing their commanders, engaging in unauthorized business activities, and advocating policies that the president himself shunned.

"I have no alternative but to have you detained," Raúl Castro said when he regained his composure. "You have broken every single rule in the military code."

For a fraction of a second, everyone in the room froze. Then, the defense minister turned and ordered the head of his personal guard to come forward. *"Por favor,"* he said with a wave of his hand. "Take him away."

The news of Division General Ochoa's arrest spread instantly through Cuba's tightly knit military hierarchy that Friday night. Everybody knew a major purge would follow.

Fidel Castro had a more pressing problem: how would he explain Ochoa's arrest to the army and, more precariously, to the population? Under no circumstances could he afford conceding that there was growing discontent among some of Cuba's top generals about the treatment of the Angola veterans and the country's failure to embrace Perestroika. A convincing reason for Ochoa's arrest was needed. After all, Castro had nothing solid to charge Ochoa with. The business deals did not suffice. Everybody in Cuba's military knew that generals enjoyed discretionary powers to handle money affairs.

Fidel Castro ordered all MININT and MINFAR counterintelligence chiefs to report to his office on Sunday afternoon. The meeting lasted fourteen hours. The Cuban leader ordered that all the evidence against Ochoa be laid out before him. He heard detailed accounts about the Patricia De La Cruz charges, about Ochoa's secret account in Panama, about the black-market deals in Angola, and about the sales of diamonds and ivory through Col. Tony De La Guardia.

That was it! As soon as the generals left the room, the Cuban leader told his brother that he had a solution to their problem.

They would announce that Ochoa had been arrested for "moral crimes" and "corruption." At the same time, they would arrest Tony De La Guardia and charge him with the same crimes—plus drug trafficking. Taking advantage of Ochoa's close ties to the De La Guardia brothers, the government would consolidate the two cases in a sweeping anticorruption campaign.* Cuba would be seen abroad as taking drastic measures against cocaine smuggling. And the government would seize the opportunity to clean up the entire Interior Ministry hierarchy.

Division General Ochoa's first hours in custody were marked by confusion. At 10 A.M. Saturday, June 10, after spending his first night in detention, he was told he would be allowed out for the weekend:

---

* *In his July 9, 1989, address to the Council of State, Castro said, "When Patricio and Tony De La Guardia are arrested, they are arrested for the Angola operations, and for the collaboration between the brothers and Ochoa in ivory and diamond trafficking. . . . We had discovered that they were not only implicated in activities such as [wild] parties and other things, but also in criminal activities: . . ." Castro said the De La Guardias' drug operations were discovered hours after their arrest, but this contradicts his own testimony—and that of General Prosecutor Juan Escalona—that the MINFAR and MININT investigations were closing in on the MC Department as far back as in May, when they detected suspicious radio communications to drug smugglers originating from Havana's Seventh Avenue and 66th Street, where the MC was located.*

Raúl Castro was sending a pass for him to spend the weekend at the MINFAR vacation retreat of Topes de Collantes in Santa Clara province. Puzzled, Ochoa asked if he could take somebody with him. The general and his guardians then picked up Ochoa's lover, Michelle, at her home, and headed for the military retreat.

At 8:30 A.M. on Monday, June 12, the couple returned to Havana. Not knowing that his fate had been decided at Fidel Castro's office a day earlier, Ochoa felt he was in a legal limbo. Was he to report back to Raúl Castro? Should he go home? He asked his driver to drop by Patricio De La Guardia's home.

Patricio was not there. His wife, Cucusa, told him Patricio and Tony were at Amado Padrón's office around the corner. By the way, would Ochoa join them that night for dinner? At midnight they would celebrate Patricio and Tony's birthday, since it fell on the next day. The party would take place at the home of Patricio's aide, Lt. Col. Michael Montaner, who would buy a lobster and enchiladas for the occasion. Ochoa assured her he would be there at 8 P.M. and went off to Padrón's office.

What happened next could have saved Ochoa's life—and delivered an unprecedented blow to the Castro revolution.

At about 9 A.M., Ochoa and the other three officers left Padrón's office, got into Tony's car, and drove off to the Border Troops seaport of Jaimanitas on the outskirts of Havana. Walking slowly, engaging in casual conversation, they headed toward the docks. Tony pointed to a big cigarette speedboat, which he had recently seized from drug smugglers. He had the keys with him. Let's take a look, he said.

The four men, fearing they might be followed, cracked jokes and tried to look relaxed as they boarded the speedboat. When they were all inside, they looked one another in the eyes.

This was their chance to flee! But they were nervous. The joint defection of Cuba's star military and intelligence officers to the United States would mark the Castro regime's biggest embarrassment ever. They knew Cuba would send its fastest navy and air force units after them instantly. They would either make it to Miami, or die in the attempt.

Acting naturally, as if he was about to go on a weekend outing, Tony turned the key, switched on the military communications radio, and waved to Padrón to untie the boat's docking line. Nobody said a word. It was just when Padrón laid his hand on the rope when a frantic radio alert message stopped the four men cold.

"Alerting all units, alerting all units!" the voice said. "Four suspects are boarding a boat for an unauthorized trip at the Border Troops' marina in Jaimanitas. There are MINFAR and MININT officers on the boat."

Tony let his head fall forward, like a child caught with his hand in the cookie jar. He grabbed the radio microphone.

"This is MININT Colonel Tony De La Guardia," he shot back. "What kind of bullshit is this? Who is talking about an unauthorized trip? This is me and generals Ochoa and Patricio De La Guardia. We're here taking a look at the boat I turned over last week to [interior vice-minister] Brigadier General Pascual Martinez Gil. We're not going anywhere."

Minutes later, the four officers were driving back to town in silence.

◄►

At eight o'clock that Monday night, Patricio De La Guardia and his wife, Cucusa, were sitting next to his aide's dinner table waiting for the other guests. Neither Tony nor Ochoa had shown up.

About an hour later, Cucusa called Tony's house. No one answered. She then tried reaching Ochoa at his Nicaraguan girlfriend's house. Michelle said Ochoa had been called for an urgent meeting at the MINFAR scheduled for 8 P.M. Ochoa had said the meeting wouldn't be long. They would go to the birthday party as soon as he returned.

At ten o'clock, Patricio, his wife and the hosts sat down at the dinner table and began to eat, a sense of dread hanging over them. Tony's wife, Marilena, called shortly thereafter: Tony had been summoned to a meeting at the MININT at 8 P.M., and had not returned. As soon as she hung up, the phone rang again. This time, it was the De La Guardias' mother: Brigadier General Martinez Gil had called her looking for Patricio, asking that he show up as soon as possible at the MININT. At that point, Patricio knew it was all over.

"Don't worry, Cucusa, everything will be fine," he tried to comfort his wife on his way out. "They'll give us a few slaps on the wrist, and we'll be back home soon."

◄►

Col. Antonio "Tony" De La Guardia, Cuba's James Bond, and his twin brother, Brig. Gen. Patricio De La Guardia, were Castro's top secret agents before they fell from grace and were tried on drug-trafficking charges in 1989. Here, Tony and Patricio are welcomed by Fidel upon returning from a mission abroad in the late 1970s.

At their trial, Col. Tony De La Guardia and his twin brother, Brig. Gen. Patricio De La Guardia, pleaded guilty to cocaine-smuggling charges. Unbeknownst to the public, Castro had visited Tony at his cell earlier and had promised him leniency if he agreed to take all the blame for Cuba's drug trafficking. Tony did so, but was executed anyway, on July 13, 1989.

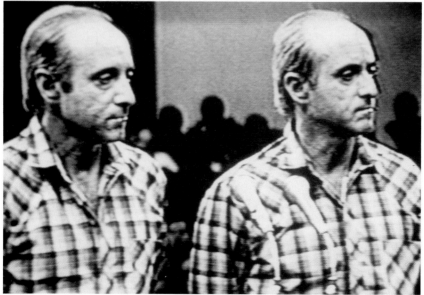

3   During one of their missions abroad in 1988, Patricio De La Guardia, here with his wife, Maria Isabel, and his twin brother, Tony De La Guardia, took time off for a vacation in Madrid. It would be their last vacation together.

Div. Gen. Arnaldo Ochoa said at a year-end party at his House No. 1 of the Cuban military mission in Luanda, Angola, in 1988, "Fidel has gone crazy. He's completely gaga." In a picture taken that night, Ochoa is shown with his wife, Maida, on his lap, Brig. Gen. Patricio De La Guardia, and his wife, Maria Isabel.

Writer Norberto Fuentes and Div. Gen. Arnaldo Ochoa in Luanda, in 1988. As a token of their friendship, the writer had given Ochoa his Rolex watch. "Fidel saw Ochoa as a charismatic leader in the making," Fuentes would say later. "Fidel could not tolerate that."

Cuban generals "Polo" Cintras Frias, Abelardo Colome Ibarra and Arnaldo Ochoa in Luanda in December 1988. Months later, Colome Ibarra would vote for Ochoa's execution at the Council of State and would be appointed as Cuba's new interior minister.

Colombia's Nobel Prize–winning novelist Gabriel García Márquez, one of Fidel Castro's closest friends. He tried to persuade Fidel in the late 1980s that Soviet *glasnost* would mark the birth of a new socialism with a human face. But Fidel replied, "No, Gabo, believe me, it's going to be a disaster."

[BELOW] To get by in Cuba, one had to have extra money to buy off-the-books foodstuffs in neighborhood grocery stores. Managers of Cuba's bodegas, like this one on Linea and H streets in Havana, routinely set aside part of their state-supplied stock to sell at premium prices to select customers. "Resolver" (to solve) was the code word for getting things under the table.

7

8

Fidel Castro ordered the "mobilization" of 200,000 Havana residents to agricultural farms in 1990. Construction brigades such as this one in Artemisa, thirty-five miles southwest of Havana, worked around the clock to build dormitories for them. But the city "volunteers" spent more time partying than solving the revolution's food shortages.

Enrique "Enriquito" Hernández Armenteros, seventy-four, Cuba's most prominent government-backed Santería priest. He made a fortune from performing initiation rites on foreigners at his home. About half of Cuba's Santería priests worked for the regime's intelligence services, according to one Cuban state-security defector.

No hay salida. No way out. Cuba had become a gray, bored, stagnant society. There was nowhere to go, nothing to do. Like the people standing in bus lines on Havana's 23rd Street in December 1991, Cubans seemed resigned to a prolonged state of collective zombiedom.

Castro opened a monumental Center of Genetic Engineering and Biotechnology on the outskirts of Havana, and announced that Cuba would become a world power in biotechnology. But Castro's plans to bank Cuba's economic future on biotechnology were seen by industry analysts as an outlandish dream.

As the economy collapsed in 1991, the number of Cubans fleeing the island soared. Nearly 2,400 Cubans made it to Miami in 1991 on inner tubes like these, up from a total of about 400 a year earlier. Hundreds are believed to have died in the shark-infested waters.

With Soviet oil supplies dwindling, the regime replaced many delivery trucks with horse-drawn carts. The Mixed Gastronomic Enterprise of Havana's Marianao suburb started using carts for daily food distribution to four dozen cafeterias. Overworked horses were exhausted at the end of the day.

Pablo Guevara, twenty-six, one of revolutionary hero Ernesto "Che" Guevara's nephews, described himself as a revolutionary, but conceded that he rarely performed "voluntary" work. "I don't think that after having studied [performing arts] for five years . . . it makes much sense for me to work in agriculture," he said.

Canek Sanchez Guevara, seventeen, the grandson of revolutionary hero Ernesto "Che" Guevara, was the epitome of a new generation of Cubans who wanted a radical break with communism. Canek wanted to be a heavy-metal rock musician—and to emigrate. "This revolution is in ruins," he said.

Popular singer Carlos Varela, one of the heroes of Cuba's new generation of disaffected youths, whose song "William Tell"—an allegory about Fidel Castro—was greeted with standing ovations. "Mine is a generation of people who are tired of being treated as if they were stupid," Varela said.

17

18

By 1991, more than 55 percent of the Cuban population was born after the revolution. To most young people, Castro's revolution was something out of history books. They were bored by Castro's Marxist dogmas and constant calls for greater sacrifices. They wanted to enjoy life.

You could find the youth sitting at the waterfront Malecón Boulevard every day: thousands of young men and women necking, chatting leisurely or looking at the sea, killing time, waiting for something to change their lives.

19

When the results of the Fourth Congress's secret vote for the Party's top authorities came in, it was learned that three delegates had voted against Fidel Castro's re-election. The show of dissent was a first: no delegate to a Cuban Communist Party Congress had ever before cast a vote against the Maximum Leader.

20

21

Raúl Castro, the number-two man in Cuba, had long been a hard-line Communist. But in the early 1990s he tried to project himself as a moderate. "What worries me . . . is what will happen if we don't make much-needed changes now, and if we don't make them under Fidel," he said at a closed-door meeting.

THE KEY MEMBERS OF CUBA'S POLITBURO

Carlos Lage. Born October 15, 1951. Cuba's economic czar and Fidel Castro protégé. A reformer.

Roberto Robaina. Born May 18, 1956. Head of the Communist Youth Union. A reformer.

Abel Prieto. Born November 11, 1950. Head of the Writer's and Artist's Union. A reformer.

Carlos Rafael Rodríguez. Born May 23, 1913. Vice-president of the Council of State and Council of Ministers. A reformer.

Carlos Aldana. Born April 12, 1942. Communist Party ideology and foreign relations chief. Sometimes a reformer, sometimes a hard-liner.

José Ramón Machado Ventura. Born October 26, 1930. Communist Party administrative chief, led the Party's hard-line old guard.

Russian leader Boris Yeltsin's views on Cuba made a 180-degree turn after his visit to Miami in September 1989, when he met and posed for a picture with exile leader Jorge Mas Canosa. "There was an immediate affinity among us," Mas Canosa would recall later. "We shared a visceral repudiation of the Communist system."

23

24

Miami-based presidential son Jeb Bush, in a guayabera shirt, with his Mexican wife, Columba Garnica Gallo. With close ties to Miami's Cuban exiles, Jeb adopted the anti-Castro cause with unusual zeal and played a key role as an informal liaison between the anti-Castro exiles and the White House.

25

Alina, Fidel Castro's only known daughter, who became increasingly critical of Fidel. Interviewed for this book, Alina called her father a "tyrant" and described him as a man out of touch with Cuba's reality. "He doesn't listen to you; he explains things to you," she said.

Human rights leader Gustavo Arcos Bergnes was being simultaneously attacked by the government and by exile leaders who resented his calls for negotiations with the regime. "The Cuban people want a peaceful change, a political settlement," Arcos Bergnes said. "Nobody wants violence."

27

Panamanian strongman Gen. Manuel A. Noriega, interviewed by the author at his office on September 15, 1988, long after Cuba had begun a massive secret airlift of weapons to Panama. "Cubans? What Cubans?" Noriega said. "Besides, what kind of advice could the Cubans possibly give us?"

Castro had warned Nicaraguan President Daniel Ortega against holding a democratic referendum in his country. When Violeta Chamorro won the election, Ortega would regret he hadn't followed Castro's advice.

28

During Soviet President Mikhail Gorbachev's visit to Cuba on April 2, 1989, the Soviet leader and Fidel Castro put on a show of unity to dispel rumors of a Soviet-Cuban rift. But behind closed doors, Soviet Vice-President Vladimir M. Kamentsev was delivering the bad news to Cuban officials.

In private conversations with foreign diplomats, Fidel Castro was always expressing his misgivings about Soviet President Mikhail Gorbachev's democratic reforms. In public, Castro praised Gorbachev as a "modern" and "brilliant" world leader. This photo was taken during Gorbachev's address to Cuba's National Assembly on April 4, 1989.

"Destiny has turned us into the standard-bearers of the world revolutionary, progressive and democratic movement," Fidel Castro told the Fourth Communist Party Congress. Even if Cuba was left as the lone keeper of the Communist flame, it would fulfill its historic duty, he insisted.

"It's good that we talk about democracy, once and for all," Castro told the Fourth Congress of Cuba's Communist Party in October 1991. "So-called Western democracy has nothing to do with real democracy. It's complete garbage."

Fidel Castro was a master at turning seemingly calamitous situations to his advantage. He had pulled similar tricks before. In the early 1960s, when Cuba's secret services discovered Rolando Cubela's CIA-backed plot to assassinate Castro, Fidel had used the occasion to send dozens of potential political adversaries to prison and clean up the corruption rampant in his government.

Using the title of the famous Italian movie of the time, the Cuban leader said Cubela was a symptom of *la dolce vita*, a wave of licentious behavior that was corrupting Cuban officials. Instead of focusing on Cubela's political motivations, he had *Granma* publish a statement saying that Cubela's "moral decay" had made him vulnerable to the CIA's approach.

In a public letter to the prosecutor in Cubela's trial, Fidel wrote, "It is much more useful for the revolution not to eliminate individuals who engage in acts of treason, but to eliminate the vices that engender such behavior." He added, "What must be done is to eliminate the roots of cronyism, favoritism, the various forms of parasitism, the enervating tendencies to accommodation and even corruption."

An anticorruption campaign was immediately unleashed. Hundreds of government officials were sent to jail. Plans were launched for what would be inaugurated in 1965 as the Military Units to Aid Production (UMAP)—an army of people in need of "ideological rehabilitation," thousands who would do forced labor in the countryside. What had started with a single assassination attempt ended with a free workforce for the revolution.

◄►

Granma's official version of the Ochoa–De La Guardia arrests, which appeared weeks later and was edited by Fidel himself, stated that when the two officers were arrested, "there was no information on drug-trafficking-related activities. The investigations were geared at illicit activities and businesses, corruption, immoral behavior and other faults and irregularities by Ochoa, to which Patricio and Tony De La Guardia appeared to be closely linked."

The day after the arrests, MININT and MINFAR intelligence teams raided the homes of dozens of high-ranking officers. Maida Ochoa was sweeping the floors when about a dozen security agents stormed into her house. She had mentally prepared herself for their visit. She sat down on the hall couch, and watched the men open every drawer in the house. She even volunteered to show them whatever valuables Ochoa kept at home. There was some money in the safe deposit—$28,500 in cash—which Ochoa had told his wife did not belong to him. There were a dozen trunks of ivory in the garage, which Ochoa had brought from Angola. That's all they would find, Maida told the men. The agents continued to search for about an hour and left.

On Wednesday, June 14, *Granma* carried a four-paragraph communique on Ochoa's arrest. It said, "We find ourselves with the unpleasant duty of reporting that Division General Ochoa Sanchez, who has received important responsibilities and honors from the Communist Party of Cuba and the FAR, has been arrested and placed under investigation for serious crimes of corruption and dishonest handling of economic resources."

It added that Ochoa had engaged in "grave violations of moral codes, as well as Socialist laws." The arrested general would go on trial, the communique added. He would be judged by a military honor tribunal made up of officers equal to him in rank.

Two days later, a new *Granma* editorial would announce the arrest of the De La Guardia brothers, Padrón, Martinez, and two lower-level officers.* Referring to all the detainees, it forewarned, "the inexorable weight of revolutionary justice will fall on them."

---

* *The June 16* Granma *editorial said investigators had not found the "slightest evidence" that the arrested officers had engaged in counterrevolutionary political activities, but added that their crimes "against the ethics, the principles and the prestige of our revolution" constituted "a type of treason that always, sooner or later, leads to political treason."*

3

A Trial with a Message

Nobel Prize-winning novelist Gabriel García Márquez was in his studio at his Mexico City home when he heard the news of Ochoa's arrest. He ordered his secretary, who was sitting at a small desk with a fax machine next to the door, to place a call immediately to Cuba.

Gabo, as the writer was known to his friends, was Fidel Castro's best-known foreign friend. He was the most prominent writer in a region where the political opinions of leading intellectuals carry enormous weight. Latin America's leftist intellectuals had long been the most important promoters of the revolutionary mystique in the region; within Cuba, García Márquez was considered a key source of support for the cause.

Fidel Castro treated Gabo as one would a precious commodity. He had given the writer a house with a swimming pool in the Cubanacan neighborhood, an embassy-row-like section of Havana close to Cuba's main convention center. Gabo's mansion, protocol house No. 6 on posh Fifth Avenue, was next to the protocol houses given to Robert Redford and Harry Belafonte on their recent visits to Cuba.

Gabo, however, was the only celebrity who had a round-the-year house at his disposal, fully equipped with three huge refrigerators and an overseas telephone line available only at Cuba's best hotels. García

Márquez's wife, Mercedes, redecorated the house with white couches and chairs imported from Mexico, and oil paintings from Cuba's best-known painters. Protocol house No. 6 was known in Havana as *La Casa de Gabo*—Gabo's house.

Fidel had also given García Márquez a black Mercedes-Benz 280, similar to one used by the Cuban leader himself. A driver and four maids were assigned to the García Márquez household during the writer's stays in Havana, and were on call when he was not in town. A gardener pruned the mango trees surrounding the swimming pool and mowed the front-yard lawn throughout the year.

The Cuban leader needed García Márquez badly. By the end of the 1980s, García Márquez was the revolution's last big-name friend. Intellectuals like Octavio Paz, Mario Vargas Llosa and Carlos Fuentes had long broken with Castro. The big question in Latin American literary and political circles was why García Márquez, who supported Gorbachev's policy of Glasnost in the Soviet Union, was not publicly advocating democratic reforms in Cuba.

Gabo, a man with an ego almost as big as his talent, enjoyed the attention his friendship with Castro gave him. He felt a certain pride in not abandoning a friend in need. It also kept him center stage in world intellectual circles, and made him a much-coveted interview for international journalists. Except for a few journalist friends and carefully selected reporters recommended to him, Gabo would charge U.S. and European journalists $10,000 per interview. The money would be donated to the Latin American film school he had founded in Havana.

Publicly, Gabo was not offering any excuses for his ties to Fidel. He talked about the Cuban leader with well-rehearsed admiration and reverence. But privately, he saw himself as a moderating influence on the Cuban leader. He believed Fidel respected him and that he listened to what he had to say. In fact, the Cuban leader often did: over the years, Gabo had quietly helped set free hundreds of Cuban political prisoners by asking Fidel or other top Cuban officials for their release.*

There was another reason why Gabo wanted to stay close to Fidel. The writer was a passionate political broker who thrived on his close-

---

* *"There are more than two thousand former political prisoners in the United States that I helped set free, and I did it quietly," García Márquez said in his first public admission of that humanitarian role at a press conference in Bogotá, Colombia, January 17, 1992. "Sometimes they didn't even ask me to do it or they didn't know about my interceding. Some of them, once freed, have turned against me."*

ness to heads of state and guerrilla leaders. His greatest source of pride was playing the role of a behind-the-scenes mediator in major international crises. His ties to Fidel gave him a leverage no Latin American leader had. When the presidents of Colombia or Venezuela needed help in obtaining the release of prominent politicians kidnapped by leftist guerrillas in their countries, they would invariably ask Gabo to talk with Fidel Castro on their behalf. And Gabo, who was planning a definitive return to Colombia after several decades of living abroad, was eager to help stop the political violence in his country.

"It's much more important for Latin America that I remain friends with him than for me to break with him," the writer explained to me once, matter-of-factly.

During García Márquez's long stays in Havana, Fidel would regularly drop in at his house on Fifth Avenue, sometimes as often as three times a week. No invitation was needed. Fidel simply drove by the house on his way home late at night, and knocked on the door if the lights were on. Sometimes, he would bring a bottle of brandy or a can of Russian caviar for Mercedes.

In recent times, the conversation between the two men had almost invariably focused on the political changes in the Soviet Union. García Márquez was an enthusiastic supporter of President Gorbachev's liberalization program. Castro, who publicly endorsed the Soviet president and called him a big friend of Cuba, was skeptical.

"Don't get me wrong, I'm not against the principles of Perestroika," Castro told García Márquez during a late-night meeting in the writer's living room in Havana in January 1989. "But it's an extremely risky policy. It's leading the Socialist world back to capitalism."

"Perhaps it's the beginning of true socialism, of socialism with a human face . . . ," replied García Márquez, trying to avoid a head-on dispute with the Cuban leader.

"No," said Castro. "Believe me, Gabo, it's going to be a disaster."

The Cuban leader explained himself. First, Perestroika would bring about major cuts in Soviet aid to the Third World. Countries like Cuba, which relied heavily on Soviet cooperation, would be badly hurt. Even if Gorbachev had the political will to maintain his alliances with the Kremlin's Third World allies, his policies would leave the Soviet economy in such a state of disarray that the aid inevitably would be disrupted.

Second, the Soviet Union was cutting its military spending so drastically as part of the new economic restructuring program that it would soon cease to be a world power. That would be a disgrace. It would destroy the balance of power. There would be only one superpower left in the world: the United States. Imperialism would have a free hand to do whatever it wanted.

Third, the Soviet Union's new freedom of expression would unleash long-simmering national and ethnic tensions. Gorbachev was making too many concessions, and once you start making concessions, Castro said, you are no longer in control. The Soviet Union could be pulled asunder by the waves of regional and ethnic movements demanding independence.

The discussion, which was taking place ten months before the fall of the Berlin Wall and at a time when few were predicting dramatic changes in Eastern Europe, ended inconclusively. It was past 3 A.M. The Cuban leader reminded Gabo of the political bets he had won in the past—this would be no different. He patted Gabo affectionately on the arm, and left.

Five months later, the day Ochoa's arrest was announced, García Márquez was desperate to know the truth. Had the general led a pro-Perestroika uprising? He knew he would receive calls from politicians and journalists throughout the region, and he wanted the facts.

When he got through to Havana, he was told that Raúl Castro would deliver an important speech that evening—it would explain everything. García Márquez hung up and instructed his secretary to book a seat on a flight to Cuba that very weekend.

Raúl Castro's improvised speech to the nation from the main hall of the Defense Ministry that evening, June 14, 1989, turned out to be his most disastrous public appearance ever.

Instead of shedding light on the reasons for Division General Ochoa's arrest, which the whole nation was awaiting anxiously since that morning's announcement in *Granma*, he delivered a rambling three-hour speech full of insults, contradictions and incoherent thoughts, which did nothing but raise more questions about the whole affair.

Looking pale, as if he hadn't slept in days, and with an angry gleam in his eyes, Raúl Castro began by telling the twelve hundred officers in the room that, due to the extraordinary nature of the day's events, the Central Committee had decided to transform what was to have been an address commemorating the 28th anniversary of the Western Army into a televised speech to the nation.

Having said that, Raúl Castro peered down from the podium, apparently distracted by a voice. He berated a reporter: "To the journalist around there who is talking a lot: Please be quiet! Or the photographer, excuse me." He looked back at the audience, but he had clearly lost his train of thought. From then on, he rambled through dozens of unconnected issues, visibly agitated, but leaving his audience—and the whole country—wondering what he was trying to say.

Ochoa, Raúl Castro said, had begun "feeling above others," and was engaging in "populist politics" that were becoming a growing threat to the revolution. While stressing that there were no political motivations behind Ochoa's ouster, Raúl Castro implied Ochoa was a supporter of Glasnost, a critic of Fidel, and thus a "charlatan," "nitwit" and a "liar."

Nowhere in the speech did he charge Ochoa with having engaged in drug trafficking. He made only vague mention of unauthorized business deals. His rage seemed directed at Ochoa's lack of discipline and his open questioning of official policies. Listening to him, many television viewers wondered whether Ochoa had begun conspiring against the Cuban leader—the very idea Fidel Castro wanted to dispel.

Pounding on the podium, Raúl Castro said Ochoa and his friends were "grouping against the figure of our commander in chief." Recalling the May 29 meeting with Ochoa at his office, he left no doubt that Ochoa had openly criticized Fidel: "I said to General Colomé Ibarra: Why don't they invent all those things against you? Why don't they say those things against you? Naturally, they know against whom they are doing it: Against our living symbol . . . , the most important symbol we have, whose name is Fidel Castro." The army officers in the audience applauded. They began to chant, in chorus: "Fee-del! Fee-del!"

As the speech went on, an increasingly mixed-up Raúl Castro found himself repeatedly saying the very opposite of what he was trying to convey. At one point, he asked the audience of MINFAR officers whether there was democracy in Cuba. When the audience responded with a polite "*Si*," Raúl Castro asked:

"Are you saying this because the minister is saying it?"

"No," responded the audience, like a model class.

Raúl Castro laughed, somewhat nervously. Looking at the television camera, realizing that the audience was responding under pressure, Raúl Castro said:

"When they said *Si* and *No*, they were joking," he said. "They look like elementary school students. It could be interpreted that way. Sometimes we teach elementary kids in such a way that when one says such and such, they all answer yes or no. Nobody ever disagrees. That is what happened to you now."

The officers in the audience now moved uncomfortably in their seats, not knowing how to react. In their homes, television viewers looked at one another in disbelief.

If one thing came across clearly from Raúl Castro's speech that night, it was that the regime would not tolerate open discussion within the military about the fate of the Cuban revolution.

"This is the moral we have to learn: regardless of the stars one wears on one's shoulders, and the stars that come with the Honorific title of Hero of the Cuban Republic, no one can put himself above the people." By now, Raúl Castro was shouting at the audience. "No one should feel above anything here, and I think the examples of these past few days are enough to prove that."

In Miami, the home of about seven hundred thousand exiled Cubans and the capital of anti-Castro activity, the news of Division General Ochoa's arrest created a frenzy. Poland had fallen. Anti-Communist street rallies were rocking other Eastern European countries. Cuba would be next.

El Nuevo Herald, the Spanish-language edition of the *Miami Herald*, began carrying banner headlines about the Ochoa case, with its commentators speculating that it was the beginning of the end of the Castro regime. A prominent recent defector, Cuban Air Force Gen. Rafael del Pino, proclaimed that Castro had arrested Ochoa to prevent disgruntled officers from carrying out "an uprising against the regime."

Miami's Spanish-language radio announcers called feverishly on their audiences to start preparing for a popular uprising on the island. Members of the Alpha 66 Cuban exile brigade, clad in combat gear and toting AR-15 semiautomatic rifles, gathered in a South Florida swamp near the Everglades National Park to begin crash weekend military training courses for new volunteers. Exile activist Tony Cuesta began organizing an "air attack" on Cuba with 1,050 helium-filled balloons carrying 16,000 anti-Castro pamphlets. The propaganda attack would be carried out several months later, but erratic winds whisked the balloons and their cargo into the hands of intrigued inhabitants of various English-speaking Caribbean islands.

Mainstream media in south Florida began to speculate about what the area would look like if Castro fell, and hundreds of thousands of

Cubans returned to their homeland.* "For Sale" signs began popping up everywhere in Miami: many exiles, fearing a sharp drop in real estate once the revolution started in Cuba, rushed to sell their homes ahead of the pack. The selling stampede brought about a 15 percent drop in real estate prices in heavily Cuban parts of the city.

Major companies in Miami began reassessing their business plans, contemplating a period of turmoil that would transform the city. Barnett Bank, one of Florida's largest, announced it would finance investments in post-Castro Cuba. The Port of Miami, anticipating a boom in trade with Cuba, began making plans for construction of new warehouses to store Cuban-bound cargo.

Washington kept its cool—up to a point. The Bush Administration said that it suspected there was something behind the Ochoa case, but it wasn't clear what.† The State Department's hierarchy had its mind on Eastern Europe, and its Latin American experts were busy with Nicaragua's leftist Sandinistas and Panama's strongman Gen. Manuel A. Noriega. Cuba was not on the front burner.

<>

By June 25, 1989, the opening day of a military tribunal to judge Division General Ochoa, Fidel and Raúl Castro had spent nearly seven days at the Defense Ministry offices—night and day—trying to find a way out of the crisis.

By then, they already had detailed information from Cuba's counterintelligence services on Colonel De La Guardia's unauthorized cocaine-trafficking activities. Although there was no evidence that Ochoa had gone beyond planning a drug deal, the Castro brothers were confident that prosecutors would manage to make a convincing case that he, too, had been a big-league cocaine smuggler.

The state security raids into the homes of the arrested officers had turned up evidence that could help implicate Ochoa in De La Guardia's drug trafficking operations. At the home of Captain Mar-

---

* A poll published by the Miami Herald *months later showed that 20 percent of the city's nearly seven hundred thousand Cubans planned to go home the minute Castro fell. "Poll: 1 in 5 Dade Cubans would go," the* Miami Herald, *February 20, 1990.*
† *U.S. intelligence had picked up a message from Panama's General Noriega to Castro alerting him about a possible military rebellion in Cuba two weeks before the Ochoa–De La Guardia arrests, according to U.S. Deputy Assistant Secretary of State for Inter-American Affairs Michael G. Kozak's testimony to a House Foreign Affairs subcomittee on August 1, 1989. But the information was too sketchy and confusing to back up a conspiracy theory, Kozak said. In an interview on June 5, 1991, Kozak told me he had not received any new information that would support a coup attempt theory.*

tinez Valdes, security agents had found a business card indicating that Ochoa's aide-de-camp had been in Colombia. Under questioning, Martinez Valdes confessed that he had met with Medellín cartel boss Pablo Escobar, and that Ochoa had approved the trip.

Having decided to consolidate the cases of Ochoa and De La Guardia, Fidel Castro planned a series of highly public trials that would impose harsh sentences on fourteen defendants. All of the accused would plead guilty, in exchange for promises of leniency. Subsequently, the Ochoa-De La Guardia case would be used as the launching pad for an unprecedented purge of the Interior Ministry and other agencies suspected of weak loyalty to the regime.

The trials would begin with a "military honor tribunal," made up of Cuba's forty-seven highest-ranking officers. The next step would be a summary court-martial on drug trafficking and corruption charges by a three-member military court. Then, the Council of State, made up of the twenty-nine highest-ranking political leaders in the country, would set the final sentences. The state prosecutors would request the death penalty for Ochoa and the De La Guardia brothers. The defendants would be advised to state their unconditional loyalty to Fidel in front of the television cameras throughout the process.

The participating generals, admirals and ministers—including the defendants' best friends—would be required to support the death penalty for Ochoa and some of the other prisoners. Their speeches would be carried on national television, and their signed statements would be published by *Granma*. A show of unity was essential to show the world that this was not a unilateral vendetta by the Castro brothers.

In a never-disclosed episode, a court instructor who identified himself as Major Pino visited all the defendants in their respective cells at the Villa Marista State Security headquarters on the eve of the trial. Major Pino brought personal messages from Fidel Castro: the Comandante wanted them to cooperate.

The visiting official gave precise instructions on how they should behave during the trial, according to De La Guardia family members. Major Pino laid out two guidelines: First, the defendants should stress at all times their commitment to Fidel and to the revolution. They would be tried exclusively on drug charges. They were expected to help dispel rumors that the trial was politically motivated.

Second, Pino said, they should keep their answers brief, and never bring up names other than those mentioned by the prosecutors.

If they complied with every guideline, their lives most likely would be spared.

"Consider this as one more mission you're being asked to carry out," Major Pino told Tony De La Guardia. "Help us, and you'll be helping yourself."

◄►

For the next several nights, Cubans watched with fascination the edited videotapes of the "honor tribunal" and the court-martial that ensued. The proceedings provided Cubans and the world with an unprecedented glimpse into the inner workings of the Castro regime.

Raúl Castro opened the event with a litany of charges against Division General Ochoa. The general sat with his head down, in the posture of a punished schoolboy. Television close-ups revealed him cleaning his fingernails and brushing lint from his uniform distractedly. When his turn to testify came, a contrite but distant Ochoa stood to make his long, drama-filled confession.

Standing firm in front of the tribunal, head bowed, eyes on the floor, hands folded before him, he said: "I want to tell my comrades-at-arms that I believe I betrayed my country. And I say in all honesty, that one pays for treason with one's life." He went on to say that neither Fidel Castro nor his brother Raúl had known anything of his business deals, dispelling any possible complicity of the leadership in corruption cases. He rejected foreign press reports that his trial was politically motivated. "I have never been opposed to the revolution—quite the contrary," Ochoa said.

His final statement to the tribunal was even more dramatic: "I firmly believe, while I am totally conscious of my guilt, that if I can be of any help to the revolution, even as a bad example, I'm at the revolution's service. If I should be condemned to a firing squad, I promise all of you that, in that moment, my last thought would be of Fidel, and of the great revolution he has given our people."

Col. Tony De La Guardia was called to testify on the second and final day of the tribunal. He was to be questioned as a witness in the Ochoa case, not as a defendant. He would be tried, with all the others, a few days later. But the prosecutors used the occasion to bombard De La Guardia with questions about his drug-trafficking deals.

"Did you at any time think this would be discovered?" asked the stern tribunal president Division General Rosales del Toro. "Had you considered the consequences of everything you did?"

"I never considered the consequences . . . ," responded De La Guardia, his eyes on the floor. "I was motivated by my interest in making money. I was given a double task: to break the U.S. blockade . . . and to support my organization with convertible currency. In my zeal to excel, to advance, to attain these goals, I did not stop and analyze what I was doing."

After short deliberations, the tribunal closed its sessions with a recommendation that Ochoa be "dishonorably discharged" from the armed forces, and stripped of his title of Hero of the Cuban Republic. It further recommended that Ochoa be tried on charges of "high treason to the fatherland."

Ochoa left the room looking genuinely repentant. De La Guardia looked on, clearly trying to assess what the tribunal's ruling meant in terms of his own upcoming trial.

Ochoa knew he would be fired and stripped of all honors, but he hoped his good performance at the tribunal would ultimately save his life. After all, Fidel had promised him leniency if he cooperated, and no high-ranking Cuban officer had been sent to the firing squad in nearly three decades. Hadn't Cubela—the man hired by the CIA to murder Fidel in 1963—been pardoned shortly before he was to be executed?

<>

The court-martial, whose edited versions were broadcast on national television for more than a week, would again bring the nation to a halt.

The proceedings took place at the huge Universal Hall auditorium of the MINFAR headquarters in Havana. At center stage, next to the Cuban flag, sat the three generals making up the court, dressed in their light-brown dress uniforms. In the middle was court-martial president Div. Gen. Ramón Espinosa Martin, the fifty-year-old chief of Cuba's Eastern Army. He was a low-key functionary, who would say little and give prosecutors a free hand throughout the trial.

On a desk to his right sat the chief prosecutor, Cuba's Justice Minister Brigadier General Escalona Reguera. The fifty-nine-year-old minister, a medium-height, overweight man who had started his career as army lawyer heading court-martials of political prisoners after the revolution, was a protégé of Raúl Castro. During the revolution, he had been a member of the pro-Moscow Socialist People's Party, which at the time showed little enthusiasm for Castro. Escalona had been the victim of at least one purge in the sixties. Raúl Castro had given him a second chance in the mid-seventies by offering him a job in the MINFAR's high command, and Escalona had risen through the ranks until he became justice minister in 1983.

To the left of the court-martial president's desk, facing Escalona, was a group of nine state-appointed defense attorneys. They were mostly lower-ranked army officers whose names were largely unknown even in military circles. There was one colonel, six majors, one captain, and one first lieutenant.

The fourteen defendants were seated in the auditorium's first row of seats, a few yards from the stage. They sat stiffly, without talking or looking at one another. Most were clad in jeans and plaid shirts or guayaberas: they had been stripped of their military status and were no longer entitled to use their uniforms. Behind them was a sea of uniformed officers in their light-brown military attire.

One by one, the defendants walked up to the stage to submit themselves to the chief prosecutor's relentless questioning. The defense attorneys watched silently from their desk, taking notes. Chief Prosecutor Escalona spent hours berating the defendants for their crimes against the revolution. He seemed to play his role with uncharacteristic zeal.

He had known Ochoa for nearly three decades, since the two had served together in the Eastern Army in the early sixties. Only the year before, Ochoa had invited Escalona to spend the night at his home in Luanda during the justice minister's visit to Angola. Until then, the two generals had been on a first-name basis. Now, the prosecutor was referring to Ochoa formally by both last names, "Ochoa Sanchez," as if he had just stumbled upon his name on a piece of paper.

The accused admitted their guilt and did their best to sound apologetic. But, in contrast to their testimony at Division General Ochoa's military honor tribunal, their mea culpas were now mixed with explanations and excuses. It was clear to them from the tone of *Granma* editorials in recent days that the government was out to get them. Their lives were on the line. Some defendants, including Ochoa, denied key charges from the prosecution. Others went so far as to hint that their actions had been cleared by their bosses—perhaps even by Fidel himself.

Late one night, Col. Tony De La Guardia received an unexpected visit at his cell. It was Fidel Castro himself. The Comandante spent at least three hours talking with his one-time protégé. After some small talk about Tony's family, the conversation shifted to the trial. Fidel was worried about the defendants' testimonies.

Castro, whose visit to De La Guardia in jail was never revealed by the Cuban regime, promised leniency to his former friend if he agreed to take all the blame for Cuba's drug trafficking. De La Guardia was asked to clear his superiors—Abrantes and Fidel—of any responsibility. When De La Guardia agreed, Fidel gave him a compassionate tap in the arm.

"Don't worry, everything will remain in the family," Fidel told De La Guardia, as he was preparing to go. Tony De La Guardia told his daughter Ileana about Fidel's promises when she visited her father in jail shortly thereafter. De La Guardia told her to cheer up: there was reason to hope that his life would be spared.

"My father seemed relieved," Ileana recalled later of that conversation with her father, one of the last ones before his execution. "Fidel had told him that, if he stayed away from implicating his superiors, everything would be all right."

Tony kept his word. At his next appearance in court, he said: "I want to underscore that I have the greatest responsibility. . . . That none of my bosses knew anything of this, that on various occasions they asked me if I knew or had participated in any of these operations, and that I always told them that no, I didn't have anything to do with this."

<>

One of the court-martial's most dramatic moments came when Captain Ruiz Poo—tears flowing down his cheeks and choking between sobs—said Ochoa's assistant, Captain Martinez Valdes, had told him that Cuba's cocaine-smuggling operations had been approved "at the highest levels." Television viewers across Cuba asked themselves, Had Fidel okayed the drug shipments? No one in the audience was sure.

The defendant said that, after learning of the internal government investigation into Cuba's drug connections, the MC Department got in touch with Martinez Valdes to ask that he stop all contacts with the Colombians.

"Martinez told me," Ruiz Poo recounted, "I don't have any problems whatsoever. Everything I do, absolutely everything I do, is discussed by my boss at the highest levels. I'll never forget his words. He said that, verbatim."

Looking down at the front row of the auditorium where Martinez

Valdes was sitting, Ruiz Poo added: "I would dare Martinez to have the guts to come forward right here, and tell me that I'm lying. He did say that!"

Ruiz Poo broke down in tears. He could not continue talking.

"Can you go on?" asked the chief prosecutor.

The defendant looked as if he was going to faint at any second. Escalona adjourned the session. It was near midnight.

<>

Major Pino, the court instructor, was asked to have another serious talk with all the defendants, especially Ruiz Poo. When the session resumed the next day, Escalona asked Ruiz Poo to clarify his statements about the alleged high-level green light for the drug-trafficking operations.

The chief prosecutor said Ruiz Poo's earlier testimony had raised disquieting questions among the population. Did Ruiz Poo think he could answer with serenity and calm today? The defendant nodded.

Ruiz Poo now said he was convinced that at no time had Fidel Castro or his brother known anything about the drug dealings. Martinez Valdes had lied to him to convey a sense of security, perhaps to calm his own fears, he said.

"Martinez led us to have that impression," Ruiz Poo went on. "We did not have ties to the MINFAR. How should we know what was going on in the army's high command?"

Escalona called Martinez Valdes to the stand.

"Defendant Martinez, is it true that you told defendant Ruiz Poo that you were sure that all your actions were discussed by your boss, Ochoa, at the highest levels?"

"No."

"Never?"

"Never."

<>

It was only the first of a series of discrepancies between the defendants' testimonies. When the chief prosecutor began to press the accused about Martinez Valdes's trip to Colombia, a key part of the government's plan to inflate Ochoa's involvement in the drug business, he received an array of contradictory answers.

Martinez Valdes said he had made the trip to Colombia as an emissary of De La Guardia, who had been originally invited to a meeting with Pablo Escobar. But De La Guardia denied the story. He said he had never been invited to Colombia, and suggested that Martinez Valdes had gone there on his own.

When Ochoa was interrogated, he conceded that he had been informed in advance of Martinez Valdes's trip to Colombia, but denied that there was any intention to team up with Escobar to smuggle cocaine through Cuba. In fact, he had specifically warned Martinez Valdes against accepting any deal that would involve trafficking through Cuba, Ochoa said.

At the most, Martinez Valdes was to try to put Escobar in contact with a Mexican businessman. If the Colombians and the Mexican did some drug-trafficking operations through Mexico, they would be invited to launder their profits by building tourism hotels in Cuba, he said. Ochoa had already contacted Cuba's tourism agency Cubanacan to inquire about possible investments in Cuba, he said.

"What did Martinez propose to Escobar?" the prosecutor asked.

"Martinez proposed to Escobar?" said Ochoa. "I don't know."

"So what did Martinez go to see Escobar for, then, if you authorized the trip?"

"To explore, to see what he wanted, to see what could be done."

"What Escobar wanted?"

"Yes."

"But Escobar had sent you a message?"

"No. Martinez made contact with Escobar's people in Panama, and they invited him to go there."

"And what came out of that exploration?"

"Well, I believe that nothing ever came out of it."

While accepting that he had been corrupted and had forgotten his revolutionary principles, Ochoa appeared more defiant than in his appearance before the honor tribunal. He pleaded guilty to trafficking in ivory, diamonds and weapons. He admitted having ordered his assistants to sell goods at Angola's Candonga black market, refraining from saying that all his predecessors in the job had done it. But he attacked the core of the prosecution's charges by denying any participation in the Ruiz-De La Guardia cocaine-smuggling operation.

"Well, in fact, I didn't have any knowledge," Ochoa said of De La Guardia's activities. "Tony never told me he was doing drug-trafficking operations. He talked to me about tobacco operations, work-of-art operations, and, about a month and a half ago, about an operation involving fighting cocks. But drug trafficking, he never told me anything about that."

Ochoa, like De La Guardia before him, spoke with the careful determination of a man who wanted to set the record straight, without antagonizing his judges. By then, the defendants knew the chances they would get away with a light sentence were small.

The trial was a sham. Escalona's questions led in one direction only: the defendants had done irreparable damage to Cuba, and to Fidel Castro. In trafficking with drugs, they had lent credence to CIA campaigns against Cuba, and had destroyed years of great effort by the revolution to convince the world of its innocence. That was nothing short of treason—the worst kind of treason anybody could commit.

◄►

"De La Guardia, you have children, right?" Chief Prosecutor Brigadier General Escalona Reguera asked.

"Four children."

"Four. Have you ever thought of the consequences of your drug operations on the youth all over the world?"

"I really didn't think about that. . . . I didn't think about that."

"But you have traveled extensively throughout the world."

"Yes, sir."

"You have seen the misery."

"Yes, sir."

"You have seen the consequences of drug trafficking."

"Yes, sir."

"You have seen what it does to the youth."

"Yes, sir."

"You are aware that drugs are the scourge of mankind in our days."

"Yes."

"And that you are part of this disgrace to mankind."

"Yes, sir."

"And your conscience, De La Guardia?"

"Bad . . ."

"That's all, Mr. President."

◄►

"Escalona, you're a son of a bitch!" yelled an infuriated Marilena De La Guardia, Col. Tony De La Guardia's young wife, standing up from her seat in the audience as the chief prosecutor concluded his questions. "Where did you get that Rolex watch on your hand?"

The other young woman next to her, Maria Isabel "Cucusa" De La Guardia, stood up at the same time.

"You have no shame, Escalona!" she shouted. "You have no shame!"

About a dozen female security guards rushed to the two women from all corners of the room. The defendants' relatives were taken away to a small room next to the court. The courtroom shouting scene was edited out of the trial's television broadcast. Instead, Cuban television showed a quick glimpse of the relatives' sad faces.

<><

The defense attorneys were so confused about their roles that they often seemed to be working for the prosecution. Most didn't ask any questions, or simply asked their clients to expand on the crimes they had committed.

Col. Alberto Ruben D'Toste, the defense attorney for Martinez Valdes, buried his client in an even deeper mess.

"Here, in the prosecution's charges, it is rightly stated that you were involved in one of the most serious, reckless and irresponsible acts ever committed," the defense attorney said. "Are you aware of that?"

"Yes," answered Martinez Valdes, lowering his head.

D'Toste's final arguments were even more astounding. He said, "In the first place, we have to make clear that we're defending the defendants, but not the grave crimes they have committed." He added, "We wouldn't deserve the dignity of occupying this chair if we interpreted the defense's mission that way. The defense attorneys, the prosecutor, the court for sure, the whole people, must be deeply angered and hurt by the actions carried out by the defendants in this case."

<><

In his closing remarks after several days of cross-examinations, Chief Prosecutor Escalona showed no mercy for the defendants. He devoted much of his written speech to Division General Ochoa. Adjusting his glasses and looking up to the television cameras for greater drama in key parts of his statement, he said Ochoa had committed the worst kind of treason: undermining Fidel's credibility.

"By assaulting Fidel's credibility, Ochoa and the other defendants have stabbed the fatherland and the people in the back. Fidel is our voice, our representation, the person we go to for help in difficult moments. He has the credibility at home and abroad, before foreign governments and international organizations, to explain the real situation in our country. . . ."

"By rejecting Fidel, Ochoa rejected Cuba, and left the people at the mercy of the enemy's attacks, dramatically weakening the defense of the revolution."

There could be no compassion for officers who had brought about such shame and danger to the revolution.

Ochoa and the thirteen other defendants sat petrified in the front row, some of them covering their eyes with their hands. Colonel De La Guardia, one hand on his right leg and the other holding his chin, occasionally looked at the chief prosecutor out of the corners of his eyes.

The court-martial's final verdict made headlines around the world. All fourteen defendants were found guilty. A brief communiqué in *Granma* July 10, 1989, listed their sentences.

Div. Gen. Arnaldo Ochoa: death.

Capt. Jorge Martinez Valdes: death.

Col. Antonio De La Guardia: death.

Maj. Amado Padrón: death.

Brig. Gen. Patricio De La Guardia: thirty years in prison.

Capt. Miguel Ruiz Poo: thirty years in prison.

The remaining eight defendants, most of them low-level officers of the MC Department, were sentenced to prison terms ranging from ten to thirty years. Antonio Sanchez Lima, Eduardo Diaz Izquierdo, Alexis Lago Arocha and Rosa Maria Abierno were sentenced to thirty years in prison. They were the Tony De La Guardia aides who had been most active in helping Ruiz's boatmen load their cocaine cargos in Varadero.

Luis Piñeda Bermudez, Gabriel Prendes Gómez and Leonel Estévez Soto were sentenced to twenty-five years in prison. Antonio Rodriguez Estupiñan, an aide to Ochoa in Angola who had supervised the Cuban mission's black market transactions, was sentenced to ten years in prison. The harsh sentences could only be commuted by the Council of State, Cuba's highest-ranking political body, the announcement said.

José Llicas, the Ochoa aide who sold Cuban sugar and other goods at the Candonga black market in Angola, was never charged with any crime. Div. Gen. Abelardo Colomé Ibarra, the top MINFAR official who had reassured Tony De La Guardia that nobody would be punished for the MC Department's transgressions, was never considered an accomplice. He was not among the generals who participated in the military honor tribunal, nor in the court-martial. He reappeared a few weeks later as Cuba's new interior minister.

Division General Abrantes, the man whom U.S. drug enforcement officials had identified as Cuba's top drug smuggler, was later charged with negligence—allegedly for failing to act on a tip he had received in February 1989 about his aide Col. Tony De La Guardia's drug-related activites. Indicting Abrantes on drug charges would have been too explosive. The interior minister was too close to Castro.

At about 1 A.M. that night, desperate to prevent her father's execution, Tony De La Guardia's daughter Ileana went to see García Márquez at his protocol house in Siboney. The young woman, accompanied by her husband, Jorge Ricardo Masetti, an Argentine-born Americas' Department agent who had most recently worked as a De La Guardia aide in Angola, made an eleventh-hour effort to have Gabo plead with Fidel for her father's life.

The knew Gabo well, from several gatherings with Tony. They knew that if anybody could save Tony's life this late in the game, it would be García Márquez.

But when the two got near Gabo's protocol house No. 6, they ran into half a dozen soldiers and a military vehicle posted at the corner. In front of Gabo's house, there were several other vehicles, and a few dozen troops, many of them with hand radios. Only Fidel kept that kind of security in Cuba. The Cuban leader had arrived there first. Ileana and her husband, knowing they would be stopped if they tried to get nearer, decided to wait a few blocks away.

Fidel Castro had rung the bell at García Márquez's house around midnight, unannounced as was his custom.

Gabo was alone. He had just finished dinner, and was reading in the living room. The Cuban leader looked angry and worried. The two men sat on a sofa next to the chimney dominating the room, and exchanged small talk. For the next hour, neither of them dared discuss the possible execution of Division General Ochoa and Col. Tony De La Guardia.

Journalists throughout the world were begging Cuba's embassies abroad for visas to get into the country and cover the Ochoa affair.

There were reports that several world leaders, including Pope John Paul II, were preparing statements asking clemency for the convicted men.

Fidel Castro feared raising the subject with Gabo. He knew that the writer was against the death penalty, both as a matter of principle and, in particular, as it had been applied to the four Cuban officers. Gabo had made it known in conversations with Castro's top aides that he was anxious to see that the four men's lives were spared. And Castro was well aware that García Márquez was a close friend of Tony De La Guardia.

The Interior Ministry colonel, an amateur painter and lover of the arts, had been a frequent visitor to Gabo's house. In fact, Tony De La Guardia had often sat in the same seat Fidel now occupied. A naive landscape painting by him hung in the entrance hall of Gabo's house. As Fidel and Gabo talked, the writer wondered whether the Cuban leader had recognized the De La Guardia painting on his way in.

At about 2 A.M., Fidel called it a night. Gabo was leaving the next morning for France, where he had an appointment with President François Mitterrand. As the two men stood at the front door, ready to say good-bye, García Márquez approached the touchy subject. He pleaded for the defendants' lives in the way he thought would be most effective.

"I wouldn't want to be in your shoes. Because if they are executed, nobody on earth will believe that it wasn't you who gave the order," Gabo said.

Fidel Castro leaned his hand on the threshold, and looked pensively at his friend.

"You think so? Do you really think that people would see it that way?" Castro asked.

Castro was a blind believer in the revolution he had created, unused to hearing skeptical views about its internal checks and balances. Like all leaders who end up believing their own campaigns of disinformation, Castro thought his regime had well-oiled mechanisms to check his own powers. He was lucid enough to know his regime was highly unpopular, but he blamed its troubles on a longstanding CIA campaign of economic sabotage and propaganda. The idea that his revolution had become a military dictatorship, where everything depended on the Comandante's whims, sounded to him like just another fabrication of enemy propaganda.

Standing in the doorway of Gabo's home, moving his hands to emphasize his words, Fidel began to explain the fairness of the legal proceedings that had ended with the court-martial's verdict. It had been the unanimous opinion of the court that Ochoa and Tony De La Guardia deserved to be executed, he said. "I have checked with all the state institutions, and I find an overwhelming majority are for their execution."

"Don't you think they say that because they think that's what you want?" García Márquez asked candidly.

"No, I don't think so," Fidel responded.

García Márquez was in a sad mood when Fidel said good-by and walked away. He was convinced that the Council of State would not spare the lives of Ochoa, Tony De La Guardia and their aides. Months later, reflecting on the executions and his conversation with Fidel on the doorstep of his house, Gabo told me: "I've known many heads of state, and there is one common denominator among them all: No ruler believes he's being told what he wants to hear."

As soon as Castro's caravan left, Ileana and her husband knocked on the door at Gabo's house. The writer and his wife, Mercedes, were still awake. They invited the couple in, and offered them coffee.

Ileana, tears in her eyes, asked the novelist to save her father's life. Gabo was sympathetic. He tried to comfort her, and told her he had already done it.

"Could you give him a letter of mine," Ileana pleaded, taking an envelope from the back pocket of her jeans. "I have tried to get it to him for several days, but nobody will pass it on."

"I'm leaving for Paris tomorrow morning, but I'll make sure it gets to him," Gabo said.

Ileana and her husband left the house at 3 A.M. They felt a little bit better. Gabo's help in forwarding the letter would add weight to it, they thought. It was their best shot at saving Tony's life.*

---

* After the executions, Ileana De La Guardia reacted bitterly against García Márquez for not doing more to save her father's life. "He was baffled, he said this couldn't happen, that nobody wanted these executions," Ileana said, recalling the late night conversation in Gabo's house. "He said Fidel would be crazy if he allowed the executions. He told me not to worry, that he personally would keep trying to persuade Fidel not to go ahead with the executions."

Gabo has a different recollection of the conversation. "I told her I had pretty much done whatever I could possibly do. I promised her I would deliver the letter, and I did. After leaving the country on the next morning, I made sure that the letter got into Fidel's hands."

The twenty-nine-member Council of State was convened for 3 P.M., July 9, 1989, two days after the court-martial issued its verdicts. Fidel Castro made sure that nobody missed the meeting, and that all the top officials of his regime shared responsibility for the group's final decision.

Council members Juan Almeida Bosque and Roberto Robaina, respectively the head of the Communist Party's Central Committee and the first secretary of Cuba's Communist Youth, were summoned overnight from an official tour to Pyongang, North Korea. Education Minister José Ramón Fernandez was told to cancel his official trip to Argentina to represent Cuba at the inauguration of President Carlos Menem. Not one single council member could be excused for this occasion.

Castro, sitting next to his brother at the head table of the Havana convention center's conference room, opened the council's session by asking that each member answer separately whether the death sentences should be commuted. Fidel Castro would be the last speaker.

One by one, in front of the state television camera, the twenty-four men and four women making up the council delivered their verdicts. They all nervously read from prepared statements, hardly lifting their eyes from their written remarks, their voices often trembling.

Unanimously, they endorsed the death sentences, their prepared statements elaborating on the same message: the defendants had stabbed Fidel and the revolution in the back.

Citing alleged letters and statements from their constituents, they said that angry factory workers, students, peasants and intellectuals were demanding the death penalty for the traitors. The leadership could not defraud them, nor allow their magnanimity to weaken the revolution. The culprits had to be executed.

Raúl Castro avoided another embarrassing intervention like his June 14 address to the Western Army by speaking slowly and not departing a comma from his prepared text. With an expression of deep concern, he told the nation that the incidents of the last few weeks had been so serious that they had created great stress for Fidel. The Cuban leader had spent 153 hours in the defense minister's office in the previous days, devoting his entire energies to this problem, Raúl said.

Raúl Castro himself had been deeply hurt by the whole process, he added. On one of the many sleepless nights when the two brothers were investigating the Ochoa case at the defense minister's office, Raúl found himself crying for Ochoa and his family.

"Deprived of sleep, I circled my desk, and went to the bathroom behind my office to brush my teeth; looking in the mirror I realized that tears were flowing down my cheeks," Raúl said.

<>

Finally, a seemingly heartbroken Fidel Castro was quick to dispel any hope that he would grant a last-minute pardon to the defendants. In a nearly four-hour speech, he went out of his way to stress that he had no alternative but to validate the collective will of the country.

"This case has been characterized by its exceptional honesty," he told the nation. "I do not think it would be an exaggeration to say that there has never been a judicial process that involved such large participation, so much information, so much clarity, and so much equitability."

Never had judges been able to make up their minds with such freedom, Castro said, only to contradict himself seconds later by conceding that during the legal proceedings he had "exchanged impressions" about the trial's outcome with members of the Communist Party Politburo, the Communist Party's Executive Committee and the Council of State—many of whom were the same people who made up the courts that tried the case.

Of the 162 Central Committee members present at a meeting during the trial, 141 had supported the death penalty for the defendants, Castro reported. Of 402 members of the National Assembly who were queried, 401 voted for the death penalty. What's more, the people's representatives had complained that the sentences had been too lenient.

"I believe that the military tribunal was generous," Castro said. "I believe that virtually all the defendants could have been given the death penalty."

But the tribunal had reached a wise decision, he said: it was better for people to complain that it had been too generous, that for people to criticize it for being too harsh. He concluded with an emotional reference to the thousands of Cubans who had died to defend the fatherland and the revolution. The government, he said, could not betray their memories, and it could not ignore the people's demands to bring the traitors to justice.

At the end, Castro requested a formal vote on the sentences.

"Those who support ratification of the sentences issued by the military tribunal raise your hands," he said.   Two seconds later: "Those who oppose it."

"By unanimous decision of the Council of State, the military tribunal's sentence is ratified. The session is over."

<>

The executions of Division General Ochoa, Colonel De La Guardia and their two aides were announced in a one-paragraph box in *Granma* on July 13. In the following weeks, there would be a widespread purge of Interior Ministry officials, their friends and others whom the Castro brothers wanted out of the way. An increasingly insecure Fidel Castro was in fact dismantling the Interior Ministry, and putting his brother's men in charge of it.

Little more than two weeks after the executions, Fidel Castro's longtime personal security chief and interior minister Abrantes was arrested with another three top former MININT officials.

Abrantes, a full member of the Communist Party's Central Committee, had been fired from his job at the beginning of the Ochoa trial, and was replaced by Raúl Castro's protégé Division General Colomé Ibarra. The ousted interior minister was charged with negligence and "corruption or tolerance of corrupt behavior," for his failure to act on the February 1989 tip about Tony De La Guardia's drug smuggling. He was sentenced to twenty years in prison.

Brig. Gen. Roberto González Caso, only a few weeks earlier Cuba's immigration chief, Oscar Carreño Gómez, the former customs chief, and Lt. Col. Rolando Castañeda Izquierdo, another senior ministry official, were arrested on similar corruption charges. A separate announcement said that former Transportation Minister Diocles Torralba, the late Col. Antonio De La Guardia's father-in-law, was sentenced to twenty years in prison on charges of corruption.

Five Interior Ministry brigadier generals were demoted and forced to retire, including Brig. Gen. Amado Valdes Gonzalez, head of Cuba's Border Troops, and Brig. Gen. Miguel Bermejo, the man in charge of Cuba's fire brigade.

Dozens of other mid-level Interior Ministry officers would be retired in coming months. The purge was expanded to the Ministry of Culture, the Ministry of Agriculture, the Ministry of Construction and independent government agencies such as the Tourism Institute and the Movie Industry Institute. The free-spending, mostly liberal Interior Ministry officers and their friends throughout the government were out. MINFAR officers replaced those fired.

<>

García Márquez returned to Havana shortly after the conclusion of the Abrantes trial. He saw Fidel Castro briefly on the day after his arrival. Later that week, Castro showed up at his home, late at night. More than half a dozen of Castro's bodyguards entered the house with the Comandante, and placed themselves around the living room.

As it happened, Gabo had guests that night. Instantly, Castro was the center of everybody's attention. He would stand, his body leaning against the wall, or he would move back and forth in the living room delivering his thoughts on issues ranging from the decline of the Soviet empire to the latest techniques for milk pasteurization. The writer and his friends were sitting around the table, most of them listening open-mouthed to Fidel's thoughts. Gabo seldom contradicted Castro in public. When addressing the Cuban leader, he referred to him as "Comandante"—never as "Fidel." Then, to reduce the emotional distance, he used the familiar Spanish-language *tu* form.

On some occasions, Gabo's shyness in front of Fidel was a major disappointment to his guests. Some considered García Márquez a far more interesting personality than Castro. The Cuban leader, in fact, was not very different in private than in public: he could bore people to death with unending technical details about a new vaccine Cuban scientists had allegedly discovered, or about a new technique for banana growing he had just learned about.

Once, more than a year before the Ochoa affair, Castro had spoiled a cheerful New Year's party at Gabo's house. It was well after midnight. A select group of artists and Cuban cultural officials were chatting cheerfully and dancing to salsa music on the patio, by the pool and its mango trees. Fidel Castro showed up with a big smile and a bottle of champagne.

In a matter of seconds, the small crowd circled the Cuban president. In the forefront were Culture Minister Armando Hart and Culture Vice-Minister Antonio Nuñez Jimenez. Others, in the outer ring of the circle, were stretching their necks to hear what the Cuban leader was saying.

Castro was holding forth about his visit to a hospital that afternoon. One of the guests, unable to follow his words over the music, signaled to have the volume of the music lowered. García Márquez turned off the tape recorder. What began as small talk soon developed into a serious dissertation by Castro: he had witnessed an autopsy at the hospital, and proceeded to give a detailed description of the mortician's hand movements within the dead man's body.

Antonio Valle Vallejo, García Márquez's young assistant at the film institute, had been one of the guests trapped in the circle of listeners. He was unable to move: going to the patio for a drink or making any other exit—no matter how good the excuse—would have been considered in very bad taste. He wished Castro had never shown up. A joyful year's-end party had turned into a gruesome press conference.

But more than a year later, when Castro dropped in at Gabo's house for the first time after the Abrantes trial and the Ochoa–De La Guardia executions, the novelist had decided he would not let his respect for Fidel get in the way of his sentiments for a dead friend.

Tony De La Guardia had been degraded, stripped of his military honors, and turned into a nonperson in Cuba. All traces of his existence had been wiped out. Yet García Márquez still had De La Guardia's painting hanging from the wall at the entrance hall of his Havana home—Fidel, who was familiar with Tony's art, could not have missed it when he strode in.

Days before, García Márquez had considered taking the picture down, and transporting it to Mexico with him when he left Cuba. But he changed his mind. In the end, he decided to leave the last vestige of Antonio De La Guardia hanging in its customary place.

Ochoa's widow, Maida, was sitting in a rocking chair in her dark-lit living room, moving back and forth, measuring her words carefully as we talked late into the night about her husband's fate.

We had been talking in the dark since the sun had gone down at about 7 P.M. I didn't dare to ask her whether it was because she was trying to save on electricity—Cuba had just imposed drastic cutbacks on home energy consumption—or because she was afraid to be seen through the windows talking with a foreigner.

Several months had passed since the executions, and she had begun to lead a more normal life. The Ochoa case had been replaced in the headlines by daily announcements of the new economic austerity measures brought on by the collapse of the Soviet bloc and the end of Socialist countries' foreign aid programs. Security around Ochoa's house on 24th Street was more lax.

Maida had gone back to teaching chemistry at the Instituto Pedagógico. The government had taken all of Ochoa's cash, as well as his elephant trunks and medals, but they had left her the Lada car. One MINFAR officer had come to the house a few weeks earlier, on the fourteenth birthday of Ochoa's son Alejandro, to ask if the child was all right and renewing an offer for first-rate psychiatric counseling if he needed it.

Clearly, the emissary had been sent by Fidel Castro. The Co-mandante, who was known for his incredible memory for people's birthdays and special anniversaries, had not forgotten the Ochoa family. Ochoa had become a folk hero in Cuba, as the 8A graffiti attested, and a cause célèbre abroad. It made good sense for Castro not to antagonize his widow.

Had Ochoa conspired against Fidel Castro? I asked. The short answer was yes and no. She said her husband had been victimized because he had grown impatient with Cuba's grim reality, and was increasingly outspoken about it. His strong talk at the dinner party with Patricio De La Guardia and his wife, Cucusa, in Luanda was just one example of Ochoa's growing anxiety over the country's future.

The Socialist bloc was crumbling. The Third World was embracing free-market policies. The whole world was changing. Life in Cuba was deteriorating by the day, and the Castro brothers—surrounded by yes men—were sticking to old Stalinist policies that had proven to be a failure. Ochoa had not conspired against the revolution, she said. Quite the contrary, he wanted an economic opening to save the revolution.

"Arnaldo used to say that we depended too heavily on the Socialist bloc; that we needed to find new markets; that we needed to develop tourism; that we needed to strike deals with countries in the capitalist world," she told me. "He wanted the same things that most Cubans want, and that the government itself began talking about a few months later."

She was talking about her husband with a mixture of cold political analysis and personal affection. Depending on the nature of her thought, she would refer to him alternatively as "Arnaldo" or as "Nine," the General's nickname at home, which she pronounced in Spanish as "Nee-neh."

His mistake, she went on, was to talk too openly. "I would often tell him: Nine, be careful what you say. You talk too much," she recalled. "He wouldn't listen. Perhaps he was a bit childish, or overconfident. He never thought he would be arrested."

After his arrest, she only saw him twice. The last time was three days before his execution. It was late at night, while the whole country was watching the televised hearings of the Council of State's appeals proceedings. She and the kids had been picked up at home by MIN-FAR agents, and driven around the city for more than an hour before they arrived at the military garrison where her husband was kept.

Ochoa was in an air-conditioned room, with a television set and a VCR. Two guards were at the door as the family walked in. They embraced, and cried. Ochoa seemed to know what the outcome of the council session would be. He sensed that he would not see his family again.

Ochoa took his son Alejandro, the thirteen-year-old, by the arms. Looking him in his eyes, he asked him to be good to his mother, and to study.

"It was all very quick," Maida recalled. "He bid farewell to the boy, and told us he loved us all," she said. "After that, I'm told he said he didn't want to talk to anybody else."

On July 13, 1989, hours after the executions were announced, a MINFAR officer knocked on the door at Maida's house. He brought Ochoa's death certificate. Reading it was "the worst moment" of the family's ordeal, she recalled. The certificate read, "Arnaldo Ochoa Sanchez; Profession?: unemployed; Married?: unknown; Cause of death?: unknown."

Ochoa, the former Hero of the Cuban Republic, was buried shortly thereafter in an unmarked grave at Havana's Colón Cemetery. It was grave No. 46,672, a small white tombstone on the cemetery's K Street, not far away from another unmarked grave, No. 46,427, containing the remains of Tony De La Guardia. Maida was informed about the tomb's number and location, but was not allowed to write her husband's name onto the stone. Eventually, she placed a small plaque on the grave. It reads, "*A Nine de su familia*"—To Nine from his family.

<>

A month after the executions, Reinaldo Ruiz was sentenced by a Miami court to seventeen years prison. He felt cheated. In several phone calls and letters that he sent me from his prison cell over the year that followed, he said he had been fooled by the U.S. government.

He had hoped his disclosures about the Cuban Interior Ministry's involvement in drug trafficking would help reduce his sentence. It hadn't. At fifty-two, he had already suffered a heart attack. His medical record also listed hypertension, diabetes, angina pectoris and shortness of breath. He would be sixty-nine years old when he was due to be freed. Ruiz was deeply depressed; felt lonely and forgotten. He had split with Colette, who was now living in Los Angeles, still looking for a way to return to Cuba.

In mid-December, 1990, I got a Christmas card from him. It was the last I heard from Reinaldo Ruiz. Later I learned that he died in his prison cell on New Year's Eve. His heart had given out.

◄►

The other key surviving witness in the Ochoa–De La Guardia affair, former interior minister Div. Gen. José Abrantes, suffered a fatal heart attack only three weeks after Ruiz's death. Abrantes's death raised suspicions among anti-Castro Cubans. At fifty-eight, he had no history of heart disease. As Col. Tony De La Guardia's boss, he was the only survivor of the Ochoa–De La Guardia group who could one day shed light on whether Fidel Castro had authorized the Interior Ministry's cocaine deals.

Abrantes was serving his twenty-year prison sentence at the Guanajay jail, a prison camp twenty-five miles southwest of Havana. It was the same prison where Patricio De La Guardia was serving his sentence. On Monday morning, January 21, 1991, Abrantes asked to be excused from his work schedule. He had been feeling bad for two days.

He asked for permission to call his wife, Natasha. He had married the young woman while in prison—it was his fourth marriage—and she had borne their first child a week earlier. He had not seen the baby girl. Natasha, still recovering from a caesarean section, had a visitors' pass, but it did not allow her to come to the prison until the following Friday.

"Try to get a permit to come sooner," Abrantes told her. "I'm not feeling well. And I want to see the baby."

Two hours later, Abrantes told a prison mate that his chest pains were getting worse. Minutes later, he fainted. About a dozen prisoners began shouting for help. When nobody came, they started banging against the walls. The prison guards rushed to the cell, but did not know what to do. They feared a riot, or an attempt to escape. The jail director was out, and they had been instructed not to open the cells under any circumstances.

"You're letting him die! You are killing him!" Abrantes's cellmates shouted, pounding frantically on the iron bars of their cell door.

Half an hour went by. When the prison director arrived, Abrantes was lying on the floor, unconscious but still breathing. Three guards placed him on a stretcher and rushed him to the street. As they moved him onto the back seat of the prison director's blue Moskvich car, Abrantes's body fell forward. He was dead.

<>

Had Abrantes ever told his cellmates to what extent he had known about the MC department's cocaine operations?

In Havana few months later, I asked Maria Isabel "Cucusa" De La Guardia to pose that question to her husband, Patricio—now the only survivor among the key figures of the Ochoa–De La Guardia affair—on her next visit to the Guanajay jail. When she returned, she told me that Abrantes had indeed confessed to Patricio that he had approved of several—although not all—drug shipments.

Abrantes and Patricio De La Guardia had often discussed their case while in jail. The last time had been only two days before the former interior minister's death—on Saturday, January 19, 1991. The two inmates were working in the Guanajay prison's vegetable garden; Abrantes was planting lettuce, De La Guardia was pushing a wheelbarrow. During the lunch break, as they had done so often in recent months, the two men tried to put together the pieces of the puzzle that had landed them in jail.

Abrantes said that he had authorized Tony De La Guardia's drug deals, but had not known of the subsequent cocaine shipments engineered by Amado Padrón. The MC Department's drug operations had taken on a life of their own, far beyond what had been officially sanctioned.

Did Fidel Castro know? Yes, Abrantes had said. Fidel was aware that Cuba was occasionally allowing cocaine shipments to go through its territory, and had at least once ordered a drug sale. In 1988, the Comandante had asked Abrantes to sell ten thousand kilograms of cocaine that was in storage at Havana's Cimeq Hospital, if possible through Eastern European countries. Abrantes was to seek $50 million for the cocaine, which had originated largely from Cuban coast guard seizures.

Abrantes had told Castro about the first De La Guardia–Ruiz drug shipment as an exceptional, top-secret operation. But Fidel had warned against more operations on Cuban soil, and had blown up when he learned that the MC Department had later engaged in large-scale drug smuggling on Cuban territory behind his back, Abrantes had said. Cuba's government-sanctioned drug smuggling had spun out of control.

"There were some authorized drug deals, and others that weren't authorized," Cucusa De La Guardia said, quoting her husband. "The whole thing blew up when the unauthorized operations were discovered."

When Castro decided the drug operations had to be denounced before the U.S. government made public new evidence in the case, Tony De La Guardia agreed to take all the blame for the drug trafficking. As Tony had told his daughter, Ileana, he had been promised that everything would stay "in the family."

"Tony died betrayed by Fidel," Cucusa said. "He didn't think things would turn out that way."

There is a virtual consensus in Cuba's Interior Ministry intelligence circles that the official story of the Ochoa–De La Guardia affair was ludicrous: Castro could not possibly have been shocked to find out that his top aides had been engaged in cocaine smuggling.*

In reality, Castro had long condoned occasional drug-trafficking deals when he considered them justified on national security grounds, such as in the case of the drug-for-weapons shipments to Colombia's M-19 guerrillas. What happened this time was only a matter of degree: the MC Department's large-scale drug smuggling had gone beyond the limits set by Fidel.

When it became clear that the U.S. government was about to uncover Cuba's role in drug smuggling, Castro moved swiftly to preempt the move. Castro used the opportunity to crack down on disaffected MINFAR and MININT officers who were becoming a major threat to Castro's leadership. Ochoa and the De La Guardia brothers represented a reform-minded movement that was gaining strength within Cuba's military. At the same time, Ochoa and the De La Guardia brothers were accumulating enormous economic power. If they weren't stopped immediately, they would start making demands. Their grumbling would turn into defection or outright rebellion.† A pre-emptive strike was needed.

After the four officers made their Monday morning visit to the port of Jaimanitas and boarded the cigarette boat, Fidel Castro and his

---

* *The behind-the-scenes accounts of the Ochoa–De La Guardia affair by Ochoa's widow, Tony De La Guardia's daughter and Patricio De La Guardia's wife coincided with the testimonies of more than half a dozen former Interior Ministry intelligence officers whom I interviewed in Havana, Miami and South America over a two-year period.*
† *Granma, in its June 16 editorial on the Ochoa–De La Guardia case, implied that much in its passage referring to the moral crimes committed by the defendants, when it said, "This kind of treason leads always, sooner or later, to political treason."*

brother Raúl decided they could waste no more time. The four men were arrested the same night. Preparations for the show trials began immediately.

When I asked chief prosecutor Brigadier General Escalona about the Ochoa–De La Guardia executions after the case had vanished from the headlines, at first he stuck to the official line that there were no political motives behind the trials. But when I took the case to a personal level and commented to him that passing the death sentences must have been a traumatic experience for him, his demeanor changed. He nodded, and his face darkened. He had been friendly with Ochoa during their military duties in Cuba's Eastern Army, he told me, and they had had dinner together at Ochoa's home in Angola not long before the scandal broke.

Escalona looked me straight eyes, held a long silence, and added: "We had to do it. The revolution was at stake."

<>

By executing Ochoa and his friends, and by purging all disaffected officers from the government, Castro sent a strong warning to the armed forces, the Cuban people, and the outside world. Cuba would not tolerate the "new thinking" that had brought about the fall of Poland, and that was threatening to shake East Germany, Hungary and the rest of the Soviet bloc. Orthodox Marxism and military discipline would be preserved in Cuba at any cost.

The executions made it clear that there would be no independent thinking—let alone dissent—permitted on Castro's island. Nobody, not even Fidel's top aides, was above suspicion, as the Cuban leader and his brother had repeatedly reminded Cubans at the trial.

In times of crisis, one had to prove oneself stronger than ever, Castro told his aides. With the Socialist bloc crumbling, Cuba could not afford to show any sign of weakness.

His strategy to survive the collapse of worldwide communism was brutally simple. He summed it up three words, which he shouted defiantly in every speech over the months that followed the Ochoa case: *"Resistir! Resistir! Resistir!"* (Resist! Resist! Resist!).

4

The Purging of a Nation

It was Sunday afternoon, several months after the Ochoa–De La Guardia executions. I had arrived in Cuba only hours before, and had taken a stroll to Coppelia square on 23rd Street and L Street, the city's most popular meeting place.

The plaza was crowded. Young couples, children and long-haired teenagers were standing in more than a dozen long lines crisscrossing the park—many of the lines more than two hundred people long. They were queuing up to buy ice-cream tickets at various cashiers' booths scattered throughout the park, then queuing again to get their ice cream. The process took several hours. Most people seemed resigned to the long wait; they were silent, eyes unfocused, staring off into space.

I took a place at the end of one of the lines, behind a pregnant black woman who seemed to be in her early thirties. She was wearing a relatively new blue dress and was not very talkative. I volunteered that I had just arrived in Cuba that day.

"How are things?" I asked.

"Tough," she answered, shrugging without turning her head. Later, she told me she had been in line for three hours. She came to Coppelia every Sunday. There was nothing else to do, she said. *"No hay nada que hacer."*

She began talking about food shortages, bus delays, the hazards of daily life. She did not blame any of these shortcomings on the government. If anybody was listening to our conversation, she could have safely said she was griping about the U.S. embargo against Cuba, or on any number of American aggressions against her country.

"Well, perhaps things will get better soon?"

"No way," she responded, without abandoning the blank expression on her face. "We're screwed. *No hay salida.*" (There's no way out.)

Over the next few days, I would hear that phrase wherever I went. *No hay salida.* No way out. I would recognize it in the way people shrugged, smiled or opened their arms in a sign of silent resignation. Cuba had become a gray, bored, stagnant society. There was nowhere to go, nothing to do. Like the people standing in line at Coppelia, Cubans seemed resigned to a prolonged state of collective zombiehood.

The events of the summer of 1989 had left the country in a catatonic state. Glimpses of hope that Cuba would embark on the radical reforms that had swept the Soviet Union had been quashed. In the aftermath of the Ochoa–De La Guardia affair, the Castro regime had unleashed a nationwide crackdown on independent thinking and private entrepreneurship.

The revelations of widespread corruption that had come out during the Ochoa–De La Guardia trials had demonstrated the need of "a continuous and systematic national purge," Raúl Castro had said in his speech to the Council of State at the end of the trial. Ideological deviations, corruption and "even the smallest signs of lawlessness" would be crushed "at all levels of society, down to the grass roots," he had warned.

To the outside world, Fidel Castro emphasized the official line that the four military officers had been executed for drug trafficking. Internally, he used the Ochoa–De La Guardia case to make it brutally clear to his island nation of 10.5 million that he would not open the gates to political or economic change. The maximum leader had drawn the line.

In every speech that summer, Castro would reiterate his resolve to stick to Cuba's one-party Communist system, crush any effort to resurrect independent farmers markets, and to prohibit artists, craftsmen and other entrepreneurs from engaging in private businesses. He summed up his stand in a new slogan with which he would close every speech after the Ochoa–De La Guardia executions: "Socialism or Death!" Cubans on the street, displaying their natural talent for black humor, would joke that the slogan was redundant.

Castro's speeches turned increasingly apocalyptic. Cuba would begin preparing itself for major sacrifices in the face of a drastic decline in Soviet bloc economic aid, he announced. Cubans should prepare themselves to cook with firewood, and live with sharply reduced electricity. Rather than acknowledge the extent of the outside pressures, he flexed his muscles and embarked on a messianic crusade to save Marxism.

"Now that the capitalists and imperialists think that the ideas of socialism, communism and Marxism-Leninism are collapsing, we are more confident than ever in the ideas of Marxism-Leninism," he told Havana construction workers on November 7, 1989. Weeks later in a speech honoring Cuba's dead in Angola, he insisted that it was Cuba's destiny "to carry out the role that history has assigned to us . . . as unbending first-line defenders of the poor and exploited of this world."

Had Castro's chronic megalomania turned worse with age? Did he seriously think that communism would make a comeback in the rest of the world? Did he really believe that his small Caribbean island had been chosen to become the lone keeper of the world's Socialist flame?

If Cuba's history is any indication, he probably did. Castro was not a historic aberration, but an almost natural by-product of a long tradition of Cuban politicians with an exaggerated sense of their importance. He was not the first Cuban to believe himself a world leader, nor the only one to make a cult of uncompromising idealism.

Nearly a century earlier, another Cuban dreamer-politician, independence hero José Martí, had talked about Cuba as if it were a key to world peace. "A mistake in Cuba is a mistake in the Americas; a mistake in modern mankind," he had said. Martí contended that Cuba's freedom from Spain and North America would help preserve "the equilibrium of the world." It was a rather grandiose statement for a political leader on a Caribbean island colony of only 1.5 million. To understand the origins of this grandiloquence, one must take into account the relative importance of Cuba in its small corner of the world.

Since its discovery by Columbus in his first voyage to the Americas, Cuba was the Pearl of the Antilles for the Spanish crown. The island soon became the obligatory stopover for convoys traveling between the kingdom and the New World. Spanish cargo ships and their escort vessels—essential to keep pirates away—needed it as a point of resupply and communication with the rest of Latin America. As Spain and Britain escalated their battle for the New World's riches, Cuba turned into a strategic outpost for the Spanish crown.

In the seventeenth and eighteenth centuries, Cuba's importance grew as the biggest supplier of sugar to the Spanish kingdom. It is hard to imagine nowadays how critical Cuba's sugarcane was at the time. While many countries today extract sugar from beets or substitute artificial sweeteners for it, sugarcane was the only known source of sugar at the time.

It wasn't a coincidence that Cuba was the last Latin American colony to obtain its independence from Spain. Spain fought harder to keep it, and many within Cuba supported the Spanish crown with greater devotion than those in other colonies. Not surprisingly, the Spanish in the nineteenth century referred to Cuba as "*la isla siempre fiel*"—the always loyal island.

Cuba only achieved its independence in 1902—nearly eight decades after most Latin American countries. One measure of Spain's efforts to keep Cuba in its domain was the number of troops it sent to the island—nearly 200,000 of them, or more than it shipped to all the Latin American colonies together, from Mexico to Buenos Aires. To this day, the Spaniards use a saying to give comfort to someone who has lost much: "*Más se perdió en Cuba.*" (More was lost in Cuba.)

The length of Cuba's war for independence gave rise to a schizophrenic political culture. Perhaps because it was so conscious of Spain's extraordinary efforts to keep it under its wing, or because its late independence made it feel inferior, Cuba developed a grandiose vision of itself. Its leaders embraced their political causes with unusual passion.

Martí, like many Cuban politicians who succeeded him, was not bluffing when he said he stood ready to die for the fatherland. Although a scholar and poet with little military training, he returned to Cuba in April 1895, after fifteen years of exile politics in the United States, and joined the rebel army with the rank of major general. He was killed four weeks later in the battle of Dos Ríos. From all accounts, his death was near suicidal: he led a charge alone on his horse, well ahead of his men, against a whole company of Spanish troops.

Cuban history is full of cases of political zeal leading to acts of self-immolation. Cuba's independence heroes Antonio Maceo and

Máximo Gómez were known to lead frontal attacks on Spanish forces, which left disproportionate numbers of victims.

On August 5, 1951, Senator Eduardo Chibás, the leader of the opposition against President Carlos Prío Socarrás, shot himself on the air in an attempt to change the course of Cuban history. He had just made a radio speech in which he called on Cubans to "awaken" in the name of "economic independence, political liberty and social justice," when he turned a revolver on himself and shot himself in the stomach. On his way to the hospital, where he died eleven days later, Chibás whispered, "I am dying for the revolution. . . . I am dying for Cuba. . . ." Shortly thereafter, in the struggle against strongman Fulgencio Batista, Castro's fellow revolutionaries died like flies when they swarmed head-on against the Palace of Government and the Moncada barracks.

Castro's inflated vision of himself had been key to his victory over Batista. At one point, shortly after his invading guerrilla army had been whipped in the December 1956 battle of Alegría de Pío, Castro found himself hiding in a cane field with two fellow combatants, one of whom had lost his boots in the retreat. The Batista regime's fifty-thousand-man army, navy, air force and secret police were combing the island in search of Castro.

The three men—all that was left of Castro's rebel army—lay next to each other under the foliage, communicating in whispers, when Castro cleared his throat and murmured triumphantly: "We are winning. . . . Victory will be ours!"

Castro would escape from the cane field, regroup his devastated forces and take power three years later. Writer Tad Szulc, who described the cane field anecdote in detail, said Castro's guerrilla war at that point was "by any reasonable standards a monumentally demented enterprise." Yet Fidel prevailed.

In addition to the length and intensity of Cuba's fight for independence, there was another major factor that contributed to the country's tradition of messianic politics: the fluky way in which Cuba's independence finally came about. Unlike most other Latin American nations, Cuba did not achieve freedom by military victory.

It was an American invasion following an 1898 declaration of war on Spain that prompted the Spanish withdrawal. Spanish troops surrendered to U.S. marines three months after the start of the conflict. The island was turned over to a U.S. military governor under a Spanish-U.S. peace treaty.

The Cuban Constitutional Assembly of 1901, partly a concession to obtain independence, voted to include in the new constitution a clause—the Platt Amendment—that gave the U.S. government the right to intervene in Cuban affairs at any time. It was a spine in the throat of the newly independent nation—a humiliation few other Latin American countries had to live with. Perhaps because the post-independence struggle was harder, Cuban nationalism became a no less passionate and quixotic venture in the twentieth century.

Not surprisingly, Martí's quotes about Cuba's key role in world affairs appeared in bright red letters on Havana walls in late 1989—Castro's Communist Youth Union had put them there. In an apparent effort to defend Castro's megalomania from public ridicule, the Cuban regime's propaganda chiefs seemed to be reminding the people that if Fidel was crazy, he was not crazier than other Cuban leaders before him.

There was little Castro could offer in the way of compensation for support of his crusade in behalf of orthodox communism. As Cuba's Eastern European allies began to suspend their economic cooperation agreements with Cuba, growing shortages of food, clothing, and virtually all consumer goods began to plague the people.

Because of declining food imports, the regime had no choice but to reduce each Cuban's monthly supply of foodstuffs. Under the state's rationing card system each person received: five pounds of rice, 10 ounces of red beans, 20 ounces of lentils, a half-pound of cooking oil, four pounds of sugar, three small cans of condensed milk, three 12-ounce portions of chicken, and one 12-ounce serving of beef. There was also an allotment of five eggs a week per person.

Even these goods, which Cubans were scheduled to get at the beginning of the month at state-run grocery stores known as "bode-gas," were often missing. A popular joke went: "What do you call the 'bodega' supplies? Answer: The Americans. Why? Because they always say they're coming, but they never do!"

Eggs, which were more often available than other foodstuffs, quickly became known as *"salvadores"*—saviors. They got you out of trouble whenever you didn't have anything else around for a main course.

The regime's newspapers, television programs and movie theaters offered little distraction from the island's grim reality. Following Castro's statement during the Ochoa–De La Guardia trials that the revolution was in danger, government censors had become more stringent than ever.

Granma, the only daily newspaper in town, was beating all records of dullness. Its front-page stories were most often stodgy chronicles of Castro's daily activities, articles about factories meeting their production goals or Cuba's achievements in health care and education.

"Fidel receives congressional delegation from Mozambique," read a typical banner headline. "Fidel to speak tomorrow at anniversary of Federation of Women Workers," read a lead story on the following day. One of my favorite front-page headlines, appearing in *Granma* a few days after a Castro speech that had already been printed in full by the newspaper and run several times on radio and television, read: "Booklet with Fidel's latest speech to be presented tomorrow."

Bookstores offered little more than Castro's speeches. There were dozens of them, in various covers and designs, recording streams of oratory from more than thirty years. Some contained full speeches; others snippets from hundreds of talks, selected chronologically or by themes.

In case these weren't enough, there were also scores of books by Cuban scholars on particular passages in Castro speeches—often quasi-Talmudic interpretations of the Cuban leader's words aimed at justifying his frequent political flip flops over the years.

At La Moderna Poesia, Havana's largest book store, the bestseller section featured a book entitled "Annotations for the History of the Young People's Communist and Pioneer Movement in Cuba."

Buying a book was an agony in itself. You couldn't just take it to the cashier and pay for it. You would be directed to another line. There, a young woman would write tickets with the title of the book, the publishing house, and the price. Then you would take the book and the ticket to the cashier's—and only then were you allowed to pay.

The process seemed to take forever. I had chosen the book about the Cuban pioneer movement, only because I couldn't find anything more exciting. The woman writing the tickets laboriously began to scribble its title on a slip of paper. She stopped after the word "Annotations" to chat with another clerk.

When she resumed her work and was about to get to "the Young People's Communist and Pioneer Movement in Cuba," she was interrupted by a phone call. As time dragged on, I was going out of my mind. Yet nobody in the line behind me complained. About a dozen people waited sheepishly for their turns, as if there were nothing worth hurrying for anyway.

Several Havana movie theaters either were closed for lack of spare parts for their long-outdated projectors, or showed slow-paced Soviet movies that few Cubans wanted to see. The latest releases in Havana movie theaters at the time were the pre-Perestroika Soviet movie, *Moscow, You Are My Love,* and the Bulgarian production *Time of Violence.*

On television, except for a popular Sunday evening double-feature of pirated American movies—those featuring Charles Bronson were a big hit in Cuba—there was little to watch. A typical evening news program on the official Tele-Rebelde channel would show a stone-faced anchorman reading a string of reports about the revolution's latest achievements.

"The 'Girón Victory' Scientific Production Center of Jaguey Grande is nearing a record crop of 7 million quintals this year," said the lead story of one evening's newscast. The second story was, "The Vladimir Ilyich Lenin Hospital of Holguín has introduced a new technique for the diagnosis and treatment of pigmentary retinosis."

Havana's nicest restaurants, cabarets and hotel bars were out of bounds for Cubans, even for those who could afford them: they were for the exclusive use of foreign tourists. Cuban youths in ragged jeans would hang around the entrance of Havana's hotels anyway—often just to watch the smiling *extranjeros* in their designer clothes. Occasionally, security agents in civilian dress would ask them to disperse. Invariably, the youths would be back in a matter of minutes.

At the tourists-only restaurant, a black-suited maitre d' would meet you at the door and ask, "Do you pay with dollars?" If you didn't (it was illegal for Cubans to possess U.S. dollars)—you couldn't get in. It was part of Cuba's drive to collect much-needed foreign currency at a time when Eastern European countries were cutting off their foreign aid, officials explained.

At a small number of restaurants that catered both to Cubans and foreign tourists, such as at old Havana's La Bodeguita, Cubans had to go through the humiliating experience of waiting in line for hours in hopes of getting one of the handful of tables assigned to the locals, while watching Spanish or Canadian tourists walk in and be seated at once at any of the dozens of tables reserved for foreigners.

There was a third class of less pretentious restaurants where only Cubans went, such as the Castillo de Jagua on Havana's 23rd Street.

But these were often closed. A sign on the door would say they were shut for repairs. Cubans knew better: the restaurants had simply run out of food for the day because of the shortages.

Even Coppelia, the revolution's main source of culinary pride, was losing its glamour. In the early years of the revolution, Castro had praised Coppelia's fifty-four ice cream flavors as a wonder of the revolution's new production techniques, proclaiming that the Cuban ice cream parlor offered "more flavors than Howard Johnson's." Now, on the Sunday afternoon I joined the thousands on Coppelia square, the establishment was offering only four flavors—chocolate, pineapple, orange and melon.

The fall of East Germany's Communist government had resulted in a sudden cut of that country's milk and fruit essence shipments to Cuba, the Cuban government explained. Coppelia's ice creams were not immune to the effects of communism's collapse.

I had visited the island several times before, in the early and mid 1980s. On those occasions, there had been excitement in the air. Government officials at the time had talked proudly about Cuba's "tropical" socialism.

The country was experimenting with small private enterprises then, shifting away from the Soviet Union's rigid Marxist dogma. Once, in 1984, a Cuban Foreign Ministry official proudly escorted me to an Old Havana street where an elderly man had set up a machine to cover ID cards with plastic coating. The man had been licensed to operate as a private businessman. For the first time in many years, scores of farmers, artists and mechanics were allowed to operate independently.

But Castro had turned sharply toward orthodox communism in his 1986 "campaign of rectification of errors," which he launched just as Soviet President Mikhail Gorbachev started his economic reforms in the Soviet Union.

In his rectification campaign, Castro argued that Cubans had reacted too enthusiastically to the island's economic opening in the early eighties. State workers had been too eager to abandon their public jobs to join the fledgling private sector, where they could double their salary, he complained. Construction workers had stolen tools and materials from their government jobs to do lucrative after-hours work for private contractors.

In the Ochoa–De La Guardia affair, an alarmed Castro had seen his back-to-basics rectification campaign threatened by a group of young officers who had become skilled capitalist entrepreneurs. They were only the tip of a huge black-market iceberg in Cuba. He reacted promptly—and brutally—to kill the trend.

<>

Castro's speeches after the summer of 1989 not only brought about a general feeling of hopelessness, they unleashed a wave of fear. Fidel's rage over Ochoa's off-the-books deals in Angola, and his public fits over the MC Department officials' possession of black market–purchased homes, motorcycles and television sets left the Cuban people bewildered.

Didn't Fidel know that everybody in Cuba was guilty of those charges? Wasn't he aware that you couldn't survive in Cuba *without* resorting to the black market? Was he about to crack down on black marketeers? If Castro's dearest aides had been punished so harshly, who would be safe from now on?

There was hardly a Cuban in military or civilian life who didn't resort regularly to the black market. It was an unavoidable—and until then widely tolerated—part of daily life.

If your house's water pipes sprang a leak, you had no other recourse but to call an illegal plumber—the state provided no such service. If you needed a gate to protect your home, you had to call an illegal handyman—there were no government-licensed workers doing that job.

If your roof was falling down, you spread the word among your friends that you needed a roofer, and somebody would soon come up with an unlicensed worker to do the job. There was no such thing as a government-run service for roof repairs. Roofers, plumbers and handymen in general were a black hole in Cuba's Socialist system.

Everyone knew that these and all other unlicensed workers used tools and materials stolen from the state—there was no legal way of buying those things in Cuba. But since even government officials routinely hired such workers for repairs at their own homes—and word of that spread fast through a neighborhood—there was a general presumption that the practice was safe.

A senior government official, admitting the state's failure to come up with a solution to the repairmen issue, confessed to me over dinner one night that he had no choice but to contract a black market handyman to install a new door in his home.

"Why doesn't the state simply allow these people to work privately?" I asked.

"Because there would be a massive shift of workers to the private sector, and every one of those private construction workers would steal materials from the state. It would result in an enormous economic drain . . ."

"But, this way, you are encouraging people to break the law," I protested.

"It's the lesser of two evils," he replied. "Better to turn a blind eye."

<>

Government-tolerated lawbreaking had long been the norm, rather than the exception, in Socialist Cuba's daily life. If Castro had suddenly decided to enforce his ideologically-inspired rectification campaign, he would have had to militarize every corner of economic activity. To begin with, he would have to evict tens of thousands of Havana residents who had acquired their homes through black market transactions.

If you lived in Havana and wanted a bigger house, you had to break the law by offering money to a potential seller. Under the law, home sales were prohibited. The state only authorized *permutas*—property exchanges—with no money changing hands.

Why would somebody move from a bigger house to a smaller one, if it wasn't for profit? The official answer was that people were willing to move to smaller homes out of revolutionary altruism, or because circumstances such as a death in the family encouraged them to find smaller places requiring less work.

That, of course, was hogwash. In real life, people traded their homes for money, space or location—here as in anywhere else in the world. There was a thriving illegal real estate market that operated in broad daylight in Central Havana.

If you wanted to move within the city, you simply went to the Del Prado Avenue plaza, Havana's real estate marketplace. Hundreds of people gathered every morning in a tree-covered square in the middle of the wide avenue. Men and women—many of them elderly people—would sit on the colonial benches or walk around holding signs. "Have three-bedroom apartment in Vedado. Looking for one-bedroom apartment in same area," read a typical one. The minute you inquired about a possible exchange, the seller would say: "I'm open to proposals," code for, "How much are you willing to pay?"

Milling around the plaza were illegal real estate agents, carrying thick notebooks under their arms. If you didn't find a sign to satisfy your housing needs, you approached one of the agents, and told him what you were looking for. The man would check his notebook and most likely find your dream house there. The middleman would then arrange a meeting with the potential seller.

If the transaction went through, the realtor would get a 5 percent commission on the off-the-books purchase price. As far as the government was concerned, the two properties had been traded without one centavo ever changing hands.

<>

If you needed soap, shampoo or shaving blades—shortages of these goods became more severe as Soviet bloc shipments dwindled—you bought them on the black market. It was the easiest thing imaginable.

There were about twenty-two thousand African, Asian and South American students on free scholarships in Cuba, part of Castro's program to increase the Cuban revolution's political influence in Third World countries. The students had free access to the Diplotiendas, Cuba's well-stocked stores for diplomats, tourists and other international visitors. So even foreign students became large-scale suppliers to the black market, supplementing their meager monthly stipends with juicy profits from their business deals.

I once saw an Angolan student in his late teens walk into the Havana Libre Hotel shoe store, and buy two dozen plastic beach sandals—all the store had. He paid one dollar a pair. He probably sold them that same day to an underground Cuban salesperson for three times as much. The going black market price for imported beach sandals in Havana was eight dollars a pair.

Wives of the more than five thousand Soviet technicians based in Cuba had also become clandestine wholesalers of Diplotienda products in their neighborhoods. Longtime experts in the art of *speculatzia* at home, Soviet women were known to supply their neighbors with Bulgarian canned meat and other foodstuffs they bought in the foreigners-only stores.

When the Soviet Union began to repatriate its technicians from Cuba in 1989, Cubans became increasingly worried about their underground food suppliers. Who would get them canned meat if the Soviets left? Until then, Cubans moving to a new neighborhood needed only to ask where the nearest Soviet family lived, and they would most likely find an immediate supplier of foodstuffs.

The practice was so widespread that Soviets who didn't engage in it felt they owed people an explanation. In Havana's upscale suburb of Siboney, a Soviet diplomat put a sign on his front door. Playing on words with Fidel's motto, "*Aquí no se rinde nadie*" (Nobody surrenders here), the Soviet's sign read, "*Aquí no se vende nada*" (Nothing is sold here).

For a sizable part of the Cuban population, the black market had long been a prime source of food and clothing. With luck, the government's monthly ration of rice and eggs lasted only three weeks in most homes. The regime's allotment of one pair of shoes and one pair of slacks a year for each Cuban was far from enough to satisfy the population's needs. The ration-card system was largely a safety net to keep the poorest of the poor from starvation.

The key word to get by in Cuba in the late 1980s and early 1990s was *resolver*—to solve—a code word for procuring things outside the legal system. "Brother, I need some extra rice for a dinner party I'm having next weekend. Could you help me solve that problem?" a client would tell the neighborhood's grocery store manager in a bid for an under-the-table purchase exceeding the person's ration-card allocation.

Another key word was *inventar*—to invent. "*Compañero*, I don't have water at home, and they're not allowing me to place my own water tank on the roof of the building. Could we invent something to get water to my place?" an apartment dweller would tell an illegal plumber in a quest to divert water from somebody else's pipes.

The third most-widely used word in Cuba at the time was *escapar*—to escape. If you asked somebody how he was doing, the answer would be, "Escaping." If a neighbor wanted to tell you she had found a dozen tomatoes in the black market, she would tell you, "I escaped with a dozen tomatoes."

If Cubans at the time were better off than Cuba's official statistics would suggest, it was because everybody found an extralegal way to "solve" problems, or "invent" solutions to them. In an unspoken deal that had not been questioned until the Ochoa scandal, the regime would look the other way, and the people would be grateful for its leniency.

In fact, the regime's blind eye to Cubans' daily little crimes had long been a subtle tool of political control. It had kept people living in permanent fear that the government could legitimately crack down on them. Cubans, in effect, were on a permanent probation status.

The nature of repression in Castro's Cuba was more sophisticated than the simple caricature of a bloody police state often painted by critics of the revolution abroad. While the government was ruthless with political dissidents, it relied mainly on positive reinforcements to keep the majority of the population in check.

Under a carefully balanced mix of rewards and punishments, the system provided numerous incentives for political loyalty. If you wanted to get ahead in Cuba, you had to voice—or fake—your loyalty to Fidel. That made you an *integrado*—a person integrated into the system. Being an *integrado* was essential in order to get by, because the government took into account your political performance in making key decisions affecting your life. In Cuba, the government decided where you would work, whether you would get a promotion at your job, permission to travel, or a chance to buy low-priced domestic appliances at your workplace's credit union. It even had the last word on what you would study: high school graduates could list four career choices, but the government made the final decision based on the country's needs.

The Castro regime would try to reward Cubans who played it by the rules by accommodating their wishes. Conversely, it would be ruthless with those who crossed the line to political dissent. Castro himself had admitted holding about eight hundred prisoners for "counterrevolutionary activities," while human rights groups estimated the real figure at more than three thousand. And the dissidents were often beaten in prison. Many were sentenced to three years behind bars for such things as scrawling "Down with Fidel" on a wall. Others were imprisoned on "illicit association" charges for joining human rights groups.

But, for many years, when hundreds of thousands of Cubans had gathered at the plaza to listen to Fidel, it wasn't that all of them had gathered there spontaneously to express their love for the Comandante, nor that they had been dragged at gunpoint: most would go just to be seen by their Communist Party political commissar, and to score points toward a promotion at the office or the purchase of a color television set.

One midlevel Communist Party official showed me an astounding document that revealed to me the subtleties of Castro's carrot-or-stick system. It was a one-page confidential personnel form for midlevel managers applying for promotions at state companies.

The official, a young man who described himself as a political realist, allowed me to photocopy it: he wanted to convince me that Cuba's system of political intimidation was near perfect—and that there would not be a popular rebellion in Cuba anytime soon. The form, of restricted use for personnel chiefs and Communist Party political commissars, was titled "Biographical Data of the Cadre." It read as follows:

POLITICAL ACTIVITIES:
   —Association with the insurrectional process (before 1959):
   1. Have you ever collaborated with revolutionary organizations?
   2. Have you ever belonged to a revolutionary organization?
   3. Have you ever been in prison for political motives?
   4. Have you ever fought with the rebel army?
   —Association with the previous regime:
   5. Did you vote in the 1958 elections?
   6. Did you collaborate with the tyranny?
   7. Did you hold political jobs or government jobs?
   8. Did you belong to the armed forces of the tyranny?
   —Political-revolutionary activities (starting in 1959):
   9. Have you had responsibilities in political organizations or mass organizations?
   10. Have you studied at political schools?
   11. Have you participated in voluntary work on a permanent basis?
   12. Have you participated in the literacy campaign?
   13. Have you had responsibilities in the (National Assembly of the) People's Power?
   14. Have you participated in the people's sugar harvest on a permanent basis?
   15. Have you participated in internationalist civilian missions?
   16. Have you participated in other military mobilizations?
   17. Did you participate in the mobilization for the October crisis?
   18. Did you participate in the mobilization of December, 1960?
   19. Did you participate in the mobilization of April, 1961?
   20. Have you ever taken part in internationalist military missions?

21. Have you ever participated in the "fight against the bandits"?
22. Did you fight in Girón?

SOCIAL DATA
1. Do you have religious beliefs?
2. Have you participated in or do you belong to fraternal or religious organizations?
3. Have you received or applied for a passport with the intention of leaving the country?
4. Have you resided abroad?
5. Have you had another citizenship?
6. Have you been repatriated?
7. Do you have close relatives who have been indicted in court?
8. Do you have relations with disaffected elements or people who have tried to leave the country?

HEALTH DATA
1. Do you suffer from a chronic ailment?
2. Have you been admitted at a medical center because of illness (not checkups)?
3. Have you had or do you have psychiatric treatment?
4. I hereby certify that the content of this document is strictly accurate.

Once the form was filled out, signed and dated by the applicant, the political commissar would start checking the accuracy of the answers with the person's neighborhood block committee and previous job supervisors. When there was reason to suspect that the job applicant was hiding something, the political commissar would inquire with state security.

"You see, the minute you engage in activities against the revolution, you can forget about a promotion, or any perk," the official told me. "Even if you don't go to jail, you become a pariah."

For those accepting the rules of the game, the Castro regime had not looked like an ironfisted policeman ready to arrest citizens the minute they broke the law. Rather, it had been perceived by many as a distant inspector who simply watched—and took note. Each transgression was silently added to one's state security dossier. If you behaved yourself and didn't challenge the legitimacy of Castro's rule, you had nothing to fear in Marxist-ruled Cuba, many would say.

At the same time, because Cubans knew they were constantly breaking the law, they all lived with a collective sense of guilt and fear of reprisal. If you became a troublemaker, the state could always bring out your dossier—there was plenty there to incriminate you.

"There is an unwritten social pact," one University of Havana professor meditated aloud as we were walking around the campus's park one afternoon. "The government pretends not to see the nasty things Cubans are doing, and Cubans pretend not to see the nasty things the government is doing."

Under the see-nothing, hear-nothing agreement, the government could go on pretending the revolution had created a new society. Most Cubans, in turn, were polite enough to pay lip service to the official myth. Prostitution on Havana's Malecón boulevard was beginning to spread fast in 1989, yet Castro's speeches kept talking about those shameful prerevolutionary days when one could find prostitutes on the streets of Havana. Officially, there was no prostitution in Cuba.

The Cuban leader spoke proudly of the New Man created by the revolution—a citizen more motivated by moral than material incentives—yet a foreigner could hardly walk outside a downtown hotel without being subjected to relentless solicitation by black market foreign-exchange dealers.

While massive Soviet aid allowed the Castro regime to offer low-cost goods and free social services, it had paid for a sizable part of the population to shrug off Fidel's grand internationalist schemes, or his wild claims about the New Man. As long as he let them buy food and jeans on the black market, or exchange dollars with foreigners, Fidel could make as many Marxist-Leninist speeches as he wanted, many Cubans would tell you with a scornful shrug.

But following the Ochoa–De La Guardia case, people on the street were wondering whether the game was over. Would the "national cleansing" campaign announced by Raúl Castro break Cuba's longtime social pact? If the regime carried out its vow to repress even the smallest felonies at all levels of society, how would anyone manage to live in Cuba? No one was immune from the regime's new threat.

<=>

The most widespread criminal activity in Cuba was the off-the-books sale of foodstuffs in neighborhood grocery stores. Managers of Cuba's bodegas, or small supermarkets, routinely set aside part of their state-supplied stock to sell at premium prices to select customers. If they ran short of products to supply the ration-card food quotas, they would simply say the delivery truck had not arrived.

At the Coppelia ice cream store, which served thousands of people a day, employees had found a clever way to elude state controls. Each Coppelia ice cream stand was given several ice cream drums a day, calculated to suffice for a determined number of servings. To get more servings out of their allocated supply and sell the remainder under the table, Coppelia workers scooped the ice cream so that the middle of each ice cream ball was empty. Often, when you were half-way through an ice cream cone, your tongue would hit a hole. By serving thousands of hollow ice cream balls a day, the workers saved enough of their stock to do their own business at the end of the day.

Cheating was only one way of making ends meet. Another way was stealing. Because there was a shortage of light bulbs, an engineer friend of mine had taken three light bulbs from his office for use at home. The alternative was living in the dark, he said.

Because there was virtually no paper nor pencils available in stationery stores, employees plundered whatever they could get their hands on at work. State companies, after all, could always request new supplies. And if they didn't get them, Oh, well . . .

At times, thefts at Cuba's state enterprises reached bizarre proportions. My first encounter with employee plundering took place at the four-star Hotel Presidente, a 144-room hotel on Havana's spacious Paseo de los Presidentes Avenue, where I once stayed for several weeks. It was one of those rare hotels catering both to foreigners and privileged Cubans, such as newlyweds getting a three-day stay as a gift from their workplaces.

On my first day at the hotel, I called room service at 7:30 A.M. for a continental breakfast. It came nearly an hour later—not a surprising delay by Cuban service standards. An agitated man clad in jeans knocked on the door, left the tray on the top of my nonfunctioning Soviet TV set and left after pocketing his tip.

When I was ready to start eating, I saw he had forgotten to bring a spoon and a knife. Faced with the prospect of having to wait another hour for him to come back, I ended up using the back side of my toothbrush to stir my coffee and to spread butter and jam on the toast.

On my second day at the hotel, I again ordered continental breakfast. The same agitated young man showed up some time later, left the tray on my bed, and rushed off. As I reached to fix my coffee, I found that the silverware was missing again. I jumped off the bed and ran to the door in an effort to catch him. He was gone. I used my toothbrush.

On the third day, I promised myself I wouldn't let it happen again. As soon as the waiter showed up, I asked him to wait while I examined the tray carefully. Once more, there was no spoon, nor knife.

"Listen, brother, you're not bringing me any tableware . . . ," I protested as politely as I could, bearing in mind the experts' advice to be nice if you want to get things done in Cuba. "How am I supposed to stir the sugar? How am I supposed to spread the butter?"

The young man nodded, as if he knew he would be confronted with the question sooner or later.

"You're right, sir. You'll have to forgive us. We're trying hard to be more efficient. . . ."

"But why is it so difficult to remember to bring a knife? Three days in a row . . . ?" I kept pressing. "If you have a list telling you to bring coffee, milk, sugar and toast, why not add a knife to it?"

Defeated, the man confessed.

"What happens is that the *compañeros* who usually bring breakfast to the rooms are coming in late because of the bus delays, and the kitchen doesn't have tableware. I work as a kitchen aide, and I can bring you breakfast, but I can't bring you any tableware."

"I don't get it," I said.

"You see, the *compañeros* who bring the breakfast each have a set of tableware. They are responsible for it. They keep it in their lockers. If they don't show up, we don't have any silverware."

Now it all began to make sense. The locked tableware system had been imposed because the hotel personnel and Cuban patrons had stolen much of the hotel's silverware, the young man explained. To stop the plundering, the hotel management had given each waiter a numbered set of forks, knives and spoons, for which they were responsible.

There was tableware inspection each Friday, at which each waiter had to produce his stock. Socialist management techniques had solved the tableware theft problem at the expense of my breakfast.

<>

When I told the missing silverware tale to a sociologist friend and his wife during a long chat at their home, they both exploded in laughter.

"That's nothing," said Liliana, a university teacher. "You should see what they did with the tableware at the pizza place at the corner of 12th Street and 23rd Street!"

"What did they do?" I asked.

"They attached the knives and forks to the tables. With chains!" she exclaimed. "I swear it's true. I saw it with my own eyes!"

The Pizzeria 12 y 23, a big corner pizza parlor next to Cuba's Film Industry Institute building, had chained the tableware to the tables in an effort to stop the plundering of forks and knives. The chains were secured to hooks bolted to the lower side of the tables, so they could be unhooked every time the utensils had to be washed.

But the system didn't work. With the constant movement of the chains back and forth to the kitchen and the inevitable pulling by curious customers, the fragile chains soon broke up. In a matter of weeks, many of the chains were reduced to half their original length. Customers were forced to eat their pizzas with their heads hovering over their plates. There were angry protests. Some patrons threatened to take their complaints to the Communist Party hierarchy—even to Fidel. Before the chains became a scandal, the place's management discontinued them.

By the time I visited the pizzeria, the system had been replaced by a less conspicuous one. After dinner, the waiter took away my tableware, and gave me a little piece of paper with a number on it—an official certification that I had returned my utensils. I had to deliver it to a guard at the front door.

My piece of paper had a number 2 on it—two utensils. The guard took the paper, threw it in a basket, and nodded. I could leave.

<>

Renting a car at the Havanautos car rental office in downtown Havana's Vedado section provided me with another precious glimpse into black market economics in Cuba.

I went in search of an economy car in reasonably good shape. There were eight brand-new 1989 Nissan cars sitting in the garage. The office manager told me, however, that they needed to pick a good car because most of them had mechanical troubles. Mexican tourists had brutalized the engines, he complained.

After they selected a four-door yellow Nissan and began readying it for me, they discovered it didn't have a spare tire. A mechanic opened the trunk of the car next to mine, but it didn't have a spare either. He repeated the operation with each of the next six cars, then came back shaking his head. None of them had a spare tire. They had all disappeared.

"Don't worry, we'll find one," the office manager told me.

He talked for a few seconds with two mechanics, then they placed a jack under one of the waiting cars, took one of its rear tires out, and left two bricks in its place. They put the free tire into the trunk of my car.

That wasn't all. After they had taken my Nissan to the car wash and given it a quick cleanup, the engine wouldn't start.

"It's the battery," one of the mechanics diagnosed. The two mechanics then walked to another sitting car, opened the hood, took its battery out, and installed it in mine. A few minutes later, as they were checking the list of car accessories in my contract, they discovered my vehicle was missing a jack. Again, they took it from another car.

When I drove out of the Havanautos agency in my yellow Nissan, I left behind a fleet of crippled vehicles. One of the cars was sitting on bricks, another had its hood gaping, a third one had its trunk door wide open. A smiling employee waved good-bye to me. Where had all the missing parts gone?

<>

Just as Castro's diatribes against the black market during the Ochoa–De La Guardia trial raised eyebrows among the population, his references to Ochoa's sexual "immoralities" left most people puzzled.

What was the big deal if Ochoa had slept with a young woman in Angola? Didn't Fidel know that sexual escapades—in the absence of other forms of entertainment—had become Cuba's national sport? Was he about to crack down on that, too?

Sex was Cubans' favorite escape from the hardships of daily life. Even by Latin American standards, promiscuity and extramarital affairs were rampant. Changing spouses was so common that few couples bothered to get married. By 1989, a whopping 61.2 percent of all birth certificates in Cuba were issued to babies born out of wedlock, according to government figures quoted by the weekly *Bohemia*.

In school, workplaces or on the street, flirting was a given. Lovers usually met at *posadas*—special hotels where you paid five pesos—the equivalent of fifty U.S. cents at the time—for three hours of privacy. After that, the telephone next to your bed would ring, and a male voice would announce, "*Turno!*" Your time was over.

In Havana, there were *posadas* for all tastes. Government officials and professionals who had their own cars often went to El Monumental, a highway motel about seven miles west of the city. There, you usually had to stand behind a line of cars and couples on foot sandwiched between them. An elderly waiter in a worn-out tuxedo periodically walked up the line, offering drinks—if there were any. At a sign from the office, he would allow the first couple in, and tell them their room number. There was no registration. You paid on your way out.

Despite widespread reports of AIDS among Cuban soldiers coming from Angola, the use of condoms was rare. The most common birth-control method was abortion. State hospitals performed—free of charge—about 160,000 abortions a year, a third of them on teenagers, according to official estimates. But many Cubans said the real figure was higher. One high-school teacher told me her students often announced openly in class that they wouldn't be coming to school on the next day, because they were going to have an *interrupción*—as Cubans referred to abortions. A middle-aged waitress claimed to me that she had had more than twenty abortions. That wasn't uncommon, she said.

Prostitution was widespread, and increasingly overt. As I drove along Havana's baronial Fifth Avenue every day, young women posted at most corners wearing designer jeans obviously procured from foreigners would recognize my rental car and try to stop me. Some raised their hands. Most threw kisses.

Whether or not they were professional prostitutes was the focus of a major debate. The government claimed they were free-lance amateurs who would go to bed with a foreigner in exchange for a trip to the Diplotienda to buy a pair of jeans or a bottle of shampoo.

But, increasingly, the *jineteras*—as the streetwalkers were known—stopped leaving their pay to their clients' discretion. They asked for twenty U.S. dollars, plus an escorted trip to the Diplotienda. Foreigners, especially older Spanish and Mexican businessmen, were in their glory. In Havana's dollar restaurants, you regularly found Spanish businessmen in their sixties happily entertaining attractive Cuban girls who could be their granddaughters.

The Marina Hemingway, a seaside development for diplomats and visiting businessmen on the outskirts of Havana, was the most desirable hangout for *jineteras*. The women made their way through the compound's entrance checkpoint by bribing guards with a pack of Diplotienda cigarettes or a bottle of scotch. Once in the bar, they were free to contact some of the richest foreign visitors in Havana.

Olga, a beautiful black woman in her mid-twenties, made no bones about what she was doing at the bar. She was a regular. She had worked until a year ago as the manager of a pharmacy, but she was a single mother, and could not live on her salary and support her two-year-old daughter, too. She had started dating foreigners after work, first for Diplotienda food, then for dollars.

After a few months in the business, she had met Ignacio, a sixty-five-year-old Spanish businessman, at the Marina Hemingway bar. She was very grateful to him, she said. He had given her the money to purchase a house.

"How much?" I asked.

"One thousand pesos. I traded my old place for a much better one for that."

I made a quick mental calculation. It was less than a hundred dollars—the equivalent of an evening's dinner. The man had probably charged it to his company. With that, he had gotten Olga's promise to be with him full time whenever he came to town. Ignacio was happy. And so, it seemed, was Olga.

Castro's hard-line rhetoric in the aftermath of the Ochoa–De La Guardia affair also left its mark on Cuba's artistic and intellectual life. Avant-garde artists who had become increasingly outspoken in the late 1980s were forced to shelve their works. Culture Minister Armando Hart gave dozens of them six-month exit visas to Mexico in an effort to keep them happy—and silent—while Cuba's political atmosphere cleared.

An exhibit entitled "Sculptured Object" at the Center for Development of Visual Arts in Havana was closed down by police on its opening night after a young artist named Angel Delgado performed a scene that became the talk of the town for several months.

Delgado, twenty-three, a slender, blue-eyed young man with a ponytail, walked into the center of the room of the forty-nine-artist exhibit and silently began to form a circle of animal bones on the floor. Then, when an intrigued crowd had gathered around him, without saying a word, he spread that day's *Granma* in the middle of the circle, placed himself on top of it, took down his pants, and defecated on it. The crowd exploded in screams of horror, and ran in all directions. Delgado calmly buttoned up his slacks and left for home.

Two days later, Delgado was fired from his job. When he returned home, the state security police were waiting for him. He was charged with "public scandal," and sentenced to six months in prison (his lawyer had tried the unlikely defense line that the young artist had felt an urge to use the toilet, but hadn't been able to find one).

Show organizers tried to get the exhibit reopened, arguing that Delgado was an intruder. They never got a positive answer. The woman who had organized the exhibit was reassigned to a lesser job. Several heads rolled at the Culture Ministry hierarchy. Authorities hadn't found Angel's performance funny.

More than a year after he had served his sentence, I ran into the young artist one Saturday evening on Havana's Fifth Avenue. He was sitting on a bench with his girlfriend, where somebody pointed him out to me. Why had he done something so dramatic? I asked. Did he think of his action as art?

"It was an act of political desperation," Delgado said. "I wanted to draw attention to the absence of freedom of expression in Cuba. I wanted to express myself against censorship."

All works of art submitted for exhibition at the show had to be approved by a Communist Party–dominated screening commission, he explained. He had objected to submitting his paintings to the politically charged commission. "I wanted to do something that would infringe the system of prior censorship," he said.

Since his release from prison, Delgado had not been able to exhibit his works anywhere. Fidel Castro and his cadre of aging comrades in the Central Committee were putting a clamp on all forms of independent thinking.

<>

Censorship had its own rules, however. It was okay for Cubans to complain about the food shortages, or about the bad service at government companies. People could openly voice their frustration in food lines, and most often nothing would happen to them. Dozens of intellectuals and academics, in private conversations, would even go as far as to voice serious doubts about "the system."

There was only one major exception to their freedom of speech: the figure of Fidel Castro. You could blame any wrongs on the government, but never on Fidel. That was the line nobody was supposed to cross. If things didn't work, it was because officials were not following Fidel's orders, or because the Comandante was not being thoroughly briefed by his aides.

Foreign journalists were subject to similar unwritten guidelines when they visited Cuba. The Castro regime did not allow working

U.S. journalists to live in Cuba—there was a parallel restriction on the U.S. side—and would only occasionally allow visiting reporters for short periods of time.

Most often, the visas were only good for seven days. During their stay in Cuba, U.S. reporters were often accompanied by a Foreign Relations Ministry (MINREX) escort, a kind of bilingual babysitter who would set up interviews and sit through them.

After the reporters' tour was over, their articles were closely scrutinized by the MINREX's team of U.S. media analysts. If the stories contained direct attacks on Castro, the reporter would most likely be penalized by not being allowed into Cuba for years—the worst punishment for a journalist worried about his competitors' access to a major story. You were not supposed to mess around with the boss.

A veteran journalist with the official Prensa Latina wire agency, trying to help me make contacts in government circles, once gave me what he described as the golden rule to keep the doors open for one in Cuba: "Remember this," he said. "You can play with the chain, but don't touch the monkey."

<>

Indeed, despite a general discontent in Cuba, virtually no one dared criticize Castro in public. There were no anti-Castro graffiti on the walls—especially after dissidents had been sentenced to three years in prison for writing "*Abajo Castro*" on a Havana street in late 1989.

The closest thing to an anti-Castro sign I saw at the time was a graffiti in the men's bathroom of the University of Havana's Faculty of Philosophy. The legend, scribbled with a pencil on the inside part of one of the toilet doors, read "Down with You Know Who." The anonymous writer had not dared to spell out the name of the Cuban strongman, or perhaps wanted to be able to claim that he was referring to the President of the United States.

Except for a few dozen human rights activists who were known abroad and kept in regular touch with Western embassies, most Cubans would not utter a word against the Cuban leader even in the company of trusted friends. There was an endemic fear of hidden microphones.

A strange ritual flourished throughout Cuba as a result: political sign language. I first noticed this peculiar phenomenon in a conversation with José, a welder at a factory in the southern city of Cienfuegos. I had met José in a crowded ice-cream line next to Cienfuegos's largest movie theater. He was in his early thirties, and clearly unhappy about Cuba's deteriorating economy. He seemed eager to talk with a foreigner. I invited him to dinner that night.

We met at the 1819 restaurant, which faced a promenade lined with colonial lampposts and park benches in the city's charming downtown area. At first, we talked about Cienfuegos and about his job at the factory. The conversation went smoothly. Nothing out of the ordinary.

But then, when we began talking about the political situation in Cuba, I noticed that José was jerking his hands through the air: he was talking with them. His only words were monosyllables, prepositions linking the signs together.

To refer to Fidel, he would take his fingers to the chin and close them as he moved his hand downward, as if showing a beard. When he talked about the military, he would place two fingers on his shoulder, as if to show a uniform's epaulets. To tell me that people feared repression, he would move his hand horizontally under his head, as if imitating a hatchet cutting through his neck.

To explain to me that people often said one thing and thought another, he made a falling-curtain sign over his face, as if every Cuban had a mask. He would make all these movements in rapid succession, with complete spontaneity, and would cap each of his body messages by raising his eyebrows and opening his hands, as if saying, "You get it?"

On my return to Havana, I noticed how complex the Cubans' political body-language had grown. At a Saturday night coffee party at the house of my sociologist friend, all the guests switched to body language when the conversation turned to Cuba's main topic of conversation—Fidel Castro.

But there was one sign I couldn't understand. The young man who was doing the talking—or rather the gesturing—would periodically take his hand to his head, and close his fingers in the air while moving his hand upwards, as if painting a dunce cap in the air. What is that weird sign? I asked.

It was a reverse beard sign, my friend explained.

"Everybody knows the normal beard sign by now," he said. "So when people talk on the street, they are using this one."

Fear had not only prompted creation of an underground sign language, but it had also led to the invention of countersigns as an added precaution.

<><>

Fear was not the only reason why there wasn't any open defiance against Castro. The rapid deterioration of Cuba's standard of living following the 1989 changes in Eastern Europe had a paralyzing effect on most Cubans' political activism. Having to stand in line for hours every day to buy bread or take a bus, most Cubans were just too busy trying to survive.

A late-afternoon conversation with a middle-aged woman outside the Mercadito Linea y H supermarket helped me understand what was in the minds of most Cubans at the time.

The woman, looking totally exhausted, was walking out of the shop with a plastic bag displaying the clear outline of a chicken. More than two hundred worried-looking people—mostly women and older men—were still in line to buy poultry. Every so often, a nasty argument broke out when somebody tried to cut in the line. It was already 5:30 P.M.

I asked the woman with the chicken how long she had had to wait in line. She had been there since 6 A.M., she said.

"Aren't you furious?" I asked, feeling the outrage for her.

"Furious? Are you kidding? I'm delighted. I got a chicken!" the woman shot back, dangling the trophy. "Last Tuesday, I stayed in line from 6 A.M. until 7 P.M., and the delivery truck didn't even show up." Survival was a time-consuming endeavor.

◄►

One of the lone public voices against the executions of Brig. Gen. Arnaldo Ochoa and Col. Antonio De La Guardia came from Cuba's usually meek Roman Catholic Church.

In August 1989, shortly after the executions, Cuba's Archbishop Jaime Ortega read a homily entitled "The Death Penalty." Using unusually direct language, he lashed out against the regime.

An icy silence reigned at the cathedral in Old Havana as the green-eyed archbishop stood and read his homily. More than three hundred people, a larger-than-usual crowd, had gathered that Sunday.

"The painful events of the past few days, which culminated with the death sentences and execution of four high-ranking officers of the Cuban army, have dramatically brought to our nation's attention the issue of the death penalty," he began.

"For us Catholics, there is special reason to reflect, since the press office of the Holy See has announced that Pope John Paul II asked Cuban authorities to grant clemency to the defendants, on humanitarian grounds," he said. It was the first time the population had heard that the Vatican had pleaded for the four officers' lives—a news item the official press had suppressed.

Perhaps to justify his incursion into politics, Ortega said he was reacting to government claims that Catholics had backed the death sentences. He concluded by saying that, as a Christian, he could not forget that Christ had been condemned to death and crucified, and that his last words had been "Forgive them, for they know not what they do."

It was a daring speech by Cuban church standards. Unlike the church authorities in El Salvador, Chile and other Latin American repressive regimes, Cuba's clerics rarely attacked the government. After a fierce public argument with the revolution's leaders in 1961, in which church authorities were accused of ties to the country's vanishing oligarchy, the church had adopted a largely submissive public stance.

Priests justified their position by saying that the church in Cuba was much weaker than in other Latin American nations. According to Cuba's Conference of Bishops' estimates, only about a hundred thousand Cubans—or 1 percent of the population—were going to church at least once a year. The Cuban church had no access to newspapers, radio, television, or any other way to get its message out.

In addition, only half of Cuba's estimated 250 Roman Catholic priests were Cuban. Most were Spaniards, in the country on temporary work visas. If they didn't behave themselves, there was no guarantee they would be let back into the country on their return from vacations at home. It was a church that saw itself as hostage to threats it had no way of controlling.

<>

In late 1989, the Castro regime decided to leave the Ochoa affair behind, and to focus its propaganda machine on the upcoming celebration of a new anniversary of the January 1, 1959, revolution.

Government-controlled newspapers began bombarding the population with reminders of the Castro revolution's greatest achievements. On top of the list were phenomenal successes in health and education. The stories were often accompanied with news items from Eastern Europe, on how people were losing their hard-won social conquests as their countries moved to market economies. *Granma* editorials would stress that Cuba would never walk away from the revolution's accomplishments.

The official data were impressive. Judging from the government propaganda, Cuba had been transformed over the past three decades from a backward Caribbean island to a model for Third World development. Cuba's health standards, for instance, were among the world's highest.

Infant mortality was 11 children per 1,000 births—lower than in Washington, D.C., as an exuberant Fidel would often note in his speeches. Cuba's literacy rate was 98 percent—the highest in Latin America, and higher than that of many industrialized countries. Ninety percent of the children of high-school age were in school—one of the lowest drop-out rates anywhere.

Government propaganda articles cited stunning successes in virtually every field. The number of hospitals in Cuba had soared from 95 before the revolution to more than three times that figure by 1989. The number of physicians had risen from a shameful 6,000 to nearly 40,000 over the same period. There were more doctors per capita in Cuba than in any developing country. The number of Cuban teachers had gone up from 26,000 in 1959 to 300,000 thirty years later. There were no barefoot children in Cuba. The list of achievements was long.

In fact, some of the government's claims were legitimate, even if exaggerated. That was why many Cubans were still finding positive aspects in a revolution that was otherwise marked by economic failure.

It was true that in the Cuba of the late 1980s you didn't find the pockets of misery you stumbled on in virtually any other Latin American country. There were no beggars on the streets—at least no full-time ones. Everybody seemed to have a pair of shoes, and a T-shirt—no matter how worn out. Cuba had eliminated misery at the cost of imposing a general poverty.

Most people seemed reasonably educated: illiteracy had dropped from nearly 40 percent before the revolution to virtually zero. Street crime was rare compared with the situation in other Latin American capitals. On the other hand, there were few cars on the streets, and store shelves were near-empty most of the time.

Institutionalized racism marred many Latin American cultures, but it was not unusual to run into black doctors, architects or engineers in Cuba. College and postgraduate education was free, and there were large numbers of working-class students at universities. Often, when I asked young professionals if they supported the revolution, they would give me the same answer: "My father was a peasant. If it weren't for the revolution, I would have never gotten a university degree."

You didn't have to look hard for examples of upward mobility in revolutionary Cuba. Emilia, a maid at the Hotel Presidente, was one of many Cubans of peasant background who had seen their children climb up the social ladder since 1959. A short, sixty-four-year-old black woman with thick reading glasses, Emilia had two children who were, respectively, a kidney surgeon at the Cira García Hospital, and an electric engineer.

"Before 1959, black people couldn't get to the university," Emilia told me one day, touching her forearm with her index finger to emphasize the color of her skin.

"You had to be a real genius to get accepted," she added. "That's why we often say that if you find a black Cuban doctor who graduated before the revolution, you've got to go to him: he's probably better than any other."

Many special schools for handicapped children thrived in Cuba. At the Abel Santamaría school for blind or visually-handicapped children in Havana, there were sixty specialized therapists for 208 children. The children had special desks, Braille machines, and large-size custom-made notebooks—everything provided by the state. At a warehouse near the classrooms, a group of high-school students with limited vision were being trained in carpentry with special saws.

In fact, the revolution's greatest success had been in providing a first-class health care system for free. Whatever health needs Cubans had, whether a pregnancy test or a heart-bypass operation, they could have it for the asking. And because health care was the revolution's greatest pride, the state's magnanimity was unlimited: even cosmetic surgery and orthodontic treatments were performed without charge.

Under an ambitious plan established in the mid-1980s, the state expanded its network of hospitals by setting up small family-doctor clinics throughout the country. The idea was to take the doctors to the people, just in case the people failed to go to the doctor. The plan was carried out with extraordinary zeal. By the late 1980s, more than ten thousand family doctors were scattered throughout the island, about half in cities and half in rural areas.

Typically, a family doctor was a recent graduate assigned to provide medical attention to an estimated 150 families in a certain neighborhood or rural area. Usually, the doctor was given a two-story house, with a small clinic downstairs and living quarters on the upper floor. The doctor's duty was to see patients who came for checkups, provide them with medical treatment, or transfer them to the nearest hospital whenever it was necessary.

Each family doctor was responsible for the health care of his or her 150 families. If one of the families didn't show up for a routine medical check, for instance, it was the doctor's duty to knock on their door and examine them at home. Because the doctor lived and worked in the neighborhood, he or she was bound to be in constant touch with the patients.

In addition to the family doctor program, there was an elaborate network of in-house physicians at the factories and government offices. These doctors were either permanently assigned to a workplace or made regular visits to it. They carried out eye, respiratory and blood-pressure tests on all employees, whether workers wanted them or not.

Nobody could fall through the cracks of the government's health care program. If you weren't checked by your family doctor, another doctor would catch you at work. The system was a model of preventive care, if enormously expensive.

There were the loopholes. Alfredo, a family doctor I had met through a friend, invited me to accompany him during a morning's work at his home-clinic in Central Havana. He was a young man from a middle-class family, most of whose members had moved to the United States after the revolution.

He was no friend of the revolution, and had mixed feelings about Cuba's health care system—not the least because he had heard stories about the salaries made by doctors in the United States. Alfredo was making 325 pesos a month (800 dollars a year at the black-market exchange rate), about the same as a Cuban college professor.

Despite his opposition to the regime, Alfredo conceded that Cuba's health care system was probably better than any other in the developing world. What bothered him, however, was its paternalist nature. It was as if the state had outlawed illness, expecting doctors to go about eliminating disease as if they were law enforcers.

Each year in the month of April, for instance, Cuba's family doctors were asked to carry out the government's polio vaccination campaign. The Health Ministry handed Alfredo a list of 100 children in his neighborhood who needed to be vaccinated. Alfredo was expected to go from door to door, checking off each child's name as he carried out the task.

"I have to meet the quota, just as if I was working in a potato factory," Alfredo complained. "If I can't find five of the children because they have moved to another neighborhood, it's a nightmare. I have to run all over the city to locate them."

What happened if he didn't find them? He would be forced to start a lengthy bureaucratic process to explain his failure to vaccinate all the children on the list. Authorities could then decide that he hadn't performed his job well, and issue a written reprimand. That could make it more difficult for him to be accepted for postgraduate studies and become a specialist, Alfredo said.

So what did he do if he couldn't vaccinate all children on the list? "Well, you invent something," Alfredo explained. "You turn in your polio campaign papers as if you'd paid a visit to each of the children . . . and then you pray that nobody will ever find out."

Although the revolution's health crusade was marched out as a point of pride, the problem with Cuba's three-decade-old revolution was that it had increasingly fewer things to offer to the sizable part of its population that wasn't ill. As the government reduced food rations because of declining Soviet bloc shipments, most Cubans' concern over their daily meals overshadowed their satisfaction with the revolution's health and education programs.

I didn't quite realize how meager Cubans' monthly rations were until I was invited for a late lunch one Sunday afternoon at the home of Gustavo, a commentator at one of Cuba's radio stations. He was a nice man in his late thirties, married to a teacher who was expecting the couple's first baby. I had met him in Miami a few months earlier. He was one of the few privileged Cubans who had been allowed to travel abroad for academic research.

Gustavo had invited his two brothers and their respective wives for the occasion. We would have a long, comfortable talk about whatever I was interested in, I had been promised. I accepted gladly.

At 2 P.M., we were all sitting around the modest table at Gustavo's home. While his wife, Maria, finished cooking a chicken, we drank rum. The other guests bombarded me with questions about life in the United States. Was it true that Coca Cola cans in America have a gas inside that turn them cold when you open them up? somebody asked. No, at least not at the time I had left, I responded.

When lunch was ready, Maria placed the food on the table, and we began to eat. Chicken. Rice. Red beans. Inevitably, the conversation turned to food shortages. Gustavo explained the food ration system to me. He listed the quotas of chicken, rice, and lentils, citing each product's ration in pounds, ounces or liters. Confused by the avalanche of data, I asked:

"How much is that? Give me an idea of how many chicken pieces or rice bowls you get a month."

There was a long silence. Gustavo and his brothers looked at one another searching for a graphic comparison. Finally, Maria, the hostess, shrugged and said with a gentle smile: "Well, what we get for a whole month is pretty much what we've eaten here just now." I felt the last piece of chicken get stuck in my throat.

The group spent the rest of our time together trying to comfort me, saying I shouldn't worry for them, that they were making good money and could always get extra food in the black market. It didn't help much. I only felt better after I bought them a basket of food at the Diplotienda the next morning.

<><>

A joke making the rounds in Havana in 1989 described the curious mix of unhappiness and docility that characterized most Cubans' attitude at the time.

The U.S. president sent a CIA spy to Cuba to obtain a first-hand report on the situation. After spending several weeks in Cuba, the spy returned home with the following report: "Mr. President, the situation in Cuba is as follows:

"There is no unemployment, but nobody works. Nobody works, but all production quotas are met. All production quotas are met, but there is nothing in the stores. There is nothing in the stores, but everybody eats. Everybody eats, but people are complaining all day long. People are complaining all day long, but they all go to the plaza to cheer Fidel. Summing up, Mr. President, we have all the data, but no conclusions."

<><>

But as Cuba prepared to celebrate the 31st anniversary of its Marxist revolution, there were growing questions about how much longer the joke would work. Would Cuba be able to maintain full employment despite its deepening economic crisis? Would there be enough food in the black market to compensate for the meager government food rations? Would the regime crack down on people buying or selling in the black market? Would Cubans continue going to the plaza to cheer Fidel?

As the Socialist world crumbled, it was becoming increasingly harder for the Castro regime to control growing discontent without showing its ugly face. The Ochoa–De La Guardia executions had marked a dramatic break in the bond of mutual tolerance between the government and the people—the unwritten social pact the University of Havana professor had talked about. The psychological foundations of the revolution had begun to shake.

MAROONED

<<<<<<<<<<<<<<<<<<<<<<<<<<<<<<<<<<<<

**Panama, Nicaragua and
the Soviet Pullout
(1989–1990)**

5
Exit Panama

◄◄◄◄◄At 12:30 A.M. on the night of December 20, 1989, while Cubans were in a holiday mood in anticipation of festivities for the new anniversary of the Castro revolution, more than twenty-two thousand U.S. troops invaded Panama. Troopers from the 82nd Airborne and Army Rangers jumped from U.S. aircraft into Panama City in what was at that time the largest American military intervention since the Vietnam war. Tracers and fires lit the sky. Bomb explosions rocked the city.

Panama's military ruler Gen. Manuel A. Noriega was with one of his occasional girlfriends in a suite at the Panama Defense Forces' La Siesta hotel near the airport when he was shaken by the first explosions. Noriega's top personal guard, Capt. Iván Castillo, ran outside. He returned seconds later, nearly out of breath.

"The sky is full of paratroopers!" Castillo reported to Noriega. "They're everywhere!"

Noriega's guards rushed to the phones. The whole city was under siege. U.S. Blackhawk helicopters were hovering above the city looking for Noriega and his top aides. Noriega and his guards changed into civilian clothes, jumped into a four-door Hyundai and a Toyota Land Cruiser, and drove to the house of Noriega's close friend Balbina de

Periñan in the working-class district of San Miguelito. The group thought the Americans would not look for them there—at least not at first.

Noriega's secretary, Marcela Tasón, who joined the general hours later, called the Cuban ambassador to Panama, Lázaro Mora. She asked for Cuba's military assistance to resist the invasion. Impossible, Mora said. That would give Washington an excuse to invade Cuba. But Noriega and his family were welcome at the embassy or at the Cuban ambassador's residence any time.

For the next five days, Noriega moved constantly between homes of friends and relatives, eluding U.S. roadblocks and helicopter searches. He sat on the floor of his various hideouts to avoid being detected by neighbors. His eyes were red from lack of sleep. His vision was blurred by alcohol.

The general was a nervous wreck. He could no longer give orders through his military radio—any call was sure to be monitored by U.S. forces and reveal his location. As days went by, it became increasingly clear that he had no army left. On television, he saw his top officers walking one by one into U.S. detention centers with their hands on their necks. Most, seeing no way to escape, had turned themselves in.

On the evening of December 23, Noriega's secretary called the Cuban ambassador, once again.

"Can we go?" she asked, nearly out of breath.

"Things have gotten more complicated," Mora answered. "The embassy is surrounded by American troops. The residence isn't, but there are U.S. troops three blocks away. I don't think it would be a good idea. . . ."*

On December 25, Noriega walked into the Vatican embassy, seeking political asylum. Days later, he was pressed by the papal nuncio to surrender to U.S. troops. Escorted by U.S. Army troops and DEA agents, he was flown to the United States to face two 1988 drug-related indictments in Florida. Cuba had just lost a key ally in Latin America.

* *"I told her it would be crazy to try to get into the [Cuban] residence, because they were probably waiting for Noriega to make the move," Mora told me in an interview in Havana November 2, 1991. "More so, because we were talking on a regular telephone line, which I was sure was being monitored by the Americans."*

American forces detained thousands of members of Noriega's Defense Forces in the aftermath of the invasion, but didn't catch one single Cuban adviser to the Panamanian regime. By the time U.S. troops landed in Panama, the Cubans were all safe at the Cuban embassy, or at Mora's residence in the exclusive neighborhood of Altos del Golf. The top Cuban intelligence adviser in Panama had left for Havana on a Cubana de Aviación airliner hours before the invasion. Had the Cubans obtained advance notice of the U.S. attack?

Judging from their preparations, they seemed to be expecting it. On December 19, Cuban Ambassador Mora had summoned all Cuban diplomats, military and intelligence advisers in Panama for an urgent meeting at 4 P.M. at the Cuban embassy. More than five dozen people gathered in the embassy's lobby. It was exactly two hours before President Bush, who had maintained a deliberately tranquil public countenance throughout the day, made his first phone call to American congressional leaders to notify them that a military operation was afoot.

Mora, a light-skinned black man with intense blue eyes and white hair, had a worried look in his eyes when he walked into the room. He greeted everybody with a short nod. A veteran diplomat, he was known as a laid-back man of few words. Yet on that occasion, he stood stiffly, his hands thrust into his pockets, to deliver his ominous message.

"Compañeros, we have reason to believe that there will be a U.S. invasion tonight," the ambassador said. "Everybody must go home, get their dependents together, and pack a small bag with essential personal belongings. You should be ready to be picked up by the embassy bus at any time. We're in a state of maximum alert."

The Cubans left in a hurry. Hours later, they began to arrive at the embassy building in downtown Panama City and at the ambassador's residence in the Altos del Golf. They carried small suitcases, some bulging with VCR machines, short-wave radios and electronic appliances not available at home. They sat on the floor of the austere building, and waited. Within six hours, the first U.S. aircraft would begin dropping paratroopers on Panama.

How did the Cubans know? By a mixture of good intelligence and good instincts, Ambassador Mora told me over dinner in Havana several months later. There had been widespread rumors of a possible American strike against Noriega since December 16, when Lt. Robert Paz, U.S. Marine Corps, was killed at a roadblock outside the Panamanian Defense Forces headquarters after a shouting match with the

Panamanian soldiers who had stopped his car. Hours later, a Cuban-trained Panamanian military spying team at Howard, the American air force base, detected an increase in landings of U.S. C-141 military aircraft. The information was passed on to the Cubans. By December 19, C-141's were arriving at a frequency of one every ten minutes.

Noriega didn't seem very concerned about the landings. He saw them as another American scare tactic. He did not believe Washington would launch an all-out military invasion. Rather, Noriega expected a surgical strike to kidnap him. He had built up a sophisticated security guard around himself, in the belief that he—not Panama's Defense Forces—would be the target of U.S. military force. Unlike Noriega, the Cubans understood that the new reinforcements meant trouble.

"We had seen this kind of activity at the base twice before in previous months," Mora said, referring to earlier reinforcements sent to U.S. military bases in Panama amid tough talk from the Bush Administration. "But this time, we noticed a big difference: they weren't showing it on the U.S. Southern Command's [public] television channel. It didn't sound like another psychological operation."

The fall of Noriega was a major blow to the Cuban regime, at a time when Fidel Castro was being pounded with bad news from almost everywhere. By the closing days of 1989, as a handcuffed Noriega was being flown to the United States, Romanian President Nicolae Ceausescu had been executed after a sudden popular rebellion; the Berlin Wall's Brandenburg Gate had been opened amid huge street celebrations on both sides of the border; Solidarity had taken over the Polish government and vowed to turn Poland into a capitalist country; and the Hungarian Parliament had renounced communism. In a matter of days, the earlier symptoms of change in Eastern Europe had developed into a general stampede away from communism.

Noriega's ouster not only increased Cuba's diplomatic isolation, it also deprived the Cuban government of its main economic outlet to the capitalist world.

In the late 1980s, Panama had become to Cuba what Hong Kong was to Communist China. Much of Cuba's foreign trade with the Western world went through Panama, or was negotiated through Panama-based front companies. As reform-minded Soviet bloc governments began to reduce their economic assistance to Cuba, Cuba's reliance on Panama became even greater. Cuba needed dollars and industrial equipment to replace the cuts in Soviet bloc aid, and Panama was the natural window to obtain both.

It was in Panama that Cuba's Interior Ministry had set up CIMEX Corp. and dozens of other trading firms aimed at circumventing the U.S. trade embargo. These firms were essential to maintaining the flow of foreign goods to Cuba, without which the island's tourism industry could not survive.

Cuba's Panama-based trading firms supplied virtually all of the island's hotels and foreigners-only Diplotienda stores, allowing the Cuban revolution to maintain a semblance of affluence in the eyes of foreign visitors. At the Diplotienda of the Havana Libre Hotel, you could buy Colgate-Palmolive toothpaste, Kellogg's cereal, or virtually any other product found in American supermarkets. A Cuban tour guide would proudly tell you that the economic situation was bad—but not that bad. Many tourists visiting the island would leave without fully realizing the shortages with which ordinary Cubans had to cope.

Official records showed that Cuba purchased more than $61 million a year worth of goods in Panama. In reality, the figure was much higher. Panamanian boats and aircraft would go back and forth to Cuba carrying millions of dollars worth of American products that would never appear on Panama's official records to prevent possible U.S. complaints of trade embargo violations. Some of these shipments would go on Panama's Air Force Boeing 727—courtesy of General Noriega.

The Castro regime's trading firms in Panama were also a major outlet for Cuban exports to the Western Hemisphere. Several joint Panamanian-Cuban companies, such as Transit S.A. and Servinaves S.A., sold Cuban rum and tobacco in Panama, and re-exported it to several countries.

The sixty-five-vessel Cuban shipping fleet in Panama's port of Vacamonte exported shrimp, crab and lobster to the United States through Panamanian front companies. It was a perfect scheme: the Cuban fishing boats caught the shellfish, and sold it to Panamanian-registered fish exporters in Vacamonte. These exporters sold the cargo to trading firms that shipped it to Miami or Los Angeles. By then, the cargo carried made-in-Panama labels.

Panama had also long served as a regional command center for Cuba's political activities in Latin America. With a staff of twenty-four officials and dozens of support personnel, the Cuban embassy in Panama was Castro's conduit to guerrilla movements and leftist political parties throughout the hemisphere.

In the late seventies, Panama had been a key bridge for Cuban arms shipments to Nicaragua's Sandinista guerrillas. Under a 1978 agreement between late Panamanian military leader Gen. Omar Torrijos and Castro, half a dozen Panamanian officers—including Intelligence Capt. Felipe Camargo and air force pilots Rodolfo Castrellón and Augusto Villalaz—made several trips to Cuba on a Panamanian DC-6 plane to pick up Cuban arms for Nicaragua. After the 1979 Sandinista victory, Nicaragua would become Cuba's closest political ally in the region. Panama, however, would remain Cuba's main business link to the rest of the region—an operations center as well as a convenient alternate route for Cuban arms shipments to insurgent groups.

Leaders of Colombia's M-19 guerrillas and El Salvador's Farabundo Martí National Liberation Front, among others, would meet regularly with their Cuban contacts at the Continental Hotel on Panama City's commercial Via España Avenue. The hotel was run by Panama's Defense Forces, and was relatively safe from U.S. spies. Late-night meetings to coordinate weapons shipments and military-training courses usually ended at Jimmy's, an open air barbecue restaurant in the seaside San Francisco quarter. Unlike leftist Nicaragua, a close-knit society that was under heavy scrutiny from U.S. media, Panama offered an international setting where these meetings could be held without drawing anybody's attention.

At the Cuban ambassador's walled-in compound in Altos del Golf, only a short walk from Noriega's mansion, huge rooftop antennas kept a constant monitor on U.S. diplomatic and military communications. The U.S. Southern Command, the 13,000-member Panama-based headquarters for U.S. military activities in Latin America, was only a few miles away. Part of the Cuban fishing fleet off Vacamonte was equipped with listening devices that intercepted U.S. telephone communications, and beamed them to the Cuban ambassador's residence.

When Panama's relations with Washington nosedived following the 1988 indictments against Noriega, Castro became increasingly worried about his Panamanian ally. The Reagan Administration was in the midst of a much-trumpeted war on drugs and Noriega's ouster was becoming a focal point of U.S. foreign policy. It was clear that Cuba risked losing its biggest trading center in the Western Hemisphere. Noriega needed help.

<>

Castro neither liked—nor trusted—Noriega. The two men had never developed a warm personal relationship, such as that existing between the Cuban leader and late Panamanian military leader Gen. Omar Torrijos. Torrijos, like Castro, suffered from insomnia and enjoyed all-night geopolitical discussions. But Noriega was no statesman. A hard drinker, he was rarely sober after midafternoon. He had a short attention span. He had no ideological pedigree: he had adopted a revolutionary rhetoric only after the U.S. government had decided to dump him.

Who knew whether Noriega would not turn against Cuba the minute his troubles with the U.S. government ended? The Cubans knew that Noriega had been on the CIA payroll for at least a decade. U.S. press reports had detailed Noriega's CIA links as early as 1986. Among other things, he had authorized CIA flights carrying weapons for the U.S.-backed Contra rebels in Nicaragua to pass through Panama airports unmolested. And until about a year before the American invasion, Castro had always assumed that Noriega would pass on to U.S. intelligence services any information obtained from Cuba.

In most cases, he did. Panama's G-2 intelligence service, for instance, had installed a copy machine at Panama's Omar Torrijos International Airport in the early eighties to make copies of the passports of all Cuban and Libyan nationals passing through Panama. Arrangements were made for a photocopy of each to be passed on to the CIA. The Cubans had reasons to be equally distrustful of Noriega's top officers. Despite their anti-American rhetoric, none was a true revolutionary. The Cubans did not know when they would turn against their boss—or against Cuba.

José Blandón, one of Noriega's most trusted political advisers and for many years his liaison with Castro, had defected as Panama's consul general in New York in January 1988. Since his defection, Blandón had made countless public statements about his meetings with Castro over the previous five years. Especially damaging to Cuba was Blandón's insistence that Castro had mediated in a 1984 dispute between Noriega and Colombia's Medellín cartel over $4.6 million of drug booty.

After Blandón's defection, Castro became so distrustful of the Panamanians that he would not talk with any Panamanian envoy without witnesses. He would invite other Latin American visitors to sit in on the meetings and have a secretary take notes of the conversations. Often, he would tape the meetings as well.

"He once told me that, quite frankly, he was taping our conversations to protect himself," Maj. Felipe Camargo, the Panamanian Defense Forces' intelligence officer who replaced Blandón as Noriega's chief liaison with Castro in 1987, told me at the Panama prison cell where he was jailed after the U.S. invasion. "He was furious at Blandón's charges, and didn't want it to happen again."

But Castro needed Panama, and could not afford to lose Noriega. Since mid-1987, when the Reagan Administration suspended military and economic aid to Panama, Castro had watched with interest the escalating war of words between the Panamanian leader and Washington. Noriega's growing dispute with the United States was bound to move him closer to Cuba, Castro thought. So the Cuban leader had decided from the outset that, with some limits, Cuba would help him.

The full extent of Cuba's military involvement in Panama has never before been revealed. Key details are contained in more than five hundred pages of classified documents from the U.S. Southern Command's 470th Military Intelligence Brigade. The documents, copies of which I obtained in Panama, contain the U.S. Army debriefings of Noriega's top military aides—including his Cuban liaison officers—following the invasion.*

The documents show that, despite his mixed feelings about General Noriega, Castro poured massive military assistance into Panama in the last two years of Noriega's regime—much more than U.S. officials ever thought. Among other things, Castro shipped more than 80,000 weapons to Panama, trained hundreds of Panamanian officers in sabotage operations, and helped set up a huge intelligence agency in Panama. Much of Cuba's military assistance was cleverly concealed and went undetected by U.S. intelligence services until the invasion, according to senior military intelligence officials.

One of the many interesting points emerging from the classified U.S. papers, in addition to the massive size of Cuba's military assistance, was its timing. The Cuban weapons airlift to Panama began at least two months before the February 1988 U.S. indictments against

---

* *I corroborated much of the information in personal interviews with nearly a dozen of Noriega's top officers at Panama's maximum security prison of El Renacer, and in later interviews in Havana with former Noriega aide Luis Gómez, and senior Cuban foreign ministry officials.*

Noriega, which according to most analysts at the time marked the turning point in the growing U.S.–Panamanian dispute.

Panamanian air force (FAP) flight logs recovered by U.S. forces after the invasion show that the first weapons flight from Cuba to Panama took place on the FAP's Boeing 727 on December 7, 1987—nearly eight weeks before the American indictments brought Noriega to the world's front pages. The timing suggests that, contrary to conventional wisdom, the Panamanian strongman had already thrown in his lot with Cuba when U.S. prosecutors charged him with drug smuggling.

The Panamanian military plane that transported the Cuban weapons to Panama was piloted by Panamanian Air Force Major Augusto Villalaz—the same man who had helped ship Cuban arms to Nicaragua a decade earlier—and Capt. Juan Luria. The two men picked up a 29,476-pound cargo of AK-47 rifles and ammunition at Havana's José Martí airport, and carried it to Panama that same day, the logs show. Major Villalaz recalls that, when he arrived at Havana's airport, the Cubans had already prepared half a million tons of weapons for shipment to Panama. Preparations for the Cuban arms airlift to Panama had begun months earlier.

As it happened, Fidel Castro received the first formal Panamanian request for military assistance in September 1987. The Reagan Administration had just cut military aid to Panama in response to Noriega's crackdown on Panama's democratic opposition. The U.S. government was further enraged by an attack on the American embassy in Panama by a mob of pro-Noriega demonstrators.

Foreseeing an escalation of tensions with Washington, Noriega sent Panamanian Army Intelligence Major Felipe Camargo to Cuba, with instructions to seek help from Castro. Camargo, a robust man in his mid-thirties, was a regular visitor to Havana. He had first met Castro in the late 1970s, when, as an assistant to Torrijos, Camargo helped organize the Cuban weapons airlift for Nicaragua's Sandinista guerrillas. The Panamanian officer had acted as Noriega's liaison with Cuba ever since.

As usual when he arrived in Havana, Camargo was welcomed at the José Martí airport by a Cuban army delegation. From there, he was driven to a protocol house in El Laguito, on the outskirts of the city. Hours later, he was at the Cuban leader's office.

"Good seeing you," Castro greeted the Panamanian envoy, as he led him to a long conference table at one corner of his office. Fidel seldom sat at his wood desk, especially when receiving friendly guests. Camargo explained his mission: he was there to request Cuban military aid in anticipation of a definitive break in U.S.–Panamanian relations.

"We are embarking on a nationalist struggle against the United States," Camargo said. "General Noriega has the support of the Panamanian people and is determined to resist the attacks of U.S. imperialism. We need your help. We know all of Latin America will support us. We would very much appreciate if Cuba were among the first to help us."

Castro listened attentively. He knew already from Mora, the Cuban ambassador to Panama, what the Panamanians would ask for. He had a ready response. Cuba would help Panama—up to a point. It would give Panama large quantities of AK-47 rifles, mortars and grenades.

"What about troops?" Camargo asked.

"No, chico, we can't send you troops. That would invite an immediate U.S. intervention. We have to maintain a low profile. That would be best for us, and for you too."

Fidel suggested a two-step military-diplomatic strategy to help Panama beat a possible U.S. offensive. First, Castro said, Panama should arm itself to its teeth, and create militias to defend the Noriega regime. Of course, Panama could not win a war with the United States. But that wasn't the point.

All Panama's Defense Forces and civilian militias needed to do was effectively resist a U.S. invasion for several days—until the United Nations could bring about a cease-fire. Cuba would then demand an immediate cessation of hostilities, and the Soviets would most likely back the motion. Then, the U.S.–Panama conflict would shift from narcotics to politics: Panama would be a courageous David fighting a war-mongering Goliath. Cuba and the Third World would rally behind Panama, and both Panama and Cuba would emerge as the clear diplomatic winners.

The Cuban leader emphasized the need to arm the Panamanian population, both as a psychological weapon to turn American public opinion against a U.S. attack on Panama and to elevate the human cost of a U.S. invasion if there was one. The idea of forming the "Dignity Battalions"—as the pro-Noriega civilian militias were named—had been proposed first by Nicaragua's Sandinista military officers during a seminar at Panama's Río Hato army academy. Castro proposed a way to implement that idea.

Under Castro's plan, the massive Cuban shipments of Soviet bloc AK-47 rifles would go exclusively to the Panamanian Defense Forces, which would hide them in their barracks. The military, in turn, would pass on its American-made M-16 rifles to the civilian militias. By arming these militias with U.S. weapons, Panama would avoid sounding alarm bells in Washington that the Panamanian people were being armed by Cuba. And by inviting the international press to watch the Dignity Battalions as they trained, Panama would get the message across to the American public that a U.S. invasion would cost thousands of lives.

Camargo took note of Castro's suggestions and took them home to Noriega. Fidel is an old fox, the Panamanian leader told Camargo with an admiring smile.

The plan was set in motion immediately. Panamanian Air Force Major Villalaz received a call from Noriega's office on December 6, 1987. He was told to have the Air Force Boeing 727 ready for takeoff the next morning at Panama's Río Hato military base. He was to make a highly confidential trip to Cuba.

Early next morning, Villalaz and his copilot, Captain Luria, prepared the 150-seat aircraft for an early takeoff. They would only carry three passengers: Camargo, fellow G-2 intelligence officer Lt. Benjamin Ku, and a Panama-based Cuban intelligence officer, MININT Lt. Col. Antonio Diegues. The two pilots were in military uniform. The two intelligence officers and their Cuban counterpart wore civilian clothes.

Major Villalaz didn't think much of Camargo. The air force pilot resented Camargo's arrogance. The intelligence officer was a mere captain at the time, yet he was giving orders right and left. Appointed head of the delegation to Cuba, Camargo was taking his role a bit too seriously. He showed up at takeoff time wearing mirror sunglasses, took a seat in the first row of the near-empty airplane, and waved haughtily to Villalaz. *"Cuando quieras!"* he said. (Whenever you're ready.)

When the Panamanian Air Force 727 arrived in Havana's José Martí airport two hours later, it was directed to a military section at the end of the civilian runway. A handful of Cuban officers in military uniforms were waiting.

The highest-ranking officer was Interior Ministry Brig. Gen. Alejandro Ronda Marrero, an old acquaintance of Camargo's. The two had carried out a similar secret mission ten years earlier, when transporting Cuban weapons to Nicaragua's Sandinista rebels.

Now Ronda was the chief of the Cuban Interior Ministry's Special Troops, a title once held by MININT Col. Antonio De La Guardia. Next to Ronda was José "Justo" Gonzalez, the Panama case officer of the MININT's Directorate General of Intelligence (DGI), who spent part of the year in Panama.

It was only then that Villalaz learned what they were doing in Cuba. The Cuban officers took the four Panamanians to a military cafeteria at the airport, offered them coffee, and began to talk business. Ronda informed Villalaz that they were to ship a half million pounds of arms to Panama. The weapons were in more than 10,000 numbered boxes, which they had to begin loading on his plane right away.

It was a staggering cache, including 20,000 Chinese and North Korean AK-47 rifles—much more than needed by Panama's 15,000-member Defense Forces. Among the other weapons: 50 mortars of 82 mm; 200 Soviet-made RPG-7 rocket-propelled grenades; 200 Chinese-made RPG-2s; 5,000 antipersonnel mines; 5,000 antitank mines; 300 light machine guns; 100 heavy machine guns; 10,000 hand grenades, and 7,200,200 rounds of ammunition for the AK-47 rifles. Needless to say, there was no charge for the weapons: it was a matter of solidarity among revolutionaries.

"How many flights will it take to ship the whole cargo to Panama?" Ronda asked. "For security reasons, the faster the better."

"I don't know. I'll have to do some numbers," Villalaz answered, taking a pen from his pocket and beginning to scribble numbers on a napkin.

"Also, it would be better if all the flights were done by the same crew," Ronda said. "The whole operation should be kept within the tightest security."

The Boeing 727, model 100, was a passenger plane that could carry a maximum of 32,000 pounds of cargo per trip. It would take at least sixteen round trips to deliver all the weapons in Panama, Villalaz said. But under international flight-safety standards, one single crew could not make the sixteen trips in a short period of time, as the Cubans wanted. Ronda raised his eyebrows. He asked Villalaz to make as many flights as he could, and left the timetable up to him.

They walked back to the aircraft there and then, and supervised the loading of the cargo. The first flight left hours later, with more than 400 wooden boxes filled with weapons. To keep U.S. intelligence services from detecting the weapons, the plane was unloaded at Panama's Río Hato military base—far away from the capital's closely watched Omar Torrijos International Airport.

◄►

Five days later, on December 12, 1987, Villalaz and Camargo left on their second trip to Cuba. This time, they were to pick up an additional cargo arriving from Libya. As they departed from the Río Hato military base, a smiling Camargo volunteered that the mysterious shipment was $50 million in cash. It was a donation from Libya to Panama, via Cuba.

"Can we carry that much in one trip?" Camargo asked.

"I don't know. I've never seen what one million looks like, let alone fifty," Villalaz answered, somewhat amused.

Seconds later, the two men were laughing and joking about the situation. Fifty million dollars in cash! What if they simply ran away with the money? They could simply veer to the right and land in Miami . . . The Americans would roll out the red carpet . . .

When the plane arrived in Havana's José Martí airport, Brigadier General Ronda was waiting for them. After the customary warm handshakes, Ronda directed the Panamanians to the warehouse where the Cuban weapons were stockpiled. When the Panamanians asked about the $50 million, Ronda seemed surprised.

"What $50 million?" The Cuban general didn't know what they were talking about.

Camargo asked to be taken to the Palace of the Revolution to clear up the confusion. Once there, he learned—to his dismay—that the money had never arrived from Libya. Cuba's ambassador to Libya had sent a message to Havana saying that Libya had made the promise—but had failed to deliver. Muammar Khadafy was adding evidence to his mounting reputation in leftist revolutionary circles as a phoney.

◄►

Shortly after the beginning of Cuba's weapons airlift, Castro sent the first military advisers to Panama. Their mission: to help train Panama's Defense Forces in the use and maintenance of the Cuban-supplied AK-47 rifles and RPG-7 rockets.

The first Cuban adviser to arrive in Panama in early 1988 was a black lieutenant colonel who quickly became known by his trainees as

"Tío Pepe." He was based at Panama's Defense Forces' 5th Military Zone in the remote northwestern province of Chiriquí.

A quiet, introverted man in his late forties with a round face and a moustache, Tío Pepe wore a Panamanian Defense Force uniform without rank or any other insignia. He lived with the Panamanian troops in the barracks, rarely left the military base and spent his free time reading and writing letters to his family in Cuba.

Tío Pepe was soon joined by "Rogelio," another black Cuban officer in his late forties. Rogelio was a slightly overweight chain smoker, an extremely sloppy man. For much of 1988, the two Cubans trained the Diablos Rojos and Paz Battalions of Panama's Defense Forces.

Their presence was a virtual secret: the Panamanian troops in Chiriquí were well isolated from the capital, and the two Cubans lived a secluded life within the military garrisons. Even if an occasional foreign visitor arrived at the base, the Cubans would hardly be detected in their Panamanian army uniforms: their Spanish accent, like that of most Cubans, was very similar to the Panamanians'.

When I asked Noriega about rumors of Cuban advisers in Panama during a two-hour interview on September 15, 1988, he laughed at the question.

"Cubans? What Cubans?" Noriega said, opening his hands widely. "We're such a small country that everybody notices when there are any Russians, Americans or any other foreigners around. People would have already seen them . . . Besides, what kind of advice could the Cubans possibly give us?"

In late 1988, Castro agreed to increase Cuba's military training assistance to Panama. In various meetings with Noriega's envoys, it was agreed that it would be easier to keep such a large-scale training secret if it was carried out in Cuba rather than in Panama.

Between October 1988 and January 1989, an elite group of twenty-nine Panamanian officers from the Diablos Rojos, Machos del Monte and Hombres Rana battalions led by Capt. Evidelio Quiel were flown to Cuba for a "special operations" training course. The course focused on how to stage commando attacks against military installations, electric power plants and other sabotage targets. Another twenty-one Panamanian officers of the 5th Military Police Company were trained in Havana in the use of police dogs to detect explosives and narcotics. Other groups of Panamanian officers flew to Cuba in early 1989 for courses in scuba diving, electrical engineering, and military communications.

<>

But Castro's most ambitious plan in Panama was to set up a Cuban-run intelligence service that would operate outside the jurisdiction of the Panamanian military's G-2 information-gathering agency. This way, Cuba would be in control of an alternate secret service that would report directly to Noriega, and would have a key influence on the Panamanian strongman's decisions.

Noriega, who until then had resisted Cuban involvement in his intelligence apparatus, changed his mind after a March 1988 coup attempt against him. Several senior officers of the G-2 had participated in the aborted coup attempt. Noriega could no longer trust his secret service.

Shortly after the failed rebellion, the Panamanian ruler asked the head of his personal guard, Capt. Eliecer Asunción Gaitán, to form an elite counterintelligence service that would operate independently from the G-2. The new service would be set up with the help of Cuban advisers, and modeled after Cuba's own counterintelligence services. Its main targets: the Defense Forces hierarchy and the U.S. military in Panama—the two forces that represented the greatest threat to Noriega.

Gaitán, a short, quick-witted and extremely ambitious officer in his early thirties, enthusiastically accepted the assignment. Over the next year and a half, until the day of the U.S. invasion, he would become the second most powerful officer in Panama's Defense Forces. Not only did he have Noriega's ear, but his domestic spying responsibilities quickly turned him into the most feared officer in the Panamanian military. The young captain could decide the future of higher-ranked officers by simply questioning their loyalty to Noriega.

The first Cuban instructor for Noriega's alternate intelligence service arrived in Panama in October 1988. The Cuban colonel introduced himself as "Eladio." His passport bore the name Rigoberto Gonzalez. He and his wife moved into apartment No. 4 on the third floor of the Banco General building on Panama City's Via Argentina Avenue.

For the next two months—ten hours a day, six days a week—Eladio trained a group of eight Panamanian officers at his apartment. Much of his course dealt with surveillance and wiretapping techniques. Even while taking their half-hour lunch—sandwiches Eladio's wife would bring for them from Via Argentina—the men would go over the morning's lessons. Toward the end of the course, a second

Cuban intelligence adviser named Gregorio arrived in Panama, and began teaching a similar course to an expanded group of Panamanian officers. There wasn't any time to waste.

By early April 1989, the training of the first group of Gaitán's men was finished. Eladio considered the group prepared to start surveillance missions. Capt. Nino Vaprio, Gaitán's top aide and the leader of the Panamanian trainees, was asked to oversee the group's day-to-day operations, and each of the men in the group was assigned a mission. One was deployed at Panama's Immigration Office at Howard, the American air force base, to monitor U.S. troop movements and new weapons' arrivals. Another was assigned to spy on Panamanian employees at the U.S. embassy in Panama. A third was to infiltrate Panama's political opposition.

Vaprio was to report his men's findings to Gaitán and Eladio. They set up a safehouse in the back room of the Medagalia Jewelry store next to the Ejecutivo Hotel in Panama City's banking area, and furnished it with a computer, so that the group could issue regular reports. A copy of each of Vaprio's reports would go to Eladio—and from there to Havana.

Among the first targets of the Cuban-trained intelligence service in Panama were the U.S. embassy officials. The Cubans wanted to find out who among them were CIA agents. To do the job, Eladio asked Vaprio for a list of all American diplomats accredited in Panama. When he got the list in late 1989, the Cuban agent sent it to Cuba to run it by the Cuban intelligence central registry, as well as by the records of other Soviet bloc intelligence services.

The Cuban plan was to pinpoint suspect CIA agents, follow them, and discover which anti-Noriega Panamanians were collaborating with them. This would have the additional advantage of establishing U.S. intelligence service movement patterns, so that they could be arrested on a moment's notice. Panama would take the CIA agents hostage if there was a U.S. attack on Panama.

A few days after sending the list, Eladio received his answer from Havana. Cuban intelligence had identified more than fifty U.S. diplomats suspected to be CIA agents. But it turned out most had long left Panama. The handful remaining in Panama were targeted for surveillance. Vaprio's team, wearing police uniforms or posing as night-watchmen, were posted in buildings near the U.S. embassy on Panama's seaside Balboa Avenue, and began to keep detailed logs on American movements.

As weeks and months went by, the new intelligence service began to produce bigger and better reports. By late 1989, Noriega asked the Cuban instructor, Gaitán and Vaprio to plan for a major expansion of the new spy agency. The service would be renamed Dirección de Inteligencia Nacional y Contra-Inteligencia (DINCI), or National Directorate of Intelligence and Counter-Intelligence, and was to replace the G-2 as Panama's main secret service.

According to a seven-page secret document found by U.S. troops after the American invasion, the new DINCI agency was to be modeled after the Cuban MININT's Directorate General of Intelligence (DGI). Among other things, it would perform activities that would be of great help to the DGI, such as "collection of intelligence against hostile intelligence services," including the CIA and the 470th Military Intelligence Brigade. Copies of the DINCI units' reports would be passed on regularly to the Cubans.

As a gesture of good will, the Cubans began sharing their own intelligence. About once a month, Eladio would give the Panamanians a diplomatic pouch containing up to fifty DGI reports. The Cubans would send them from Havana to the Cuban embassy in Panama, then embassy intelligence officer Jesús García would pass them to Eladio, who in turn handed them over to Vaprio.

The reports contained specific information about American diplomats and military officers in Panama—mostly telephone intercepts recorded by the Cuban monitoring stations aboard the fishing vessels off the port of Vacamonte. By early December 1989, about two weeks before the U.S. invasion, the DINCI was ready to make its official debut. A full reorganization of Panama's security agencies was to be launched with the beginning of the new year. Cuba, in effect, was about to begin running Panama's entire intelligence apparatus.

By late 1989, Castro was also encouraging Noriega to revamp Panama's newly created Dignity Battalion militias. The eight-thousand-strong civilian force had turned into something far different from what Castro had envisaged a year earlier.

The Panamanian militias had become a joke: not one single leader of Noriega's ruling Revolutionary Democratic Party (PRD) was a member, nor would any one of them take time off from their weekends to watch the battalions train. The militias were largely made up of unemployed civilians—many of them street bums—with little ideological motivation, hardly what the country needed to scare off a possible U.S. intervention.

In Cuba, senior government officials were expected to donate part of their time to Cuban militias, and to do "voluntary work" in agricultural farms several times a year. This was supposed to serve as a morale booster for the population. In Panama, nothing of the sort was taking place.

"Your Dignity Battalions are becoming dumping grounds for the unemployed," a top Cuban official told a group of Panamanian officials visiting Cuba months before the invasion. "If you don't get PRD leaders to participate in them, the battalions will lose all legitimacy."

In the last months of the Noriega regime, Cuba invited dozens of Panamanian politicians to attend classes at the Cuban Communist Party's Ñico Lopez school for political leaders in Havana. Perhaps looking at Cuba's political-military defense system, the Cubans thought, the Panamanians would learn to improve theirs.

<>

Despite all the cooperation, however, there was one major sticking point between the Cubans and the Panamanians. Noriega was desperately seeking fifty SA-7 surface-to-air missiles. He was convinced that the missiles would be his best defense in the event of a U.S. military intervention, and he was determined to obtain them at any cost.

Noriega believed the SA-7s would allow Panama to stave off an American attack for a few days—long enough to take the conflict to the U.N. Security Council and ask for a cease-fire, as Castro had proposed. If Panama was able to shoot down a few U.S. warplanes, images of the wrecks—or of captured U.S. air force pilots—would make headlines around the world, Noriega told his aides. Antiwar protests would erupt everywhere. At the United Nations, Latin American nations would naturally side with Panama against the aggressor. All that Panama needed was to maintain a reasonable air defense for a few days.

But Fidel Castro was reluctant to provide the sophisticated SA-7 missiles to his unreliable ally. The Cuban leader had told Noriega's envoy Camargo so in early 1988. Too risky, he had said: sending Cuban troops or SA-7s would give Washington a pretext to invade.

Noriega was thus forced to look for the missiles elsewhere. He sent envoys on secret missions to obtain the weapons from Libya, the Soviet Union and the Palestine Liberation Organization. Along the way, he would always go back to the Cubans to renew his pleas. Wherever he went, he was met with empty promises or polite rejections. The story of Noriega's quest for the SA-7s offers a rare glimpse into secret dealings among the world's most radical revolutionary regimes—a tale of mutual suspicions, broken promises and surprising tension.

<><>

In late March 1988, a few days after the failed coup against General Noriega, the Panamanian strongman sent his first envoy to Libya— Maj. Humberto Melara, a forty-one-year-old Peruvian-trained military communications expert. Melara was to talk directly with Muammar Khadafy, and to seek the missiles from him.

Melara spent only three days in Libya. After a two-day wait in Tripoli, the Libyan capital, he was flown to a military base where Khadafy was staying. The meeting took place in a huge tent and lasted no more than ten minutes. Melara presented Khadafy with a machete, as a token of the two countries' friendship. The Libyan said he would consider providing the SA-7s to Panama.

But several months went by without a yes or no from Libya. In November 1988, Noriega sent Melara to Libya again, this time with a personal note requesting the missiles. The Panamanian envoy was accompanied by Maj. Mario del Cid, a Noriega confidant who was to report to the Panamanian strongman on whether or not the Libyans felt comfortable dealing with Melara.

Dealing with the Libyans was a headache. Melara and Del Cid first went to Madrid, and checked in at the Princesa Plaza Hotel, where they were to wait to be contacted by a representative from Libya's intelligence service. The Libyan agent, a man who identified himself as Ibrahim, showed up six days later and asked the Panamanians to fly to Zurich. There they were to wait for another Libyan agent at the Zurich Hotel. Three days later, the new agent showed up, only to tell them there would be a delay before they could fly to Libya. They finally left for Tripoli on December 8, 1988.

The Panamanians were welcomed at the airport by three Libyan officials and were taken to the Al-Kabbir Hotel. A day later, they were received by a high-ranking official. He was introduced to them as Lieutenant Colonel Sanusi, Khadafy's brother-in-law—the officer in charge of Khadafy's personal security. Sanusi said Libya was willing to give the missiles to Panama, but that his country had not yet found a ship from a friendly nation that could deliver the weapons safely— and secretly.

In general, the Libyan official was full of complaints about Cuba. First, he told the Panamanians, Cuba claimed there was no space on

Cuban cargo ships calling on Libya. Then, a previous container full of Libyan weapons had gone out on a Cuban sugar ship bound for Panama a few months earlier, but the vessel had arrived in Panama without the weapons. The Cubans had seized them.

"We will send you the SA-7s as soon as we can find a cargo ship that will not raise the suspicions of the United States," Sanusi told the Panamanian envoys.

"We would very much appreciate if you could find one as soon as possible," responded Melara.

That night, the two Panamanian envoys had dinner at the house of Cuba's ambassador to Libya, Enrique Trujillo, a diplomat who had recently been posted in Panama. The Cuban ambassador was four years into his current assignment and claimed to know the Libyans well, but didn't trust them. He exploded in anger when Melara hinted that the Libyans had accused Cuba of failing to deliver the missiles to Panama.

"The ambassador blamed the Libyans for the failure," Del Cid recalled in his debriefing by U.S. officers. "He claimed the Libyans were quite disorganized and erratic in the way they went about their business." One could not do business with the Libyans. They were just not serious.

Melara asked the Cuban ambassador if there were Cuban ships calling on Tripoli any time soon. Castro had refused to provide the SA-7s, he thought, but maybe he would not object to helping transport somebody else's missiles. Trujillo informed him that some Cuban sugar ships were due to arrive soon, but he did not volunteer to try to place the missiles on them. The Panamanians left the Cuban ambassador's residence with a clear impression that the Cubans were not ready to provide any help—no matter how small—with the missiles. On December 15, 1988, Melara and Del Cid returned from Tripoli to Panama—empty-handed.

<>

Noriega resumed his quest for the SA-7 missiles in late 1989. There was mounting speculation about a possible U.S. invasion of Panama, and he was in a hurry to obtain the weapons. This time, he tried to get them through the PLO.

Noriega's security chief Captain Gaitán had spread the word through Arab diplomatic circles that Panama's military ruler was eager to contact PLO chairman Yasir Arafat. A few months later, Ali Kassem, a young PLO militant who had studied in Panama, called

Gaitán's office to say an Arafat envoy would soon arrive in Panama. A few days later, Palestinian businessman Tarik Salameh arrived on a Cubana de Aviación flight from Cuba. He checked into the downtown Continental Hotel, called Gaitán, and told him he was bringing a message from Arafat to Noriega. Gaitán arranged for a meeting at Noriega's office the next day.

Tarik Salameh was a big man with a smooth manner. He always carried a pipe, but not for smoking. He would fill the bowl with aromatic powders and sniff at it periodically. Based in East Berlin, Salameh ran an import-export firm named Al Khobar. It was a front for PLO arms shipments.

The meeting with Noriega was short and cordial. It was agreed that the PLO representative would maintain regular contact with the Panamanian strongman through Gaitán. That afternoon, Salameh made a call to Tunisia, and said a second PLO representative named Tarik Mahdi would fly to Panama immediately. He was the man with the right contacts to procure the missiles.

Mahdi arrived in Panama a few days later with the PLO ambassador to Cuba. The three men met with Noriega, and said they would work around the clock to get the SA-7s. The next day, they left. On October 4, 1989, a day after the failed coup attempt against Noriega, Gaitán received a fax from East Berlin with the letterhead "Al Khobar Kuwait." The fax, handwritten in English and sent to Gaitán's office at Building No. 8 in Fort Amador, read as follows:

Dear Friends:

On behalf of Mr. President Yasir Arafat, the Palestinian people, and myself, we are congratulating commander general Manuel Noriega and the Panamanian people for smashing the conspiracy. We hope you all successful times.

Yours,
Tarik Mahdi
Tarik Salameh

On October 25, 1989, Gaitán received a telex from East Berlin, with the sending indicators of ALKHO, for Al Khobar. It was written in Spanish, and addressed to "Esteemed friend E. Gaitán and B. Ku." The telex read: "My chief is very pleased to invite you to Tunis to meet you personally. You are invited to be his guest. Please give me a date that would be convenient for you to fly to Tunis. Possibly you can come to Berlin, and then we can fly together from here. . . . Your friend, Tarik." In an ensuing telephone call, Tarik Salameh informed the Panamanians that "two containers are ready with the merchandise."

Gaitán left in late November 1989, for Algiers, where the missiles supposedly were. But once again, Gaitán had no luck in finding a ship to take the missiles to Panama. From Algiers, he flew to East Germany, where he took an InterFlug flight to Havana. The Cubans would not come up with a solution. On his return to Panama City, Gaitán asked his aide, Lt. Benjamin Ku, to set up a meeting with the KGB agent in Panama. Perhaps he could persuade Moscow—and through them, the Cubans—to ship the missiles.

The KGB representative's name was Nikolai, and he was a fluent Spanish-speaker who had lived many years in Cuba. A KGB colonel, he had been transferred to Panama under the cover of correspondent for the Soviet Novosti news agency. Nikolai was a stocky, balding man in his late forties—a jovial, backslapping character who chain-smoked Marlboro cigarettes. The few times that he spoke seriously with his Panamanian contacts, he made no bones about his politics: he was no friend of Perestroika.

Ku told Nikolai that Panama needed his help in bringing two containers from Algiers. When the Soviet asked what was in the containers, Ku laughed.

"Let's say it's tractor parts," the Panamanian said.

"I see, that's what they call them now," Nikolai smiled back.

The Soviet said he needed a few days to consult with his superiors. They convened a meeting with Gaitán on December 19, 1989. In the United States, troops were already assembling on bases for the invasion of Panama that night.

At 9 A.M. December 19, Gaitán and Ku met with the Soviet agent at the headquarters of the Panamanian Defense Forces' Institute of Historic and Geopolitical Studies. The two-story house, a former Buddhist temple in Panama's El Cangrejo neighborhood, was known in Panamanian-Cuban intelligence circles as El Manguito—the little mango tree—after the tree in its patio. It was the main meeting place for Cuban, Soviet, and Libyan agents in Panama.

At the meeting, Nikolai said the Soviets had no ship going from Algiers to Panama. The missiles would have to go through the Soviet Union or through Cuba, which was the normal travel route for Soviet cargo ships. He was still awaiting an answer from Moscow.

The answer didn't come in time. That afternoon, at about 5 P.M., six hours or so before the start of the U.S. invasion, a visibly agitated Nikolai returned to El Manguito. Across town, the Cuban ambassador was gathering his staff at his embassy to put them on maximum alert. Nikolai asked for Lieutenant Ku.

"I have received a message from my service that I should try to keep all Soviet citizens in their respective homes," the Soviet said.

"Is anything going on?" asked Ku.

"I don't know. I've got to run," Nikolai said. It was the last time the Panamanian officers saw the KGB agent.

A few hours later, U.S. troops would begin their massive attack on Panama. After several days in hiding, Noriega and Gaitán would seek asylum at the Vatican embassy. There, a distressed Gaitán would tell fellow asylum-seeker Jaime Simmonds, the head of the government's Savings and Loans Credit Union: "If the ground-to-air missiles had arrived on time, it would have been a different story."

<><>

Why did Castro hold back on the SA-7 missiles? There were many reasons. First, as he himself had said, he did not want to give Washington a pretext to invade Panama—and possibly even Cuba. Second, Cuba's SA-7 missiles were Soviet-made, and had strings attached: they were not supposed to be delivered to third parties without Moscow's approval. The Soviets were not willing to ship sophisticated weapons to Noriega, and Castro did not want to start a squabble with Moscow. Third, Castro did not trust Noriega's judgment to use these weapons responsibly.

When U.S. military debriefers asked Panamanian envoys Camargo and Vaprio what reason the Cuban leader gave them for not producing the missiles, the two Panamanian officers agreed that Castro was afraid of an irrational action by Noriega or his troops. Long after the Panama invasion, Cuba's Politburo ideology and foreign-relations chief Carlos Aldana corroborated their presumption.

"A soldier with a weapon like that could just as well shoot down a military aircraft or a commercial airliner," Aldana told me. "Can you imagine the political consequences for us had we found ourselves linked to a massive killing like that?"

In a separate interview, a senior Cuban Foreign Ministry official in Havana said with a broad smile, "Fidel may have also feared that Noriega would sell the missiles to a third party. . . . There was so much corruption among the Panamanian officers, that we always kept our hands in our pockets when dealing with them."

<>

Two weeks after the invasion, the U.S.-installed Panamanian government of President Guillermo Endara allowed all the Cuban diplomats and advisers who were holed up at the Cuban embassy to leave the country. Sixty-four Cubans, including women and children, left Panama January 4, 1990, on a Cubana de Aviación airliner.

Eladio, the Cuban instructor who had been the brains behind the new DINCI intelligence service, was not among them. He had left Panama for Cuba on December 19, 1989—hours before the U.S. invasion. He would have been a major catch for American forces.

While the Cuban regime may have wanted to get Eladio out of Panama as rumors about a possible U.S. invasion grew, Eladio had made his own plans to leave weeks earlier. It wasn't that he feared a U.S. strike, but that he wanted to take a Christmas break. The Cuban adviser to Panama's new intelligence service had asked Vaprio in early December to tap the home telephones of dozens of American embassy employees. It was part of the plan to pinpoint possible CIA agents and their Panamanian contacts.

Vaprio's men soon learned from the telephone intercepts that 80 percent of the U.S. embassy people were going home for the year-end holidays. Based on that information, Vaprio suggested to Eladio on December 10 that it would be a good idea for all of them to take a year-end break. "The Americans will be out of town, and Panama will come to a halt anyway during the holidays," Vaprio told the Cuban instructor. "If there is any good time for a vacation, this is it."

Eladio and his wife booked a Cubana flight to Cuba for December 19. If they entertained any thoughts of postponing their trip, they were rapidly discouraged by the escalation of tensions following the December 17 killing of the U.S. Marine. On the morning of the invasion, Eladio and his wife left for Cuba, loaded with year-end presents for their relatives.

<>

After the invasion, the dozens of Panamanian officers who were receiving training in Cuba were asked to leave the country. Panamanian Sgt. Augusto Cesar Sanchez, alias "Manteca," one of Vaprio's intelligence officers who had just arrived in Cuba for training, found himself abandoned two days after beginning his course at a MININT's Special Troops house in Siboney.

Activities at the house stopped. Cuban instructors disappeared.

Over the next few days, the quality of the food deteriorated rapidly. Cubans stopped handing out pocket money to the Panamanians. The senior Cuban instructor, a man identified as Major "Angelito," showed up at the house a few days later to tell the Panamanians they would have to go back to Panama. The course had been called off.

<><>

Luis "Lucho" Gómez, a former left-wing leader of Noriega's Revolutionary Democratic Party, sought political asylum at the Cuban embassy shortly after the U.S. invasion. After obtaining a safe-conduct out of the country and settling in Cuba as a political refugee several months later, he expressed great bitterness at Noriega for not following Castro's advice.

"The Cubans had long told us that Panama's salvation would be in arming the people, the Dignity Battalions, and waging what they called 'a war of all people,' " Gómez told me in Havana, confirming Camargo's testimony from the other side of the political spectrum.

"But approximately forty tons of Cuban weapons were never sent to the Panamanian Defense Forces' barracks in the countryside, because Noriega feared the military would use them to stage a coup. And no weapons were given to the Dignity Battalions, because the military high command feared they would turn into an independent army.

"The whole defense plan went bust because Noriega failed to give us the weapons," Gómez concluded, referring to the Dignity Battalions. "Noriega's historic mistake was that he prepared for a surgical strike, rather than for a military invasion."

<><>

Castro was scheduled to speak on December 21 at an awards ceremony for Cuba's most outstanding athletes. Crowded into Havana's Ciudad Deportiva sports stadium, Cubans awaited the speech anxiously. It was to be Castro's first public appearance since the U.S. invasion of Panama. How would he react?

After the official ceremonies honoring the athletes, the Cuban leader walked to the podium and started by addressing the latest events head on.

"Comrade athletes, comrade guests," he began. "During the past few hours, we wondered whether or not we should suspend this ceremony because of events of which you are aware." Always using the plural "we"—Castro never used the "I" form, as if he were only an incidental factor in the Cuban decision-making process—he said the decision had been made to go ahead with the ceremony anyway.

"However, we are not in the mood to discuss sports," he said, lowering his head in an expression of deep grief. "It is better to dedicate some words to the heroes of our America who at this moment are fighting for the dignity, honor and sovereignty of our peoples.

"The empire thought it would only last minutes, maybe hours," he said. "The real fact is that they did not want the combat to continue into the dawn. The U.S. President had prepared a speech for 0700 to announce that everything had ended. One could see the discouragement, anger, almost panic on the face of the U.S. president.

"Thus, we believe that in the past forty-eight hours the Panamanian people have achieved one of the most heroic feats in the history of the hemisphere."

Castro went out of his way not to link himself to Noriega in his two-hour speech. He didn't mention Noriega by name, referring to him only as "the commander of Panama's Defense Forces." But days later, he would have to eat his words of praise for the Panamanian people and their military.

Noriega's Defense Forces had put up only token resistance to the U.S. forces. Many of Noriega's top officers had turned themselves in within hours of the invasion. Others fled into the countryside, or hid in relatives' homes. Castro's hopes for a protracted war that would lead to a U.N.-mandated cease-fire and a political uproar throughout Latin America were dashed.

What's more, the spectacle of thousands of Panamanians welcoming the incoming American troops with white handkerchiefs—the symbol of the anti-Noriega resistance—was being reported throughout Cuba on the U.S. government's Radio Martí. Panama was lost, and even the Yanqui aggression could not be turned into a propaganda gain for the Cuban revolution.

6

Exit Nicaragua

◄◄◄◄◄Fidel Castro had only a few weeks to recover from Gen. Manuel A. Noriega's overthrow in Panama before he received another devastating blow: the fall of the Sandinista government in Nicaragua. On February 25, 1990, President Daniel Ortega's leftist Sandinista regime was crushed in the polls by a U.S.-backed coalition of fourteen opposition parties in Nicaragua's first free national elections.

Ortega's defeat took the world by surprise. Virtually all preelection opinion polls had him winning the election with ease. For Cuba, Ortega's political demise meant the loss of Castro's closest political ally in the region. If Panama had been Cuba's financial outlet to the capitalist world and its commercial center, Nicaragua had been its main ideological partner and its political operations center.

Nicaragua's 1979 Sandinista revolution had been a major victory for the Cuban revolution. The Cuban-inspired rebels had established a leftist regime in a Latin American country. It was the dream that Argentine-born Cuban revolutionary hero Ernesto "Che" Guevara and other Cuban internationalist warriors had unsuccessfully tried to realize over two decades in various corners of the hemisphere.

With the Sandinista takeover in Nicaragua, Cuba gained a foothold in Central America from which it could assist the growing Marxist insurgencies in El Salvador, Guatemala, and other countries in the region. Cuba was no longer the lone keeper of the revolutionary flame.

<>

Sandinista leader Daniel Ortega, a boyish-looking man clad in jeans and high-heel black leather boots, smiled broadly when I asked him about his dealings with Castro during his ten years as Nicaragua's president. It was early 1991, and we were talking late into the night at the patio of his office in Managua, the Nicaraguan capital. People would be surprised to learn what kind of advice Castro gave him, Ortega said.

From the very beginning of the Nicaraguan revolution, Castro preached moderation to the young Sandinista leaders. While the Cuban leader poured massive military assistance into Nicaragua, he explicitly advised Ortega in 1979 not to follow Cuba's Marxist model, Ortega told me. Castro was afraid that a drastic radicalization of the Nicaraguan revolution would trigger a U.S. invasion. The Nicaraguan revolution was too dear to him to be put at risk by an excess of ideological fervor. So he recommended among other things that the Sandinista *comandantes* maintain a mixed economy and allow the existence of opposition political parties.

Ortega spoke of Castro with a respect and admiration that I would not find in later interviews with other Sandinista *comandantes*. Speaking slowly, his eyes fixed on the sky while he chewed cardamom seeds he extracted from his pocket, Ortega recalled one of his first meetings with Castro after the July 19, 1979, Nicaraguan revolution.

At the Cuban leader's office in the Palace of the Revolution not long after the Sandinista victory, Castro explained why Ortega should not rush to make radical changes. Their revolution was under a much greater military threat than Cuba, he said. Unlike Cuba, a nation surrounded by water and impossible to attack by land, Nicaragua was surrounded by hostile neighbors. Some of them, especially Honduras, would soon actively support anti-Sandinista Contra rebels.

"Fidel told us that the gringos had an obsession with Nicaragua," Ortega recalled. "He told us that, because of the giant military threat against us, we should put much more emphasis [than Cuba] on the political-diplomatic battle."

The Sandinistas followed Castro's advice. Over the next few years, they would map their domestic and foreign policies with an eye on U.S. public opinion. Soon, they became sophisticated players in the international propaganda game. Each time the Reagan Administration pressed for aid to Nicaragua's U.S.-backed Contra rebels in Congress, arguing that the Sandinistas had imposed a Marxist dictatorship, the Nicaraguan regime would come up with new cosmetic measures showing its alleged support for a mixed economy and political pluralism. Often, it was blunt political deceit. At times, it was a genuine symptom of the Sandinistas' split political personality.

In the same 1979 talks with Ortega, Castro also argued that the Sandinistas—who included several non-Marxists in their governing junta at the time—could not afford a crack in their leadership until the revolution had consolidated itself. By allowing certain political freedoms at home, the Sandinistas would gain time to establish their power. Nicaragua's main priority was, after all, the survival of the Sandinista revolution.

Finally, Castro recommended that Ortega not further antagonize Nicaragua's Roman Catholic Church. The Sandinista media were making a big mistake in attacking the church, Castro said. Nicaragua was a deeply religious country, and the Sandinistas' verbal onslaughts would only help alienate growing sectors of the population. Castro had made that mistake in Cuba. Shortly after the revolution, he had had a nasty public argument with Cuba's church hierarchy and had alienated most practicing Cuban Catholics from the revolution ever since.

<>

During the first years of the Nicaraguan revolution, Castro had been not only the Sandinista *comandantes'* ideological mentor, but also their main source of military and logistical support. In the final months before the July 1979 Sandinista takeover, Cuba had shipped thousands of weapons through Panama and Costa Rica for the Sandinista guerrillas. As soon as the Sandinistas seized power, Cuba sent thousands of military advisers, teachers and doctors to help consolidate the new leftist regime.

Sandinista leaders and Cuban officials began to shuttle back and forth between the two countries for military and political consultations. The trips were seldom publicized—only when they involved an official ceremony.

"I used to go to Havana four or five times a year," Daniel Ortega told me, referring to his years as president. Most of these trips were kept secret at the time, in order not to give Washington more ammunition for its campaign to aid the Contra rebels.

On his arrival, Ortega was usually met at the airport by one of the

Castro brothers, and immediately taken to a protocol house in the closed compound of El Laguito. Although he had his own presidential plane, the *19 de Julio* executive jet, the Nicaraguan president would leave Managua most often on the once-a-week Monday morning commercial Aeroflot flight. He would return early the next morning on another commercial flight. His logic: the U.S.-backed Nicaraguan rebels would not dare blow up a Soviet commercial airliner—they would not risk triggering the international outrage that undoubtedly would follow.

The Sandinistas had everything they needed in Havana. Shortly after the 1979 revolution, the Cuban government had given the Nicaraguan embassy twelve elegant residences—a gift from the Cuban revolution. The Sandinista Party was given another three mansions in Havana for its own use. One of them, protocol house No. 40, was a full-fledged office that coordinated with the Americas' Department of the Cuban Communist Party on covert operations and other projects too sensitive to be handled by the Nicaraguan embassy. As was usual in Marxist regimes, party officials—not diplomats—often handled the most delicate issues.

In addition to the Mercedes-Benzes given to Ortega and other Sandinista leaders during their visits to Havana, Cuba had also made the Nicaraguan embassy a gift of eighteen cars, one van and a truck. So when the Sandinista leaders arrived in Cuba, they had a well-established Nicaraguan bureaucracy at their service. Cuba had become a second home.

There was a seemingly endless list of issues that required constant consultations between Cuban and Nicaraguan officials. By the mid-1980s, U.S. intelligence services estimated there were about nine thousand Cubans in Nicaragua, involved in every branch of the Nicaraguan government.

In addition to an estimated three thousand military advisers, there were about six thousand Cuban construction workers, agrarian reform specialists, doctors and teachers—many of them working for free in the Atlantic Coast and other remote regions of the country where few Nicaraguan professionals would go on their own. Cuba was not only sending a small army of professionals to Nicaragua, but was inviting thousands of Nicaraguans to go to school in Cuba.

An estimated three thousand Nicaraguan high school and college students received full scholarships to study in Cuba. Every year, the Cuban government paid for their plane tickets, living quarters, tuition, food and even clothing. In Cuba, each student received two pairs of pants, two shirts, underwear and one pair of shoes a year, plus a sixty-peso monthly stipend—nearly half of an average Cuban worker's monthly salary.

The Cubans' generosity with Nicaragua seemed unlimited. In Havana, the Cuban government set aside two small hospitals for exclusive use of Nicaraguans who couldn't get proper medical attention at home. One of them, the Ana Betancur clinic in Havana's Miramar section, had beds for more than one hundred patients. Cubana flights from Managua came several times a week, bringing dozens of wounded Sandinista soldiers or civilians in urgent need of medical attention. Cuba paid for the airfare, medical attention, food and lodging.

<><

The Cuban advisers would leave their mark on every corner of Nicaraguan life. In some fields, such as education, the Cubans virtually ran the Sandinista government's programs. Sandinista school texts were a case in point.

When I visited Nicaragua once in the late 1980s, a Nicaraguan woman showed me the textbooks of her three elementary-school children. The books were clearly modeled after heavily politicized Cuban school texts—only slightly adapted to Nicaragua's reality.

The Sandinistas' first-grade reading book, shortly after teaching children how to scribble the words *"mama"* and *"papa,"* asked students to write the sentence *"Toño es un niño Sandinista."* Nicaragua's first-grade math book, a virtual copy of Cuba's own, taught children to count by using drawings of Soviet-made AK-47 rifles and grenades rather than apples. Drawings of smiling children marching with rifles on their backs decorated its pages.

While the Sandinistas painted themselves as committed democrats, they were adopting Cuba's domestic indoctrination programs lock, stock and barrel. The new Nicaraguan regime set up neighborhood watch committees modeled after Cuba's Committees for the Defense of the Revolution. It soon renamed streets, factories, buildings and public works after fallen guerrillas, emulating Cuba's almost religious glorification of revolutionary heroes.

Castro offered the Nicaraguans technical and material assistance in nearly all fields—except one. He told the Sandinistas he would not send economic advisers to the new regime. "When the revolution won, I asked Fidel for an economic adviser," Ortega told me. "He said no. He told me he didn't want us to blame Cuba if the Nicaraguan economy went down the drain."

<><

Perhaps nowhere was the Cuban presence greater than in Nicaragua's Sandinista military apparatus. Only four weeks after the Nicaraguan revolution, Cuba set up its first military mission in Managua. For more than a year, Cuban and Soviet advisers would meet regularly with Sandinista army chief Gen. Humberto Ortega to map the new government's military strategy. Under the plan, the Soviets would provide the hardware, and the Cubans the military training and advice.

In November 1981, Ortega flew to Moscow to sign the first five-year treaty of military cooperation between Nicaragua and the Soviet Union. Among the weapons delivered by the Soviets: four T-55 tank battalions; four BTR-60 PB armored vehicle battalions; four 152mm cannons; three 122mm cannon-shell groups; one Mig-21 squadron; one MI-8 squadron; eight 1400 ME Griff patrol boats and 100,000 AK-47 rifles.

But the Sandinistas and their Cuban advisers soon discovered they had made a big mistake. They had built a conventional army, conceived to fight a possible U.S. invasion or an attack by neighboring Central American armies. The Sandinistas had been so confident about their popularity at home that they had left to their militia forces the task of quashing a potential popular rebellion within the country.

By 1983, Nicaragua's U.S.-financed Contra rebels had become a growing force in the countryside. Nicaragua's militias and reserve troops could not stop the guerrillas. The heavy Sandinista army was not trained—nor equipped—to face the rebels' hit-and-run attacks. Sandinista leaders were worried.

Gen. Humberto Ortega flew to Havana in late 1983 in search of help. At a meeting with Fidel Castro, he requested a battalion of 2,800 Cuban troops to help contain the Contra offensive while the Sandinistas trained in irregular warfare. "We told him we could not stop the Contras without Cuban troops," recalled Sandinista Army Maj. Roger Miranda Bengoechea, who was present at the meeting as General Ortega's personal assistant.

Castro rejected the plan as too risky. He offered instead to send Cuba's top expert in irregular warfare to head the Cuban military mission in Nicaragua: Brig. Gen. Arnaldo Ochoa. Ochoa was coming from Angola and Ethiopia, where he had commanded antiguerrilla wars for several years. After his arrival in Managua, he oversaw a complete overhaul of the Sandinista army. He presided over the creation of irregular combat units, and reoriented the army's weapons purchases to make them adequate for the new circumstances.

Gen. Humberto Ortega was impressed by Ochoa. Although he

didn't strike a close personal friendship with the Cuban general—Ochoa's Nicaraguan fishing and drinking buddy was Brig. Gen. Joaquin Cuadra—the Nicaraguan defense minister saw him as a brilliant strategist. Within months of his arrival in Managua, Ochoa became a regular visitor to Ortega's office, to the point that few decisions were made without informal consultations with him.

Over the two years that followed the October 25, 1983, U.S. invasion of Grenada, the Cuban and Nicaraguan regimes drew closer than ever. In the aftermath of Grenada, Castro began for the first time to contemplate dispatching Cuban troops to Central America if U.S. forces invaded Nicaragua. The Cuban leader and the Sandinista *comandantes* began to discuss the possibility of "regionalizing" the conflict in the event of an American attack.

It was a grandiose plan. According to General Ortega's aide Miranda Bengoechea, who defected to the United States in 1987, the Sandinista *comandantes*—in close coordination with the Cubans—drew up a contingency plan to launch air and ground attacks on the sitting governments of neighboring Central American countries if the U.S. invasion occurred. Costa Rica and El Salvador would be the first targets. Among other things, Sandinista army-tank columns would join forces with El Salvador's Farabundo Martí National Liberation Front guerrillas to march into the Salvadoran capital, while the Sandinista air force was to bomb the U.S. embassy in Costa Rica. Managua would be defended by Nicaragua's Interior Ministry troops and Sandinista militias.

"The thinking was that, with our small air force, we couldn't possibly face the gringos' air power," said Miranda Bengoechea, who helped draft the plan at the Sandinista army's high command. "So we would use our air force against the Costa Ricans, who didn't have an air force, in an effort to broaden the conflict."

The plan was approved at a Sandinista National Directorate meeting in 1985. Among the people who helped Defense Minister Ortega draft it were his top aides, Nicaragua's Interior Minister Tomás Borge, and the head of Cuba's military mission, Brigadier General Ochoa.

In Havana, meantime, Fidel Castro had gathered Cuba's top military officers at his office to plan the Cuban forces' participation in the plan. The meetings stretched out for several days. Standing in front of a huge map of Central America and the Caribbean, Castro moved pins between Honduras, El Salvador and Costa Rica as he evaluated suggestions from his high command on possible Cuban-Nicaraguan attack routes.

It was decided that all Cubans in Nicaragua—both civilians and military advisers—would be organized into battalions and brigades, and would invade southern Honduras while Sandinista forces attacked El Salvador and Costa Rica. Cuban troops would launch hit-and-run strikes against the Honduran army's main units.

"The plan was meticulously drawn by Fidel Castro himself," recalls former Cuban Air Force Gen. Rafael del Pino, who participated in the meetings. "U.S. troops would never face a regular force, but would have to spread their forces in many directions to come to the rescue of weak [Central American] armies harassed by better-equipped Cuban and Sandinista forces."

<>

Cuba also poured massive economic assistance into its new Central American ally. Under a one-way cooperation agreement, Cuba shipped $50 million a year worth of goods to Nicaragua annually. The products included spare parts for the Victoria de Julio sugar mill—a giant Cuban-built plant that Castro later donated to Nicaragua—and oil. Cuba's oil shipments to Nicaragua, which were drawn from the Soviet Union's annual oil allotment for Cuba, went up from thirty thousand tons a year in the mid-1980s to ninety thousand tons in 1989.

A separate commercial agreement between the two countries, which was negotiated by the two governments every year, was enormously profitable for Nicaragua. Under the deal, the Cubans shipped $20 million worth of goods to Nicaragua, while the Nicaraguans were only obliged to ship $10 million worth of goods to Cuba. While Cuba sent huge quantities of medicine and industrial tools, Nicaragua made only sporadic shipments of blue jeans and shoes.

"We were delighted with our trade agreements with the Cubans," one Sandinista *comandante* recalled. "They were so advantageous to us, that Western European and Latin American diplomats used to jokingly ask us how they could get similar deals for themselves."

Whenever Nicaragua was in urgent need of certain industrial spare parts, fuel or raw materials, the Sandinista leaders would declare it a national security issue and rush to Cuba for help.

"We would take the first Cubana flight to Cuba, and the Cubans most likely came forward with a solution," a Sandinista *comandante* who traveled regularly to Cuba in search of economic aid told me. "If they didn't have what we needed, they would get it from somewhere else. But they would always bail us out."

What did Cuba expect from Nicaragua? Commercially, there was not much the small Central American country could offer—only wood and a few other raw materials. But the emergence of a new leftist regime was crucial to Cuba—as a means to end its diplomatic isolation and to advance Castro's old dream of creating a growing revolutionary bloc in the Americas.

For Cuba, exporting the revolution was also a strategy of self-preservation. Under Fidel's slogan of "One, two, many Vietnams," the emergence of Marxist revolutions would divert the attention of Washington, and keep it from concentrating its forces on a single enemy.

The Sandinistas embraced the theory wholeheartedly. Convinced that Washington would sooner or later intervene militarily to stop their Socialist experiment, they began funneling weapons to leftist guerrillas in El Salvador and Guatemala. The Reagan Administration insisted that, in this, the Sandinistas were Cuban puppets. In fact, the Nicaraguan revolutionaries were acting on their own. Fidel did not need to persuade them.

<>

But, unbeknownst to the rest of the world, the Cuba-Nicaragua political marriage was beginning to suffer its first symptoms of strain in the mid-eighties—at the very height of Castro's involvement in the Central American country. The first quarrel took place in July 1985, over preparations for a Castro-convened conference of Latin American debtors in Havana. The Cuban leader wanted the meeting to repudiate the region's $360-billion foreign debt to Western banks. He hadn't been so animated about a foreign policy issue in years.

Castro sent three senior Cuban officials—Ricardo Alarcón, Alberto Betancourt and Carlos Salsamendi—on missions throughout the hemisphere to persuade state leaders to attend the debtors' summit. A Cuban Foreign Ministry official told *Miami Herald* reporter Sam Dillon at a presummit reception in Havana, "This is the most important thing that's happened in twenty-five years of Cuban revolution."

Castro asked the Sandinistas for help in using their good contacts with Latin America's social democratic parties to promote Cuba's new cause. But the Sandinistas weren't so enthusiastic. They decided that, for tactical reasons, Nicaragua would not go out of its way to assist Fidel.

"We didn't want the foreign debt issue to displace the U.S. aggression against Nicaragua as the focus of Latin America's joint diplomatic action," a senior Sandinista Foreign Ministry official told me.

"We told the Cubans we wouldn't be in the forefront of that fight."

When Castro opened the summit at Havana's Palace of Conventions, he found himself talking to a low-level audience of Latin American legislators, academics, and leftist intellectuals. No Latin American leader attended. Nicaragua sent Victor Tirado, one of its lesser-known *comandantes*. Tirado avoided calling for an all-out repudiation of Latin America's foreign debt. On his way out of the country, there were no Cuban officials to bid him farewell.

Two years later, Nicaragua and Cuba found themselves for the first time differing on a major policy issue when the Sandinistas signed the August 7, 1987, Central American peace plan with four other Central American countries. Despite their continued shows of unity, Nicaragua and Cuba would secretly argue about the peace plan during the remainder of the Sandinista regime.

The Esquipulas plan, named after the Guatemalan city where it was signed, was a two-pronged approach to end the region's guerrilla wars. It called for Nicaragua and El Salvador to start a dialogue with opposition groups and begin negotiations toward cease-fires with rebel groups. It simultaneously asked outside powers—the United States, the Soviet Union and Cuba—to stop aiding rebel groups in the region.

Castro didn't like it at all. As usual, he was careful not to antagonize the Sandinistas by criticizing their decisions, but he let it be known through midlevel Cuban officials and foreign dignitaries that he had serious reservations about the document Ortega had just signed.

Cuba supported a political solution to the Central American crisis within the framework of the nine-member Contadora group, which included Mexico, Panama, Colombia and Venezuela. By shifting the negotiations to the five Central American nations, the Sandinistas would find themselves at a smaller negotiating table where they would be more isolated, and more vulnerable to U.S. pressures, Castro argued.

Even worse, from Cuba's standpoint, the Esquipulas agreement demanded among other things a political opening, a step toward Glasnost in Nicaragua. In Cuba's eyes, the Sandinistas had opened a Pandora's box that would cost them dearly in the future.

Shortly after signing the Esquipulas peace plan, Nicaragua and Cuba had their first gloves-off diplomatic quarrel. As usual, the flap—a squabble among brothers—was kept a tight secret between Castro and the nine Sandinista commanders. President Reagan used almost any occasion to paint Nicaragua as a Cuban satellite, and neither Castro nor the Sandinistas were doing much to dispel that: any publicity about their internal disagreements would have weakened Nicaragua's military standing.

The quarrel was over Cuban ambassador to Nicaragua Julián Lopez, a veteran Americas' Department official who had been posted in Nicaragua since the 1979 revolution. Lopez was an old friend of the Sandinistas. He had helped them since their guerrilla days, when he was based in Costa Rica and was Cuba's key officer in charge of helping the rebels smuggle weapons and equipment into Nicaragua. Since then, the Cuban ambassador had spent every Christmas Eve at Gen. Humberto Ortega's house.

In September 1987, a month after Daniel Ortega had signed the Central American peace agreement, Castro abruptly recalled Lopez. The Cuban ambassador had fallen from grace at home. Rumors in diplomatic circles had it that Lopez had made a disparaging remark about Raúl Castro in a telephone conversation, and it had been picked up by Cuban counterintelligence.

The Sandinistas suspected Lopez had been sacked because of his support for the Esquipulas plan. In a move to assert their self-determination, the Sandinista commanders informed the Cuban embassy that Nicaragua would honor the outgoing ambassador with a big ceremony at the César Augusto Silva Convention Center. Lopez would be awarded with the Carlos Fonseca Order, Nicaragua's highest diplomatic award.

"Havana immediately asked that the order not be awarded to the outgoing ambassador," one Sandinista *comandante* who was in the midst of the diplomatic skirmish told me. "We did it anyway."

The tug of war over Lopez's recall didn't end there. After the ambassador's departure, Cuba appointed Brig. Gen. Sergio Perez Lezcano as the new ambassador to Nicaragua. Perez Lezcano was well known to the Sandinistas. In the early 1980s, he had headed Cuba's first group of military advisers in Nicaragua. But the Sandinista junta rejected the Perez Lezcano appointment.

"We told them no," the Sandinista *comandante* recalled. "We said that appointing a Cuban general as ambassador would send the wrong message abroad at a time when we were trying to implement the Central American peace plan, and when the United States was doubtful of our sincerity."

Castro backed off. On November 24, 1987, a new Cuban ambassador presented his credentials to Nicaraguan President Daniel Ortega. He was Norberto Hernandez Curbelo, a diplomat who had served as ambassador in Venezuela until 1980, and who—like the outgoing ambassador—was a top aide to Cuban Communist Party Americas' Department chief Manuel "Barbarroja" Piñeiro. The first serious clash between the two revolutionary regimes had come to an end. But it would not be the last.

As the Central American agreement moved forward, the Sandinistas agreed to a growing number of opposition demands. Over the two years that followed the signing of the Esquipulas accords, they authorized anti-Sandinista street rallies, allowed the reopening of the opposition daily *La Prensa,* and tolerated a resumption of fiercely anti-Sandinista radio programs on Radio Catolica. In order to achieve their goal—to pressure the United States into stopping its aid to the Contras—they embarked on an all-out political opening.

The Sandinista neighborhood watch committees were soon allowed to fade away, victims of public indifference and a lack of government determination to keep them functioning. The wave of nationalizations, which had come to a halt in the mid-1980s, was in some cases reversed to return property to its prerevolutionary owners.

Finally, in early 1989, the Sandinistas made a dramatic decision that left the Cubans dumbfounded—to hold free elections in 1990. By then, the U.S.-financed Contra guerrilla war and the collapse of the Nicaraguan economy had pushed the Sandinista *comandantes* to seek an immediate political solution to the Nicaraguan crisis.

The Sandinistas' original scheme of maintaining a democratic façade to win the war in the political battlefield had taken a life of its own. Many of the Marxist *comandantes* who had once supported the Esquipulas plan as a ploy to disarm the Contras were now choosing to believe their own democratic pledges.

They didn't have much of a choice. Inflation in 1988 had reached 35,000 percent. A U.S. trade embargo continued to strangle the Nicaraguan economy. There were shortages of food and gasoline. Managua was out of water three days a week because of broken down pipes that couldn't be replaced for lack of funds. Strikes were spreading throughout the country.

The Sandinistas realized they could not get control of the situation without imposing an all-out dictatorship, which would only isolate them more. World conditions were not favorable for a hard-line option. The Soviet Union was moving toward a normalization of relations with the United States. Eastern European countries were moving away from Marxism. Cuba itself was increasingly isolated and in no condition to increase its support for the Sandinistas.

In late January 1989, Nicaragua's beleaguered Sandinista *comandantes* decided to convene national elections in early 1990—and to win them. They agreed to take a daring proposal to Caracas, Venezuela, where Central American leaders, Fidel Castro, and U.S. Vice-President Dan Quayle were to gather a few days later for the inauguration of Venezuelan President Carlos Andres Perez.

Under the Nicaraguan proposal, the Sandinistas would convene the elections in exchange for an internationally supervised disbanding of the Contra rebels and American recognition of the election's results. At a February 1, 1989, private meeting at the new Venezuelan president's suite at the Caracas Hilton Hotel, Ortega broke the news to his Latin American counterparts.

"We understand that it is important to hold elections in Nicaragua, but also consider that it is essential that the Contras turn in their weapons and join the election process," Ortega recalls telling the other presidents. Perez, Honduran President José Azcona and Guatemalan President Vinicio Cerezo said they supported the Nicaraguan proposal. Castro, sitting in one corner of the room, nodded approvingly.

"Fidel said, 'I'm all for that.' He was in total agreement with our decision to call elections," Ortega recalls.

Two weeks later, at the February 14 summit of Central American presidents in Costa del Sol, El Salvador, Ortega committed himself to holding internationally supervised elections by February 25, 1990. In exchange, the four other Central American leaders agreed to close down Nicaraguan Contra rebel camps in their territories. Nicaragua's electoral process was set in motion.

Publicly, Castro applauded the Costa del Sol agreement as an important step toward solving the Central American crisis, just as he had done in Caracas. Castro also told Ortega privately he respected the Sandinistas' decision to hold elections. In reality, the Cuban leader didn't like at all what his Nicaraguan friends were getting into.

Castro and Ortega discussed the planned Nicaraguan elections thoroughly during a quick visit by the Nicaraguan president to Havana a few weeks after the Central American summit. The two presidents sat at opposite sides of the conference table in Castro's office, flanked respectively by Nicaraguan Foreign Minister Miguel D'Escoto and Cuba's Americas' Department head Manuel Piñeiro. Everybody sipped Cuban-style espresso coffee except the Nicaraguan foreign minister, who always carried his herbal tea bags with him.

Castro was nearly twenty years Ortega's senior, and—since the time the Nicaraguan had come to Cuba for military training as a young guerrilla nearly two decades before—treated him as a father would a son. To the Cuban leader, Ortega was "Daniel." To the Nicaraguan president, Castro was still "Comandante."

But Castro was sensitive to American charges that the Sandinistas were Cuban puppets, and so he was extremely careful not to complain about Nicaragua's election plans. As he often did, Fidel kept the conversation casual, and peppered his opinions with humor. "This is what I think," he would say as a preamble to his recommendations, then he would add immediately with a malicious smile, "Of course, I'm sure you'll do exactly the opposite."

On that occasion, rather than argue against what the Sandinistas had already decided, Castro offered advice on how to win the Nicaraguan elections.

"If I were you, I would abolish the draft. That would give you a lot of votes," Castro said, referring to the widespread popular opposition to the military draft in Nicaragua. "You've got to do better grass-roots work, and go back to a volunteer army."

"We can't, Comandante," replied Ortega. "If we do, we won't have enough manpower to stop the Contras. They will descend on the cities. They will force us to cancel the elections. That's exactly what they want . . . then the whole world would blame us for not holding the elections."

Ortega was confident the Sandinistas would win by a landslide. Public opinion polls were giving them a huge margin. The Sandinistas controlled most of Nicaragua's radio and television stations, had a campaign budget several times larger than the opposition, and could use state-owned vehicles to mobilize tens of thousands of people in the countryside. The Sandinistas would win, Ortega assured Fidel.

The Cuban leader wasn't convinced. He suggested that Ortega shouldn't be so confident. The elections were being held under extremely unfavorable conditions for the Sandinistas, Castro said. The U.S. trade embargo was crippling Nicaragua's economy, creating widespread discontent. The United States was still providing financial aid to the Contra rebels, and forcing the Sandinistas to maintain the highly unpopular military draft. It was hardly the ideal political climate for Ortega.

"Elections are a risky business," Castro said. "If you get into the game, you should be prepared to lose."

The Nicaraguan president was taken aback by Fidel's pessimism.

"We will win, Comandante. If we do things right, we will win."

"Well, who knows . . . ," Castro said, continuing with his previous train of thought. "Perhaps, losing would be the best thing for you. It would solve all your problems."

The four laughed. Ortega left the meeting pondering Fidel's warnings. It was the first time somebody whose judgment he respected had voiced doubts about a Sandinista victory. As he left the room, the Nicaraguan leader wondered, Could Fidel be right?

In subsequent conversations with the Nicaraguan president, Castro never crossed the line of friendly advice. But, at the same time, he directed his top aides to do whatever they could to convince the Sandinista leaders to cancel the elections. The pressure started out as casual conversations, and ended with a full-blown diplomatic offensive to get the Sandinistas to scrap the voting.

It was one of those hot summer days in Havana when people disappear from their offices by early afternoon. Cuban Foreign Minister Isidoro Malmierca, a big, heavyset man better known for his obedience than for his wit, had invited Nicaraguan Foreign Minister Miguel D'Escoto to his home for lunch.

Malmierca's wife Maria Helena and her mother had spent the morning cooking a chicken broth and a pork stew with rice and beans in honor of their Nicaraguan visitor. It was to be a small gathering, a good occasion to discuss the latest events in Central America in an informal setting. The only other guest was Lázaro Mora, Cuba's ambassador to Panama. He had just arrived in Havana on a routine visit. It was July 1989, and Nicaragua's Sandinista government had already embarked on the campaign for the 1990 elections.

Over lunch, Mora told the Nicaraguan foreign minister that the Sandinistas were taking a big gamble by going to the polls. In Panama, Gen. Manuel A. Noriega's regime had just held elections a few weeks earlier, and the opposition had won by a landslide. Noriega had been forced to send troops into the voting places to stop the tallying process and nullify the elections. It had resulted in a major international embarrassment for the Panamanian regime.

"The Panamanians' experience with the May 7th elections was disastrous," Mora told D'Escoto, while Cuban Foreign Minister Malmierca backed him with a nod. "Look, Noriega controlled the country's television, radio and print media, and none of that did him any good. The opposition had U.S. media advisers. They ran much slicker ads. . . . You can't beat the gringos at their own game."

D'Escoto disagreed. The Sandinistas enjoyed widespread popular support in Nicaragua, he said. And they had U.S. advisers, too. They would run a sophisticated campaign, and they would win. Nicaragua's economy would be in somewhat better shape by election day. There would be more consumer goods on the shelves.

"You're worrying too much," D'Escoto said. "We'll win. You'll see."

"Don't forget that you've been in power for ten years now. That produces political fatigue. . . . That can cost votes," the Cuban ambassador to Panama countered.

"We're aware of that. We have taken that into account."

As the three men were finishing their coffee and Malmierca's wife began to clear the table, Mora excused himself for a minute. He returned immediately from the entrance hall with a small present for D'Escoto. It was a book entitled *Voting Images*, written by an Argentine political advertising expert. Its main point: a good advertising campaign with sophisticated media techniques is more effective than total control of a country's mass media.

"Read it," Mora said. "You'll see what I mean. The [Nicaraguan] opposition will have the best U.S. campaign advisers behind it. They will clobber you."

D'Escoto thanked Mora for the book, smiled, and insisted once again that the Sandinistas were well aware of the difficulties they would face, but that they were confident they would win.*

---

* *In 1991, when Mora was back in Havana as head of the Cuban Foreign Ministry's Latin America Department, I asked him what exactly had he tried to get across to the Nicaraguan foreign minister at that luncheon, since the Sandinista regime had already committed itself to holding elections by then.*

    Mora was silent for a long while, then cited the American trade embargo, Washington's aid for the Nicaraguan Contra rebels, the U.S. National Endowment for Democracy's financial aid to the Chamorro-led opposition coalition, and other conditions adverse to the Sandinistas' electoral hopes. "They could have canceled the elections in light of the U.S. interference. They could have put off the voting until the U.S. aggression was over," he said.

    D'Escoto remembers the conversation, but does not recall Mora explicitly asking for a cancellation of the elections. "On that occasion, we were talking among close friends," the former Sandinista foreign minister said.

<>

Castro's exasperation grew in mid-1989, when the Nicaraguan regime adopted a stringent economic austerity plan to curb the country's five-digit hyperinflation before the elections. The measures included sharp cuts in public spending, which left tens of thousands of government workers on the street. The cash-starved government announced a major devaluation of Nicaragua's currency. State-run industries were given greater autonomy to raise prices in an effort to reduce government subsidies.

The Cuban leader was flabbergasted. What were the Sandinistas doing? Did they think they would win the elections by laying off public workers? In conversations with foreign diplomats and visiting Latin American officials, Castro questioned the wisdom of adopting such economic measures before the elections. What's more, he insisted, the Sandinistas' shift toward free market policies was a recipe for disaster.

Nicaragua's would be "the most right-wing economic policy in Latin America," he complained bitterly in a private meeting with a Western European ambassador.

<>

In the summer of 1989, senior officials of Castro's Foreign Ministry and the Communist Party's Americas' Department were conveying their misgivings about the Nicaraguan elections to the Soviet Union.

Yuri Pavlov, the Soviets' top Latin American policy assistant, was in Cuba on a routine visit to discuss regional matters with his Cuban counterparts. Pavlov, fifty-eight, was a reformer. His father, a Communist Party functionary, had been imprisoned by Stalin's secret police in 1938. Pavlov had read whatever he could find about Stalin's 1930s trials. He had no appetite for dictatorships. After holding several obscure jobs since joining the Soviet foreign service in 1954, he had obtained his first ambassadorial posting in Costa Rica in 1982.

Five years later, Pavlov was picked by the new Soviet foreign policy elite to head the Foreign Ministry's Latin American Department. Since then, he had struck a good working relationship with his American counterpart, U.S. Assistant Secretary of State for Inter-American Affairs Bernard Aronson. The Cubans knew that Pavlov and Aronson considered themselves good friends. Aronson's was the only American home Pavlov had ever visited.

In one of several meetings at the Cuban Foreign Ministry in Havana, Cuban officials tried to talk Pavlov against going ahead with ongoing Soviet-American talks for a political settlement in Nicaragua. At the time of Pavlov's visit to Cuba, the Soviets had already obtained assurances from the Bush Administration that Washington was ready to settle the Nicaraguan war through negotiations, and would respect the results of free Nicaraguan elections.

"The Cubans pointed out to me their doubts about the wisdom of going to elections," Pavlov recalls. "One of their main arguments was, 'You can't trust the Americans.' They argued that the Americans would never normalize relations with the Sandinistas, even if the Sandinistas won free elections."

"Our line was, 'Look, the Americans have made certain promises. It is our belief that it serves the purposes of U.S. policy, as formulated by the Bush Administration, to stop the war in Nicaragua and settle the Nicaraguan crisis through political means.' "

The conversation at the Cuban Foreign Ministry had reached a dead end. Hours later, Pavlov was going through the same argument with Cuban officials at the Americas' Department. The two sides stuck to their lines. It was too late to make a difference, anyway: the Soviets had already made the firm decision to back the Nicaraguan elections. They wanted Nicaragua to return to normal life, so the Kremlin could start reducing its economic aid to that Central American country. They hoped Washington and Western Europe would help rebuild a democratic Nicaragua.

Top Castro aide Carlos Aldana, the Cuban Communist Party's ideology and foreign relations chief, conceded to me two years later that Cuba had indeed voiced its opposition to the Nicaraguan elections in behind-the-scenes talks with Nicaraguan and Soviet officials.

"We told whoever wanted to know, or asked our opinion, that you don't call elections to lose them. We told them that an election was enormously risky, especially in a country where a majority could vote against the Sandinista Front in hopes of ending the military draft, the war, and an asphyxiating economic situation. . . . We told them it was almost impossible to win."

But Sandinista hard-liners who were tempted to follow the advice and cancel the elections—Nicaragua's Interior Minister Tomás Borge among them—soon discovered they would have nowhere to go for help.

The Soviet Union, which had provided Nicaragua with nearly $1 billion in military and economic assistance in previous years, was rapidly cutting its aid. In December 1989, when a superpower summit in Malta approached, Soviet officials were clearly more interested in improving their ties with Washington than in keeping the Sandinista leadership happy.

When the Sandinistas went to Moscow in late 1989 asking for emergency aid to arrive at the election day with their economy in better shape, they were kindly told that the Kremlin could not offer more than it was already giving.

"They wanted money to put consumer goods in the stores, so that they could portray the economic situation as improving and attract voter support," said Pavlov, who received the Sandinista request. "We didn't think it was a good investment."

Sandinista hard-liners realized they could only expect worse reactions from the Soviets if they decided to cancel the elections. "The Sandinistas also knew that we would have growing difficulties in continuing our oil supplies to them. They could not expect much help from us," Pavlov said.

Even the Cubans, despite their pressures on the Sandinistas, could not offer much help. Their own economy was in deeper trouble than ever. By 1989, Cuba was not only unable to increase its economic assistance to Nicaragua, but was secretly preparing to reduce it. The way the Cubans saw it, the Sandinistas had to step up ideological fervor at home, so as to overshadow their deepening economic crisis with a wave of popular support for the revolution's social conquests.

In secret talks in mid-1989, Castro had warned visiting Sandinista *comandantes* that Cuba would no longer be able to ship food, medicines and toys for fifty thousand residents of Nicaragua's remote Atlantic Coast. At least four Cuban ships laden with these goods had arrived in Nicaragua's poverty-stricken Atlantic Coast city of Puerto Cabezas every year since 1985.

The ships had carried enough food to provide for the town's basic nourishment year-round. Now, the Cuban leader was telling the Sandinistas that the last shipment would arrive in Puerto Cabezas shortly before the elections. Cuba itself was short of food and clothing. It could no longer afford to be so generous, Castro said.

But the worst news was still to come. In a never-reported conversation in mid-1989, Castro told Sandinista *comandante* Henry Ruiz,

Nicaragua's minister of economic cooperation, that Cuba would also have to suspend its oil shipments to Nicaragua immediately after the 1990 elections.

"We can continue giving you oil until 1990," Castro told Ruiz at the Cuban leader's office. "After that, we won't be able to ship you a single drop. We're screwed. The Soviets are cutting back on their shipments to us, and we'll be having major oil shortages ourselves."

Ruiz, a nice man of working-class origin who was known in Nicaragua as "Comandante Modesto" for his unassuming character, was flabbergasted. Castro's announcement was the worst news the Sandinistas could possibly get, even if it included the promise to maintain supplies until election day.

Cuba's oil shipments of 90,000 tons a year represented 14 percent of Nicaragua's already sharply reduced annual oil consumption at the time. The Soviet Union, which provided the bulk of Nicaragua's oil, had already told the Sandinistas it would start cutting back on its shipments. Eastern European countries had already cut off their oil supplies. Mexico had just stopped its own oil deliveries to Nicaragua for lack of payment. If even Cuba—Nicaragua's best friend—cut its oil shipments to Nicaragua, the Sandinista regime would have to close factories, and lay off thousands of workers. And if word of the cutbacks got out, Sandinista campaign claims that things were bound to improve after the voting would backfire. Ruiz decided not to take no for an answer.

"Well, Comandante, we've got to discuss this at a later date," Ruiz said, swallowing hard. "Let me just submit to you that Cuba's oil shipments shouldn't be viewed in our bilateral relations as a trade issue. It's really a political issue. That oil is vital for our survival."

Castro and Ruiz left it at that. They only agreed not to talk publicly about the oil problem.

The issue never came up again. Cuban oil shipments were discontinued after the Sandinistas' defeat in the polls. In their post-election statements, Sandinista leaders never mentioned Castro's warnings of an imminent oil cutoff. But at least two senior Sandinista leaders conceded to me that Castro's secret notice was the last straw in an escalating series of frustrations that drove the Sandinista *comandantes* to accept the idea of elections—and their ultimate outcome.

"There were some Sandinista *comandantes* who were considering calling off the elections and imposing a war economy," one Sandinista leader told me at his office in Managua. "But the prospect of an imminent cut in Cuba's oil supplies convinced them that we would have nobody to count on."

◄►

A new behind-the-scenes diplomatic brawl erupted in July 1989. This time, the dispute centered on Div. Gen. Arnaldo Ochoa. At the beginning of the trial, when Ochoa was stripped of all his military honors, Raúl Castro called Nicaraguan Defense Minister Humberto Ortega. Castro suggested that Cuba would be pleased if the Sandinistas withdrew all military honors they had bestowed on the disgraced Cuban general.

The Sandinistas had awarded Ochoa with the Orders of Camilo Ortega and Hilario Sanchez, the two highest honors conferred by the Sandinista military. The awards had been conferred on Ochoa on March 8, 1986, a day before the Cuban general ended his three-year assignment in Nicaragua. Acting President Sergio Ramirez had presided over the ceremony—President Daniel Ortega had been away on a week-long visit to Cuba—escorted by Gen. Humberto Ortega and Nicaragua's entire high command.

Humberto Ortega decided to ignore the Cuban petition. Nicaragua never withdrew Ochoa's military honors. Ochoa had been indispensable in training the Sandinista army in unconventional warfare, and most Sandinista *comandantes* had developed a warm loyalty to him.

When Ochoa was executed a few weeks later, Sandinista leaders were shocked. They had always been skeptical of the drug charges leveled against him and suspected he had been eliminated because he had advocated a political opening at home. The execution reinforced the feeling among them that Castro was out of touch with the new Socialist world.

◄►

In the closing weeks before the February 25, 1990, elections, the Nicaraguan regime made major new concessions that fell like a cold shower on Havana.

One of them hurt the Cubans especially. At the December 13, 1989, summit of Central American presidents in San Isidro de Coronado, Costa Rica, President Ortega signed a regional agreement that for the first time flatly condemned the Cuban-backed Farabundo Martí National Liberation Front (FMLN) guerrillas in El Salvador.

In exchange for regional pressure on the U.S. government to cut aid to the Contras, Ortega had agreed to sign the document that among other things made a "vehement call on the FMLN to immediately and effectively end hostilities." It also made an urgent demand on the FMLN "to publicly renounce any kind of violent action that directly or indirectly affects the civilian population."

The two clauses were near-verbatim copies of El Salvador's President Alfredo Cristiani's proposal. Ortega had handed the newly elected rightist Salvadoran president a major political victory.

Hours later, the FMLN guerrillas issued a communique expressing outrage over the San Isidro document. "The Central American presidents have supported the fascist policy of the Salvadoran government," the rebels protested. In a rare public criticism of their former Sandinista allies, they accused Ortega of having "sold out" the Salvadoran rebels. Radio Havana, the Cuban regime's overseas radio station, broadcast the Salvadoran guerrillas' statement several times over the following days.

The Cuban government did not make an official comment on the San Isidro document, and Cuban media were instructed not to talk about the document. Such a sensitive moment in the relationship of Latin America's three largest leftist movements required vigorous but quiet diplomacy.

Castro sent Americas' Department head Manuel Piñeiro and his top Nicaraguan expert, Luis Hernández, on a secret trip to Managua. As soon as the two Cuban officials arrived, they headed for a meeting with the nine-member Sandinista junta to discuss the San Isidro agreements.

Piñeiro expressed the Cuban leadership's sadness over the blow to the FMLN. "What's done is done," he told the Sandinistas. "But was it really necessary to accept that language?"

"Yes, we didn't have a choice," answered one of the Nicaraguan *comandantes*.

The Sandinista *comandante*, who was present at the meeting, said in a later interview in Nicaragua: "For us, everything was riding on that Central American agreement. We wanted to win a clean election, end the war, defeat the Contras in the polls, and win the support of capitalist countries. We could not afford to be fundamentalists. We told him [Piñeiro] that we had had no choice but to be pragmatic and sign that document."

There was a chilly atmosphere at the crowded Cuban embassy's New Year's Eve party in Nicaragua December 31, 1989. The open-air dance party in the garden of Managua's César Augusto Silva Convention Center was an annual event; the Cuban diplomatic mission in Nicaragua celebrated both the New Year and the anniversary of the Cuban revolution.

Over the past ten years, it had been the biggest diplomatic bash in town—and one of the most fun. There was usually Cuban rum, and a good salsa music band. Hundreds of Cuban residents in Nicaragua—teachers, physicians and military advisers—were invited to attend, along with foreign diplomats and international journalists. It was a precious opportunity for outsiders to take a peek into the close-knit world of the Cubans in Nicaragua.

But that New Year's Eve, less than two months before the Nicaraguan elections, there was a subdued atmosphere at the Cubans' party. Hundreds of guests in white guayabera shirts and long summer dresses exchanged small talk under a huge Seiba tree next to the center's Olympic pool.

The salsa band was playing at full gear, but the dance floor was nearly empty. Only three of the Sandinista *comandantes*—Daniel Ortega, Tomás Borge and Henry Ruiz—showed up, and each stayed only a few minutes. Other Sandinista officials and Cuban diplomats could be seen only engaging in polite conversation—a far cry from their enthusiastic, almost conspiratorial, conversations of a few years earlier. The *New York Times* reported that the Cuban party "had the markings of a political wake."

Victor Hugo Tinoco, at the time Nicaragua's vice-minister of foreign relations, was one of the Sandinista officials in attendance. He dropped by only long enough to say Happy New Year, then rushed off to another party.

"We now had fewer things in common," Tinoco told me, recalling the atmosphere at the party. "We had gone separate ways. Once we decided to embark on elections, the Cubans couldn't offer us much advice. We had taken a path that wasn't theirs. We didn't have that much to talk about anymore."

In the final days before the elections, Ortega campaigned like a born-again Social Democrat. In an effort to shed the warmongering image of the Sandinistas, he traded his olive-drab uniform for jeans and colorful Hawaiian shirts. He paid a courtesy visit to conservative archbishop Miguel Obando y Bravo, a frequent critic of the Sandinistas. The Nicaraguan president started going to church, and appeared in a front-page picture at the opposition daily *La Prensa* kneeling before a priest at the Coronado church, taking the host like a devout Catholic.

The Sandinista campaign was fashioned after American electoral races. Huge loudspeakers beamed rock music at Sandinista rallies. Tens of thousands of "Daniel Presidente" baseball caps and T-shirts were distributed on the streets. A Sandinista National Liberation Front campaign poster showed the naked legs of a man and a woman embracing with a rose at their feet. The poster, aimed at the tens of thousands of Nicaraguan youths who were voting for the first time, said: "It's better when you do it the first time with love—vote FSLN."

"The time has come to put away the olive green," Ortega told reporters a week before the election, explaining his decision not to wear his guerrilla commander uniform. Ortega's campaign manager, commander Bayardo Arce, told a group of American reporters that the Cuban model was passé, and that "the country we like the most in social-economic terms is Sweden."

In their determination to win the elections and gain the acceptance of the Western world, the Sandinista *comandantes* also allowed the U.S. Agency for International Development to disburse $9 million for the Nicaraguan elections, knowing that much of the money would go to the fourteen-party anti-Sandinista National Opposition Union. The funds, channeled through the National Endowment for Democracy, a group funded by the U.S. Congress, were supposed to pay for various election expenses, but U.S. officials conceded that at least $1.8 million went directly to the Chamorro campaign coffers. It was a tough nut for the ultranationalistic Sandinista *comandantes* to swallow.

In a conversation with Gabriel García Márquez in January 1990, during one of their late-night chats at the writer's home in Havana, Fidel Castro again expressed his deep worry about the Nicaraguan elections. The Cuban leader was shaking his head as he openly wondered why the Sandinistas had made so many pre-electoral concessions to the Nicaraguan opposition.

"Fidel did not oppose the election, and would have been incapable of giving any order to the Sandinistas not to hold them," García Márquez told me later that year. "But he was scandalized by the concessions Daniel Ortega had made in the campaign. For instance, when Ortega allowed himself to be photographed next to Cardinal Obando y Bravo, or when he talked about dropping his olive green uniform. Fidel thought he was making too many concessions."

Sandinista *comandante* Bayardo Arce, Ortega's campaign manager in the 1990 elections and one of the Nicaraguan leadership's most frequent travelers to Havana, described Castro's attitude this way: "Fidel understood our realities very well. He was perfectly clear that in Nicaragua we could not repeat Cuba's model of a one-party system. He had always supported the idea of a multiparty system as a correct response to Nicaragua's needs. But some things during the electoral campaign were just too much for him."

The U.S. dollars for the opposition, for instance. "His main objection was our allowing the North Americans to send that money," Comandante Arce recalled. "He told us that was absurd; that it was a blatant intervention in our internal affairs."

Castro gave the first public hints about his misgiving over the Nicaraguan elections in a late January 1990 speech to the Confederation of Cuban Workers. On that occasion, he obliquely referred to the Sandinista political opening in a wide-ranging analysis of the political openings in most Socialist countries. His main point: the liberalization process was leading to the collapse of revolutionary regimes everywhere.

"There are some who would like to save socialism by making concessions," Castro said. "What little do they know about the voracious, monstrous mentality of imperialism and of reactionary forces. If you give them so much as a little nail, they will want a piece of your little finger; if you give them a piece, they will want the whole finger; if you give them the finger, they will ask for the forearm; if you give them the forearm, they will ask for the arm, and when you give them the arm, they will chop off your head."

<>

Castro's fears about the Sandinistas turned out to be prophetic. On election day, while virtually all independent polls were forecasting a Sandinista victory, Ortega suffered a devastating upset. Opposition presidential candidate Violeta Chamorro won a stunning 55 percent of the vote; only 41 percent went to the Sandinista Front. Pollsters scrambled for explanations. A crushed Ortega, his tearful wife holding his hand, conceded defeat in a nationally televised speech early the next morning.

In Havana, there was a long official silence over the results of the Nicaraguan elections. The first reaction to the Sandinista defeat came in a *Granma* article two days later. The story, reflecting Castro's views, blamed the election results on Nicaragua's catastrophic economic crisis and the pressures from the U.S.-backed Contra war. Nicaraguans had voted for Chamorro in the belief that a Sandinista defeat would mean the end of the war, and would move the United States to lift its trade embargo, the article said.

Cuba had lost its closest ideological ally in Latin America. Within days after the Sandinista defeat, Castro ordered a gradual withdrawal of the more than a thousand Cuban internationalist workers and advisers still based in Nicaragua.

Among the first to go were the military advisers. About 160 Cuban military men and their families boarded two Cubana de Aviación flights to Havana on March 23, 1990. In previous departures of Cuban military personnel, there had always been an official farewell ceremony. The Sandinista military high command would gather, the national anthems of Nicaragua and Cuba would be sung, medals would be awarded. Emotional speeches would follow. Nothing like that happened on that occasion. Sandinista army Brigadier General Cuadra drove alone to the Cuban compound in Managua's Monte Tabor neighborhood on the eve of the Cubans' departure, and casually bade them farewell.

"The Cubans left overnight, abruptly, almost through the back door," recalled Nicaraguan air force chief Col. Javier Pichardo Ramirez, who had attended various farewell ceremonies for the Cubans in previous years. "I didn't find out about their departure until a few days later."

A major chapter in Cuba's military presence abroad had come to an abrupt end.

<>

Almost simultaneously, Cuba was closing its fifteen-year military involvement in Angola. Under a bilateral agreement signed in New York in December 1988 with the endorsement of the United States and the Soviet Union, Cuba began to withdraw thousands of soldiers from the Marxist-ruled African country in early 1989. The Angola accord called for the withdrawal of fifty thousand Cuban troops from that country by July 1, 1991.

At first, the Castro regime billed the Angola accord as a major triumph for the Cuban revolution. The international settlement also called for the independence of South Africa–ruled Namibia, long used as a haven by anti-Communist Angolan rebels. Cuba boasted that its presence in Angola had helped bring about the independence of Namibia.

But it soon became clear that Angola's Marxist President José

Eduardo Dos Santos had little support at home, and was under growing pressure to come to terms with the rebels. Months later, Dos Santos would begin secret negotiations with U.S.-backed guerrilla leader Jonas Savimbi. Back in Havana, many began to ask themselves—as the late Div. Gen. Arnaldo Ochoa had done a few years earlier—whether thousands of Cuban soldiers in Angola had not died in vain.

<>

By early 1990, Castro found himself abandoned by his closest allies. In Panama, Gen. Manuel A. Noriega had been replaced by U.S.-installed President Guillermo Endara. In Nicaragua, Ortega had been voted out of power. Angola's once-radical regime of President Eduardo Dos Santos was preparing to call free elections, and analysts were giving Savimbi a good chance of winning.

More ominously, the Soviet bloc was crumbling. The Berlin wall had already fallen. Critics of Cuba's Stalinist rule were beginning to be heard within the Soviet Union, by far Cuba's largest economic benefactor. Soviet publications such as *Moscow News* and *Izvestia* were beginning to question the Kremlin's $3 billion-a-year subsidies to the tropical island at a time of widespread food shortages at home. The Soviets were openly saying they would have to revise their terms of trade with Cuba, and that Castro would have to begin paying part of his Soviet oil imports in hard currency.

On March 6, 1990, shortly after 8 P.M., American diplomats and a small group of Cuban exiles exploded in cheers as the United Nations Human Rights Commission in Geneva, Switzerland, voted for the first time in favor of a U.S.-sponsored resolution to investigate human rights abuses in Cuba. The news that most shocked Castro, however, was how the American diplomatic victory had come about: Czechoslovakia and Poland had cosponsored the U.S. resolution. Hungary and Bulgaria had been among its backers. Major Latin American countries such as Argentina, Brazil and Colombia, which in the past had blocked U.S. attempts to investigate the Castro regime's human rights abuses, had abstained this time. In the end, the U.S. proposal had won by 19 to 12 votes, with 12 abstentions.

When Castro made his next public appearance two days later at a long-scheduled speech at the Fifth Congress of the Federation of Cuban Women, he was fuming. Castro started out in a low, weary voice, listing the advances made by Cuban women since the revolution. About an hour into his speech, his voice in a continuous crescendo, he addressed the latest events in Panama, Nicaragua, and Geneva.

"At this time, when the imperialists threaten other Latin American countries . . . when they threaten to intervene anywhere . . . Poland and Czechoslovakia cosponsor the document! Bulgaria and Hungary, members of the [U.N. Human Rights] Commission, vote against Cuba!" he shouted, pounding the podium with his fist. "They are feeding the imperialists' triumphalism, the imperialists' warmongering, giving the imperialists justification and excuses to be more aggressive against our country!

"That is why one day, if one day they dare to invade our country . . . those countries—governments that until yesterday were part of the Socialist bloc—will also be responsible for the blood that is shed here. The blood will also fall on Poland and Czechoslovakia. . . . And it will fall on Hungary and Bulgaria. . . . It will fall on their leaders, their governments, which have been capable of writing such a vile page in history."

Fidel's tantrum didn't end there. Later in his speech, he lashed out against the products that Cuba imported from Eastern European countries—the same goods he had long praised as wonders of Socialist technology and international solidarity. By now, he was raising his hands wildly, pointing his index finger high in the air, and pounding his fist on the podium in increasing rage.

"We are the only ones who buy those Bulgarian forklifts!" he shouted. "They are such worthless things and have so many problems that we are the only ones who buy them. . . . The Hungarian buses travel six kilometers on a gallon of fuel. They fill the city with smog. They poison everybody. We could get the data: We could get statistics about the number of people killed by Hungarian buses!"

Over the next few months, Castro repeated his tirades against his former Socialist allies again and again. He was like a betrayed lover unable to get over a broken affair. Worried and bitter, Castro had lost the near majestic self-confidence he displayed a few years earlier. He had become the odd man out.

But an even bigger shock to the Cuban regime would come later in 1990, when the magnitude of the Soviet retrenchment from Cuba began to make itself apparent. Few in Castro's inner circle would have ever imagined that their longtime Soviet benefactors would reduce their presence in Cuba so much, so soon. It just hadn't seemed possible.

7

The "Bolos" (Soviets) Pack Up

◄◄◄◄◄ It would be an unforgettable scene for the more than one thousand Soviet schoolchildren gathering at the basketball court of Havana's Soviet School. The mostly blond, blue-eyed children had just walked down from the classrooms on the building's second floor. In class, they had marked the occasion with chocolate cake and cold tea. Now, the whole school was assembling in the main patio to give more than two hundred Soviet students a formal farewell ceremony. They were going home.

Standing firm in their white uniforms, the children faced the convent-like building, which had once served as an Ursuline nuns' school before Fidel Castro presented it to the Soviets in the heyday of Cuban-Soviet relations.

Principal Vyacheslav Sholok, the stern-looking man directing the ceremony, made a sign with his head. The music teacher stepped forward, raised her hand, and the entire school took up the strains of "Gosudarstvenny Gymn," the Soviet Union's state anthem. Afterward, a chorus of thirty sang the popular songs "Katiusha" and "Moscow Nights." Girls, with flower garlands around their necks, performed a folk dance. A grammar teacher made a short farewell speech.

Finally, Sholok asked all the departing children to step forward.

They were to receive a souvenir from their classmates and teachers remaining in Cuba. The more than two hundred came forward, their faces showing a mixture of excitement and fear. Each was given a flower. Dozens in the audience—teachers and students—had begun to cry.

It was near the end of the 1990 school year, and hundreds of Soviet technicians and their families were being sent home. Others were being advised that they would have to start packing soon: the Kremlin was scaling down its massive subsidies to Cuba. The Soviet School's ceremony would be only the first of many farewell parties throughout Cuba over the next few months.

<>

By 1989, there were more than twelve thousand Soviet technicians and military support personnel in Cuba; with their families, they made up the largest foreign group in Cuba. Most of them were happy to be there. It wasn't just the sun. It was a privileged life.

The Soviet Union was suffering from food shortages and mounting political turmoil as it inched toward a market economy. In Cuba, the Soviets had nothing to worry about. They had access to the Diplotienda supermarkets, where they could buy food and American and Western European goods that they couldn't dream of purchasing at home. Even money wasn't much of a problem.

Ever since Perestroika, the technicians were making a fortune by Soviet standards, because they were earning salaries in dollars. About half their monthly wage was deposited in rubles at home. They received $100 in U.S. currency plus 500 Cuban pesos (another $100 at the black market rate) a month if their programs were sponsored by Cuba, and $200 in U.S. currency plus 650 Cuban pesos (another $130 at the black market rate) if their contracts were sponsored by the Soviet Union. It was much more than they could possibly spend: their rent, telephone, water, electricity and health care bills were taken care of by the Cuban government. Their spouses often generated a sizable extra income by playing the *speculatzia* game—purchasing goods at the foreigners-only stores and reselling them at a profit in their Cuban neighborhoods.

Most of the nearly 5,000 technicians on the island were engineers, chemists or economists working at Soviet-financed projects such as the Karl Marx concrete factory, the Cienfuegos nuclear plant and oil refineries, steel mills and nickel plants scattered throughout the island. Hundreds of other technicians were in Cuba to service the

Soviet-made cars, and the tractors and industrial equipment that Cuba imported almost exclusively from the Soviet bloc. Of the estimated 7,700 Soviet military based in Cuba, 2,800 were part of the Soviet combat brigade in Santiago de las Vegas, about ten miles south of Havana; 2,600 were technicians assigned to the Soviet-run Lourdes electronic intelligence gathering post in El Chico, on the outskirts of Havana; 1,500 were military advisers attached to more than a dozen Cuban military facilities, and the remaining 800 were civilian technical advisers.

The Soviets had their own restaurants, social clubs and sports facilities. In Havana, most lived in the downtown Focsa skyscraper, the waterfront Sierra Maestra Hotel, or at houses in the residential Reparto Kohly neighborhood. Each Soviet institution had its own social club. The military would gather at the club La Amistad, while members of the commercial office and the Soviet embassy would have their own clubs. They lived a secluded life in Cuba. Despite three decades of government rhetoric about the eternal brotherhood between the Soviet and Cuban peoples, the two didn't mix.

<>

Not knowing much about Soviet life in Cuba, I was surprised to learn of this apparent segregation. To satisfy my curiosity, I went to the huge Soviet School in Miramar where the farewell ceremony for the departing Soviet students had taken place a few months earlier, and asked to talk to the principal.

The employee at the front door, a plump, middle-aged woman, didn't understand me. I tried Spanish, German, and English, to no avail. She asked me to wait, and came back with a Russian interpreter. Thirty minutes later, I was sitting in principal Sholok's office.

I was lucky that the interpreter happened to be there that day, for Mr. Sholok didn't speak a word of Spanish. I soon learned that he was no exception: the school had seventy teachers, all of them Soviets, of which only one—the translator sitting at my side—happened to speak Spanish. The school's cooks, maids, maintenance staff, physician, nurse, switchboard operator, and car mechanic were all on assignment from the Soviet Union. None of the support staff could communicate in Spanish, either.

"It makes things easier," principal Sholok explained to me, when I expressed my surprise at not seeing any Cubans around. "It's easier to work with one's own people than with foreigners."

He took me on a tour of the former Catholic school. As we crossed the patio, he showed me the tomb with a stone cross where three prominent Catholic bishops were buried, squeezed between the basketball and volleyball courts. He did not know their names, but they had been very famous, he said. A handful of students were shooting baskets a few yards away. Every now and then, a stray ball would hit the bishops' tomb. Mr. Sholok's interpreter, detecting a smile in my eyes, assured me that the graves were being maintained with great care.

We walked through the school's second-floor corridors, under the building's big Gothic windows. Mr. Sholok invited me into a junior-high biology class in progress. The students, about thirty boys and girls in blue and white uniforms, stood up as the principal opened the door. Mr. Sholok introduced me to them. I was an Amerikansky journalist visiting the school, he said. The kids looked at me with curiosity, nodded, and sat down at a sign from the teacher. The class went on. When the principal asked me a few minutes later if I wanted to put any questions to the class, I asked, "How many of you speak Spanish?"

Of the thirty students, only one raised his hand. He was a light-skinned black boy, with curly hair—one of the few in the room that wasn't blond. He was the son of a Soviet technician and a Cuban woman. He had learned Spanish at home.

"Very few take Spanish," principal Sholok explained to me. "The vast majority study English."

Except for the one boy, the rest of the children had lived in Cuba for several years, and didn't speak a word of the language. Hadn't they ever played with a Cuban kid? I knew that Soviet diplomats lived in secluded compounds in the United States and other supposedly hostile Western countries. But in Cuba?

As I was getting into my rental car and ready to leave, a crowd of students rushed into the street. The bell had just rung and school was over. I recognized the black boy I had met in the biology class, and waved him over. After asking him for directions, I asked how his Soviet classmates communicated with their Cuban friends.

"I don't know, I don't mix with the Soviets very much," the boy shrugged. "The only ones who speak Spanish are the Czechs and the Hungarians, but most of them are gone by now. The Soviets hang out with each other."

<>

Perhaps nowhere did the Soviets live in greater isolation than in Cuba's interior, where thousands of them worked on major energy and manufacturing projects. In Cienfuegos, where nearly two thousand Soviets were stationed to help run the Soviet-built nuclear plant and a huge Soviet-financed oil refinery, there was virtually no contact between the foreign technicians and the local population. At the refinery, the Soviets had their special restaurant; Cubans were not admitted. Cuban managers and technicians ate at the Cubans' cafeteria, together with the rest of the workers.

At their homes in Cienfuegos, it was as if the Soviets had transplanted a section of Moscow to the tropics. They lived in a four-square-block section of Reparto Pastorita, a tree-lined neighborhood on the outskirts of the city. There were four all-Soviet apartment buildings there, each of them eight stories high. One building was for Soviet singles, another for young married couples, and a third one for senior managers. Next to one of the buildings was the Technomarket, a supermarket exclusively for Soviet technicians, filled with foodstuffs that were not available on the street. Not far away was the Technostore, a shop selling clothes and electronic goods that was also exclusively for the Soviet advisers. In both stores, they could pay in dollar- denominated coupons, which they received at work as part of their salary.

Behind the apartment buildings was the Soviet-Cuban Friendship Club. It was one of the best-equipped sports clubs I have ever seen. There was an Olympic swimming pool, a sauna room, several tennis and basketball courts, a huge soccer field, a restaurant and two bars. At one side of a big building was a wing with ten classrooms for summer camp. Inside the main building was a 300-seat auditorium, with a modern stage made of fine woods. In the back of the room, a mural covered the entire wall. It was a picture of the Kremlin.

When I visited the club on a hot summer afternoon, the place was almost dead. Only two Soviet girls were playing in the huge Olympic pool. The tennis courts, soccer field, bars and restaurant were empty. The club's new Cuban administrator explained to me that most of the Soviets had left Cienfuegos in recent months. There was virtually no activity now. The Cuban government had appointed him to replace the Soviet manager who had run the club until then, and who had left a few weeks earlier. The club was about to be opened for Cuban workers from the nuclear plant and the refinery, while continuing to serve the Soviets remaining in the city. It was only then that it dawned on me that the Soviet-Cuban Friendship Club had been closed to Cubans until then.

As I walked through the club's various facilities, I knew any visiting Cuban would feel as lost as I felt. Once you entered the place and left the big Spanish banner behind at the main entrance, you would not find one single sign written in the Roman alphabet. All indications leading to rest rooms, sports facilities and restaurants were written in Russian, as were the swimming pool safety rules and tennis-lessons schedules on the walls. The restaurant's menu had no Spanish translation.

It was a major problem for the new Cuban administrator. The man raised his hands in desperation as he showed me a Russian-language instruction sheet on the back of the sauna room's entrance door. He was supposed to maintain the sauna room, yet he couldn't even read the instructions. The Soviet administrator had left without explaining the maintenance procedures to him, and he had not a clue as to what to do.

"In Cuba, we don't even know what a sauna is," he told me, half-amused at the very idea of somebody wanting to get a good sweat going. "This is a tropical country. If you want to sweat, you just go outside."

In 1990, the Soviet technicians quietly began to leave Cuba as the cash-starved Soviet Union decided not to renew their contracts. At least twelve hundred Soviet technicians and their families left that year, according to Soviet embassy estimates. At first, their departure went unnoticed. Only in the tightly knit community of the Soviet School in Havana or the Soviet-Cuban Club in Cienfuegos were there symptoms of an impending Soviet exodus from Cuba.

As the numbers of Soviets leaving the island grew, Cuban house-wives suddenly found themselves without their longtime black-market food suppliers. One Cuban woman, the mother of a Cuban academic I visited, told me she used to buy ten packages of canned meat a month from a Soviet woman in the neighborhood, to distribute among her four children.

"I don't know what I'm going to do now," the professor's mother lamented. "The Soviet woman is leaving. We have to find some other foreigner who can get us the meat . . ." The massive Soviet pullback would soon leave its mark on all aspects of daily life.

The Soviet Union was Cuba's economic lifeline. More than 90 percent of the island's oil consumption was supplied by the Soviets under heavily subsidized oil-for-sugar agreements. Until 1990, the Soviets shipped thirteen million tons of oil a year to Cuba, slightly more than what the island needed. The Castro government sold the excess on the world market to earn up to $500 million a year in much-needed cash. In all, Soviet subsidies to Cuba amounted to more than $3 billion a year.

Much of Cuba's basic foodstuffs came from the Soviet Union and other Eastern bloc countries under subsidized barter deals, most of them involving Cuban sugar. All of Cuba's bread was made out of Soviet wheat, for instance. According to Cuban Foreign Trade Ministry estimates, Cuba in 1989 depended on the Soviet bloc for 100 percent of its wheat consumption, 100 percent of its vegetable cooking oil, 100 percent of its soybeans, 63 percent of its powdered milk, and 40 percent of its rice. About 40 percent of all the island's food was imported from Soviet bloc countries.

When it came to raw materials, fertilizers, industrial equipment, or spare parts, it wasn't any different. The Soviets operated about four hundred major public works in Cuba, including the Cienfuegos nuclear plant, oil refineries, steel mills, sugar refineries, and nickel plants throughout the island. Soviet-built factories accounted for 80 percent of the island's steel, 50 percent of its fertilizers, and 50 percent of its mechanical industry production. These factories, most of them gigantic facilities, were almost entirely reliant on Soviet equipment and spare parts.

Consumer goods such as cars, refrigerators, television sets and radios, were mostly from the Soviet Union. On Havana's streets, all but the tourist rental cars were Soviet-made Lada or Moskvitch cars. Cubans had no choice but to buy Soviet television sets or portable radios, although they were terribly out of date compared with what Cubans could see in Western movies or in the magazines tourists would bring to the island.

In all, more than 70 percent of Cuba's worldwide foreign trade in 1989 was with the Soviet Union, while another 17 percent was with other Soviet bloc countries. Only 13 percent of the island's commerce was with the West.

It hadn't always been like that. Until the mid-1970s, the Castro revolution's commercial transactions with the West had accounted for more than 40 percent of the island's foreign trade. But in 1976, Castro joined the Soviet bloc's Council on Mutual Economic Assistance (COMECON) economic community in an effort to reverse Cuba's economic troubles. As part of COMECON, Cuba became a cog in the Socialist world's system of trade. Cuba's role would be to supply the Soviet Union and Eastern European countries with sugar, nickel, citrus, tobacco and rum. If they delivered on their part of the bargain, they wouldn't have to worry about the rest. The Soviet bloc would take care of them.

Soviet technicians, who had been coming to Cuba in relatively small numbers since the early sixties, began arriving by the thousands to build the huge sugar and steel mills geared to supply COMECON members. The Castro regime erected apartment buildings and sports clubs for the visiting technicians and their families near Soviet-sponsored public works. By the late seventies, there were large Soviet communities in Havana, Cienfuegos and Santiago.

To adapt to the bloc's economic alliance, Castro turned the Cuban bureaucracy upside down. A new Cuban government structure was set up to mirror the Soviet Union's institutions, with which Cuba would now have to deal on a daily basis. The new entities were to negotiate five-year trade and cooperation plans with their counterparts from other COMECON nations. Castro created a Soviet-like Council of State, which would be the highest government institution, a Soviet-like Council of Ministers, and dozens of parallel Institutes, Committees and Academies.

Many of the new institutions duplicated the work of existing ministries, or of other newly created entities. It was hard to tell the difference between the State Committee for Science and Technology and the Academy of Sciences, each of which was given a giant building and a staff of thousands. The Cuban government's administrative bureaucracy grew from 2 percent of the work force in 1973 to more than 7 percent in 1985.

By the late 1980s, as Eastern Europe was reneging on Marxism and the Soviet Union was shifting to a market economy, Castro was confronted with the worst possible scenario. Cuba had given up its previous economic policies aimed at self-sufficiency in favor of Soviet bloc oil and food supply commitments that were now being cut. Most members of the COMECON agreement were beginning to question the group's very existence. Cuba's former Socialist allies were pulling the rug out from under the island's economy.

<>

The much-publicized visit by Soviet President Mikhail Gorbachev to Cuba on April 2, 1989, marked the beginning of the Soviet Union's economic retrenchment from Cuba. But one couldn't have told it from the two leaders' public statements.

Gorbachev's three-day visit was a long-awaited event. It was the first trip to Latin America by the reformist leader and the first to Cuba by any Soviet leader since Leonid Brezhnev's trip in 1974. There was widespread speculation that Gorbachev would press Castro to embark on major political and economic reforms. Gorbachev's visits to Eastern European countries had been followed by the collapse of their Communist regimes. Would the same thing happen in Cuba?

More than a thousand journalists from around the world, including two hundred television anchors and producers, had arrived in Cuba for the occasion. Downtown Havana was flooded by newspeople, all too recognizable by their camouflage shirts and multipocket slacks, with their cameras, laptop computers and portable telephone systems in tow.

The blue-and-white Aeroflot jetliner landed at 6 P.M. that Sunday at the José Martí International Airport. The late afternoon sun had just emerged after a brief but heavy shower. Fidel Castro, at the time sixty-three, and wearing his usual olive green military fatigues, welcomed the fifty-eight-year-old Gorbachev—clad in a gray business suit—with a warm embrace. It was a strange scene, as if the roles had reversed: for the first time, Cubans saw an aging Castro greeting a younger, more dynamic Soviet leader.

After a military band played the two countries' national anthems, and an honor guard fired a twenty-one-gun salute, the two leaders climbed into an open car with Cuban and Soviet flags flying on the hood. Their motorcade's fifteen-mile trek to the city was cheered by more than half a million people. A smiling Castro talked animatedly and almost continuously with his guest, pointing at a building here, a "Viva Gorbachev" there.

Gorbachev and Castro carried out a hectic schedule over the next two days. They laid a wreath at the monument of José Martí at the Plaza de la Revolución, held a similar ceremony at the Lenin monument in Havana's Lenin Park, toured the Biotechnology Center and visited various medical centers. Through it all, the presidents spoke about the "unbreakable friendship" between the two countries, and posed before reporters clasping their hands in the air like triumphant prizefighters. In his speeches, Gorbachev emphasized the right of each Communist country to interpret socialism in its own way—making it clear that he was not pressuring Castro into adopting his Glasnost policies.*

At the opening night reception for Gorbachev in the marble hall of the Palace of the Revolution, the two stood together greeting a long line of special guests. Novelist García Márquez was among the many foreign dignitaries in the queue. When Gorbachev spotted him about four places away from the beginning of the line—the two had met briefly in Moscow shortly before—the Soviet leader waved his hand and smiled. As García Márquez walked over, Castro turned to the Soviet leader, grabbed his arm, pointed at the writer, and said jokingly:

"That guy over there is coming to demand his book royalties in the Soviet Union."

Gorbachev laughed and extended a warm handshake to the novelist. Then, turning to García Márquez, Fidel added, "I'm trying to get the Soviet Union to pay you royalties for your books. You'll have to pay me a commission for this."

"Mr. President," García Márquez said to Gorbachev, continuing the joke. "I would be happy to pay a commission to you if you could convince him [Castro] to have Cuba pay all the royalties it owes me."

The three men celebrated the exchange. To his great relief, Castro was hitting it off with Gorbachev.

The two leaders had had little personal contact before. Relations between them had been formal and somewhat cold, insiders say. They had met briefly during Castro's 1984 trip to Moscow for the funeral of Soviet Premier Yuri V. Andropov, but during that visit, Castro was busy trying to meet the men surrounding new Soviet Party leader Konstantin U. Chernenko. Few suspected Gorbachev would rise to power one year later.

Following Chernenko's death and Gorbachev's appointment as new Communist Party secretary general in March 1985, Castro had called the new leader to congratulate him. Late that year, Gorbachev had made his first telephone call to Havana, to ask Castro if Cuba needed any extra help in the aftermath of a devastating hurricane that

---

* *In his address to Cuba's National Assembly, Gorbachev did say that the Soviet Union was "against any theories or doctrines that justify exporting revolution," but the jab at Castro's internationalist policies was overshadowed by his repeated assurances that the Kremlin would not put pressure on Cuba to embark on a political opening.*

had just swept the island. The conversations had been short and to the point.

In private, Castro was already expressing his misgivings about Gorbachev's planned reforms. To Latin American and European diplomats, he expressed his concern that Gorbachev's Perestroika economic reform policies would lead the Soviet Union to political and economic chaos. In public, Castro praised Gorbachev as a "modern" and "brilliant" world leader. It was flattery bred from necessity.

Castro and Gorbachev's first lengthy meeting had been in March 1986, during Castro's visit to Moscow for the Twenty-seventh Communist Party Congress. Gorbachev, busy with his party's internal politics, had little time for Castro during the proceedings. So he invited Fidel to chat with him in the Kremlin on a Sunday afternoon, which happened to be the Soviet leader's birthday. Despite the weekend atmosphere, the three-hour talk was strictly business.

Now, three years and several telephone conversations later, there was a semblance of personal chemistry between the two heads of state. Everything seemed to bode well for the Cuban leader.

<>

While going out of his way to charm his prominent guest, Castro was determined to show the world that it was he who was in command of the situation. At one of their largest news conferences, when a Moscow-based reporter for the Spanish news agency EFE asked Gorbachev if he intended to collaborate with President Bush on the Central American crisis, Castro broke into the questioning and prevented the surprised Soviet leader from answering.

Castro scolded the reporter, saying her question violated the dignity of small countries and assumed that the United States had rights to dictate its will in Latin America. The Soviet leader, seemingly embarrassed, made a move with his hand in an apparent effort to intervene. Castro continued talking, not noticing—or pretending not to notice—the gesture.

"It wasn't very tactful on Fidel's side," recalls Yuri Pavlov, the Soviet Ministry Latin American Department director, who was accompanying Gorbachev. "We pretended we hadn't seen anything."

At another evening reception, as the two leaders shook hands with guests, American TV news anchormen Peter Jennings, Dan Rather and Tom Brokaw stopped them to ask questions. But before they could get anything out, Castro began berating them for their handling of previous interviews.

"I give you hours and hours of interviews and you always chop them up into a few minutes on the air. You get rich and I don't get paid. I should start charging for them," Castro said, as he walked away, inviting Gorbachev to shake hands with other guests.

The next morning, when Gorbachev was to address the National Assembly, Fidel Castro rose first to make a few unscheduled introductory remarks. He spoke for forty-five minutes. He was determined not to be upstaged by the Soviet leader.

<><>

But while everything seemed to indicate that Castro had managed to turn Gorbachev's visit into a success for Cuba, behind-the-scenes talks between the Soviet leader's top aides and Cuban officials were pointing to turbulent times.

On the afternoon of Monday, April 3, as Gorbachev and Castro were touring the city, Soviet Vice-President Vladimir M. Kamentsev sat down with his Cuban counterpart Carlos Rafael Rodriguez to discuss the upcoming five-year economic agreement between the two countries. It was a formal setting: Kamentsev's six-man Soviet delegation and Rodriguez's six-member staff faced one another across a massive conference table rigged especially for the occasion. All men sported suits and ties—a Cuban concession to Soviet protocol.

As soon as the talks began, the Soviet side made it clear that there would have to be a major revision of their economic ties. The Soviet Union wanted Cuba to begin paying for Soviet goods in dollars. Subsidies had to be reduced. The trade imbalance had to be narrowed. A delegation would be sent to Cuba soon to discuss details.

The Soviet notice came just as Cuba was receiving the first threats from other COMECON members; unless Cuba paid more—and in U.S. dollars—their shipments would be canceled. Hungary had just given Cuba an ultimatum: if the Cubans didn't pay 20 percent more than the previous year for the Ikarus buses assembled on the island, and 40 percent more for them over the next five years, the contract would be rescinded.

It was an unprecedented demand among Soviet bloc members, which until then were doing all their trade on a barter basis protected under five-year plans. Given the sorry state of Cuba's bus fleet, the Castro regime had to accept a six-month contract under the new terms. Now, Cuban officials viewed the events with a rising sense of panic. Were the Soviets serious about their demands that Cuba pay for Soviet goods in dollars?

Publicly, Gorbachev made only a passing reference to Moscow's new toughness. In his address to the National Assembly, he stated that Soviet-Cuban economic ties should "become more dynamic, more efficient, and render better results to our two countries." The line was buried in a speech in which the visiting leader told the world that Moscow would not impose its political reforms on Cuba. But Cuban officials understood the message clearly. Gorbachev, unlike more liberal Party leaders in Moscow, did not dislike Castro, but the process of economic reforms he had unleashed in the Soviet Union was bound to hurt Cuba. The party was over.

<><>

Within months after Gorbachev's visit, officials at the 100-member Cuban commercial office in Moscow began to feel the pinch of the new Soviet trade policies. The Cubans were told that Gosplan, the Soviet Union's central planning office, was no longer authorized to negotiate international trade agreements on behalf of Soviet firms. Hundreds of Soviet enterprises had been declared autonomous, and would conduct their own foreign trade operations independently. From now on, Cuba would have to deal with each of these companies separately.

The first shock to the Cubans came when they tried to claim their annual shipment of 108,000 Soviet home refrigerators. When Cuban officials knocked on the doors of the Gosplan office in Moscow to make shipping arrangements—as they had for years—they were referred to the Atlant refrigerator factory in the city of Minsk. In fact, that factory had long been the sole supplier of refrigerators to Cuba, but its managers had never seen their Cuban buyers face to face. All contracts had been signed in Moscow between government officials.

The day the delegation of Cuban trade officials showed up in Minsk to renew the refrigerator contract, it was told by Atlant managers that the firm would be delighted to continue its trade relations with Cuba—but only if the Cubans paid in dollars.

"Our people protested, saying they had signed an agreement with the Soviet government guaranteeing the supply of refrigerators," said Ramón Gonzalez Vergara, at the time Cuba's ambassador to the Soviet-Cuban Council for Mutual Economic Assistance in Moscow. "The factory manager said, 'I'm sorry, but that doesn't mean anything anymore.' The Cubans returned to Moscow empty-handed."

News of the Minsk case spread rapidly within the Cuban trade bureaucracy. Asked for explanations, the delegation that had traveled to Minsk could offer little but expressions of frustration.

The second eye-opener came shortly thereafter, when the Cu-

bans were notified that they would not receive 128,500 Soviet washing machines that were scheduled to be delivered under the ongoing
five-year trade agreement. This time, the Aurica washing machine
factory in Kishinev, the Moldavian capital, had sent a telex to the
Cuban trade office in Moscow advising that the models it had long
shipped to Cuba were being discontinued.

The factory had entered a joint venture with an Italian firm to
produce a new model, the fully automatic Aurica 110, the telex said.
The Aurica management was sorry to inform them that it would have
to cancel the contract with Cuba because the new Italian-Soviet model
was "not suitable" for Cuba's tropical climate.

"It was their way of saying they would no longer accept rubles or
Cuban goods as a form of payment," said a Soviet trade official in
Havana who was close to the case. "Soviet companies are looking for
any excuse to get their foreign clients to pay in dollars."

◄►

Fidel Castro looked into the television camera with an air of scorn. It
was January 1990 and he was speaking to the Cuban people about the
forty-fifth conference of COMECON countries that had just ended in
Sofia, the Bulgarian capital.

"It used to be customary in COMECON meetings to call those in
attendance 'comrades,' " he lamented. "Now the word 'comrade' has
been abolished by a few members. Others do not even call them
'comrades,' they call them 'gentlemen,' and 'ladies,' or 'miss' . . . as
if there were one [gentleman or lady] there. . . ."

Fidel had good reason to be outraged. The two-day COMECON
meeting had approved radical changes. From now on, the entire ten-
country Soviet bloc trading association would officially adopt the hard-
currency trade transaction mode that had been pioneered by some of
its members. COMECON was adopting the standards of the capitalist
world's international trade community.

The move was hitting Cuba especially hard: the Cuban peso was
not convertible into Western currencies, and Cuban exports to
COMECON countries—largely sugar and citrus—were much cheaper
than the imported goods for which Cuba would now have to pay in
dollars. Cuba needed a waiver from the new rules—urgently.

Cuban Vice-President Rodriguez, who led the Cuban delegation
to the COMECON meeting, pulled Soviet Prime Minister Nikolai
Ryzhkov aside at the end of the session. Rodriguez, seventy-six, an
old Communist Party boss who had been Castro's troubleshooter with

Moscow since the early days of the Cuban revolution, asked Ryzhkov for a chance to meet privately.

The two men sat together on a couch outside the auditorium. The Cuban argued for a grace period. Cuba was a special case; it had a special relationship with the Soviet Union, he said. The Kremlin could not abruptly cut off three decades of cooperation. A gradual approach to the changes was needed.

With a wave of his hand and two consecutive nods, Ryzhkov gave the Cuban representative the guarantee he sought. The Cubans returned home deeply worried, nevertheless.

"A forty-year period comes to an end," Bulgarian Prime Minister Georgi Atanassov told reporters at the end of the conference. "This meeting marks a new beginning."

◄►

Gorbachev's first envoy to discuss new economic terms with the Cubans arrived in Havana on April 13th, 1990. He was Leonid Abalkin, the deputy chairman of the Soviet Union's Council of Ministers, a reformist economist who was known to favor a drastic cut in aid to Cuba. Abalkin's first statements as he emerged from his Aeroflot flight at Havana's José Martí airport sounded ominous. "Our relations must be built on the basis of reciprocity," he told reporters.

In Moscow, the Soviet press and several deputies in Congress had begun to openly question the Soviet Union's subsidies to Cuba. The first all-out attack on the Castro regime had been published by the independent liberal weekly *Moscow News* a month earlier. Correspondent Vladimir Orlov, poking fun at Castro's criticism of changes in the Soviet Union and Eastern Europe, wrote that the Cuban leader aimed "to take on the role of a wise man who alone knows the true path." The story told about widespread political repression in Cuba, noted growing opposition to the Castro regime among the population, and ended with a call to support Cuban dissidents in their request for a referendum in Cuba.

The article opened the doors for a blunt public discussion on Soviet aid to Cuba—an issue that had been taboo in the Soviet press over the past three decades. Conservative and liberal papers and radio stations engaged in a bitter fight over the Cuban aid issue.

The battle lines were clearly drawn. Reform-minded economists, worried about the Soviet Union's giant public deficit, called publicly for a cut in subsidies to Cuba. On the other hand, conservative politicians, leaders of the KGB and the armed forces, were determined not to lose one of the Soviet Union's most strategic bases abroad. They resisted any drastic retrenchment in Cuba.

Orthodox Marxists at the Kremlin, shocked by the fall of Eastern Europe, saw Cuba as one of the last remaining symbols of the Soviet Union's status as a superpower. The Soviet military argued that Cuba was essential for maintaining the Lourdes intelligence-gathering base, servicing Soviet submarines, and to keep an air base for Soviet reconnaissance planes in the Americas. They portrayed Cuba as a huge Soviet aircraft carrier sitting at the doorstep of the United States. In wartime, U.S. navy ships would have to pass it on their way to Europe.

But Abalkin, a prominent academician suddenly propelled into diplomacy, mellowed his line substantially during his stay in Cuba. Fidel Castro gave him the royal treatment. The Cuban leader never left the Soviet's side, going all-out to convince him that Cuba had impressive economic potential—and a lot to offer the Soviet Union.

Castro accompanied Abalkin to the clinic he had offered for the treatment of up to ten thousand Soviet children, victims of the Chernobyl nuclear plant accident. Among other places, they toured nickel plants, steel mills, oil refineries, and the construction site for the 1991 Pan American games. Wherever Abalkin went, he would find workers in feverish activity. Plant managers would explain they were working fourteen-hour shifts, of their own will, in response to Fidel's call to help the revolution in times of need.

Abalkin's week-long visit ended with the signing of a one-year bilateral trade protocol for 1990 that was much better than the Cubans had expected. It called for a continuation of Soviet shipments of grain, raw materials, equipment and spare parts at existing levels, and for a slight increase in Cuban medicine and biotechnology exports to the Soviet Union. A proud Castro was able to announce an 8.7 percent increase in the volume of the $14 billion bilateral trade pact.

"Abalkin came preceded by a reputation that he wanted to put an end to the Soviet Union's trade relations with Cuba, to cut Soviet aid to Cuba," remembers Cuba's Vice Minister of Foreign Trade Miguel Angel Castillo. "When he arrived, he discovered that Cuba was capable of exporting biotechnology, medicine, tourism, etc. He changed his mind. When he returned home, he became one of the most vocal supporters of a continuation of trade ties with Cuba."

In Moscow, they saw things differently. On his return, Abalkin came under fire in the Soviet Congress. He had "surrendered to his [Cuban] partners all the positions that had already been won," *Izvestia* commented.

"Fidel charmed him," recalls Yuri Pavlov, who was the Soviet Foreign Ministry's Latin American Department director at the time. "The agreement Abalkin came back with was seen by us as unrealistic. We could not deliver that much, that soon."

<>

Cuba had won a one-year respite. But it would be its last. In early June 1990, a new Soviet delegation headed by Soviet Foreign Trade Minister Konstantin Katushev arrived in Havana to begin discussions for the upcoming 1991–1996 five-year plan. Katushev, a senior Party apparatchik, was an old Cuba hand at the Kremlin. He had been Moscow's ambassador to Cuba, and had in recent years followed Soviet-Cuban trade relations closely from the Trade Ministry in Moscow.

When Katushev sat down with Cuban Foreign Trade Minister Ricardo Cabrisas, he delivered a dire message: there would most likely not be a five-year plan. Because of political uncertainty at home, the Soviet Union would only negotiate a one-year trade agreement for 1991.

Also, the new trade agreement would begin phasing out barter trade and demanding cash payment for Soviet goods. Finally, Cuba would have to begin paying for part of the freight costs of Soviet shipments to Cuba.

"Right now, a fifth of our merchant marine fleet does nothing but bring Soviet goods to Cuba," Katushev told the Cuban trade minister. "Hundreds of our ships are tied up because of this. You need to start paying for this service as soon as possible."

For the next six months, half a dozen Cuban-Soviet trade commissions met alternately in Havana and Moscow to negotiate new agreements on oil deliveries, food shipment, transportation and foreign aid.

<>

In mid-December 1990, a twenty-member Cuban delegation led by Cabrisas flew to Moscow to negotiate the last details of the agreements.

A tense, somber atmosphere pervaded the various conference rooms of the Soviet Foreign Trade Ministry when the talks began. The fiercest debate during the twelve-day negotiations was to determine which products would be considered of strategic value—and thus continue to be provided by the Soviet government.

Under the new Soviet rules, the one-year trade agreement for 1991 would only include seventy of the estimated seven hundred products that the Soviet Union exported to Cuba annually. Among the strategic products were oil, wheat, rice, and spare parts for vital industrial equipment. The remaining products would have to be negotiated by Cuba independently with each Soviet factory. The Cubans protested, fiercely.

"What about motor oils and other engine lubricants," a Cuban delegate stammered as he went down the list of strategic goods a few days before the scheduled signing of the new agreement. "How are we supposed to keep our engines going?"

"We're sorry, it can't be included," the Soviet representative at the other end of the table responded. "All our motor oil companies have already been turned into autonomous firms. We can't negotiate for them."

"What about pork fat," another Cuban delegate was asking in a room nearby, where food shipments were being discussed. "We use it instead of cooking oil, to fry our food. It's a first-necessity item. How are we going to do without it?"

"Well, you can always knock something else from the list," the Soviet side said. "But, remember, we have to keep it down to seventy items . . ."

The size and price of Soviet shipments were also major sticking points in the talks. Cuba wanted assurances that the Soviets would deliver 1.5 million tons of grains over the next twelve months. The Soviets, facing food shortages at home, did not want to commit themselves.

<>

On Saturday, December 29, 1990, Katushev and Cabrisas signed the first Soviet-Cuban agreement reflecting the Kremlin's new economic policies. It would have a dramatic impact on the Cuban economy.

Under the new deal, the Soviet Union would send 10 million tons of oil in 1991, a 25 percent drop from previous years; Soviet exports would begin to be paid in U.S. dollars under a clearing arrangement; Cuba would start paying 10 percent of the total freight costs incurred by the Soviet company Morflot in transporting goods to Cuba; the Soviet Union would withdraw about two thousand technicians from Cuba, leaving only those necessary to complete an estimated eighty projects; the Soviets would commit themselves to deliver grains only for the first six months of the upcoming year.

The Cuban delegation didn't have much to celebrate that icy Saturday evening in Moscow. After the agreement was signed by

Katushev and Cabrisas, a waiter brought champagne to the room for the customary celebration of a new commercial accord. But the men swallowed their drinks in a hurry, shook hands, and were out of the room within five minutes.

"We had worked around the clock for the past two days, because we all wanted to be at home on New Year's Eve," remembers Vice-Minister Castillo, a member of the Cuban delegation. "When we finished work on December 29th, we quickly drank a glass of champagne, and rushed from there to the airport."

Back in Havana, after the New Year holidays, the Cuban regime's economic hierarchy found itself in total chaos. Top officials did not know where to begin restructuring their bureaucracy to deal with the new Soviet trade mechanisms.

"Whereas in the past we conducted our trade with sixty-two Soviet (government) institutions, we will now have to deal with some twenty-five thousand Soviet organizations that have already been authorized to engage in foreign trade," Cuban Foreign Trade Minister Cabrisas conceded to *Granma*. "And where we were formerly able to get things done through a single firm with centralized authority, we will now have to deal directly with suppliers."

Cuba's Vice-President Carlos Rafael Rodriguez, perhaps the most candid man in Castro's inner circle, was more blunt. "The word to define Cuba's relationship with the Soviet Union is uncertainty," he said. "We don't know what will happen in the long run. The only certainty is that, in the immediate future, the situation will worsen."

Cuban trade delegations began flying throughout the Soviet Union to touch base with newly independent producers. Often, the Soviet companies were in the process of setting up new market working mechanisms themselves. The Cubans were told to come back in six months, when the situation would be clearer to all.

Cuba's State Committee for Economic Cooperation, a huge bureaucracy set up to deal with the Soviet Union's foreign aid apparatus, suddenly found itself out of a job. There were no new Soviet aid packages, and many existing Soviet projects were being frozen. Often, technical assistance projects were abandoned midway: the Soviets would announce their withdrawal by stating that Cuba's own professionals had reached such levels of technical sophistication that Soviet help was no longer needed.

Castro had little choice but to go along with the Soviets' new policies—and hope that orthodox Marxist forces at the Kremlin would stage a coup against Gorbachev.

<>

I ran into Ernesto Meléndez, president of the Cuban Economic Co-operation committee, at a cocktail party in the residence of the British ambassador in Havana. A tall, friendly man in a white guayabera, Meléndez summed up Cuba's economic drama.

Cuba's former Socialist allies were dismantling their barter trade system to start new business relationships based on market prices and were closing lines of credit to Cuba. Western banks, on the other hand, refused to make loans or finance trade with Cuba because the island had suspended payments on its $6.2 billion foreign debt in 1986.

"We have been left outside the world's two economic structures," Meléndez explained. "We're hanging in the air, trying to find a new place to insert ourselves."

<>

Soviet companies in Cuba whose products would no longer be sold by the Soviet government found themselves in a similar state of turmoil. Many of them decided to close down their offices in the first months of 1991.

Hundreds of their technicians, whose job was to service Soviet cars, refrigerators and television sets sold to Cuba, were ordered back home in anticipation of declining exports. If needed, they would be sent on one-month trips to the island, without their families.

Some companies, such as the Electronintorg group of electronic goods firms, chose to keep sales offices in Havana open in an effort to compete with Japanese and Canadian exporters, but it wasn't easy. Electronintorg set up a showroom on Havana's posh Fifth Avenue so that Cuban trade officials could have a firsthand look at its products. In three long tables at the firm's waiting room, there were dozens of watches, lamps, and electronic toys on display.

"We have been spoiled for a long time," office manager Sergei Komarov told me through an interpreter as he showed me through the exhibit. "In the past, the Soviet government sold our goods, and we were simply here to service them. Now, we have to sell our products like any other international exporter. We have to convince the Cubans that we are competitive."

Komarov had been forced to change his job overnight from a repair shop manager to an international trader. Sales were plummeting, but he was still trying to figure out how to do his new job. None of his people had had any experience in selling. Of his eleven-person staff, all were Soviets, and only one—the interpreter—spoke Spanish. Even the nightwatchman was a Soviet. The office had only two Cubans as support personnel: Komarov's driver and the building's gardener. Wouldn't it be easier to do business in Cuba with Spanish-speaking officers?

"Yes, we're thinking of hiring a Cuban commercial assistant," Komarov conceded. "But we have a lot to learn. This is all very new to us."

One of the first visible signs of the Soviet pullout from Cuba came when Soviet propaganda magazines disappeared overnight from Havana newsstands in early 1991. Until then, the Soviet Union had more than half a dozen Spanish-language magazines, most of them produced by the Soviet news agency *Novosty*, in Cuba. Because they were the only foreign publications allowed to circulate on the island, they had long been one of the few windows to the outside world for millions of Cubans.

But in December 1990, the Kremlin's budget-cutters reduced *Novosty*'s twenty-five-member Havana staff by half, and discontinued all the Spanish-language propaganda. *Novosty* immediately suspended publication of its daily Spanish-language bulletin "News from the URSS," which went to four hundred Cuban media and had long been a major source of news stories for Cuban journalists. Moscow also suspended publication of *Novosty*'s forty-thousand-circulation monthly *URSS*, a lavish magazine that included regular features on Soviet economic cooperation with Cuba.

Sputnik and *Moscow News*, two widely read Soviet Spanish-language magazines, had been prohibited by the Cuban regime more than a year earlier, because of their criticism of the Cuban revolution. By early 1991, Soviet newspapers and magazines had vanished from Cuba's newsstands.

There was no consternation in Cuba as thousands of Soviets began their silent exodus from the island. In fact, despite the inconveniences brought about by the departure of Soviet black marketeers, most Cubans were indifferent. The Soviets had not left major marks: intermarriages between Soviets and Cubans had been rare, and neither their music nor their art had caught on among Cubans. After three decades of state-imposed Soviet influence in all walks of life, Cubans were as hooked on American movies, music, literature and fashion as they had been before the revolution.

In fact, the Cuban revolution had a long history of political schizo-phrenia regarding the Soviet Union. Castro had clashed with Cuba's Communist Party chiefs before he had come to power, and had gone through major ups and downs in his dealings with the Kremlin ever since. He had been furious at Soviet Premier Nikita Khrushchev's secret dealings with Washington to solve the October 1962 missile crisis without Cuba's input; then his relations with the Kremlin blos-somed after Cuba endorsed the 1968 Soviet invasion of Czechoslova-kia. Ever since Gorbachev began implementing his Perestroika and Glasnost policies in the late 1980s, however, things had only gone downhill.*

<>

Cuba's official rhetoric continued extolling the virtues of the Soviet Union, but on the streets of Havana, you would be surprised at the Cubans' disregard for anything Soviet. Cubans had a contemptuous attitude bordering on racial prejudice toward the Soviets. They called them *"Bolos"*—a coined word that came from *bolas* (balls) and de-scribed the Soviets' round physical appearance, as if they looked like bowling balls.

One night in early 1991, I had a long chat about the Soviets with two senior Cuban officials at the house of Alfredo Muñoz Unsain, a veteran journalist for the Agence France Presse news agency who had lived in Cuba for nearly three decades and was by far the best-connected foreign journalist on the island.

Muñoz Unsain, a gourmet cook, had prepared an exotic dish made of fish eggs. There was plenty of first-class Argentine wine on the table. The Cubans were surprisingly candid in that atmosphere. One was a prominent economist with a cabinet-level job, the other headed a major government publication. When the conversation turned to the Soviets, they couldn't be stopped.

The Soviets living in Cuba were the most unsophisticated people

---

* *In a videotaped address to the Communist Party's Directorate of Orientation and Propaganda, Castro described the Soviet leader as a "traitor" to the international Socialist movement. In another videotape shown to Party cadres shortly after he had banned* Sputnik *and* Moscow News, *Castro said, referring to the Soviet Union, that "poisonous information is now coming to us from the very Holy Spirit," according to two influential Communist Party members who saw the tapes.*

on earth, they said. The Soviets didn't dress well; didn't use deodorant; were usually dirty and didn't know how to drink without making fools of themselves, they said, echoing the most widespread Cuban prejudices against the Soviets.

"I've been several times to the Soviet Union and, believe me, it's like living in Antarctica," said the economist, who was part of numerous Cuban delegations to Moscow that had made unending toasts to Soviet-Cuban friendship over the years. "That's not a country made for people; it's a country made for seals."

A few days later, I recalled that conversation over lunch with Roberto Fernández Retamar, the poet and president of Casa de Las Americas, the Cuban regime's foreign-oriented culture and propaganda outlet. Long regarded as a hard-liner by liberal intellectuals, he had been one of the top promoters of Soviet books, movies and art exhibits in Cuba.

Now, Fernández Retamar was agreeing that Soviet culture—and Soviets themselves—had never been fully accepted in Cuba. Thirty years is nothing in the cultural life of a country, he said. The state-imposed Soviet culture—85 percent of Cuba's imported school texts came from the Soviet Union—and even the compulsory teaching of Russian in Cuban schools had not made a dent in the Cubans' natural affinity for Western culture, he conceded.

"Political changes are quick to happen, but cultural evolution is slow," Fernández Retamar said. "Any of us can get along fine with an American, even if we disagree politically. But we find it much harder to get along with a Russian, even when we agree politically. Our cultures are different. We are on different wave lengths."

Fernández Retamar, a highly cultured man with an exquisite sense of humor, was up to date with the latest developments in the U.S. publishing world. He was eager for news. Like most of the regime's top officials, he spent much of his time lashing out against the enemy, yet he was fascinated by it.

"I always tease Armando Hart, the culture minister, that he doesn't know the world's capital, because he's never been to New York," he told me. Then, as an afterthought: "I have been in New York."

Toward the end of our conversation that day, I asked Fernández Retamar what would come of the more than thirty years of massive Soviet cultural influence on the island; of the avalanche of Soviet books, movies, and educational programs that people like himself had forced onto Cuba over decades.

He thought it over for a few seconds, shrugged, and said he could sum up his answer in two words: *"Casi nada."* Almost nothing.

With the collapse of its closest allies in Latin America and the retrenchment of its longtime Soviet benefactors, the Castro regime scurried to draft plans for Cuba's survival without foreign aid.

In preparation for a possible total cut in Soviet oil shipments, Castro would soon launch sweeping energy-saving measures. Anticipating drastic drops in Soviet food supplies, he prepared to move large numbers of Cubans to agricultural farms in the countryside. Within months, Castro's survival programs would force millions of Cubans to radically change their lifestyles.

8
Bicycles, Oxen and Potato Jam

◄◄◄◄◄In May of 1991 I was in my rented Nissan driving down a narrow street of Old Havana when I almost hit a mature woman who was obviously on her first outing on a bicycle. She was riding along in front of my car and suddenly lost control. The front wheel of her bike shifted wildly from left to right before she hit the ground. The woman sprawled on the pavement as I screeched to a halt only six feet away.

"Momee, I warned you not to try it!" her daughter yelled frantically from her bicycle behind, as I was trying to recover my breath in my driver's seat. "How many times did I tell you not to try it!"

The poor woman had only been doing her part to save the revolution. Cuba was more than twelve months into Fidel Castro's "Special Period for Times of Peace," a wartime-like austerity plan to help Cuba survive with shrinking Soviet oil supplies. The oil shipments were already 25 percent down from what Cuba had received from the Russians in 1989. Castro's draconian energy-saving plan sounded like a blueprint to drag the country back into the nineteenth century.

Under the special period program, Cuba's gas-guzzling buses would be replaced by bicycles. Oxen would be substituted for tractors. Food delivery trucks would be replaced by horse-drawn carts. Hundreds of factories would be closed down to save energy. Manufacturing plants and administrative offices would cut down their energy consumption by up to 50 percent.

There would be a weekly "special effort day" when factories and government offices would operate without electricity. All lights would go off, and all the cooking would be done with firewood. Up to two hundred thousand Havana residents would be "mobilized" to the countryside for three-week working stints on farms. Tens of thousands would be fired from the government bureaucracy, and moved to work permanently in agriculture. Cuba would return to a subsistence economy.

The program was designed both to deal with smaller oil supplies and to convince everybody that Castro would remain firmly in control of the country—a key move to discourage organized dissent. Although Castro's oxen-and-bicycles program was not taken seriously by many at first, it soon became evident that the Cuban leader wasn't kidding.

By mid-1991, Havana was dotted with huge street signs showing an electricity plug with the legend "Save Energy." Cuban factories, offices and private homes were always in the half dark. Supermarkets had disconnected most of their ceiling fluorescent tubes, and customers wandered down aisles in darkness. Chandeliers in restaurants operated with most bulbs unscrewed, and diners were left to deal with the dimly lit atmosphere. At many workplaces, employees were let go at 3 P.M., when the sun stopped filtering through the windows.

On the streets, you could see fewer and fewer cars—gasoline rations for private vehicles had been reduced to about ten gallons a month. Lines in front of bus stops grew longer and more bicycles appeared. Here and there, there was a horse-driven cart carrying food or passengers. Government dissertations about the new measures filled the pages of *Granma*. The term "special period" became the most widely used expression in Cuba. People would utter it with a resigned smile or shrug—a catchword for anything they couldn't obtain or deliver.

Castro's arguments in support of the austerity program were often bizarre. On nightly television appearances, he maintained that bicycles and oxen were a sign of progress—an indication that the Cuban revolution had reached a stage of development only comparable to that of the wealthiest nations on earth. Even rich countries like the Netherlands were phasing out automobiles and tractors to help protect the ecology, he argued.

Bicycles became his obsession. After *Granma* announced the importation of two hundred thousand of them—the first leg of a wider program to purchase a total of seven hundred thousand—the Cuban leader proclaimed the "era of the bicycle" had begun. Bicycles would solve most of the country's energy, pollution and health problems, he insisted in every speech.

The government started distributing Chinese "Forever" and "Flying Pigeon" bikes at schools and workplaces. The recipients, mostly young people who had never ridden bikes before, enthusiastically welcomed the black, sturdy Chinese contraptions. In a matter of weeks, there was turmoil in the streets. Cubans had taken to the new means of transportation with characteristic zeal.

Havana's few motorists—mostly foreign tourists—had to veer sharply every few seconds to keep from hitting the cyclists. Long-haired youths zigzagged through the streets, driving their Flying Pigeons without their hands, or doing pirouettes to impress passersby. Middle-aged men painfully pedaled their way to work down the very middle of the street, forcing motorists to slow down and honk their horns to avoid hitting them. The matron I nearly hit was only one of an army of grandmothers riding bicycles for the first time in their lives, weaving wildly down the nation's roads and into lampposts or trees.

Hospital emergency rooms were flooded with victims of bicycle accidents. The Havana weekly *Tribuna* reported 171 bicycle accidents in the first five months of 1991, which left a toll of 26 dead and 180 wounded. Doctors privately put the death toll at more than twice the official figures.

But Castro couldn't stop congratulating himself publicly for the idea of introducing Cubans to the bicycle. "Could anything be more healthy?" he asked at a nationally televised press conference. "Many people have worried about how they could do exercises when they got home [from work]. Now they will have already exercised on their way home. . . . We now have learned that the Netherlands has about twelve million bicycles. It is a very developed country, but it did this for ecological and health reasons. It is a healthy custom, a very healthy custom."

The Cuban weekly *Bohemia* asserted in an editorial that, with Fidel's introduction of the bicycle era in Cuba, "we join the latest trend in the world." The editorial contended in all seriousness that it was more comfortable to go to work on a bicycle than to ride a bus.

"With the bicycle, we can mellow down the aggression that comes when hanging on a bus; we improve our silhouettes; we make better use of our time and we can even observe the landscape better, humanizing our habits," *Bohemia* said. "To expand the use of bicycles among us is an indication of cultural progress, a gesture of respect toward nature. . . . With bicycles, we will improve the quality of life in our society."

<>

In the same spirit, the government ordered the domestication of three hundred thousand oxen by the end of 1991. The animals would substitute for thirty thousand gas-guzzling Soviet tractors, many of which were already idle because of shortages of spare parts.

During one of my trips to Cuba, my government-appointed tour guide insisted that I see the oxen at work. He was eager to convince me how the country was ready—and able—to live in total isolation. We drove to an agricultural cooperative near Artemisa, a town thirty-eight miles west of Havana, and saw hundreds of oxen working the fields. "Oxen are better than tractors," my minder commented, only half-jokingly. "They don't need spare parts."

At the Nuevas Tecnicas El Morro factory in Havana, the regime ordered construction of three hundred wagons designed to be drawn by horses. Other factories elsewhere built hundreds more in various designs, shaped to accommodate two or more passengers. The idea: to use these carts instead of company delivery trucks.

My government escort took me to Havana's working-class district of Marianao to see the horse-drawn carts at work. At Marianao's Le Van Than food production company, two carts—drawn by one horse each—had begun delivering chicken salad and *bocaditos*, snacks, to forty-six cafeterias in the area.

"We are saving a lot of gasoline this way," Herminio Mederos, the pudgy manager of the Le Van Than Production Center, told me. "We have quit using one of our two trucks altogether, and we are using the second one only to pick up raw materials in faraway places."

The company's three horses—named Bombón, Satanás and Bayo—left every day at about 7:30 A.M. from the Le Van Than Production Center, and delivered about twenty-five thousand food units daily to the area's cafeterias, Mederos stated with Socialist pride. Because the carts were too small to accommodate all the cargo, they returned to their bases three times a day to reload about forty food boxes at a time each, he said. In all, the horses worked ten hours a day, six days a week.

Weren't they being overworked? No, said manager Mederos. The horses got Sunday off, and were allowed frequent rest periods during work hours. Judging from their sorry appearance, it didn't seem like Bombón, Satanás and Bayo would agree with that assertion.

Didn't the food get spoiled in the open carts on Havana's steamy streets?

"On the contrary, the products are better preserved this way," Mederos replied. "Our trucks were never refrigerated. Now, the food is exposed to ventilation, and arrives much fresher."

<>

During this time, more than sixty apartment buildings were built in Havana province's agricultural areas by revolutionary Microbrigades— groups of workers from all walks of life who were temporarily shifted to construction work. The buildings were to house the estimated two hundred thousand city residents who would be doing "voluntary work" in the countryside, rotating in three-week shifts of twenty thousand people each.

Most Havana residents asked to do this work had little choice: while instances of direct punitive measures against those who refused to go were rare, you could not expect to advance at work or at school if you didn't fulfill your patriotic duties.

The dorms were usually one-story buildings with dozens of rooms each, and recreation areas with a Ping-Pong table and domino games. The *mobilizados*, as the transferred agricultural workers were called, slept in groups of ten—men and women separately. Each group's 12-by-18-foot room had five bunk beds, and two ceiling fans.

During a government-organized visit to the La Esperanza farm in a banana-growing region near Artemisa, we were shown hundreds of *mobilizados* from the city who were learning to pick bananas and potatoes.

The manager at the Empresa de Cultivos Varios de Artemisa, a bureaucrat with a sheepish look, explained to me that the *mobilizados* were badly needed because Cuba didn't have enough agricultural laborers to harvest the crops. The government was planning to double the potato and plantain production over the next two years and needed large numbers of extra hands.

Could city residents who had never worked in the fields do such hard work? Hardly, the manager conceded. But even if they produced less than half what the agricultural workers produced, by their sheer numbers, they were getting the job done, he said.

In fact, the *mobilizados* at the camps seemed to spend more of their energies partying than solving the revolution's food shortages.

At some camps, such as that of the Communist Youth in Guines, there was an unusually festive mood among the young temporary workers. There were rock-music parties every night. The talk focused almost exclusively on sex. There were late-night bargaining sessions over who would stay out of his room to allow a couple an hour of privacy. One could only wonder how much concentration the *mobilizados* would have left for the next morning's potato-picking session.

◄►

A few hours into my visit to the agricultural camps, my brain was completely addled. The Foreign Relations Ministry (MINREX) minder who escorted me had filled my head with political buzzwords I had a hard time following. The revolution's special period program had created a terminology that not even the most fluent Spanish-speaking outsider could possibly understand.

"You see, these are *mobilizados*," my MINREX minder told me as we drove through the countryside and saw a group of people working on a field. "They are living in the dorms built by Microbrigades."

"The Microbrigades . . . they are the same as the Contingents, right?" I asked.

"No, no," my minder replied, almost offended. "The Microbrigades are *like* the Contingents, but they don't work in the country-side. They are more like the *Colectivos*, or Collective workers' groups, where people work near their respective nucleus."

"Oh, I see . . . the *nucleus*," I said, fearing that any new question would lead us to a whole new category of special period jargon.

Hours later, when my minder kept talking about the nucleus, I ventured to ask what that meant. Was he referring to the family?

"Well, yes," he replied. "I guess you could also call it that."

◄►

In 1991, the Castro regime was forced to choose between ice cream or butter. The authorities of newly reunited Germany had sent a telex to Cuban Trade Minister Ricardo Cabrisas advising that East German shipments of powdered milk to Cuba would be suspended by December 31, 1990.

Under an agreement with East Germany, Cuba had long bartered thirty thousand tons of Cuban animal feed annually for twenty thousand tons of powdered milk from an East Berlin factory. The powdered milk was used both for Coppelia's ice-cream factories and to supply butter-production plants.

Now, newly reunited Germany was saying it didn't need animal feed. West German factories were producing enough to meet the new country's needs. The Cuban regime had to make a choice. Top aides to Cabrisas said that, considering the social impact of the first alternative—closing down Coppelia would do away with one of the few remaining pastimes in town—they decided to eliminate butter. No more butter would be seen in Cuba for a long time.

Next to disappear from supermarket shelves was beer. Germany and Czechoslovakia respectively terminated other barter deals that had long provided Cuba with forty-five thousand tons of malt a year. The shortage of malt forced Cuba to cut its beer production by 90 percent. Other Eastern European food imports that were quick to vanish: canned meat, cooking oil, fish products and cereals.

But the trade dislocations resulting from the fall of Eastern Europe were minuscule compared with what came after the December 1990 Soviet-Cuban trade agreement. Shipments of Soviet raw materials, industrial equipment and spare parts plummeted in 1991, affecting production of virtually everything made in Cuba.

In a matter of months, there were growing bread shortages because of delays of Soviet wheat shipments. Clothing factories were idle because of a lack of Soviet zippers. Construction works were suspended because of shortages of Soviet cement. Food distribution networks had to be overhauled because spare parts for Soviet trucks were no longer arriving. Cuban newspapers and magazines were closed down for lack of newsprint and pulp. The magazines *Bastion*, *Verde Olivo*, *Mujeres* and *Opina* were shut down altogether. Circulation of *Granma* was cut by a third to four hundred thousand copies, and was reduced from seven days a week to five.

Because of deep cuts in the sixteen-thousand-ton annual Soviet shipments of soda ash, a vital raw material for glass production, Cuba had to reduce production of bottles and glass jars. As a result, the island had to cancel its 1991 commitments to export bottled tomato products.

"We are stuck with a lot of tomato we can't export because of shortages of raw materials to make glass jars," a senior trade official told me at the time. "Rather than wait for a solution and let it get spoiled, we're dumping it all into the domestic market."

A tomato-eating propaganda campaign was launched. TV spots aired every ten minutes featured a Spanish-language rap musician exhorting the population to eat tomato. Either raw, cooked or mashed, tomatoes made for a wonderful main dish, the singer intoned rhythmically as a cartoon character devoured a series of tomato dishes.

The tomato crusade lasted about three months, until the red vegetables began to disappear from the markets. They were quickly replaced by potatoes. The massive crop of potatoes picked by the *mobilizados* began to arrive in Havana in early 1991. For several months, potatoes became the main—and often only—readily available dish for most Cubans. State media now promoted potatoes as the ultimate delicacy.

<><

Nitza Villapol had arguably the second most difficult job in Cuba. She was a television cooking star in a country facing starvation. Her once-a-week "Cooking in a Minute" program was an institution in Cuba. It had first appeared in 1951, when it was sponsored by American food companies and taught Cuba's society ladies the secrets of haute cuisine. Four decades later, Villapol was delivering televised cooking classes—with a straight face—to a country with empty supermarket shelves.

I first saw "Cooking in a Minute" on a Saturday at noon in my Havana hotel room. Villapol, a small but vigorous woman at sixty-eight, was teaching a recipe for potato salad, a dish she said had enough nutritional value to serve as a day's main course.

On the following Saturday, I again turned on the television set at noon, curious about what she could possibly recommend. It was mashed potatoes with onions. It seemed to be made out of everything that was available in Cuban supermarkets that week. ("If you have trouble getting milk and butter, the traditional ingredients for mashed potatoes, smash one clove of garlic, add salt, mix it with orange juice and a bit of pork fat, and pour the sauce over the mashed potatoes.") It was billed as an ideal main course for dinner.

The third Saturday, it was potato mayonnaise. The dish was meant to help circumvent cooking oil shortages by replacing part of the oil with potatoes (1 egg; 1 espresso coffee cup of cooking oil; 2 medium-sized potatoes, and salt). The fourth Saturday, it was potato jam (mash two boiled potatoes with orange peels and a spoonful of salt; then add two egg yolks, and one cup of sugar. Cook and serve as spread or dessert).

How much longer could Villapol keep churning out potato recipes? When I knocked on the door of her Havana apartment, she nearly barked at me. Looking at me suspiciously, she said she was not in the business of giving interviews. She was not amused by my curiosity about her job. Did I have a Foreign Ministry authorization for an interview? No. Could she spare me the trouble of getting one? No. But later, she calmed down and allowed me in.

Hers was an odd story. She was born in New York, her parents had been staunch Communists. The family moved to Cuba when Nitza was in high school. She had taken up fast-food cooking from her mother, a feminist who insisted a woman shouldn't spend the whole day in the kitchen. When Nitza had started her program eight years before the revolution, it was an instant success. American food companies rushed to sponsor her program and cookbooks.

With the revolution, the U.S. sponsors disappeared, but her program remained on the air. She began adapting her dishes to the new realities. Now, Nitza regularly consulted with government officials when preparing her programs, to see which food would be available by the time she went on the air.

When was the last time she had taught a recipe containing meat? She didn't remember. Perhaps a year and a half ago. Perhaps two. How many more weeks would she keep featuring potato recipes? For as long as there wasn't anything else on the supermarket shelves.

As we talked in her messy living room—dirty pots and old newspapers littered the floor of her apartment—I glanced through a stack of *Nitza Villapol's Cooking in a Minute* books displayed on the coffee table. They were fancy editions dating from the mid-fifties, complete with color illustrations. The ads were from American ketchup and mayonnaise companies. Among her recipes at the time: *Rognons Sautés au Champagne*, *Filet de Boeuf à la Perigourdine*, and *Poulet à la Basquaise*.

Her last book had appeared shortly before the revolution. She did not appreciate my unconscious smile as I imagined what a Nitza Villapol cookbook for the nineties would look like (*Nitza Villapol's Hundred Best Potato Recipes*, perhaps?).

"Young man, we may not have anything left to eat, but we have kept our dignity," she berated me. "If it's necessary, we will do our cooking with firewood. We will do anything, except surrender."

On my way out, she insisted, "Make sure you write that I'm a committed Fidelista." As I was walking down the stairs, her voice still yelled at me from two stories up, "We are standing up against U.S. aggression! We are proud of that!"

Was this New York-born Cuban trying to convince her neighbors about her revolutionary credentials? Or did she really mean it? I decided she was most likely putting on a show. It was hard for me to imagine how somebody who had doted over *Rognons Sautés au Champagne* could three decades later still be proud of a revolution that had a hard time offering bread to its people. I was not impressed by her political assertions. As the saying went, in Cuba you could only believe half of what you heard—and nothing of what you saw.

I was struck by a curious phenomenon: food—except for potatoes and pineapples—was scarce, yet this was not what seemed to bother Cubans the most. What people seemed most irked about was the shortage of soap, deodorant, shampoo, toothpaste, shaving cream and perfume.

You can fool your stomach with several infusions of coffee a day, but there's little you can do to make up for soap, they would tell you. Although the government's rationing cards entitled each Cuban to one bottle of shampoo and one deodorant stick every six months, these products had vanished from supermarkets by early 1991.

Shortages of personal care products made Cubans feel insecure about themselves. Most Cubans asking foreigners to buy them something at the dollar shops did not request something to eat, but a bottle of shampoo. It was not rare for the *jineteras*—as Cuba's free-lance prostitutes were called—to ask to be paid with a box of deodorants. Dirt was getting on people's nerves.

"It's funny, but not being able to wash your hands after going to the bathroom or to shave in the morning hurts your self-esteem more than not eating well," said José, a young engineer who had a three-day-old beard when I met him. "If there's ever going to be an uprising here, it will be over soap shortages."

Produimport, the Soviet state corporation that exported most raw materials to Cuba, had long shipped one hundred twenty thousand tons of animal fats a year to the island. But in the first six months of 1991, it had only shipped one ton of that product. Cuban officials blamed domestic political turmoil in the Soviet Union. Soviet officials said Cuba had failed to pay.

At the same time, a sharp reduction in the Soviet Union's annual shipments of forty-two thousand tons of paper pulp to Cuba resulted in a widespread shortage of toilet paper. Making things worse, Havana's rusty water-distribution system left thousands of apartment dwellers without water several days a week.

At several homes I visited, residents had to fill their bathtubs whenever they had water, so they could shave, wash their hands and flush their toilets during the rest of the week. In other neighborhoods, there were government trucks delivering water from door to door.

When the trucks were late, people became irritable. Few would tell you what was wrong—Cubans are highly image-conscious people—but you could feel a collective edge in the air.

"Try not washing your hands for a day, and tell me how you feel," José challenged me. "Try not shaving for three days. . . . Your neck itches, you smell bad, you feel awful."

Cubans developed a variety of home-grown formulas to replace the missing toiletries. *Bohemia,* the weekly magazine, began publishing a "Practical Solutions" column offering formulas to make one's own products at home.

A "Make-Your-Own-Deodorant" column recommended mixing three spoonfuls of laundry soap, half a cup of alcohol, a quarter of a spoonful of bicarbonate, and a few drops of cologne. The ingredients were to be mixed, cooked, and placed in the freezer for at least one hour. The resulting concoction would make women smell "marvelous," it said.

There were dozens of apocryphal recipes for shampoo, which neighbors exchanged with great zeal. The most common ones used rain water, detergent, and honey or egg yolks. Many women added sugar: it kept their hair firmer, as if it had been doused with spray. The formula gained widespread popularity for a few weeks, until growing numbers of people began complaining about its downside: a syrupy smell that just wouldn't go away, and attracted flies.

Many men, tired of worrying about finding razor blades, began growing beards. The supply of Soviet "Sputnik" blades, long the only ones available in Cuba, was dwindling. Julio, a Havana high-school teacher, showed me a complicated shaving ritual he performed every morning: he rubbed his flat Sputnik blade several times—back and forth—against the walls of a moist drinking glass. This extended the life of the blade, he explained. He had been using the same blade for more than a month.

Cubans' ingenuity seemed to have no limits. Among the weirdest things I saw was women walking down the street with toilet paper cartons rolled into their hair. It wasn't part of a Santería ritual.

"You can't get plastic curlers anymore," said Carmen, a young grandmother of Old Havana. "These may not be too elegant, but they work just the same."

Health care—the pride of the Cuban revolution—suffered a rapid deterioration. Services continued to be free, but there were growing shortages of medical supplies. Horror stories at hospitals multiplied.

As supplies of East German X-ray plates dried up, doctors were forced to limit their use to emergency cases. Soviet bloc surgical gloves were washed and reused up to ten times. Bed sheets could not be replaced, and sometimes could not be washed for several days because there was no soap or detergent. Cotton, which had long been imported from the Soviet Union, became a precious commodity.

At Havana's Calixto García hospital, the water supply was often cut off for days at a time. Relatives of patients were asked to bring water-filled jugs to the hospital, and to use the water in washing them. Often, the emergency room didn't have tranquilizers or antibiotics—only a limited supply of aspirins. You could hear the cries of victims of burns or other wounds, whose pain could not be alleviated because of a lack of painkillers.

Rubén Pineda, a former head of the Calixto García's emergency room, often didn't have alcohol or other disinfectants for his emergency cases. In some cases, he had to make deep incisions, and had no thread for the stitches. "I had to use adhesive tape," said Pineda, who eventually fled in a raft to Miami in 1990. "That was common; it happened all the time."

Some hospitals, like the CIMEQ or the Hermanos Ameijeiras, were better supplied, because they catered largely to party members and were showplaces where foreign visitors could view the wonders of Cuba's health care system. But Cubans knew better.

The number of disaffected Cubans fleeing the island soared. Every day, small groups of Cubans—mostly young males—took off from Havana beaches on inner tubes to make the ninety-mile trek through the Florida Straits to the United States. More than one thousand Cuban rafters arrived on the Florida coasts in the first half of 1991, more than twice the total number for the previous year. Often, the rafts landed empty on Miami's beaches. The U.S. Coast Guard estimated that only two out of three Cuban rafters made it alive.*

Havana's coastal suburbs of Jaimanitas and Santa Fe quickly became known as towns of *balseros*, or rafters. A whole black-market

---

* *By the end of 1991, 2,417 Cubans had arrived in rafts or boats to Florida, up from 467 during the previous year.*

support industry developed around the escapees. Neighbors sold truck and tractor inner tubes, heavy-duty cloth that was wrapped around the bottom of the tubes, handmade oars, burned engine oil to be used as shark repellent, rubber boots and dried food. Some escapees would venture into the sea with only one inner tube, frog legs and a pair of Ping-Pong paddles they used as oars.

Despite stiff penalties for those attempting to flee—including jail terms from one to three years for those caught on the sea or people providing them with material support—there were periodic farewell parties for departing Cubans. Weeks after their departure, relatives and neighbors would anxiously await news about their fate from Radio Martí or from an occasional foreign visitor. If an escape was successful, others would begin planning their own.

"I love Miami," a teenager who stopped by a *balseros* farewell party in Jaimanitas told *Miami Herald* reporter Mimi Whitefield. He glanced down at his cutoff jean shorts and flexed his muscles. "I've got good arms for rowing. I could get a good pair of pants there."

Another young man at the party added bitterly, "This country isn't for young people. It's for old people who want to die."

Balsero success stories, celebrated by Miami's Cuban exile media, became the talk of the day in Cuba. One rafter, twenty-one-year-old textile worker Lázaro Colomé, had traveled in style: he was picked up at sea by the Queen of England's cruising yacht *Britannia*. The 412-foot royal vessel was returning to Europe after a cruise off Florida when crew members spotted Colomé's four-foot foam plastic raft.

Another escapee made it to the Florida coast on a wind-surfing board. Lester Moreno, a seventeen-year-old wind-surfing instructor, had obtained the board from an East German tourist. Blessed by twenty-mile-per-hour winds, the young Cuban made it to U.S. waters in sixteen hours. He was spotted by a Korean freighter. Its Korean-speaking crew had trouble explaining to the U.S. Coast Guard what exactly they had encountered. After several tries, they put Moreno on the radio to talk to a Spanish-speaking Coast Guard officer.

"No problem. I'm just wind surfing. Going to see my family in Miami," the officer quoted Moreno as saying.

A group of five Cubans commandeered an aging Soviet-made Antonov crop-dusting plane to Miami, flying only two yards above the water to avoid detection by Cuban radar. In an unrelated escape that same day, a group of eight Cubans armed with a toy revolver hijacked the fishing vessel *Veneciana 5* with two Canadian tourists aboard, and forced it to the Florida Keys.

The number of would-be rafters and ex-rafters who had failed in their attempts to flee grew so rapidly that Jaimanitas residents soon created an association of *balseros.* Francisco Chaviano, a former high-school math teacher, created the Council of Balseros to help people who—like himself—had failed in their attempts to escape. Chaviano, his son and a family friend had been arrested after being detected by a Cuban Coast Guard boat nine miles away from the coast. ("Enjoying a nice day on the beach?" the Cuban officer had asked Chaviano as he approached his raft.) After spending a year in jail, Chaviano had started the *balsero* group at his home on a dirt road in Jaimanitas to demand that the regime stop jailing failed rafters. By mid-1991, the group claimed thirty activists and nearly two thousand members, most of them *balseros* serving prison sentences or fired from their jobs for their attempts to escape.

Chaviano's association soon began to operate like a human rights group, compiling information about missing rafters and providing it to the Cuban and U.S. governments for help in locating them. Desperate mothers would contact the group in search of news from their children. Based on his reports, Chaviano estimated that more than five hundred Cubans had died at sea during the first half of 1991.

"We are advising young people against trying it," Chaviano said. "When I did it, the end of this regime was nowhere in sight. Now, it's around the corner—it doesn't make sense to risk one's life anymore."

Indeed, most *balseros* told hair-raising stories about their struggle to survive in the shark-infested Caribbean waters. Sharks would sometimes bang their heads against the bottom of their rafts. When that happened, you scared them away by hitting the water with your oars, they said. Most often, the sharks would flee. The *balseros'* biggest concern was bad weather. If a storm overturned your raft, you were left at the mercy of the sharks. That's how most *balseros* who hadn't made it had died, they said. In bad weather, you had to cling to your *balsa* with all your strength, or you were dead meat.

Reuters news agency correspondent Pascal Fletcher was snorkeling one Sunday afternoon on a reef several hundred yards off the Cuban coast when he stumbled into a lone *balsero* desperately waving his hands for help—his raft had been beaten relentlessly back toward the shore by wind and current. The encounter would have made a funny anecdote if it weren't for the rafter's terrifying story.

"There were four of us, all [our inner tubes] tied together," the young man said, nearly out of breath. When the wind started blowing, "the others just started drifting away." They had disappeared into the horizon.

Were people just fleeing Cuba because of the shortages? Judging from the statements of many middle-class rafters after their triumphant arrival in Miami, ideological fatigue had also been a major factor in their decision to flee. Ricardo Presas Grau, a young physician who fled on a tractor inner tube, told me he had felt asphyxiated by the regime's Communist propaganda. In light of the world collapse of Marxism, Cuba's official credo was harder than ever to swallow.

<>

Long after the fall of Communist regimes in Eastern Europe and the democratic reforms in the Soviet Union, all students at the University of Havana were still required to memorize old Soviet manuals. No matter whether you studied medicine or architecture, you had to take at least one "Scientific Communism" course a year. Students now referred to this course as "Science Fiction" class.

The outdated lectures about the inexorable triumph of the world's proletarian movement sounded ridiculous in the face of world changes that not even the official Cuban media could ignore. Yet, as a student, you were supposed to recite the Communist texts with religious fervor.

Glancing through *Foundations of Marxist-Leninist Philosophy* by F. Konstantinov, a Soviet manual that had been phased out in the Soviet Union in the late eighties but continued to be an obligatory text at the University of Havana, I was intrigued by a chapter entitled "The General Crisis of Capitalism." Could any professor teach that course with a straight face?

Another Soviet textbook that was required reading for Cuban college students, *Scientific Communism* by P. N. Fedoseev, sounded even more bizarre. It had a whole chapter devoted to the "latest stages" in the crisis of capitalism. Another chapter was entitled "The International Communist Movement: The Most Influential Political Force Nowadays." The manual's glossy-paper Spanish edition was dated USSR, 1986.

At the Fernando Ortiz bookstore, one of Havana's largest, the "new releases" section featured a September 1989 book entitled *Cuba–Democratic Republic of Germany: Brothers*. On its first page, it carried a quote by former East German president Erich Honecker: "The Democratic Republic of Germany and the Cuban Republic are linked by firm, indestructible ties, today and forever."

Honecker resigned in October 1989, a month after the book's release. More than a year later, the former East German president had fled the country, and East Germany had ceased to exist. Yet the book was still being offered in Cuba as a new release.

The most ridiculous Cuban text clinging to the Soviet Union's outdated Marxist doctrine was the Cuban Constitution. The island's 1976 Constitution stated in its preamble that the fatherland was "guided by the victorious doctrine of Marxism-Leninism" and was "based" on "the fraternal friendship, help and cooperation of the Soviet Union and other Socialist countries, and on the solidarity of the workers and peoples of Latin America and the world."

But now, statues of Marx and Lenin had come down across the Socialist world. The fraternal Soviet friendship was turning into a business relationship at best, and dollar-based at that. The "other Socialist countries" had gleefully renounced socialism. How could anyone seriously invoke the Cuban Constitution?

<>

I walked up the majestic steps of the University of Havana and turned right, straight to the Department of Scientific Communism in the Philosophy and History School. It was late April 1991. I had an appointment with a professor of Marxism. I had told him I was interested in knowing how he and his colleagues were handling the collapse of the Communist world in their classes.

The first thing I saw at the department was a new sign on the door. Where there had once been a painted sign reading "Scientific Communism Department," there was now a paper sign with the more moderate legend "Scientific Socialism Department." Was it a student prank?

"No, not at all," responded Carlos Cabrera, the Moscow-educated Marxism professor who headed the department, a young man with about as much of a sense of humor as the Soviet manuals on his desk. "We have recently changed the name of the department, to adapt it to the new realities."

Cabrera explained to me that the university was phasing out the Soviet manuals. He took me to a nearby storage room, where there were probably thousands of Konstantinov manuals gathering dust. Starting in the upcoming school year, they would no longer be used, he said. The university had not yet decided what to do with them. I was welcome to take as many as I wanted.

The young man was worried. Eastern European universities had long closed down their Marxism Departments, and the Soviet Union itself had just abolished scientific socialism as an independent academic course. Cabrera had recently returned from Moscow, and all his former colleagues had been reassigned to various other departments. Asked whether his newly named Scientific Socialism Department would survive, he said, "That's being analyzed by authorities."

Jorge Nuñez, one of the university's most prominent Marxism professors, was more upbeat. He was glad that the old Soviet manuals were being shelved. They were Stalinist manuals, which taught one model of socialism, not all possible forms of socialism, he explained. Now, professors of Marxism like himself were free to teach the Cuban revolution's own brand of socialism.

The Soviet manuals deserved to be "eaten by the cockroaches," he said. "But if you think we have a problem, go and talk with the guys teaching political economy," Nuñez said with a broad smile. "Those guys have what I would call a real problem."

At the University of Havana's Economics school, the ideological vacuum was threatening chaos. Unlike in other schools, where outdated Soviet textbooks clashed with political reality in the Soviet Union, the school's manuals contradicted Cuba's own new economic policies.

Or did they? Nobody at the school really knew. Fidel was proclaiming "Socialism or death" on one hand, yet he was also bending all Socialist rules to attract Spanish and Canadian investments. Were material incentives okay, once again? Why was strict economic planning okay in some sectors, such as tourism, and not in others?

The School of Economics faculty had set up a special committee in 1990 to write a new set of textbooks for the school. The school had abolished its Soviet manuals in 1990, following the collapse of Eastern Europe. The manuals were replaced with a *Selection of Readings*, a booklet with dissertations by Cuban economists. The *Selection* went into print, and ultimately resulted in nine textbooks designed to cover all political economy courses.

But by the time the new Cuban textbooks were to be released, they were already outdated: they still maintained the superiority of the Socialist economic system, when virtually all Socialist countries were trying to abandon it.

"When we finished writing the books after two years of hard work, we discovered they were no longer any good," said Román García, a political economy professor who was part of the committee that drafted the books. "We threw the drafts away. Now, we are writing new ones that start from the premise that true socialism hasn't been built anywhere, not even in the Soviet Union."

The course's name had been just changed from "Political Economy of Socialism" to "Political Economy of the Construction of Socialism." But students were still relying solely on their class notes. The new textbooks were scheduled to come out in six months— unless new revisions held them up. Students took the oral Marxism classes with philosophic resignation. "It's like studying Greek or Latin," one history student told me. "It's useless, but you just have to do it."

<>

If Cuba's new economic crisis and ideological vacuum was most acutely felt in any one sector of the population, it was among the island's youth.

By 1991, more than 55 percent of the Cuban population was born after the revolution, and youths aged fourteen to twenty-nine made up 45 percent of the island's working people. The vast majority were the product of a baby boom in the sixties and early seventies, when the revolution had launched its first full-employment and education programs with resources from expropriations of foreign corporations and Cuba's bourgeoisie. Birth rates dropped sharply in the mid-seventies, when the revolution proved unable to solve the country's economic troubles, and birth control methods proliferated.

Now, this generation of baby boomers was reaching its mid-twenties, creating what experts described as a huge mass of "maturing" youths. The group aged twenty-five to thirty was to become the largest bloc within Cuba's youth in the 1990s, according to Cuba's Statistics Committee.

These young adults were the most affected by the collapse of the Socialist dream. They could not buy clothes because of the growing shortages of consumer goods. They could not meet at restaurants or cafés because most establishments had closed down for lack of food. They could not enter tourists-only restaurants or night clubs. They no longer saw any reason to do "volunteer" agricultural work or stand guard at their Committees for the Defense of the Revolution, if the revolution was being regarded in the rest of the world as a dinosaur. Tens of thousands of Cuba's maturing youths had peeked into Western magazines or television sets while studying in the Soviet Union and Eastern Europe. In Cuba, they followed world events through their Soviet shortwave radios. They couldn't be fooled.

Even worse: job opportunities for them were shrinking fast. Because of Soviet oil shortages, hundreds of factories had been closed down or asked to reduce their shifts. For the first time since the revolution, there was unemployment in Cuba.

Fifty thousand veterans from the war in Angola had returned to the island in the three-year period before the July 1991 pullout. Thousands of Cuba's internationalist teachers, doctors and nurses in Nicaragua had repatriated following the fall of the Sandinista regime. Thousands more had been recalled from universities in East Germany, Poland, Czechoslovakia and the Soviet Union, either because fellowship programs had been suspended or because Cuba feared the young people might be politically contaminated.

A youth's chances of getting an internationalist assignment in the Third World disappeared, as virtually all African and Latin American countries sent the last Cubans back home. It seemed that all political doors were closed to Cuba's young. The old boys from Castro's guerrilla days, men now in their late sixties and seventies, were occupying most of the top jobs in public service, stalling the upward mobility of even those youths who still held hopes for the revolution.

The revolution had created a mass of educated youths whose expectations clashed sharply with Cuba's desperate conditions. You could find them sitting at the waterfront Malecón boulevard every evening: thousands of young men and women chatting leisurely or looking at the sea, killing time, waiting for something to change their lives.

<><>

Singer Carlos Varela was one of the heroes of that generation of disaffected youth. Varela, a short, slightly overweight young man in his late twenties, had made a career out of addressing the frustrations of Cuba's disaffected youths. More than a protest singer, he was a chronicler of the Cuban youth's long-silenced gripes. His songs—a mix of rock and Cuban folk music—were ambiguous enough to allow him to operate within the system. He was allowed to perform at Havana's huge Karl Marx theater at least once a year, and some of his ballads were broadcast on Radio Havana.

Varela's claim that he supported the revolution but wanted to correct its failures was taken at face value by the regime, perhaps because his music was judged a relatively harmless way for young people to let off steam.

I saw Varela in a concert one Saturday at the Karl Marx. The five-thousand-seat concert hall was filled to capacity. Most youths were in their late teens or early twenties. Varela appeared alone on stage, clad in a black robe and a Chaplinesque black hat. When he

grabbed his guitar and played the first three notes of a song called
"William Tell," the theater burst into cheers.

In the song, William Tell's son tells his father that the time has
come to switch roles, but the father is reluctant to do so. I did not
need to have the symbolism explained to me:

*"Guillermo Tell | Tu hijo creció | quiere tirar la flecha. | Le toca a él |
probar su valor | usando tu ballesta."* (William Tell / your son has grown
up / he wants to shoot the arrow. / It's his turn / to prove his valor /
using your crossbow.)

*"A Guillermo Tell no le gustó la idea | y se negó a ponerse la manzana
en la cabeza."* (William Tell didn't like the idea / and he refused to put
the apple on his head.) The song ended: *"Guillermo Tell no comprendió
a su hijo | que un día se aburrió de la manzana en la cabeza."* (William
Tell did not understand his son / who one day got tired of the apple
on his head.) The audience sprang to its feet with an explosion of
cheers, whistles and applause.

A few days later, I visited Varela at his apartment in Vedado. He lived
comfortably: he had a desktop computer, a printer, a record player
and a fairly new tape recorder. On the wall was a poster of songwriter
and performer Silvio Rodriguez, the father of Cuba's young revolutionary singers, who was now in his mid-forties and regarded as too
conservative and Fidelista by most Cuban youths. Rodriguez, however, had accepted the young protest singer as his protégé, and had
opened many official doors to him.

You see all these tapes there? Varela asked me. They were underground recordings of songs by John Lennon, Madonna, Miami
Sound Machine, and dozens of American and British rock singers.
They had all been made by Cuban black market entrepreneurs who
had built special antennas to receive U.S. radio stations, then taped
the music and sold the tapes.

"My generation has created a communication system that can't be
matched," Varela said. "We trade tapes, magazines, everything . . .
especially what's forbidden. This is a country where Milan Kundera
books are banned, and yet millions have read them."

Although he claimed to be a *revolucionario*, Varela was not a member of the Communist Party, nor of any Communist artists' or youth
organization. He had not done voluntary work in agriculture, and had
no intention of doing it. He did not believe he would help solve
Cuba's problems by chanting Marxist slogans or doing volunteer work
in the countryside.

"Mine is a generation of people who are tired of being treated as if they were stupid," he said. "We are a generation with our own social, economic and political proposals. It's like the clash between William Tell and his son. We're not being listened to."

How could he get away with saying these things? The regime tolerated him because Varela was not calling for violent change, after all. If somebody at one of his concerts were to shout "Down with Fidel," he would immediately suspend the show, he told me. If he didn't do that, somebody else would. Hundreds of secret police agents in civilian clothes mixed among the crowd at every one of his concerts, he said.

Did his William Tell song refer specifically to Fidel? That's up to the listener to interpret, he answered. So how did he see Fidel Castro and his old revolutionary comrades?

"The revolution was carried out with good intentions. But now, we have a huge generation of educated people who are questioning many things, and who want to try their own solutions to our new realities," he said.

Although Varela had not said it in so many words, he had come to regard Fidel as a well-intentioned grandfather who was now behind the times. Most youths didn't feel the hatred against Fidel one could see in the eyes of Miami exiles. Rather, they saw him as a benevolent idealist who had tried to bring equal rights, education and health to Cuba, but whose program had run out of steam. Now, when the whole world was moving in another direction, it was time to join the international tide. The revolution's children were getting tired of holding apples on their heads.

The young Cubans' frustrations did not translate into political activism, but were beginning to result in sporadic acts of spontaneous rebellion. By far the most defiant Cuban youths were heavy-metal rock fans, mostly long-haired teenagers who were known as *roqueros*, or rockers. Almost by accident, they found themselves at the center of one of the first politically charged street clashes with the regime's police.

It happened on April 21st 1991, when more than one thousand *roqueros* attending a heavy-metal concert in Havana fought a street battle with Interior Ministry police that left at least ten wounded. The youths were inside the Casa de la Cultura de Playa, listening to the punk rock band Metal Oscuro (Dark Metal). The band was singing the song "Holocaust"—whose entire lyric was an endless repetition of the word "Holocaust"—when word came from the street that three youths were being arrested for drinking.

Within minutes, dozens of *roqueros* were outside, protesting the arrests. Bottles flew. The police shot into the air. Soon, hundreds of youths flooded into the street, throwing rocks, chairs and tables at police. Official reinforcements moved in and shot tear-gas canisters into the crowd.

"This is worse than Pinochet's police!" one youth yelled, referring to Chile's right-wing dictator Gen. Augusto Pinochet. Another yelled, "Down with Fidel!" A third one, shouting at a group of scared Venezuelan tourists rushing to the nearby Triton Hotel, yelled: "This is the Cuba they won't show you!"

When I arrived at the scene about thirty minutes later, the street was filled with debris. Dozens of kids were still milling around. About twenty had been arrested, they said.

Neighbors on Fifth Avenue were appalled. It was the first time since the revolution they had seen something resembling a political demonstration in Havana. Although it had not been an organized protest, the *roqueros* had broken a collective barrier of fear. Cubans were beginning to speak out.

9
Che's Grandchildren

◄◄◄◄◄Comandante Ernesto "Che" Guevara's oldest grandchild had already turned seventeen when I met him in late 1991. A six-foot-tall teenager, Canek Sanchez Guevara wore his hair down to his shoulders, had a silver earring hanging from his left earlobe, and four colored leather bracelets on his left hand. Like thousands of Cuban youths milling about on Havana's Malecón boulevard, he wore faded, fashionably ripped jeans, white sneakers and a T-shirt. The grandson of Cuba's most venerated martyr didn't want to be a Marxist revolutionary. He wanted to be a heavy-metal rock musician.

To the dismay of his mother Hilda, the oldest of Che Guevara's five children, Canek composed his songs in English. His bedroom walls were covered with posters of American and British rock stars, taken from Western magazines brought to him by foreign visitors. On the little free space left on these walls, he had written the names of his favorite bands: Slayer, Death, Kreator. Canek was a *roquero*, a rocker.

Like all Cuban teenagers, he had grown up venerating his world-famous guerrilla grandfather, the martyr of the Cuban revolution following his 1967 death in a Bolivian jungle. Fidel Castro had fostered a personality cult for Che Guevara that surpassed his own, partly because he needed a deity to cement his revolution's mystique, partly because a dead rebel leader posed no threat to his hold on power. Che Guevara's ideal of the revolutionary New Man—a new generation whose social conscience prevails over selfish material interest—was the goal of Cuba's communism.

A four-story-high Che Guevara mural had long dominated Havana's Revolution Square, where Castro made his most important public speeches. Che Guevara signs could be found on the busiest avenues of Cuban cities, and his posters were displayed in millions of Cuban living rooms. Cuban children were taught to worship Che starting in kindergarten. First-grade reading books showed illustrations of the bearded guerrilla leader, with his ever-present black beret and five-point star, and a legend reading, "Who wouldn't like to be like Che Guevara?" Cuban children began every school day by saluting the flag and chanting, "Pioneers for communism, we shall be like Che!"

As one of Cuba's most important grandchildren, Canek had always been the center of attention. Whatever Cubans' feelings toward Fidel Castro's revolution were, most felt admiration for Che Guevara's idealism, and so Canek was treated with a special respect. Growing up at center stage may have helped turn Canek into a highly articulate teenager—but not one the Castro regime could exhibit at its political rallies. Like most Cubans his age, Canek had little good to say about the Castro government.

"This revolution is in ruins," he told me, with precocious self-assurance. "There's no food, there's no freedom. Dare to open your mouth, and you'll see what happens to you! People say it's all because of the Yanqui aggression, but that's a myth, as real as dragons and witches—a children's tale."

The day I visited Canek in his mother's spacious flat on the twelfth floor of a Vedado neighborhood apartment building, he was fuming. Hours earlier, he had gone to the House of Culture of Havana—the government institution in charge of issuing performing licenses to young artists—in hopes of registering a rock band he had just put together with four friends. The group's name was Mentalizer.

"They turned us down because we sing in English! Can you imagine that?" Canek said, raising his hands in a gesture of desperation. "In this country, you can't do anything without state support. You need the House of Culture to authorize your group, to let you practice at their facilities, to help you transport instruments, to perform at their concerts. But the state is only interested in subsidizing salsa musicians. Each time one of us wants to perform, they accuse us of ideological deviations, Yanqui penetration and twenty-five thousand other stupidities—all because we happen to sing in English!"

He shook his head and concluded, "In this country, *no se puede hacer nada* . . . one can't do anything."

In recent months, Canek had been stopped by police twice, and detained once for not carrying an ID card. Police usually mingled with the teenagers at the Malecón and other kids' hangout places, stopping children every now and then for questioning. Most often, the police intercepted long-haired teenagers, like Canek.

"Can you imagine? This revolution was won by people who wore beards and ponytails. Raúl Castro himself came down from the mountains with a ponytail. Now, it's as if they had forgotten their past. The police spot somebody like me on the street, and immediately ask for our documents. If you don't happen to have them with you, you spend the night in jail."

Canek was planning to move to Mexico after his eighteenth birthday, using his Mexican passport to leave the country. Although he had been born in Cuba, his mother Hilda was Mexican. She had been born in 1956, while Che Guevara and Fidel Castro were in Mexico preparing for their expedition aboard the *Granma* to liberate Cuba from Batista. The Guevara family had moved to Cuba after the revolution, but had kept the children's Mexican passports—just in case.

What could somebody like him do in Cuba? Canek asked rhetorically. Nothing. He was studying at a graphic design high school, but he described his studies as a "waste of time."

"There's no paper, no pens, and no interest on the part of the teachers to do anything. And if you graduate, there's no work in your field. They'll ask you to go to the countryside and work in agriculture. This place is hopeless."

In what kind of a country would he like to live? I asked Canek.

"First of all, I would like to live in a society that isn't so hooked on politics. In this country, whatever you say or do is perceived as a political act. Second, I would like to live in a society where private initiative is rewarded, where there is some competition, without infringing on workers' rights. Something along the lines of Sweden, Switzerland, or Belgium."

What would Che Guevara think of him if he were alive today? I asked.

"He would be proud of me. Che Guevara was a rebel. He never would have approved of what has become of this revolution. Imagine, they are saying that Cuba is the first liberated country in the Americas. . . . They are just using his image to their advantage. What pisses me off the most is how they are commercializing the image of someone who has fought for an ideal. I wouldn't want to be a hero just to have my picture sold to tourists for five dollars apiece. I would like to be a hero so that others follow my example. . . ."

Rock music was Canek's way of defying the revolution's political discipline. He had decorated the front of his electric guitar with an American dollar bill—in open defiance of a Cuban law prohibiting Cubans from holding U.S. currency. His songs were openly critical of the status quo.

He wrote his songs by hand in a notebook in the rudimentary English he had picked up in school and from reading whatever English-language publication he could lay his hands on. Some of the lyrics he showed me were clearly subversive by Cuban standards. One, entitled "Censored words, hidden thoughts," was a teenager's anxious call for freedom of speech.

The handwritten text read, "Ideas in my head / fighting to get out / forbidden words / in my mouth / discrimination / Scorned and decayed flesh / What's the truth? / Who imposes it? / Censored words, there is no liberty / hidden thoughts inside of me. . . . / I only ask / respect for me / and my thoughts. / Why can't I / think like you. / Why am I bad, / and you are not?"

Another song dealt with Adolf Hitler, his propaganda machine, and his monopoly on power. Was it an allegory of Fidel Castro? Canek smiled broadly and responded, "Draw your own conclusions . . ."

How could he speak so bluntly? Wasn't he afraid of government retaliations? Perhaps he would already be in Mexico by the time his statements were published, he said. And if he was still in Cuba, well, so be it. He was a Guevara, after all. Fear was not something that ran in the family's veins, he said, with a mixture of resignation and pride.

Canek Sanchez Guevara was not a big-name exception among Cuban youths. Although more politically conscious, critical and outspoken than many of his generation, he represented an almost universal craving for personal freedoms among Cuban kids. Their long hair, frayed jeans and marked preference for anything American amounted to a collective—often unconscious—declaration of independence. They didn't want to be the little Communist clones many of their parents wanted them to be. They didn't want to be heroes, like Che. They wanted to be themselves.

In dozens of interviews with young students, workers and intellectuals, I found a recurrent theme shared even by the small minority that claimed they supported the revolution: they were all tired of the regime's seemingly unending demands that they sacrifice "for the common good." They were tired of the political slogans they had been forced to recite since kindergarten. They wanted more freedom to travel abroad, to buy what they wanted, and to pursue the careers of their choice—regardless of the revolution's needs.

Some wanted to obtain scholarships that would allow them to continue their studies abroad. Others were competing for jobs as waiters or desk clerks at tourist hotels, which offered regular contact with foreigners and—through them—access to Diplotienda goods. Young women in the big cities were on the hunt for foreigners to marry—and with whom to leave Cuba.

Aspiring entrepreneurs were seeking a niche in Cuba's flourishing black market to become the underground providers of some much-needed product. Whatever they did, Cuban youths described it as their way to *escapar*—to escape the gray Communist life the regime had in store for them.

<>

Fernando, an eighteen-year-old in his last year of high school, asked me to wait a minute. He wanted to show me something. We were sitting in his parents' middle-class home in Havana, talking about his generation. He was a neatly dressed young man, with short hair and glasses. After a few seconds, he came back from his bedroom with a first-grade reading book. He had recently found it among a pile of old papers in a drawer. He wanted me to read it.

The textbook was called "Lectura I," or Reading I. Its first lesson, on page 10, featured a color illustration of a young girl in the uniform of Cuba's Communist Pioneers movement bestowing a medal on Fidel Castro. The Cuban leader was shown in his olive green uniform, looking down at the girl's hands as she placed the pin on his lapel.

The lesson, "What Fidel Said," read as follows: "One day, Fidel met with a group of pioneers. He told them, 'We want the organization of Cuban pioneers to be a great organization. We want our children to be the best students, to behave the best. We want our children to be the happiest. We want to feel proud of our children always.' The pioneers were moved by his words. They applauded. They applauded a lot!"

That was only the beginning, Fernando pointed out, taking the book from my hands and going through its pages to show me the illustrations of Fidel and Che, stories of the 1953 attack on Batista's Moncada barracks, anecdotes of Castro's life in the mountains as a guerrilla, and Che's adventures in faraway countries. Many lessons ended with the Pioneers' slogan, "We shall be like Che."

Fernando came to the point he wanted to make all along. He was sick of political indoctrination. He had been subjected to too much of it over the years.

"They saturated us, bombarded us. We're simply fed up with it all."

Like everybody else, Fernando faked total commitment to the revolution in front of his teachers and most outsiders. He had to, if he wanted to get a decent job from Cuba's only employer—the government. Faking it was easy, almost instinctive. All Fernando had to do was recite mechanically the well-learned collection of slogans. We shall be like Che! No big deal.

Did that mean that nothing had stuck after so many years of pervasive political indoctrination? Fernando thought about it. It was a hard question to answer, he said.

"Every time we chanted, 'We shall be like Che,' I felt like laughing. I always thought it was an insult to Che's memory. I see Che as a model, an idealist, a romantic hero. But the problem is that not all people are like Che. If everybody were, socialism would work."

And how did Fernando perceive Fidel?

"I don't like him, but I admire him. Even his enemies have to admit that the guy has guts. Not anybody can stand up to an adversary like the United States, only ninety miles away, and survive. The guy started with a handful of guerrillas, and defeated the whole Batista army. *Tiene cojones*. He's got balls. If he stepped down tomorrow, we would throw a big party. But if he walked into this room right now, I would melt."

<>

Jorge, an eighteen-year-old friend of Fernando's who was participating in the conversation, disagreed sharply.

"I used to admire Fidel when I was a kid, but not anymore," Jorge said. "The guy has gone increasingly crazier with time. He doesn't convince me anymore. I'm tired of him. I wish he'd go."

Like Fernando, Jorge looked pretty conventional with his short hair, long-sleeve shirt and leather shoes. He had just spent forty-five days in the countryside doing "voluntary work" to help alleviate

Cuba's food shortages. He participated in all political activities required by his school, and had attended a Fidel speech at Revolution Square during his summer vacation. Everybody went to the plaza when Fidel appeared—for the free beer that was given out by the Communist Youth, he said.

What did he dislike most about the Castro regime?

"This system has had its good things, like health and education, but it has become stagnant. This 'special period' we are living in, with oxen replacing tractors, is ridiculous. We're going back to the nineteenth century. The government's slogan is 'resist.' Resist? That doesn't look like a life plan to me. I want to be an artist, not a *boniato* [Cuba's sweet potato] picker. I wasn't born to pick *boniato*. Do you think my mother brought me into this world to pick *boniato*?"

Jorge saw no hope in the system—but conceded he did not want to become a martyr or a political prisoner by trying to change it by force. He would take to the streets to protest when everybody else did, he said.

He did not think the new generation of young Communist leaders that had just been promoted to the upper echelons of the Castro regime would change the system from within. Roberto Robaina, the T-shirt-clad Communist Youth leader who was a rising star in the regime's hierarchy, was an opportunist. And Carlos Lage, the physician in his late thirties who had become Castro's economic czar, also represented the old thinking despite his age.

"Imagine, he wears a guayabera!" Jorge said, smiling. "How can you trust anybody who wears a guayabera?"

Jorge's plan was to emigrate. He would not repeat his parents' mistake.

"My father is a revolutionary. But now, after all the things that have happened in the Soviet bloc, he is asking himself if it was all worth it. My parents sacrificed their personal lives for the revolution. I won't do it."

<>

Even young people who described themselves as supporters of the revolution, such as Che Guevara's twenty-six-year-old nephew Pablo Guevara, shunned the regime's political machinery.

Pablo, the son of one of Che's youngest brothers, was an actor. Like his distant cousin Canek, he had long hair, sported an earring, and wore faded jeans with sneakers. Unlike Canek, however, he still harbored sympathy for the revolution. Although much had gone wrong in recent years, the revolution's ideals of equality and justice were noble ones. In his view, the project—as he referred to the revolution—was still valid.

But Pablo was not a member of the Communist Youth, did not perform "voluntary work" for his neighborhood Committee for the Defense of the Revolution, and did not go to the countryside to serve several weeks on agricultural farms, as the regime was asking most young Havana residents to do. He just would not do it. He was an actor, not a peasant. He had a degree in performing arts from Cuba's Superior Institute of Arts. He was rehearsing for a play with a new company. He was too busy. He hoped his professional credentials— and, in all probability, his famous last name—would make up for his refusal to work in the fields.

"I'm not going to the countryside, because I don't think that after having studied for five years, and having had my studies paid for by the state, it makes much sense for me to work in agriculture," Pablo said. "I think I can better serve the country by doing what I can do best."

Pablo was not very interested in politics. He rarely watched Fidel's speeches on television. He conceded he had not paid much attention to the preparations for the Fourth Congress of the Communist Party—the much-awaited event that was to set the Cuban regime's new course following the collapse of the Soviet bloc. His life was acting.

What did he think of his uncle, Che Guevara?

"I admire him a lot," Pablo said. "But that doesn't mean that I want to be like him."

<>

There was a common denominator in what the young Cubans were saying. It wasn't so much *what* they were saying that was interesting—or the fact that they were expressing various degrees of opposition to the regime—but *how* they were saying it.

Most prevalent in their responses to my questions was the word "I." They said, "*I* want to do this; *I* want to do that." By comparison, their parents and grandparents expressed themselves in terms of "We." They said, "*We* thought that the best thing to do was this; *we* thought that the best thing to do was that."

Grownups had been part of a revolution in the making that most had accepted as a collective endeavor. They shared fond memories of the literacy campaign in the early sixties, when they had taken to the mountains to teach peasants to read and write. They had been unified by serious threats from Yanqui imperialism: they had closed ranks during the missile crisis and the Bay of Pigs. Their revolutionary ardor had been cemented by a myriad of job opportunities that had opened up with the massive flight of Cuban professionals after the revolution.

But young Cubans had grown up in a mature revolution, an institution. The literacy campaign and the Bay of Pigs were events in history books. To them, Fidel's constant warnings of the Yanqui threat were empty rhetoric. Those who had participated in the Angola war regarded it as an experience they would rather blot from memory. Whatever respect they held for the Cuban revolution, their mindset was different. Their world outlook started with the word "I."

Their parents, middle-aged Cubans, lived in a more confusing world. Many had spent the best years of their lives sacrificing personal dreams and doing the hard work required to turn the Communist ideal into reality. They were too old to forsake their past—and too young to settle for a tattered vision of a Communist paradise.

<>

Few carried a heavier political burden than Hilda Guevara, Canek's mother. She had not only been an enthusiastic supporter of the revolution, but also had received a well-known mandate from her legendary father to be a revolutionary—a demand that was prominently displayed in the revolution's history books.

On February 15, 1966, shortly after leaving Cuba to start the guerrilla war in Bolivia from which he would never return, Che Guevara sent Hilda a letter for her tenth birthday. By then, Hilda and a younger sister had been in Cuba for seven years. The letter, now part of Cuba's elementary school textbooks, reads in part as follows:

> Hildita Dearest:
>   I'm writing to you today, although this letter will arrive to you much later, because I want you to know that I remember you and hope that you spend your birthday happily. You are almost a woman now, and one can't write to you as one would to children, talking poppycock or telling little lies.
>   You must know that I'm still far away, and that I'll be spending a long time away from you, doing what I can to fight against our enemies. I'm not doing a great deal, but I'm doing something, and I think that one day you will be able to be always proud of your father, just as I'm proud of you.

Remember that many years of struggle are still ahead, and when you become a woman you'll have to do your share of the fighting. Meanwhile, one must prepare, be very revolutionary—which at your age means learning a lot, the most one can—and always be ready to support just causes. . . .

You must struggle to be among the best in school. The best in every sense. You know, in academics and in revolutionary attitude. That means good conduct, love for the revolution, comradery, etc. I wasn't like that when I was your age, but I lived in a different society where man was man's enemy. Now, you have the privilege of living in a different era, and you must be worthy of it. . . .

Okay, my dear, once again, have a very happy birthday. Give a hug to your mother . . . , and get yourself a super big and strong one that lasts for all the time during which we will not see one another.

> Your
> Papa.

Twenty-five years later, at age thirty-five, Hilda was still a revolutionary—but a very skeptical one. A short woman with native Indian features whose mother was Peruvian, Hilda worked as a librarian at Casa de las Americas, the regime's Latin American arts and propaganda center. At night, she studied for a master's degree in sociology.

Although she was bright and witty, Hilda stayed out of the limelight. Unlike her younger sister Aleida, she rarely participated in government ceremonies honoring her famous father. Hilda had accepted from the regime a comfortable two-bedroom flat, a small car and a fifty-peso monthly pension (little more than two dollars a month at the black market exchange rate) for children of martyrs of the revolution—the same amount that was being paid to the sons and daughters of Cuban soldiers fallen more recently in Angola.

I visited Hilda at her home one evening when Cuban television was to broadcast a newly made documentary about Che Guevara and fellow guerrilla commander Camilo Cienfuegos. The three-part series, "Camilo and Che, Courage and Conscience," had been announced on *Granma*'s front page that day, and had been heavily promoted for several weeks by the state-run media. I had asked a mutual friend to get Hilda to invite me to watch the series with her. It was agreed that I would buy a package of spaghetti at the Diplotienda, my friend would prepare it in Hilda's kitchen, and we would all watch the program together after dinner. It was a standard courtesy for foreign visitors in Cuba to bring food when invited for dinner.

We arrived at Hilda's home two hours before the program—more than enough time to introduce ourselves, have dinner, exchange jokes about our respective nationalities, and enter into a casual conversation about Cuba's reality. It was a privileged apartment by Cuban standards: a big living room, modern—but sparse—furnishings, and a few framed reproductions of abstract art hanging from the walls. It was also one of the few houses I had seen in Cuba with no Che Guevara poster in any visible place. Hilda kept only one black-and-white photograph of her father, smiling, next to her bed.

We were about to have coffee at the kitchen table when my friend alerted us that the documentary was about to begin. We were in the middle of a conversation about the differences between her perception of the revolution and that of her son, Canek. Fifteen minutes later, our friend hurried back into the kitchen to report that the program had already begun. Hilda was now washing the dishes, without much hurry. We would go as soon as she finished, she said. When she concluded the job, she sat back down at the table, and continued the discussion, ignoring the television program in the other room completely.

(A few days later, she would confess to me that she didn't want to watch it because she knew she would be "mad as hell." The film's last part featured a make-believe interview with Che, as if he were alive today. An actor looking remarkably like Che portrayed the guerrilla commander as still living in Cuba's mountains, standing ready to resume the fight for the revolution wherever he was needed, whenever Fidel asked. Hilda said she did not like the political manipulation of her father's memory—not by anybody.)

When I asked Hilda about her son's political views, she said she did not fully agree with Canek's radical opposition to the revolution. "I'm simply older," she shrugged. But that didn't mean she liked what was going on in Cuba.

"I, like many people, am confused, bewildered and skeptical about many things," she said. "Perestroika and the collapse of the world's Socialist bloc have brought into question many of the things in which we used to believe. It has left us totally confused."

So did she still believe in the Cuban revolution?

"I think the Cuban revolution can still be saved, but I have to confess I don't know how. To me, the dream is not dead. It's dormant; it's frozen in time." She explained, "Capitalism has regenerated itself over the years. It has adopted new forms—such as neoliberalism, for example. But communism has failed to keep up with the times. There is no such thing as neocommunism. That's what I would like. A communist system with a human face."

Hilda wanted Cuba to become more integrated with Latin America and the rest of the world, to tone down the Marxist rhetoric and to become a more efficient society. But she did not want to see Cuba become a de-facto U.S. colony, she said. That would be too much for her. She was unhappy that Canek was writing his songs in English.

"Look, for my generation, it was a major triumph to be allowed to sing in Spanish. For us, listening to [Argentina's protest singer] Mercedes Sosa amounted to a statement of support for Latin American culture at a time when the mass media were flooding us with American music. Language is the ultimate expression of one's nationality. We fought hard for it."

Yet without saying it, Hilda was proud of Canek. She was aware that I would quote his statements criticizing the Castro revolution, but she did not try to talk me out of it. Canek was within his rights to express his own opinions. "He is a free-thinker, just like my father was," she said. And she was clearly not in disagreement with many of the things he had said.

"My son is not an isolated entity in society. If he thinks the way he thinks, it must also have something to do with his being my son," she told me. "There must be a part of me that thinks that way."

If there was one woman in Cuba with a more prominent father than Hilda Guevara, it was Alina, thirty-five, Fidel Castro's only known daughter. Her life story had all the makings of a television drama.

Her mother, Natalia "Nati" Revuelta—a striking blond, green-eyed woman who moved in Cuba's aristocratic circles—had had a very public relationship with Castro in the mid-fifties, while she was still legally married to prominent Cuban heart specialist Orlando Fernandez. Alina was Castro's child, but was given the name of Alina Fernandez Revuelta to hide what would have been a major society scandal at the time.

When Fidel landed in Cuba with his eighty-two-man expeditionary force from Mexico a few months later, he asked Nati to join him in the mountains. He wanted to make her Cuba's First Lady, he said. She refused to go, saying she could not leave the baby alone. Fidel never forgave her for that. "Nati missed the boat . . . Nati missed the boat . . . ," Fidel would later tell a close associate.

Two years later, when Castro took power, Nati's husband left for the United States with the couple's other daughter. Nati and Alina were left alone in the family's big Havana mansion. Castro began to visit Nati, openly admitting to friends that Alina was his child.

He gave Nati a succession of government jobs, as well as a generous government subsidy as a veteran of the Moncada attack—in reality, Nati had only helped distribute leaflets. In 1964, he sent Nati and Alina to Paris, where Nati was given a diplomatic job at the Cuban embassy. When mother and daughter returned to Cuba two years later, Fidel's visits would be shorter, and more seldom. Castro would eventually move in with another woman, Dalia Soto Del Valle—also a green-eyed, upper-class Cubana—with whom he would have five sons.

Castro saw Alina sporadically in the seventies and eighties. He wanted her to take Russian and study in the Soviet Union, as his other children were doing, but she quit after six months of Russian lessons in Havana. She wanted to be a fashion model. Castro had paid for and attended at least one of Alina's four wedding ceremonies. But in the mid-eighties, father and daughter had a nasty falling out over Alina's marriage to a Mexican businessman, and her desire to leave the country. Since then, they had only seen one another once: at the French embassy's Bastille Day reception in 1988. Alina had sought him out among the diplomats, and the two had embraced and chatted warmly for a few moments.

A slender woman with high cheekbones who was used to being told she looked like actress Geraldine Chaplin, Alina had appeared for several years at fashion shows in Havana's exclusive La Maison boutique. She was well-connected in Cuban artistic and intellectual circles. In private, she had long shared her friends' growing frustration about the revolution's totalitarian practices.

As her demands to leave the country were consistently turned down despite her marriage to a Mexican citizen—there was speculation that Fidel had ordered immigration authorities not to let her leave—Alina was becoming increasingly impatient. She wanted to model in Paris, and to have a chance to show her teenage daughter, also named Alina, the outside world.

After two unsuccessful efforts to obtain an exit visa for a short trip to Europe in 1991, Alina began to spread the word that she would go public with her travel demands—and with charges that she was being held prisoner in her own country. She hoped that state security would report their anxiety to her father—and that he would issue orders to let her go.

A few months later, while Alina was still waiting for her travel permit, the Spanish magazine *Tiempo* ran a sensational story quoting her as saying she had once thrown her father out of her home, and that she had been known to complain that he had given her a box of soft drinks as a wedding present. She was also quoted as saying that Fidel "should be given a medal for having done such a good job destroying the country over the past thirty-two years." Alina immediately denied the story, calling it a "complete fabrication." Her friends in Cuba, however, knew that much of the story's content—especially the political statements—was vintage Alina.

When I visited her for the first time a few weeks after the story had appeared in the Spanish magazine, she looked frail and depressed. There was a fresh scar in her forehead, which she said was from a scratch from her cat. She denied rumors that she was anorexic, but conceded she had lost much weight and suffered from asthma. Her open pleas to leave Cuba had strained her relationship with her mother, who lived around the corner and feared antagonizing Fidel would only make things worse for Alina. Unemployed, at odds with her powerful father, unable to leave the country and missing her Mexican husband who had long left, Alina's life was a mess. But she didn't seem anything close to a mentally disturbed person—as government officials would soon try to hint to anyone inquiring about Fidel's rebellious daughter.

Her two-bedroom apartment in a three-story building in Havana's residential area of Nuevo Vedado was cozy. The front door had been decorated with hearts drawn in colored chalk, and the handwritten legend, "Alina y Alina." Her refrigerator was stocked with nearly a dozen cheeses, which she bought at the Diplotienda thanks to a German friend who let her in, and to the dollars sent by her estranged Mexican husband ("I live on cheese," she laughed, explaining the virtual absence of anything else in her refrigerator). In the living room, there were pictures of her mother, Marilyn Monroe, herself, and an image of Jesus Christ. There was no visible picture of Fidel Castro in the room.

Alina asked me not to discuss her relationship with her father. Castro had always maintained an obsessive secrecy about his private life—part of his tactic to project a larger-than-life image. No stories or pictures of his various wives or children had ever appeared in the Cuban press. The closest thing to a first lady in revolutionary Cuba was Raúl Castro's wife Vilma Espin, who welcomed foreign first ladies and dedicated children's hospitals in official ceremonies. Alina did not want to further infuriate her father by disclosing family secrets. She told me she would talk only about Cuba's political situation—just as any other concerned citizen would.

"What do I think about Cuba's socialism? I used to believe in it when I was very little," Alina said. "But now, Cuban socialism is a dead-end street. In my mind, I associate it with economic collapse, with food shortages."

What bothered her the most about life in Cuba? She didn't know where to start.

"It's very tiring to be on a permanent war footing for so many years. . . . Cuba is always in a state of war, either because one war is starting or because another is ending. Do you realize what that means? We have never lived in peace. . . ." She hated her father's slogan, "Socialism or Death." She said, "I think human beings are born to live, not to die."

She could not stand the systematic curtailment of personal freedoms. "What bothers me most is the disinformation. The lack of news, literature. We don't get books, we don't know what is being published abroad. . . ." She resented the government's restrictions on foreign travel. "I would like my daughter to have the chance to see other places. I have never understood why people are not allowed out of here."

Alina told me her generation—people in their thirties and early forties—was the most frustrated in Cuba. It was a generation that had no place in Cuba's revolution, she said. Their parents—people now in their sixties, like Fidel—occupied virtually all decision-making jobs in Cuba's political and economic life.

"I'm typical of my generation," she continued. "My generation is the most troubled of all. We were supposed to be the ones taking over from our parents. And what has happened? We've found that everything was done, laid out, and untouchable. They have not allowed us to do anything. . . . We feel frustrated, useless. We grew up believing in the revolution's mystique, but we later found out that our hands were tied.

"And we're screwed even more, because we know what was there before. I still remember the fancy clothes I had when I was a child, the alphabet noodle soups in various shapes and colors, the Malecón when it was lined with lit advertisements for the department stores . . .''

What would happen next in Cuba?

"There must be an immediate opening, if not an ideological one at least an economic one, and each leads to the other. I don't think people can take this level of stress for much longer. There must be an opening, and it must come from the top."

Would her father open up the system he had so carefully controlled?

She hoped so, but doubted he would. She declined to speculate who else could carry out the reforms.

Did she see Fidel Castro as a dictator?

"When people tell me he's a dictator, I tell them that's not the right word. . . . Strictly speaking, Fidel is a tyrant. I have looked up the two words in the dictionary. A dictator is a 'person who is granted absolute powers to face a national emergency on a temporary basis.' A tyrant is an 'absolute ruler unrestrained by law, who usurps people's rights.' "

Faced with a drastic cut in Soviet aid and an increasingly anxious population, the Castro regime scrambled to put together a long-term economic recovery plan. Bicycles and oxen would help Cuba survive in the short run, but Castro needed to offer Cubans—especially the island's restless youth—a more promising future.

His economic strategy would be based on development of hard-currency-generating businesses. He would soon turn Cuba's economy upside down to pump all available resources into a few selected industries, led by tourism. It would be a risky gambit.

PART

III

THE POLITICS OF SURVIVAL

<<<<<<<<<<<<<<<<<<<<<<<<<<<<<<<<<<<<

Selling Out the Cuban Revolution (1990-1991)

10
Banking on an Old Ghost—Tourism

◄◄◄◄◄The fancy tourist brochure gave high marks to the Casa de las Infusiones, a corner teahouse on Havana's scenic G Avenue. The booklet described it as a "beautiful colonial house, located in a magnificent natural setting, offering aromatic herbal teas that are very cherished in Cuba." It sounded like a good prospect for a quiet Saturday afternoon.

Indeed, the Casa de las Infusiones was a colonial house, with a big porch and a white veranda. I sat at one of its six outdoor tables—the only one that wasn't occupied. The menu on the table offered only two things: hot tea, and cold tea, for the equivalent of about one U.S. cent each.

A sleepy atmosphere hung over the place. The two middle-aged men next to me sat idly, with nothing to say to one another. One picked his teeth and looked off into the horizon. The other man was half asleep, his head resting on his left fist. At other tables, the scene wasn't much livelier.

I was thirsty. After more than half an hour, no one had appeared to take my order. Nobody else was being waited on, but nobody else seemed to mind. I began looking right and left, increasingly impatient. Where the hell was the waiter?

After an additional ten minutes, I walked back to the kitchen.

"Excuse me. Could I order something?" I asked.

"No, señor. Don't you see there's nobody out there?" one of the two women behind the counter answered, quite rudely.

"Well, *you* are here . . . I thought perhaps you could help me . . ."

"Señor, I'm not a waitress. I'm kitchen personnel," she shot back. "The waiters haven't arrived yet."

When would they arrive? She didn't know. Could she at least give me a glass of water? No. That was not within her job description. That was the waiters' job. They would do it . . . when they showed up.

I decided to get a drink elsewhere. To my amazement, nobody seemed to share my frustration. As I strode out the door, a sign with a surrealist touch caught my eye. It said: "Decree-Law No. 141: It is prohibited to occupy a table without consuming."

Fidel Castro had just decided to bank Cuba's economic survival on tourism. The service at Cuban hotels, bars and restaurants—a favorite topic of conversation among foreigners visiting the island—was no laughing matter to him. Cuba desperately needed dollars to buy the food and raw materials that it was no longer getting from its former Communist allies. Tourism offered the quickest way to obtain cash to pay for these imports.

In a sharp reversal from his previous stand—he had condemned tourism for three decades as a symbol of Batista-era decadence— Castro ordered an all-out campaign to revamp the island's tourist business.* The goal was to increase the number of foreign tourists from three hundred forty thousand in 1990 to one million in 1995.

The revolution's ideological principles were bent every which way in the bid for new tourist dollars. In 1991, for the first time since the wave of nationalizations that followed the Castro takeover, foreign companies were allowed to buy a 50 percent share of new hotels and run them single-handedly. A decade-old foreign-investment law had been quietly amended to give new investors legal protection. Under the new legislation, foreign investors paid no income taxes during their first ten years in Cuba, and didn't pay customs duties for their imports of hotel construction materials, furniture and food.

---

* *The new policy had been first outlined in 1987, but began to be fully implemented in early 1990, when Castro ordered that major resources be devoted to expand the tourism industry.*

Labor laws guaranteeing job stability, a longtime source of revolutionary pride, were quietly shelved. Foreign hotel managers, mostly Spanish firms, were now allowed to lay off workers at their will—and often did. Castro's diatribes against bourgeois decadence were quickly forgotten, as the cash-starved government invited *Playboy* magazine— long prohibited in Cuba—to produce a ten-page girls-of-Cuba pictorial photographed in various Cuban tourist resorts. A simultaneous Cuban government ad campaign featured tourist posters showing bikini-clad Cuban women under the title, "Cuba. Come and be tempted."

More than a dozen luxury hotels, including the five-star Cohiba Hotel, and nearly fifty tourist-only restaurants sprang up across the island. In Havana's Miramar neighborhood, a Spanish investor opened the $1 million Havana Club, a giant discotheque with a circular dance floor, indoor waterfalls and lots of glowing neon. Women approached foreign visitors at the front door. Inside, the dance floor was packed with elderly Spanish and Mexican businessmen dancing with provocatively dressed Cuban women, most of them in their teens.

Not far away, La Maison—an old mansion—was upgraded to offer nightly fashion shows. Blond women in haute couture evening dresses and male models in leather shirts danced up and down a ramp to the sound of tropical music. A tourist-only dollar shop offered silver tea sets, trays, and rings priced up to a thousand dollars.

The idea was to attract upscale Canadian, Western European and Latin American tourists. Since the revolution, most tourists to Cuba had been youths in Che Guevara T-shirts, with revolutionary fervor in their hearts but few dollars in their pockets. The regime was now aiming for their wealthier parents, whatever their ideology. According to the government's projections, the new wave of richer visitors would produce an income of $350 million in 1991, and this would grow steadily to reach $1 billion by the end of the decade.

To make sure the tourists felt at home, the regime started importing products that hadn't been seen on the island in decades. Among them: apples, pears, and grapes. For many young hotel workers, it was the first time in their lives they were seeing something as exotic as an apple. Even caviar was allowed onto the island for the first time in thirty years.

"If you ask, can one bring in caviar for that hotel? Yes, you can bring in caviar," Castro said when asked about the new policy. "And will caviar have to pay customs duties? No, caviar won't have to pay customs duty."

<>

By far the greatest challenge in Cuba's new tourism drive was the organization of the XIth Pan American Games, which Castro had insisted on holding in Havana in August 1991, despite Cuba's calamitous economy. The event would burden Cuba with more than $130 million in construction costs, but the Cuban leader decided to go ahead with it anyway. Canceling the games would send a signal of political weakness. Holding them would show the world that Cuba continued to be a politically stable country, a viable tourist spot, and a sports contender.

It was a pharaonic undertaking. More than three hundred thousand Havana residents were asked at work to "donate" their weekends to help build a 35,000-seat stadium, an aquatic complex, dozens of new sporting facilities, and an athletic village consisting of fifty-five apartment buildings on the outskirts of the city. A few weeks before the start of the games, when it was clear that the facilities would not be ready on time, army troops were brought in to finish the job.

Shiploads of food were brought to the island to help fill a forty-page-long list of menus for the more than seventeen thousand athletes, journalists, sports officials and tourists that attended the sport event. The massive importation of food for the visitors—there were five breakfast, lunch and dinner menus for the foreigners, each offering several choices of French cuisine dishes—shocked the Cubans.

Many could not help linking the regime's fabulous expenditures with the population's dismal food shortages. "Tocopan," the little red-white-and-blue bird that was to be the mascot emblem of the games, quickly became known in the streets as "Poco pan"—too little bread.

<>

The government's efforts to attract legions of foreign tourists to Cuba began to pay off. Package tours of Canadian, Western European and Latin American groups rose by more than 20 percent a year in 1990 and again in 1991.* The rapid growth was partly guaranteed by the big Spanish hotel chains, which were bringing in their own tourists to assure themselves a quick return on their investments.

Most of the tourists were attracted by the Caribbean sun and the low prices. Many males were also drawn by the island's tourist-loving

---

* Americans were prohibited from visiting Cuba under 1963 U.S. regulations that were further tightened with new travel restrictions in 1982.

women—a lure the government cheerfully exploited by featuring virtually naked mulatto women in Cuba's promotional tourist posters abroad.

By the end of 1991, Cuban officials were reporting a record influx of nearly four hundred thousand foreign visitors—more than had ever visited the island in any single year during the Batista era. In fairness, neighboring Caribbean countries had since done much better. Cuba now attracted only 4 percent of all travelers to the Caribbean, down from 33 percent before the revolution. But Cuba was beginning to catch up.

The main hurdle in Cuba's effort to resuscitate its tourist industry was the painfully poor service at hotels and restaurants. Getting Cuban hotel workers to stop barking at foreigners was in itself a formidable task.

During the previous three decades, Cubans had been brought up to think they were equal to—or better than—the arrogant Americans who had turned Cuba into a gambling and prostitution center during the Batista years. It had long been considered a revolutionary duty for hotel employees to lecture foreigners about the wonders of Marxism-Leninism.

Now, all of a sudden, the government was asking hotel workers to forget everything they had learned—and be solicitous to foreign visitors. Scores of "hospitality schools" were opened in Havana and Varadero, with the assistance of Spanish and German hotel-management consultants, to improve the training of tourist workers. The schools' main lesson: hotel guests were not potential revolutionary fellow travelers. Tourism was an industry and foreign visitors were clients who deserved to be pampered for their money. Once again, the customer was always right.

"We're telling our students to address foreigners no longer as *compañero*," Abraham Maciques, the businesslike general manager of the Cuban government's huge tourism corporation Cubanacan, explained to me at his office. "We're telling them to address them as *señor*, which is an internationally accepted term."

All of this was hard on the workers themselves. You could see a confusion in their attitudes, a sudden switch from rudeness to cordiality—or vice versa.

At Havana's elegant Hotel Victoria, I was once correctly addressed as "*señor*" by a waitress—only to be immediately scolded for my ignorance about the wonders of Marxism-Leninism. I had only attempted to order my breakfast.

"*Señora*," I had called the waitress, raising my hand. The woman, standing only ten feet away rearranging some coffee cups, pretended not to hear me. The hotel's small restaurant was almost empty.

"*Compañera*," I ventured, curious whether that would make her pay attention to me. It didn't. She continued to concentrate on her coffee cups, her back turned to me.

"*Camarera*," I tried next, choosing a word commonly used in Latin America to call a waitress.

This time, the woman whirled around, and strode toward me with an angry snarl on her face.

"*Señor*," she admonished me. "I'm not a *camarera*. I'm a *capitana!*"

I opened my hands asking for clemency. She informed me that the *camareras* were the ones doing room service. She, on the other hand, was part of the restaurant personnel, clearly a higher position in the Socialist workplace. She proceeded to sternly explain the rights and obligations of each category of hotel workers—and the advantages they enjoyed compared with their status in prerevolutionary times.

I thanked her for the information and asked for a continental breakfast.

"With pleasure, *señor*," she answered, switching back to her sugary, please-the-customer mode.

<><>

I once caused a major political brawl at Havana's Hotel Presidente when I innocently asked to make a photocopy. A sign at the reception desk offered the copy-machine service upon request. But the receptionist had told me that the employee in charge of it happened to be at a meeting. Could I wait for about an hour?

I couldn't. A Cuban I had just interviewed was standing next to me, with the papers I wanted to copy. He was in a rush, and wouldn't leave the papers with me. I asked the hotel employee if the copy-machine person couldn't be asked out of the meeting. I only needed to make a handful of copies . . .

The receptionist, somewhat shocked at my demand, said he didn't think it was possible. The copy-machine employee was at his Communist Party cell's weekly meeting.

Well, my need to make a photocopy was much more important, I replied, curious to put Cuba's new tourism policy at test. I was a customer at the hotel. I was paying the exorbitant sum of sixty dollars a day, and was entitled to the services the hotel was offering, I protested. Could he please talk to his supervisor?

The young reception desk employee hesitated for a few seconds, and went to the back room to talk to his superior. I could overhear the ensuing argument. The supervisor seemed to be recommending that the employee be called out of the meeting. Another person objected, saying a Party meeting couldn't be interrupted. Within minutes, several other employees had joined the discussion. The voices grew louder—and angrier.

Finally, the young concierge emerged from the room, pale and frightened. He told me the copy-machine employee would be brought down. Within minutes I was making my photocopies. The incident became the talk of the day among the Presidente's workers. It later became a case study in the hotel's staff meetings, I was told.

Unbeknownst to the rest of the world, Cuba's mighty Communist Party had just lost a small battle to the country's new managerial class.

<>

But the regime's tourism campaign was producing a dangerous social backlash. Cubans were increasingly troubled by Cuba's new apartheid system. The more new hotels, restaurants and beach resorts that were opened, the more Cubans realized they were being barred from access to them. The more foreign tourists visited the island, the more often Cubans were humiliated by having to give up their places at restaurant and gasoline lines.

At some places, such as Varadero's El Bodegón Criollo restaurant, the separation of Cubans and foreigners was reminiscent of the worst days of racial segregation in the United States. The locals were allowed in, but they were seated in a separate section, away from dollar-paying tourists.

The night I visited the restaurant, a cavelike building with graffiti on the walls, the tourist section was empty and the Cuban area was filled to capacity. About twenty people waited in line outside.

"You pay in dollars, right?" the maître d' asked me, recognizing me as a foreigner.

"Yes," I answered.

"Come on in," he said, asking the Cubans standing in line to move aside so that he could direct me to the empty foreigners' section.

But I didn't like the idea of eating alone. Couldn't I sit in the other room?, I asked.

"I'm sorry, señor, but that area is reserved for Cubans," he said apologetically.

Why weren't the Cubans waiting outside allowed into the tourist section, since it was empty anyway?

"I'm sorry, señor, but that's not possible," the maître d' said. "It's against the guidelines."

I was placed in the empty room, and served immediately. I could see the Cuban families in the other room, crowded around the tables, waiting for a single waiter to take care of them all. I ate my dinner in silence, watching them watch me.

<>

Early in the afternoon a few days later, when I approached the gas station on the corner of Havana's Linea and E streets, I saw a line of cars two blocks long waiting for gas under the scorching sun.

Curious to see what it would be like to exercise my rights as a tourist, I pulled right up to the gas pump. The attendant, seeing my Havanautos license plate, stopped the first car in line and waved me in.

As I got out of my car to give the attendant my tourist-issue gasoline coupons, a woman in the blue Lada that had been first in line emerged from her vehicle and walked over, visibly upset.

"This is outrageous! What has become of our country? Cuba no longer belongs to us Cubans! This has become a country for foreigners!" she started yelling at the half dozen people standing around the gasoline pumps.

The little audience smiled passively. A few men nodded at her, and shrugged. I decided to play the innocent tourist. I excused myself, and said I was sorry, but that people at the Havanautos office had told me that as a tourist I did not have to wait in line.

"They told me that's the law," I said.

"That's not our law, sir, that's *their* law!" she protested.

"They told me it's the law of Cuba, of you Cubans . . . ," I went on, curious to see her reaction.

"Sir, that's their law. The law *de los que mandan* . . . Of those who rule . . . !"

The game was over. I apologized, and told her she was absolutely right. She went back to her car, feeling better. Everybody smiled approvingly. It was harder and harder for Cubans to swallow the humiliations that came along with the new tourism policy.

<>

It was a song criticizing Cuba's new apartheid system that had made Carlos Varela, the government-tolerated protest singer, an instant idol. Nobody had dared to bring up the issue publicly before. When the young artist came out with "Tropicollage," his biting song about the privileged life of tourists in Cuba, audiences went wild.

The song tells of foreign tourists coming to Cuba for a week, eating at tourist-only restaurants, staying at tourist-only hotels, visiting tourist-only beaches, and taking tourist-only taxis to the airport, never getting a glimpse of how Cubans really live. It tells of Cubans trying to get into the hotels and not being allowed in. "It's all happening here, and I want to change it," says the refrain. The line would draw standing ovations from Varela's audiences, the cheering youths ecstatically venting their rage.

"The Cuban people understand that it's all right to try to earn foreign currency," Varela told me later. "But that shouldn't mean you can't enter the lobby of a hotel in your own country."

<>

Tourism was creating another problem: the emergence of a workers' aristocracy, not unlike that which had existed in prerevolutionary times among the better-paid workers of U.S. companies.

The foreign-run hotel chains soon became a magnet for university graduates in economics, psychology, history and other professions. One waitress at the Victoria Hotel told me she had a master's degree in agronomy. A young clerk at the Vedado Hotel was an economist. A room maid in Varadero was a graduate in Marxist studies. Thousands of young professionals were enrolling in three-month tourism courses to get jobs in the new hotels and join the new privileged class.

"Our hotel has three hundred twenty workers, eighty percent of whom have college degrees and the remainder has at least twelve years of schooling," Carlos Pereda Navarro, the Spanish manager of the brand new Sol Palmeras Hotel in Varadero, told the weekly *Bohemia*. "Naturally, because we are a joint venture, we pay higher salaries than elsewhere."

It wasn't just the better pay. What was much more important was that a hotel job facilitated contact with foreigners. This meant tips in dollars—a forbidden currency for all other Cubans—and a chance to get a friendly tourist to buy you soap or a shirt at the Diplotienda. Hotel workers were better dressed and better fed than anyone else in the workforce.

To many, it also meant a chance to leave Cuba: one could always become romantically involved with a tourist, and leave the island with real or faked marriage papers. The attraction was irresistible: in 1991, about thirty-six thousand young Cubans enrolled in the new hospitality schools and tourism-related university careers.

As the new generation of hotel workers learned that good service to foreigners translated into fatter dollar tips, they competed tooth and nail to work at foreigners-only hotels. Those employed at the few places that served foreigners and Cubans both soon learned to sneer at Cuban patrons.

Ricardo, a guitar player with his own Cuban folk-music group, told me that one night after his performance at the Capri Hotel cabaret, he walked over to the bar to watch the rest of the show from one of the stools there. The bartender was in a bad mood.

"You know what he told me? He said, 'What a shame. Tonight, we have mostly Cubans!' Outrageous! It seems like we've gone back full circle to the Batista days."

In addition to tourism, Castro's economic survival plan targeted a second industry: biotechnology.

In 1986, Castro opened a monumental Center of Genetic Engineering and Biotechnology on the outskirts of Havana, and announced that Cuba would become a Third World power in scientific research. The Center soon began to produce biological products for medical, industrial, agricultural and veterinary uses, mainly for Third World countries.

Like most large-scale operations in Cuba, it was born of Castro's whim. The idea had come to the Cuban leader during a 1980 chat with Dr. Randolph Lee Clark, a visiting researcher from the Anderson Hospital in Houston, Texas. Castro, known to be a hypochondriac with a ravenous hunger for medical news, was impressed by the visiting professor's tales about Interferon, a new drug for cancer patients.

Two weeks later, Castro dispatched a Cuban scientist, Dr. Manuel Limonta, to study the new drug with Clark at the Anderson Hospital. A year later, after a team led by Limonta began producing Interferon in Cuba, Castro set out to create a huge biotechnology center—the biggest one in Latin America.

More than $140 million was spent on construction and startup equipment, not including the cost of the 37-acre stretch of land on the outskirts of Havana on which it was built. The Cuban leader would show up as often as once a week after its opening, personally overseeing the progress of every experiment.

"He had read everything," Limonta recalls. "He was up-to-date on every scientific project we were undertaking."

By 1990, Castro was claiming some early successes. The Center had sold $100 million worth of its newly developed Meningitis B vaccine to Brazil that year. It was beginning to barter $240 million worth of the vaccine and other medical materials for Soviet oil and grain. The Center was also starting mass production of low-priced AIDS testing kits and a skin growth factor for burn patients, which it planned to sell massively in Latin American and African countries.

Biotechnology soon became a central theme in Castro's speeches about Cuba's future. The Center had produced a "scientific explosion" that would dramatically bolster the country's export income, he claimed. Cuban scientists were "the pillars" of Cuba's economic development, he told the nation in December 1990.

Prensa Latina, the official Cuban wire agency, claimed a few weeks later that biotechnology would make Cuba a wealthy superpower. "The era of biotechnology could do away with the frontiers that industrialization has erected to separate the First, Second and Third World countries," it said.

<>

Dr. Limonta, the no-nonsense physician-scientist who heads the Center, invited me to tour the giant scientific research complex and draw my own conclusions. I was immediately impressed by its futuristic architecture. Its two interconnected eight-story main buildings made a giant concrete fortress, which spread its tentacles into various wings.

Walking behind Limonta through the Center's seemingly endless corridors, I felt I could have been in Dr. No's secret headquarters. The institute was a full-fledged city, where 450 scientists lived and worked. Young, stern-looking men and women in white lab uniforms with ID tags crisscrossed the corridors at full speed, stopping briefly to compare notes on computer printouts, then resuming their resolute march toward some other laboratory. Loudspeakers blared announcements from every wall.

The main building housed a huge cafeteria where workers got their meals three times a day. Most ate in silence, as if their minds continued to puzzle over technical problems. Various dormitories were close by, as well as a 400-seat movie theater, which offered the latest American and European movies; a gym with two swimming pools, a track-and-field path, basketball and volleyball courts. A solar-powered hotel with 112 rooms, a discotheque and a separate swimming pool were under construction, to be used by visiting scientists.

As we walked along, Dr. Limonta showed me what was being done in the Center's nearly two hundred laboratories. In one, scientists were trying to genetically engineer a cow that could produce more milk, or one that would give milk with a healthier nutritive content. A long machine with bottles and tubes hung from the wall.

In another laboratory, they were producing hybrid fish species. Dozens of live fish were swimming inside two giant water tanks. Most looked quite normal to me, but I was assured they were all products of genetic engineering. Looking closer, I saw one with a monstrous mustache like none I had ever seen before.

In one floor's elevator hall was a giant decorative plant. It, too, was a hybrid conceived at the laboratories. Through genetic engineering, the Center had also developed a drug to hasten the process of human skin growth, and was in various stages of developing products that could slow down the aging process, increase sexual energy, interrupt heart attacks, and fight cholesterol. Cuba's scientists were making crucial contributions to mankind, Dr. Limonta assured me.

<>

Was Castro's pet project an outlandish dream? Could an island that wasn't able to offer aspirins to its population become a world power in biotechnology? At the very least, it was an adventurous proposition. Its creation had more to do with Castro's hankering for international prestige than with realistic expectations of big profits.

U.S. and Western European pharmaceutical companies spend more than $150 million to develop a new drug, according to industry analysts. Most pharmaceutical firms' research projects are abandoned, either because they prove to be ineffective or because they fail to pass safety tests. Cuba could hardly spend what it takes to develop and test drugs that could be licensed internationally.

In fact, by mid-1991, none of the Center's drugs had met U.S. and Western European licensing standards. When a major international corporation explored the possibility of buying the Center's skin growth factor for skin patients, it backed off after finding out that Cuba had not performed long-term tests on the drug's possible carcinogenic effects or the risk of birth defects.

Cuba could only hope to sell its biotechnology in developing countries whose drug licensing standards were much more lax.

And even there, the island had no marketing or distribution structure in place to sell the products. Multinational firms were not losing sleep over Cuba's plans to sell its pharmaceutical goods around the world.

"Cuba cannot afford to open sales offices abroad because it only has one or two products to sell," a Havana-based representative of a multinational pharmaceutical firm said. "You can only start your own sales network when you have hundreds of products to offer, so that if one of them gets killed by the competition, you still have dozens of others to sell."

When I asked Limonta how cash-starved Cuba hoped to outperform the big U.S. and German pharmaceutical companies in the Third World, he had a simple answer—lower production costs. The Center had a highly motivated staff of young scientists who worked fifteen hours a day, six days a week. Their small pay incentive brought their salary to about 350 pesos a month, or about $420 a year at the black market exchange rate—a minuscule fraction of a scientist's salary in the United States or Europe.

They were motivated by Fidel's call to save Cuba from its desperate economic situation, he said. "You can't have people working this hard in other countries, because they don't have the ideological motivation."

Judging from the bulletin boards on the laboratory walls, the young scientists were mostly driven by professional prestige. There were fewer pictures of Castro than at your standard Cuban government office—and more postcards from New York and Amsterdam. The Center's scientists had more professional contacts with the outside world than their colleagues in other Cuban institutions, and enjoyed more foreign travel opportunities. Working at the Center was about the best thing a Cuban scientist could show in his resumé, one young biologist told me.

But an efficient scientific research center without the circuitry to sell its products abroad amounted to little more than a costly propaganda show. As time went by, Cuban officials realized that the only way to make the biotechnology industry profitable was to enter joint ventures with foreign corporations, much like what was being done in the tourism industry. Cuba began to look for foreign firms to test and market its newly developed drugs. As much as Castro might regret it, there was no way to keep capitalism from creeping into his island's economy.

The third part of Castro's economic salvation plan was a combination of the other two: medical tourism. According to government estimates, more than thirty-five hundred foreigners came to Cuba in 1990 to be treated for vitiligo, psoriasis and retinitis pigmentosa and to receive a variety of organ transplants. More than four thousand tourist-patients were projected for 1991.

Many of the tourist-patients were Central and South Americans, seeking sophisticated medical treatments they couldn't obtain in their own countries. Cuba offered these treatments more cheaply than the United States in a series of hospitals that were rapidly converted to serve primarily foreigners. The prices were $10,000 for a coronary bypass, $3,500 for a cornea transplant, $2,500 for a face lift, and $400 for an abortion.

One of the biggest sellers was a Cuban-developed treatment for retinitis pigmentosa, an eye disease considered incurable in most other countries. Servimed, Cubanacan's health tourism division, also opened a handful of "antistress" clinics for tired foreign executives in Varadero. Altogether, by 1992, the regime expected to earn more than $10 million a year from foreign patients.

Meanwhile, Castro continued to prepare the population for the Zero Option—the possibility of a total cutoff of fuel and grain shipments from the Soviet Union. Dress rehearsals were conducted throughout the country to keep factories going without fuel. One day a week, every work center was asked to operate in the dark, and restaurants and cafeterias were made to do their cooking with charcoal.

Growing numbers of state food distribution companies began to deliver their goods with horse-drawn carts, and more than three dozen repair shops were opened in Havana to service hundreds of thousands of new Chinese bicycles. Thirty additional "new towns" were built in the countryside to house the waves of city residents assigned to work in agriculture. Biologists studied the breeding of rodents and other animals as possible food for the population in a scenario of total isolation. Government media began promoting "green medicine" herbal potions to take the place of manufactured drugs.

"The country must be prepared for even bigger limitations than the current ones, even for the zero fuel option," a gloomy Castro warned in a December 1990 speech to the Fourth Congress of the Federation of University Students (FEU). "Cuba will continue to defend socialism even if the Soviet Union disappears. . . . We're not even toying with the idea that one day Yanqui imperialists may set their indecent boots on our territory again."

<>

Would Castro's tourism-and-biotechnology economic salvation plan work? It never stood a chance—at least not in time to offset the loss of massive Soviet bloc subsidies. Cuba was an economic basket case.

Cuba's new tourism drive was producing net profits of little more than $150 million a year, and the biotechnology industry was netting profits of only about $50 million annually. The country had been shut off from foreign credit lines, because it had long suspended payments on its $6.2 billion debt to Western banks, and it owed about $16 billion to the Soviets.*

Following Castro's participation in the July 1991 summit of Ibero-American heads of state in Guadalajara, Mexico, he had made enthusiastic public vows to replace his trade dependence on the Soviet bloc with new economic ties with Latin America. But it was wishful thinking: Cuba's exports to all Latin American and Caribbean countries amounted to a pitiful 3.5 percent of the island's overall annual foreign sales. Even if the figure was doubled or tripled in future years—a dynamic enough jump—it would still amount to a small fraction of what Cuba had been shipping to its former Socialist allies.

If the Soviets started paying market prices for Cuban sugar, and tobacco and nickel exports continued dropping, Cuba would soon be left with an export income of little more than $2.5 billion—far short of the country's traditional $6 billion import bill. It was an abysmal gap.

<>

The trouble was, as usual, the Comandante was putting ideology ahead of sound economic thinking. Castro hoped that tourism and biotechnology would generate enough foreign income to keep the rest of the economy afloat, without having to extend free-market mechanisms to other industries. He was determined not to allow these islands of economic efficiency to contaminate the rest of the system.

The fall of Eastern Europe had convinced him that a wider economic opening would lead to more independent thinking and possi-

---

* *The dollar amount of Cuba's debt to the Soviets has been estimated at $10 billion to $16 billion, depending on the exchange rate for the ruble. The $16 billion figure was used by former Soviet ambassador to Cuba Yuri Petrov, in a December 1991 interview with Reuters in Moscow.*

bly a full-fledged popular uprising. The more Cubans were allowed to work for private companies, the less power the state would have to force them to show up at mass rallies, report on their neighbors or do "voluntary" work for the revolution. And if Cubans saw with their own eyes that the only companies that worked were those operating under market economy rules, how long would they keep tolerating a Marxist state that maintained that capitalism was the scourge of humanity?

Castro's top advisers were divided over which way to go. Reformers within his inner circle, led by Council of State economic coordinator Carlos Lage and Party ideology and foreign affairs chief Carlos Aldana, were pressing to allow other parts of the Cuban economy to operate with greater autonomy, at least until the island could emerge from its crisis. They recommended trimming the overblown staffs of state enterprises, and offering material incentives for increased productivity. They had a powerful backer in Raúl Castro, whose military supply companies had begun experimenting with capitalist management practices in the mid-eighties.*

"It doesn't make sense to create islands of efficiency such as tourism or biotechnology in an economy that is globally inefficient," one reform-minded Party official told me, paraphrasing a confidential report that circulated in Aldana's office. "We have to be able to invest the proceeds of our showcase industries into an efficient economy. Otherwise, we're throwing money into a bottomless barrel."

On the other side of the argument was Communist Party Organization chief José Ramón Machado Ventura, a sixty-one-year-old hard-liner who constantly voiced fears that new pockets of capitalism would undermine Cuba's socialist system. What leverage would the neighborhood committees have to mobilize crowds in support of the revolution if people no longer depended on the state for their income? the ideologues argued.

"If these pockets of capitalism are allowed to grow, our political discourse will become totally divorced from reality," a Machado Ventura follower told me. "The Party will be weakened to the point of irrelevancy, just like what happened in Eastern Europe."

---

* *In 1986, Raúl Castro authorized seventeen MINFAR companies, led by the Che Guevara mechanical spare parts plant in Villa Clara, to operate semi–autonomously. The MINFAR firms, which were exempt from revolutionary labor laws prohibiting firms from laying off workers, rapidly trimmed their workforces and became more productive. Raúl Castro's economic team, led by Lt. Col. Armando Perez, proclaimed the experiment a success. The idea to extend it to other parts of the economy was soon embraced by Vice-President Carlos Rafael Rodriguez, Aldana and Lage.*

In 1990, Castro chose a middle course: he launched a draconian austerity plan that would lay off or relocate thousands of Party officials, and he postponed a decision on whether to provide new material incentives to state company managers.

By October 1990, the Communist Party's nineteen departments were reduced to nine—the first step toward wider cutbacks that were to be extended to other government offices and state corporations. For the first time since the revolution, thousands of workers risked being left unemployed. The government offered them the option of either moving to the countryside to work in agriculture, or staying at home with 70 percent of their pay. But soon, those who didn't have strong reasons for refusing to move to the interior were told they would lose their salary altogether.

"Our government apparatus has become overblown," Vice-Minister of Foreign Affairs Ramón Sanchez Parodi told me in late 1990. "Now, it will be substantially reduced. In some places, we will cut fifty percent of the staff. We will have to do whatever is necessary to achieve the highest possible level of efficiency."

◄►

The regime's propaganda machine immediately launched a campaign to show that Cuba's economic ills were due to an inflated bureaucracy—and not to Castro's steadfast refusal to accept a market economy. Echoing the new line, a senior Communist Party official told me this joke to explain why it was impossible to find the traditional Cuban staple, pork, on Cuban supermarket shelves:

> Fidel visits a model pig farm and stops by a pregnant pig. "Beautiful specimen," Fidel says, patting the animal with admiration. "I bet it will produce at least ten piglets."
>
> Everybody nods and applauds. Fidel leaves the farm.
>
> But two weeks later, when the pig delivers, there are only six piglets. There is consternation in the farm's administrative offices. The farm manager, fearing Fidel will be disappointed by the lower-than-expected production, writes in his report that the pig delivered seven.
>
> His supervisor, the regional farm director, changes the figure to eight piglets. His boss, the national farm director, raises the number to nine. His boss, the minister of agriculture, the man who has to submit the report personally to Castro, changes the figure to ten piglets.

"Great! Fantastic!" says Fidel upon seeing his prediction come true. "We'll use sixty percent of the pigs for export, and forty percent for domestic consumption."

The joke's underlying message: if you couldn't find pork in Cuba, it wasn't Fidel's fault. Blame it on the bureaucracy. Of course, the problem in real life was much deeper: farmers didn't raise more pigs because the state paid too little for them, and because they were prohibited from growing and selling the animals privately. The net effect of the state monopoly on production was that pork—or any other meat, for that matter—was nowhere to be seen in city super-markets.

In 1990, during the nationwide meetings to help draft the agenda for the Fourth Communist Party Congress, supporters of an economic opening were encouraged by an overwhelming grass-roots demand to privatize services and small industries. As part of his March 1990 Llamamiento—or call—to the Fourth Congress, Castro had launched a one-year national poll to collect recommendations for the Congress. The economic and political proposals would then be brought before the October 10, 1991, Party Congress for possible adoption.

During the twelve-month period from April 1990 to April 1991, an estimated 3.5 million Cubans attended 80,000 assemblies in government offices, factories and schools. In meeting after meeting, workers expressed strong support for economic reforms. As food became more scarce, louder demands to legalize private farmers markets were heard. A general conviction grew that as soon as farmers were allowed to sell privately, food would miraculously appear everywhere. Cubans had seen it happen before, in the early 1980s, before Castro's 1986 "rectification of errors" campaign.

Thousands of workers spoke up at the meetings, supporting legalization of small private businesses, and asking that plumbers, builders and other laborers be allowed to work on their own. If the regime was conceding that privately run hotels were more efficient because they offered material incentives to their workers, why didn't it allow others to operate under the same rules? people asked.

Shortly before the October 1991 Party Congress, I visited liberal-minded Communist Party economist Pedro Monreal at his office at

Havana's Center of American Studies (CEA). A golden boy of the Party's reformist wing—one of Cuba's "Yummies," or Young Upwardly Mobile Marxists—Monreal was in his mid-thirties and wore U.S.-made clothes and horn-rimmed glasses. He was the only Cuban official I had met who used an American nickname. His secretary called him "Peter."

That day, Monreal was highly optimistic that the Party hierarchy would accept the inevitability of economic and political change, perhaps as soon as the upcoming Party congress. In addition to the people's demands, there were growing economic pressures pointing in that direction, he said.

To his mind, the tourism and biotechnology industries had set an unstoppable trend toward greater economic freedoms. Eventually, hotels would have to begin purchasing their food, furniture and other supplies in Cuba. These goods could only be supplied in a reliable way by autonomous companies that offered material incentives to its workers and did not depend on Party directives. For Cuba to survive economically, the government would have to override the Party hardliners and authorize more and more autonomy.

"We have created a Frankenstein," Monreal said, in obvious sympathy with the monster. "The original idea that you could have a two-track economy didn't work. You can't keep market-economy industries isolated from the rest of the economy."

Could the regime stick to its orthodox Marxist rhetoric while allowing these islands of capitalist efficiency to grow? I asked. No, he said. The hard-line Communist rhetoric would have to change, or enterprising people would refuse to work, fearing government reprisals.

"It's being proven that whatever is productive in Cuba contradicts the political line," Monreal said. "People are noticing what works, and what doesn't. Unless we change the rhetoric, we will reach a point where people start questioning it openly."

Like most reformers, Monreal fully expected the Fourth Party Congress to adapt Cuba's die-hard Communist rhetoric to the island's economic realities.

11
The Zombie Factor

◄◄◄◄◄Orlando and Melba were a couple in their mid-fifties, house-keepers at the University of Havana protocol house where I rented a room during one of my extended stays in 1991. They were also living zombies.

In the morning, I would find Orlando and Melba sitting in front of the living room television set, their arms draped over the sides of their chairs, heads tilted forward, eyes half-open, watching cartoons. As I crossed the living room back to my bedroom after breakfast, I would see them absolutely unchanged, watching the morning aerobics classes. One evening, when a Tele Rebelde soap opera was interrupted due to technical difficulties and a still picture was telecast in its place, the two remained immobile, their eyes glued to the box.

From a brief conversation I had with Melba during one of her more lucid moments, I gleaned that the couple had little work to do. There had not been another guest at the protocol house since a Mexican visitor had left several months ago.

Melba told me she was a true believer in the revolution. She had grown up in the countryside, and had worked much of her youth as a maid for a bourgeois family. After the revolution, she had moved to Havana, and had worked for twenty years at the University of Havana cafeteria before being transferred to the protocol house. She had a secure job, and free health care. Her three daughters had graduated from college. She owed everything she had to Fidel Castro, she said, before turning her eyes back to the television set.

She was probably right. The revolution's full-employment policy had long provided security—if not a decent life—for a sizable part of the population. Cuba's communism had not only helped the poor but was also a paradise for the idle and the inept.

Ironically, it was this sorry constituency—rather than Che Guevara's "New Man"—that was Fidel Castro's main hope for political survival. As European communism continued to disintegrate, Castro increasingly relied on a propaganda campaign designed to make Cubans fearful of what would happen to them if the revolution collapsed.

A full-page color ad by Cuba's Communist Party on the back cover of *Bohemia*, the weekly magazine, showed the smiling face of an elderly Cuban with the legend: "To maintain the security we enjoy, let's stay united and march forward!" *Granma* and the Tele Rebelde television network, meanwhile, would carry daily stories about calamities that had befallen Eastern European countries after the fall of their Marxist regimes. One million unemployed in the former German Democratic Republic, one headline said. Communist Party members arrested in Poland, said another. Thousands evicted from their homes in Czechoslovakia, said a third.

Cuban radio commentators filled the air waves with speculation about the atrocities Miami's Cuban exiles would commit if they took over the country. Not only would there be bloodshed, but millions of Cubans would lose their jobs, houses and health care benefits, the regime's journalists said. It was either Fidel or it was chaos. For people like Orlando and Melba, the threat was real. What could possibly be their fate in a competitive post-Castro society?

Young professionals, tourist-industry workers and black-market entrepreneurs who were getting a taste of capitalism were anxious for changes in the system that would allow them to unleash their long-suppressed creativity. But for hundreds of thousands of zombies who bloated the government payroll, the revolution's propaganda scare tactics were effective.

The number of Cubans who held nonproductive jobs was staggering, even by the standards of populist-ruled Latin American countries. Of the 3.5 million people in Cuba's workforce, more than 1.1 million held what the Cuban regime's National Census Office described as "nonproductive" jobs, a category made up of white collar employees and "others" whose work government statisticians had found hard to define.

The latter included 304,000 people employed in "other intellectual work occupations" that did not include teaching, scientific research, or the arts. There were, for instance, thousands who received lifelong government salaries for staying at their homes allegedly researching topics such as fifteenth-century French classical music or ancient Chinese poetry—without even the prospect of having their work published. Some of the make-work jobs held by average Cubans looked hilarious to visitors from the capitalist world.

I didn't know quite how to react when Nelson, a good-looking man in his late thirties, told me he was a musician with the Havana Psychiatric Hospital Orchestra. Was that a group of mental patients doing music therapy, or a professional band playing for the mentally ill? Groping for an elegant way to ask what side of the padded door he knew best, I asked Nelson if he was a professional or an amateur musician.

He laughed. He was not crazy, he said. The crazies were the powerful people who had created a full-fledged Symphonic Orchestra with no other purpose than playing for the Havana Psychiatric Hospital. Nelson's story about the band, which I corroborated later, was the most bizarre tale of government waste I'd ever heard—a page right out of a Fellini script.

The Havana Psychiatric Hospital, a huge building near Havana's José Martí Airport, was run by Dr. Eduardo Bernabé Ordaz, a former physician-guerrilla in Castro's rebel army. Taking over the run-down, overcrowded asylum a week after the revolution's victory in 1959, Ordaz had turned it into a propaganda showcase for the new regime's health care system. The number of inmates had been cut in half to two thousand, and their facilities modernized.

Ordaz had also turned out to be a music lover. Having paid part of his medical school tuition playing with a band in bars and restaurants during the Batista years, he set out to create an orchestra as soon as he took over the hospital. Thirty-two years later, the Havana Psychiatric Hospital Orchestra had eighty-two full-time musicians, including three directors, eighteen clarinets, ten percussionists, ten trumpets, seven saxophones, four trombones, and five flutes. The group played Tchaikovsky, Wagner and Beethoven four times a week on the hospital patio. It never performed anywhere else for anyone else.

"I know it sounds crazy to you, but it's true," Nelson told me with a mixture of amusement and embarrassment. "If you were living in Cuba, you wouldn't find it so extraordinary."

How many mental patients attended the concerts? I asked. Of the two thousand patients at the hospital, only a few were docile enough to be allowed to attend, he said. And many of those who showed up could not sit for more than a few minutes. Some would stand, walk around aimlessly, or mimic the band players.

"But how many patients show up?"

"On a good day? Ten, perhaps fifteen, and always the same ones."

"You mean you have an eighty-two-person symphonic orchestra playing four times a week for an audience of fifteen?"

"Yes, that is, on a good day . . ."

Nelson's drama was so bizarre that he couldn't relate it without laughing. He had been playing with the Psychiatric Hospital Orchestra for twenty years. He considered himself a talented composer and player, and yet he had spent his entire professional life playing for fifteen mentally ill patients who may or may not have appreciated his music.

Nelson had asked several times for a transfer to another band, and had even tried to form a group of salsa musicians to play at Havana hotels. But his official petitions had been denied, and he could not play anywhere without a government permit. He had a wife and a child, and could not give up his 295-peso-a-month salary—$295 at the official rate, nearly twice the amount of Cuba's minimum wage—and stay at home. He was eager to flee to Miami, but couldn't bear the thought of abandoning his family. He was anxious to see Castro's regime fall, but too many zombies still backed Fidel. Nelson was in a dilemma, and going through a major depression because of it.

"Many of us would like to start our own bands, play our own music, make our own money, and stop playing for the crazies," Nelson said. "But others in the orchestra, especially the older ones, are terrified by the idea of change. They're perfectly content to receive a monthly check for what we do. They wouldn't mind if Fidel stayed in power forever."

While making millions of Cubans nervous about life without Fidel, the regime tried to lift the population's morale with promises of controlled political change.

Castro's March 1990 call for a national poll to collect recommendations for the Fourth Communist Party Congress raised hopes of significant political reforms. In its Llamamiento document of March 15, 1990, the Central Committee had called on the population to "leave behind dogmas" and make their recommendations in an atmosphere of "diversity of opinions."

At long last, there would be much-needed economic and political changes in the system, the government said. Castro promised workers, students and housewives that nobody would be punished for speaking his mind. The only untouchables were Castro's leadership and Cuba's one-party system. Everything else was negotiable.

Like the new economic program, the political strategy contemplated isolated reforms—such as accepting Catholics into the Communist Party, or allowing the appointment of nonparty members to senior government jobs. Without risking an overall political opening, it left enough room for reformers to hope for changes that would give them a greater say in the country's future.

At the very least, the Llamamiento would help the regime buy time. Castro thought the tourism-and-biotechnology program would take at least two years to produce its first results. Vice-president Carlos Rafael Rodriguez was even more pessimistic: he predicted Cuba would face "five difficult years." Castro's grass-roots program was a way of placating the population's anxiety in the meantime. Implicit in the waiting game was his assumption that the Soviet hardliners who supported continued aid to Cuba would gain the upper hand in the Kremlin once Gorbachev's reforms proved to be a failure.

During the grass-roots meetings over the next twelve months, the Party collected more than 1.1 million suggestions. They were put into the Central Committee's computers and divided by issues and recommendations. Summaries were forwarded to various Party departments to serve as the basis for the Fourth Congress's discussions. It was democracy at work, Castro said.

Since one could safely assume that state security informants attended every meeting, most Cubans were cautious in their criticism. Nevertheless, a groundswell of dissatisfaction emerged at the assemblies. Many Cubans spoke out for private farmers markets and free-market economic recipes. Thousands of workers and students called for a greater freedom of the press, arguing that the government's firm censorship only forced people to tune in to anti-Castro Miami radio stations. The meetings also produced an almost unanimous condemnation of the tourism apartheid policy, and of government restrictions on foreign travel.

As months went by, the demands grew bolder. At the University of Havana's Philosophy school, faculty members demanded direct elections for the National Assembly. At the Cuban Institute of Cinema (ICAIC), there was a proposal to appoint Fidel as Cuba's new foreign minister, and elect somebody else to run the country. Foreign relations was what Fidel was most interested in anyway, the argument went.

At the Port of Havana, several dock workers complained about the *históricos*—Fidel's fellow guerrillas during the 1950s uprising—who were now old men still occupying key government jobs. "Quite frankly, I've stopped trusting these people," one man said. "We should allow a new generation of leaders to take over."

By April 1991, the meetings were called off. The Party said it had collected more than enough opinions to bring to the October congress. The public demands were getting out of hand. If the assemblies were allowed to go on, the regime would have had to suspend from their jobs and perhaps even arrest the most outspoken critics of the Comandante. It was precisely what Fidel had promised would not happen when he had encouraged Cubans to speak out.

<><>

Other political measures were taken to mitigate an increasingly anxious population. Mandatory meetings of the Communist Party organizations were reduced to a minimum. Participation in these had turned into a physical impossibility for the millions now forced to spend much of their day in lines to buy food or catch a bus.

Until 1991, an average Cuban was supposed to donate about four days of "voluntary work" a month for various mass organizations, such as the neighborhood Committees for the Defense of the Revolution (CDR's) or the popular militias. In addition, there were monthly "study circles" in the workplace, at which Fidel's latest speeches would be dissected by a Party apparatchik; and once-a-month "orientation" meetings at the Communist Youth Union, the Federation of Cuban Women or similar Party groups. As attendance at these regular meetings plummeted, the Party gracefully scaled them down to conform to the new realities of daily survival.

In early 1991, the Committees for the Defense of the Revolution announced they would reduce their meetings to one every three months. Other Party organizations followed suit. Even hard-line Communists were relieved: most meetings, particularly the CDR's, were a waste of time. Young professionals were especially irritated by having to sit through lectures on U.S. imperialism by CDR bloc chiefs who often hadn't read a book in their lives.

Mercedes, a twenty-two-year-old economics student at the University of Havana, had developed her own notions about communism based on her experience at CDR meetings. The problem with communism, she explained to me, is not in the theory, not even in the way the theory is implemented, but in *who* implements it.

"Let me give you an example," she said. "The idea of having a CDR on each block is great: neighbors are supposed to meet regularly to decide who will man the crime watch patrols, fix the potholes, patch a faulty water pipe or make proposals to the government on national issues. But who are the CDR leaders organizing these activities? Would a doctor, an economist, a professor or anybody with a good job volunteer for that job?"

Of course not. The problem with communism, she said, was that the people volunteering for these tedious jobs were the neighborhood busybodies, who enjoyed making life difficult for anybody who didn't render them proper respect.

"The CDR is typically presided over by some resentful spinster who doesn't have anything better to do," Mercedes said. "These people end up making your life impossible."

Mercedes was happy to see her CDR meetings cut down, although the new schedule of one session every three months was still one time too many for her. She did not plan to attend. If they knocked on her door afterward, she would say she had been too busy lining up for food that day.

<>

Travel restrictions were eased, as an additional way to release social tensions. Intellectuals, the driving force behind the anti-Communist movements in Eastern Europe, were bribed into passivity with government cars—the Union of Cuban Writers and Artists (UNEAC) alone gave out more than three hundred cars to its most prominent members between 1988 and 1991—and hundreds of visas for periodic trips abroad.

Under new guidelines, the government began to authorize artists, writers, filmmakers and university professors to travel to the United

States, Mexico and Western Europe. Most were traveling outside Cuba for the first time in their lives. It was an exhilarating opportunity.

"*Viajar*"—to travel—became the ultimate status symbol in literary circles. To breathe some foreign air and return home with bags full of American products—and lots of stories to tell about life in the capitalist world—turned into the Cuban intellectuals' foremost ambition. And if the trip was to the United States, so much the better.

Some intellectuals were given visas that allowed them to live for extended periods of time abroad. Mexico City became a magnet for Cuban painters and sculptors who settled there without actually having to defect. More than fifty of them gathered around the Mexican capital's Ninarte Gallery, where they sold their works—and kept their critiques of the Cuban regime largely to themselves.

In an unspoken deal with the Cuban Ministry of Culture, they were given extensions to their six-month exit visas if they refrained from making public statements against the Cuban regime. It worked: the young artists never criticized their government publicly.

In the gallery's first-floor exhibition room, they exhibited abstract art works and decorative paintings. Cuban embassy officials would show up on opening nights, to boast to the Mexican press about the revolution's cultural achievements. Art critics would write glowing portraits of Cuba's young artists. But in their fourth floor living quarters, most of the artists hid portraits of Cuba as a prison camp and caricatures of Fidel. It was their real art, they told me.

Culture Minister Armando Hart was the man who authorized reform-minded artists and writers to travel abroad, and who often gave his blessing to artworks that went beyond the limits of loyal criticism.

As one of the few *históricos* remaining in the Council of Ministers, he had enough revolutionary credentials to play the good cop. Hart had been taken prisoner by the Batista troops in 1957, and was released two years later with the triumph of the revolution. At age twenty-nine, he had become the new regime's first education minister. Now, in addition to culture minister, he was one of the thirteen members of Cuba's Politburo and—what was even more important—one of the few top officials with direct access to Castro.

Often, when an artist got in trouble for his political stand, UNEAC president Abel Prieto—a towering young man with long hair and matinee-idol features—would ask his powerful friend at the Culture Ministry to rule on the side of artistic freedom. On most occasions, he got his way. UNEAC members, feeling there was still some support in high circles for their reformist ideas, had an additional reason not to cross the line to open dissent.

"Hart is a progressive guy," Prieto assured me once as we sipped coffee at his office. "Whenever we're under attack from the hard-liners, he comes to our aid."

Armando Hart, a chubby, pallid man in his early sixties, pulled himself up from his chair with the help of a cane when I was escorted into his office at the Ministry of Culture one rainy afternoon in April 1991. He walked with difficulty, a vestige of a bout with phlebitis several years ago. That day, he also seemed to be having a mild asthma attack. He was breathing rapidly, his forehead showing a thin coat of perspiration.

Once we sat down, I tried to break the ice with a bit of small talk: I was glad to meet him, I started. Many intellectuals I had talked to in recent days had spoken very highly of him. Several artists had described him as one of the most open-minded members of the Co-mandante's inner circle, I said, expecting to trigger a sympathetic response.

But Hart wasn't smiling. Instead, his eyebrows knit together in a mixture of amazement and anger. His breathing accelerated. His hands began to shake.

"They told you that? Who told you that? That's crazy!" he replied angrily, his voice choking. "I don't consider myself tolerant at all! I'm more radical and revolutionary than anybody!"

I excused myself, saying I might have used the wrong word. What the artists and writers had probably meant was that he was more progressive than others.

"No! No! No!" he yelled back in escalating indignation. "Don't put me in that category! I'm a radical, with very hard-line positions!" He then warned me: "Don't you dare accuse me of being tolerant, liberal, or anything like that. I'm a radical!"

From then on, the culture minister eyed me with suspicion. After an hour, he told me he had to go back to work. As he stood up to say good-bye, he came back to the theme that was most important to him all along.

"Don't you ever write that I'm a progressive!" he repeated. "Remember, *Yo soy un duro!* (I'm a hard-liner!)"

I had made a major mistake. Hart was obviously terrified he would be labeled a softie. It was an insult—a ticket to political disgrace within Castro's iron-handed inner circle. It became clear to me that, in Castro's Cuba, the kindest compliment you could pay a cabinet minister was to tell him he was a narrow-minded Communist apparatchik.

<>

Soon, the regime's largess in foreign travel permits extended to the rest of the population. In a series of decrees, the government gradually lowered the age limitations for Cubans wanting to leave the island. By mid-1991, for the first time in many years, any Cuban over the age of twenty could apply for a passport.

The response was immediate. The number of applications at the U.S. Interest Section in Havana tripled in 1991 to a projected one hundred thousand before the U.S. government temporarily stopped accepting new visa requests, fearing a massive new wave of Cuban immigrants. Thousands of others applied for visas at European and Latin American embassies. The young had found a new hope to keep them going: the possibility of getting out of their country.

About 30 percent of all Cubans traveling to the United States overstayed their visas, most of them settling in Miami for good. A new joke making the rounds in Havana told of a Cuban father asking his son: "What do you want to be when you grow up?" The son's answer: "A foreigner."

<>

Even as it was opening new safety valves for the population's growing frustration, the Castro regime set out to fine-tune the state's machinery of oppression. In early 1991, Castro created the Rapid Response Brigades—a new militia of "voluntary" members recruited at CDR's and workplaces. Their responsibility was to crack down—with clubs and stones if necessary—on any demonstrations of protest on the island.

Cuba would not make the mistake some of Eastern Europe's Communist regimes had made when they asked their armed forces to fire at antigovernment demonstrators. The troops' refusal to shoot into the crowds—or, in other cases, the soldiers' bloody repression—had led to the regimes' own undoing. And Cuba would not make the mistake General Noriega had made in Panama by not giving weapons and better training to his Dignity Battalions. In Cuba, the "people" would do the job of cracking down, not the armed forces. If the new

Rapid Response Brigades couldn't do the job on their own, security agents in civilian clothes would help them.

The revolution's repression tactics served a major psychological purpose: paralyzing dissidents with fear. The vast state apparatus, a seemingly benign institution, was also eager to assert itself as an all-powerful police state.

The psychological terror campaign against anti-Castro activism had worked for many years. When you asked government critics why there weren't any street protests in Cuba, the answer was always the same: it would be pointless. The state security was too efficient; no opposition group would ever succeed in staging mass protests. Until the early nineties, Cuba's anti-Castro militants had relatively passive goals: either to get themselves off the island, or to wait for a military coup that would topple the Comandante.

Under the Cuban revolution's laws, any assembly of more than three people—even in a private home—was punishable with up to three months in prison and a fine. Article 240 of the Penal Code established that organizers of "illicit or unrecognized groups" could get sentences of up to nine months in prison. The law's enforcement was selective. Most Cubans often invited as many friends as they wanted to their homes, and it was not unusual to discuss politics and criticize the government at these private parties. But, at the same time, people faced harsh punishment if they crossed the line to political activism.

"You can't put anybody in prison for expressing an opinion," Castro explained when asked about the arrest of four mathematics students after they had tried to start an independent student group. "Now, if they start organizing to carry out their program, you can't allow them to organize, you can't allow them to go ahead with impunity."

Because the government often charged political activists with common crimes, it was impossible to establish how many political prisoners there were in Cuba. Cuba's Attorney General Ramón De La Cruz stated that the country's prison population was about forty thousand people, of which fewer than two hundred were serving sentences for "counterrevolutionary crimes." The first figure was misleading, however, because it did not include prisoners kept at prison camps or halfway houses. The estimate of political prisoners was equally deceptive, because it did not count those arrested for political motives but charged with common crimes.

The attorney general's list of political prisoners only included people charged with "crimes against state security," such as "enemy propaganda," "rebellion" and "terrorism." It did not include prisoners held for "illegal association, demonstration and meeting," "disrespect," "illegal exit," "illegal economic activity," or a vast number of other crimes.

Roberto Bahamonde Masot, for instance, was held for three months in Havana in 1989 on charges of illicit association: he was arrested for planning a peaceful demonstration outside the Soviet embassy during President Gorbachev's visit to Cuba. While he was in prison, the regime charged Bahamonde Masot with a new crime: "illicit economic activity."

The government presented as evidence a camera it had found at his home, and charged that prior to his detention he had worked as an unauthorized, independent photographer. He was sentenced to one year in prison at the Combinado del Sur prison in Matanzas province as a common criminal. Bahamonde Masot had, indeed, free-lanced as a photographer. It was a typical case of how the regime dusted off your dossier the minute you engaged in dissident activities, and charged you with any one of the myriad crimes average Cubans commit daily.

Cuba's Commission for Human Rights and National Reconciliation (CCDHRN) estimated Cuba's total prison population in 1991 at up to one hundred thousand people, including those held in prison camps and half-way houses. At least three thousand of those were political prisoners, according to group leader Elizardo Sanchez Santa Cruz. And most of them had been arrested for common crimes.

High-school history teacher Ariel Hidalgo was relatively lucky: he was arrested on political charges, and was among those quickly adopted by international human rights organizations as a prisoner of conscience. His crime: writing a book. His sentence: eight years in prison "and that his work be destroyed by fire."

Hidalgo got in trouble with the regime during the 1980 Mariel boatlift. He was arrested while helping protect a friend who was being harassed physically by a progovernment mob that was attacking him for wanting to leave the country. Security agents searched Hidalgo's home and found the manuscript of *"Cuba, the Marxist State and the New Class."* They didn't like it.

After the professor was released three days later—the regime didn't have a solid case against him—he began to receive strange visits from long-forgotten friends. One asked him for forbidden dollars to buy a pair of shoes. Another offered to sell him black-market goods. A third invited him out for drinks and took him to a private house where an orgy was in progress. Hidalgo knew better: suspecting a government trap to arrest him on a common crime, he left the place in a hurry.

But he was arrested anyway about a year later. Not finding a common crime to charge him with, authorities returned to their original charge and accused him of producing "enemy propaganda." The state security made it look as if it had just confiscated Hidalgo's manuscript. The professor, at the time in his mid-thirties, received an eight-year prison sentence.

He spent the first twenty days under interrogation at the State Security Villa Marista complex in Havana. From there, he was transferred to the Havana Psychiatric Hospital—the same institution where luckier inmates got to hear the eighty-two-member Symphonic Orchestra—and placed in the Carbo Servia ward, one of two sections of the building reserved for most dangerous inmates.

"There were about a hundred people crammed into the high-security room, virtually all of them aggressive and mentally ill," Hidalgo recalls. "I saw everything in there: people being raped, old men being beaten, others defecating in your bed. It was a place where no policeman, doctor or anybody else from the outside world ever came in. When a second political prisoner joined me, a young pediatrician, we took turns sleeping: some of the inmates had begun setting fire to our stocking feet in the middle of the night."

Ten days later, Hidalgo was transferred to the La Cabaña prison, and a few weeks later to the Combinado del Este prison, Havana's largest. He was put in the death-row section, in an unlit cell barely big enough for his body. The prison ward was known among Combinado inmates as "death rectangle." There Hidalgo could hear the screams of the tortured, or of those—most often common criminals—about to be executed. He spent a year and twenty days there.

Only then was he transferred to the political prisoners' section at Combinado del Este, where Hidalgo met other prisoners of conscience and teamed up with them to start a human rights movement.

"Until then, I had never been a human rights activist," Hidalgo told me after he was released and put on a plane to Miami. "I was an intellectual dissident, a lonely writer, who had never belonged to an organization."

"I was also a Socialist," he was quick to add. "I believed—I still believe—in the original goals of the revolution. What I didn't believe in anymore was the revolution's leadership."

Asked about why the regime had acted so harshly in his case, he said the government probably feared—correctly—that he planned to leak his book out of the country, and try to become a Cuban-styled Aleksandr Solzhenitsyn. At the time, there were no known books critical of the Castro regime that actually had been written on the island.

"A lot of prisoners were in jail for much more innocuous things," Hidalgo said. "One, a navy lieutenant named Francisco Benitez Ferrer, was there for scribbling on a wall a phrase by José Martí: 'Every time a man is deprived of his right to think, I feel as if one of my children were being killed.'

"In Cuba, you can make a casual antigovernment comment and get away with it," said Hidalgo, who was released in 1988 after seven years in prison and set up a Cuban human rights information center in Miami. "But the minute you write a book, paint a sign or plan a demonstration, you're behind bars."

It was the certainty of swift repression, as well as the widespread belief that no secret could be kept away from the state security, that helped keep Cubans in a state of inertia as massive protests rocked the rest of the Communist world.

At times, foreign diplomats based in Havana could not help shaking their heads in frustration at what they saw as a lack of aggressiveness by Cuban dissidents. After all, people like Hidalgo had been systematically persecuted and imprisoned in virtually all Soviet bloc countries—and that had not kept dissidents there from organizing formidable opposition movements. Why was Cuba different?

That question was in everybody's mind in August 1991. The XIth Pan American Games organizing committee, following the institution's rules, had forced Cuba to open its doors indiscriminately to foreign journalists wanting to cover the event. An army of more than thirteen hundred foreign journalists, including hundreds of U.S. reporters normally barred from entering Cuba, had taken advantage of the occasion to get into the country.

For several weeks, reporters scoured the streets of Havana in search of signs of active opposition to Castro, but couldn't find any. Incredibly, not one single Cuban raised an anti-Castro flag during the sports competitions. Nobody tried to get arrested in front of cameras for distributing opposition leaflets, or painting prodemocracy graffiti on the walls. A precious opportunity to focus international attention on human rights abuses in Cuba had been lost.

Some journalists visiting Cuba for the first time quickly concluded that Castro's revolution was still popular. Foreign diplomats based in Havana, who were familiar with the growing discontent on the island, looked about them in wonder. What was holding Cubans back? Where were all the brave men and women?

"I'm not ashamed to say that I'm scared, that all of us are scared," responded human rights activist Elizardo Sanchez, of Cuba's CCD-HRN. "You talk to me about Eastern Europe, but I'm not sure there is another country in the world with a bigger repressive apparatus relative to its population than Cuba. This country is a big prison."

<>

Gustavo Arcos Bergnes, head of Cuba's Human Rights Committee (CCDH), was the best-known human rights activist in Cuba. A powerfully built man in his mid-sixties, Arcos was still remembered as one of the courageous revolutionaries who had attacked the Moncada barracks with Fidel in 1953. Arcos had been shot and wounded in the attack, and left with a permanent limp in his right leg.

After the revolution, he had served as Castro's ambassador to Belgium, until his arrest in 1966 for making disparaging remarks about the Comandante to a fellow Cuban official. In the late eighties, Arcos had become head of Cuba's CCDH, a group that—like Elizardo Sanchez's CCDHRN—collected information on human rights abuses and passed it on to foreign embassies and international organizations. He lived in a two-story house in the residential Vedado neighborhood, which he shared with at least two other families.

The day I went to see him, the living room was nearly empty: much of the furniture had been destroyed during an attack by a progovernment mob in 1990. The paint on the walls was peeling. A 1960s television set sat in a corner.

Why wasn't anybody rebelling in Cuba? I asked.

"In Cuba, we don't want bloodshed," he answered. "If there are sectors who hope there will be a violent coup d'etat, or a civil war, or a social uprising that will be crushed with force, let me tell you, the majority of Cubans don't want that."

Why wasn't anybody even painting anti-Castro graffiti on the walls?

"We're not telling our people to do that: it wouldn't serve any purpose," he said. "They would get arrested, and the block's CDR would paint over the graffiti ten minutes later. What good would that do?"

So how did he expect change to come about in Cuba?

Change would come from within the Communist Party, he said. Party leaders would reach the conclusion that there was no way out for the regime, and would hopefully propose radical changes at the Fourth Party Congress.

"Most Cubans want a negotiated solution, a national dialogue that would lead to a transitional government," he said. "We hope that delegates participating in the Fourth Congress will think first as Cubans, and second as followers of a *caudillo*."

Arcos had been harshly criticized by rightist Cuban exiles in Miami for his call for a political dialogue with the Castro regime. Leaders of the hard-line Cuban American National Foundation (CANF), the most powerful Cuban exile lobbying group, had branded the Arcos proposal as naive. Armando Valladares, a former Cuban political prisoner who had been appointed by President Reagan U.S. ambassador to the U.N. Human Rights Commission in Geneva (despite the fact that he barely spoke English) had astonished his State Department colleagues by denouncing Arcos as having committed "treason." A political dialogue with the Cuban regime would only take the pressure off Castro, and would help him buy time, Valladares and other CANF leaders argued. Their strategy called for growing confrontation—on all fronts—with the beleaguered Castro regime.

"What do the exiles know?" Arcos told me, opening his hands as he referred to the Valladares accusation. "They don't live here. They live *there*. They can have some information about what's going on in Cuba, but not nearly as much information as we have. The fact of the matter is that the Cuban people want a peaceful change, a political settlement. Nobody wants violence."

<>

That was the crux of the island's political paralysis. If there was one point in which the Castro regime and its political opponents agreed, it was that the best-known Miami exile leaders, now calling for an uprising from Radio Martí's studios, were out of touch with the island's political realities.

Cuba had become a different country from the one they had left three decades ago. More than half of all Cubans had been born after the revolution and raised under the Marxist regime. Migration to the cities had soared, to the point that more than 70 percent of the population was now living in urban areas. Most of the exiles wouldn't even recognize their old neighborhoods, where once elegant mansions had become crowded tenements housing several families each. The country's racial mix had turned significantly darker.

You could stand on any corner in Havana and notice a substantial difference between the people passing by and the Cuban exiles you saw in Miami. Most people on the streets of Havana were black or mulatto. Mixed couples holding hands were a common sight. Following the massive flight of Cuba's white elite and middle class in the early sixties, the island's nonwhite population had become a majority.

Unofficial estimates put Cuba's blacks and mulattos in the early nineties at about 58 percent of the total population, up from 45 percent in 1959. Of the more than one million Cuban exiles in the United States, conversely, more than 95 percent are white.*

Race had always been a major factor in Cuban politics, despite efforts by Cuban politicians to play down the issue. In Havana and Miami, you heard the same phrase: "In Cuba, we have never had a racial problem." In reality, discrimination was rampant on both sides. There were only two blacks or mulattos in the Communist Party's fourteen-member Politburo, and at least one was a token figure. Among the exiles in the United States, the CANF's fifty directors—often described as a government-in-waiting—were an all-white crowd.

Nonwhite Cubans on the island knew they were not represented in the Castro hierarchy, and many were tired of the Comandante's Marxist fantasies—but feared for their future if the white Miami crowd took over. In the first days of the revolution, when the white elite and members of the middle class had fled the island overnight, blacks from the countryside and the Havana slums had moved into their mansions.

By the early nineties, many of those original squatters and their children were comfortably settled and living in the magnificent homes of Havana's Miramar and Vedado neighborhoods. Other black squatters had established their homes in commercial districts. On Central Havana's Monte Street, once a fashionable shopping place for the middle class, the former Casa de las Planchas (The House of Irons)

---

* *In the 1990 Census, of the estimated 950,000 Hispanics in Dade County, most of them Cubans, only 28,372 were black. Cited in "Es la Cuba de Hoy una Cuba negra?" by Miñuca Villaverde,* El Nuevo Herald, *March 3, 1992.*

home-appliances store had been turned into a multifamily black tenement.

Like the zombie public workers who received their monthly checks for doing very little, the dark-skinned squatters of the early sixties made up a latent progovernment constituency. They were not necessarily Castro fans, but they knew that as long as Castro was in power, the original owners could not confiscate their property. To many, it didn't make sense to replace a Communist white elite that had given them jobs and homes with a capitalist white elite that would most likely take them away.

There had been a long history to Cuba's racial dilemma. If it had taken Cuba's white elite half a century longer than whites in other Latin American countries to embrace the cause of independence, it was partly because they had always feared that Cuba might become like Haiti—a country under black rule.

A little more than half of Cuba's population in the nineteenth century had been black. The white elite knew that it couldn't win an independence war without their help, but at the same time feared that the blacks would take over if there were radical political changes. To calm the elite's fears as they launched the war against Spain in 1895, Cuba's "apostle" José Martí and Gen. Máximo Gómez included a paragraph in their declaration on principles—the Manifesto of Montecristi—reassuring whites that the participation of blacks would not threaten white interests.

The situation changed after the U.S.-brokered independence in 1902, when massive waves of Spanish immigrants began to arrive in Cuba. The racial mix began to tilt again to the whites. But racial tensions did not subside: blacks felt they had been cheated of legitimate rewards for their participation in the wars of independence. A newly formed black party was banned in 1910, when the government prohibited racially based political organizations. Two years later, growing black resentment turned into a full-fledged uprising, known as the Little War of the Blacks. It was quickly suppressed by the new republic's U.S.-backed white government, but not before more than four thousand blacks had died in the fighting. Cuba became a predominantly white country, and remained so for the first half of the century.

Now, three decades after a white exodus that had turned nonwhites into the new majority, history was repeating itself, but in reverse. Just as the white upper class in the nineteenth century had feared independence would lead to black rule, Cuba's blacks now feared freedom from the Castro dictatorship would bring about a return to white dominance.

◄►

We were standing on the doorstep of the home of University of Havana professor Jorge Nuñez in the Reparto Fontanar neighborhood on the outskirts of Havana. Reparto Fontanar had been built in 1956 as a country club with two swimming pools and a basketball court. Several Batista army colonels, successful professionals and prominent artists had bought spacious homes there shortly before the revolution. The Nuñez family was among them.

Now, Nuñez was showing me what had happened since to each house on his block. Except for himself, there was nobody else from prerevolutionary times. Of the original seven hundred fifty families who had moved into the Fontanar neighborhood during the Batista era, there were only ten left.

"I was seven years old when the revolution was won," Nuñez told me. "I went out into the street and all my friends had disappeared. I came back home, turned on the television set, and that's when I saw Fidel for the first time."

In a matter of days, the neighborhood turned into a ghost town. Then Castro's guerrilla columns began their descent from the mountains into Havana. A few months later, when Castro summoned supporters from the countryside to attend his July 26, 1959, speech in Havana, hundreds of new families arrived for the occasion and moved into the empty homes. Years later, some of them were resettled to make room for professors from the nearby José Antonio Echevarria Engineering School.

By the early 1990s, the neighborhood was shared by the original peasant settlers and the engineering teachers. Many of the homes had been split in two or three living quarters to accommodate various families. The swimming pool and basketball courts had long been covered over by the tropical vegetation.

"In that mansion in the corner, there's a college professor from Santiago who came here in 1962," Nuñez told me. "What would he do if Castro fell and Miami exiles demanded their homes back? Could he go back to Santiago and claim his previous house? That would be impossible. People are asking themselves, What will happen to me if Castro falls?"

<>

They had good reasons to be scared. The news coming from Cuban-exile radio stations in Miami wasn't reassuring for the largely black masses who had benefited from the revolution. Miami's Cuban exile leaders were not only white, but most had left Cuba in the early days of the revolution. Unlike most Cubans on the island, they had never supported the Castro regime. In their breathless political speeches, they talked of returning to Cuba and restoring the country they had left. Many were already claiming what had once been theirs.

As early as in August 1990, a joint venture between the University of Miami's Research Institute for Cuban Studies and a former Dade County Commissioner began collecting data for publication of a "Registry of Expropriated Properties in Cuba." The project invited Cuban exiles to register their claims.

"When Castro falls and a new government takes over, the book could be used to recover some of these properties," Dade County Commissioner Barry Schreiber, the company's president, announced. More than a thousand people had called with inquiries a week after the story appeared in the *Miami Herald*. Cuban government media had a field day. Predictably, the story sent chills up the spines of millions of Cubans who were living in properties once owned by exiles.

By 1991, several exile groups in Miami were already fighting publicly over how they would dispose of the properties confiscated by the Cuban revolution once the Castro regime was toppled. The Cuban American National Foundation (CANF), the powerful Cuban-exile lobbying group led by Miami millionaire Jorge Mas Canosa, called for a compensation system: the post-Castro government would sell off all public assets, including houses, and pay its former owners with the proceeds.*

Other former property owners took out paid ads in Miami Spanish-language newspapers to denounce the post-Castro auction plan.

"The undersigned, farmers, landowners and ranchers, representing the legitimate owners of these lands and factories they plan to auction off without our consent . . . support and defend the right to

---

* *Mas Canosa said the post-Castro Cuban government should take no more than two years to sell off all public assets, to start paying off former owners. "You cannot return properties to their owners," he said in an interview published by the* Miami Herald *on September 29, 1991. "You must go into a compensation system right from the start."*

repossession and full restitution," said a full-page ad signed by a National Association of Ranchers and National Association of Land-owners in exile. "Nobody has more right to property than its legitimate owners."

Cubans on the island could not take the debate lightly. There was the precedent of Nicaragua, where the fall of the leftist Sandinista regime had moved thousands of Miami-based Nicaraguan exiles to file claims for their confiscated properties. Despite efforts by U.S.-backed President Violeta Chamorro to stop the return of Sandinista-confiscated homes as a way to prevent a new cycle of violence, the Nicaraguan legislature had passed sweeping laws demanding eviction or payment from thousands of property owners. A long tug of war between Chamorro and the Nicaraguan Congress ensued. Cuban government media made sure that Cubans were kept informed of every detail of these events.

Castro himself would use every opportunity to add fuel to the fire. "What would remain of the housing and other buildings the revolution turned over to the people if their former owners came back to reclaim them?" he asked the nation in late 1991. In a later address to the National Assembly, he added, "in Miami, they are already parceling out our country, and dreaming of getting everything back, but that won't happen as long as there remains one single man or woman with a sense of dignity."

Other news coming from Miami was no more encouraging. Many exiles were talking of vengeance. Their slogan at anti-Castro street rallies was, "War! War! War!" A militant rightist anti-Castro brigade called Alpha 66 was conducting weekend military training exercises in preparation for a planned assault on Cuba. The middle-aged men who participated in the exercises had no use for a negotiated solution to the Cuban crisis. Brigade leader Tomás Arencibia had stated that his life's greatest dream was "to return to my country with a rifle in hand, fighting." It was hardly the kind of message Cuban mothers wanted to hear.

One of the hard-line exiles' best-known leaders was Orlando Bosch, a sixty-five-year-old former pediatrician who had devoted his adult life to the anti-Castro armed struggle.

A former neighbor and friend of Castro's during their student days—he was only five days older than Castro—Bosch had been in and out of jail in the United States and South America for the previous two decades. He had first acquired notoriety in 1968, when he was convicted of firing a bazooka at a Polish freighter docked at the Port of Miami. Since then, he had been involved in attacks on Cuban embassies throughout the hemisphere.

In 1991, Bosch was rallying Cuban exiles through Miami's Spanish-language radio stations to help trigger an armed uprising in Cuba. At a public rally in Miami's Bobby Maduro stadium, he launched a campaign to collect $1 million to finance the rebellion.

"Let's send mix to the masons!" he told an enthusiastic crowd of a thousand exiles at the stadium, most of whom carried handwritten signs reading, *"Mezcla para los albañiles"* (Mix for the masons). "Our people do not have any arms. They lack the mix for the insurrection."

"Guerra! Guerra! Guerra!" (War! War! War!) the crowd roared back.

In Cuba, the very mention of Bosch's name drew expressions of anger and revulsion. Bosch had long been singled out by the Cuban regime as the mastermind of a 1976 bombing of a Cubana de Aviación commercial airliner flying from Barbados to Jamaica. Seventy-three people died in the terrorist attack on Flight CU-455. Among the victims was Cuba's twenty-four-member Olympic fencing team— mostly teenagers from humble families who were making their first tour outside Cuba.

Cuban media had repeatedly shown the pictures of the deceased members of the fencing team, and of their grieving parents. The Castro regime had even opened a museum in Havana—the Museum of the Fighting People—to commemorate the victims of the tragedy. Over the years, tens of thousands of schoolchildren had passed through the museum on field trips. The images they saw there had made a lasting impression on many Cubans. Even those who now were critical of the Castro regime were scandalized by the killings of innocent Cubans in the name of the anti-Castro cause.

Bosch did little to dispel the charge that he had been behind the bombing. He had repeatedly stated his moral right to fight the Cuban regime through any means—including terrorism. He had admitted being a member of the terrorist group that had planted the bomb, although he claimed he was in charge of propaganda activities and had not been involved in the actual bombing. At any rate, he had publicly applauded the bombing, on the dubious ground that Cubana's DC-8 commercial planes were also being used to fly Cuban generals and physicians to Angola.

"It was a legitimate war action," Bosch continued to maintain when I visited his Miami home in 1991. "Castro's aircraft are always military aircraft, even if he puts a Cubana de Aviación seal on them."

Bosch had no qualms about the dozens of civilian passengers killed in the bombing. The members of Cuba's Olympic fencing team "were servants of the [Castro] regime," he told me straight-faced. Asked why, he explained that a young woman member of the fencing team had praised the social accomplishments of the Cuban revolution in an interview in Venezuela days before her death. The fact that any member of an official Cuban delegation traveling abroad was expected to make such statements was no mitigating factor in Bosch's mind. "If you do make such statements, you run certain risks," he said. "We are at war, aren't we?"

As for the other innocent passengers on the aircraft, Bosch justified their deaths as necessary sacrifices in the holy war against Castro. "Thomas Jefferson said something along the lines that the tree of freedom has to be nurtured with the blood of tyrants and heroes, and I would add also with the blood of the innocent," he told me. "War is a competition of cruelties, and commiseration is pure stupidity."

Bosch had spent eleven years in jail in Venezuela in connection with the CU-455 bombing and was released in 1988 after being tried twice and acquitted both times. In Miami, where he was arrested immediately on old parole-violation charges against him, he received a hero's welcome from rightist Cuban exiles and south Florida politicians courting their votes. Half a dozen Cuban-exile radio stations launched an enthusiastic campaign to collect money for Bosch's defense. Florida Gov. Bob Martinez, later appointed drug czar by President Bush, promised to make "new efforts . . . to resolve this humanitarian case."

Since his release from jail in 1990, Bosch was again hard at work to ignite his sacred war. Even after the collapse of the Soviet bloc, he insisted that armed struggle was the only way to oust Castro, because domestic and international pressures on his regime would not be enough to bring him down. Cubans listening to his fiery speeches on short-wave broadcasts were scared. Was Bosch about to unleash a new wave of indiscriminate terrorism? A hero to a vocal crowd of Cuban exiles in Miami, Bosch was a lunatic in the minds of most Cubans I talked with on the island.

Although their message was more levelheaded than Bosch's, non-military Cuban-exile groups such as the Miami-based CANF were also seen with apprehension in Cuba. The CANF's political agenda sounded too right-wing—and too pro-American—to most Cubans who were familiar with it from Radio Martí and the CANF's own Voice of the Foundation radio broadcasts to Cuba.

The CANF was made up of the cream of Miami's all-white Cuban-exile business elite: the group had started in 1981 with fifty Cuban-exile businessmen who paid ten thousand dollars each for the privilege of serving as directors. In his impassioned short-wave radio speeches to Cuba, CANF's chairman Mas Canosa had often given ammunition to the Castro regime's claims that he wanted to turn Cuba into a U.S. protectorate.

"Americans and Cubans together again will gain the liberty and independence of Cuba," said Mas Canosa, flanked by former American President Ronald Reagan and Ambassador Armando Valladares, to a flag-waving crowd of twenty thousand Cuban exiles in a speech broadcast live to Cuba on April 28th, 1990. The speech concluded with a prayer that Cubans, "with our brothers from North America, hand in hand with President Reagan, can soon form an interminable symbolic line of free men."

Mas Canosa had made no bones over the years about his desire to become the new Cuban leader. "I know a lot of people say Mas Canosa does what he does because he wants to be president of Cuba," he said once. "Once Cuba is free, I'm going to run for everything I can. I want to make a contribution. Nobody can deny me the right to run for elective office if I choose to do that."

And he was not modest about the leading role he thought the exiles should play in post-Castro Cuba. Asked about the economic chaos that had followed the fall of communism in the Soviet Union, he said Cuba would be much better off, "because 10 to 15 percent of our people have been living in the most advanced market economy of the whole world."

Most CANF leaders talked about the foundation as if it were a government-in-exile preparing to assume a caretaker role after Castro's fall. They were being encouraged to do so by some influential Americans.

CANF President Francisco "Pepe" Hernandez wrote, following Ronald Reagan's April 1990 visit to Miami, "While we talked in private, [Reagan] told us, 'Do you know what was one of President Roosevelt's first appointments after the Japanese attack on Pearl Harbor? It was a commission to study the political and economic reconstruction of Japan for when the war was over. That's how Japan's present democracy was born. You, who are now so close to Castro's fall, should plan for the future.' '' Referring to Reagan, Hernandez added that "we, the Cuban exiles, cannot fail to pay attention to the advice of our great North American friend." The fact that Roosevelt's commission was meant for a country that was to be taken over by U.S. forces did not strike the CANF official as something that many Cubans on the island might resent.

In mid-1991, Mas Canosa unveiled a "Social, Political and Economic Program for the Reconstruction of Cuba." It included signing a free-trade agreement with the United States and sending more than ten thousand Cuban-exile professionals—accountants, lawyers, bankers and business people—to teach the islanders how to adapt virtually all Cuban institutions to a free-market economy.

"Let's rescue Cuba and Cubans from this obscure chapter of history," Mas Canosa roared to a crowd of Cuban exiles, raising his hand and circling the air with his index finger. "We Cubans in exile have demonstrated ourselves to be winners. . . . We want the same future for our brothers in Cuba."

The brothers in Cuba, however, were suspicious. To them, the fiery exile leader sounded too much like the Comandante they had at home. His thundering speeches exuded hatred and intransigence. Like Castro, he often spoke of himself in the third person—Jorge Mas wants this, Jorge Mas thinks that, he would say. Mas Canosa was widely perceived as the head of a horde of rich exiles eager to reclaim their lost properties.

Most Cubans found it preposterous that the exiles, who had done so well in Miami, were even talking about apportioning the crumbs of what was left in Cuba. They said that only the Cubans on the island, who had suffered for more than three decades and had seen their children off to faraway wars, had the moral right to inherit the country after Castro.

Even the island's best-known dissidents had little use for CANF's reconstruction program. Maria Elena Cruz Varela, a poet who led the Alternative Criterion group of anti-Castro intellectuals, summed it up this way: "First, we were a Spanish colony. Then, we became an American colony. Then, we became a Soviet colony. The last thing we need now is to become a colony of Miami's Cuban exiles."

There was also the question of Mas Canosa's credentials to play a lead role in post-Castro Cuba. Many of the things that had made him popular in Miami did not play well in Cuba.

Mas Canosa had become an American citizen, ostensibly to qualify for the Radio Martí Advisory Board and carry out the struggle against Fidel from there. His U.S. citizenship did not sit well with Cubans on the island. He was also depicted by the Cuban regime—unfairly—as a former Batista follower. It's true that, unlike many other prominent exiles who had joined the revolution and had later become disenchanted with it, Mas Canosa had never fought against the Batista dictatorship. But neither had he been a supporter of the regime.

After fleeing to Miami in 1960 as a twenty year old—most of Castro's guerrillas had been fighting for years by the time they were that age—Mas Canosa had trained for the failed 1961 Bay of Pigs invasion, but his boat never made it to Cuba. He worked as a milkman in Miami and later joined the Church & Tower of Florida, Inc. utility company–contracting firm, which he ended up buying in 1971. He bought a $700,000 home and became the proud owner of a bulletproof Mercedes, which was reported to have once belonged to the late Nicaraguan dictator Anastasio Somoza.

Frustrated by Washington's failure to act more decisively against the Castro regime, Mas Canosa and his wealthy anti-Castro friends created their lobbying group shortly after Ronald Reagan's inauguration. They would immediately become golden boys of the Reagan Administration's anti-Communist zealots. Conservatives in Washington had a natural sympathy for Miami's Cuban exiles: they saw them as living proof of their claims that minorities in America could succeed without government handouts. More important, the prosperous and fiercely anti-Communist Miami Cuban exiles were seen in Washington as a key constituency to support the administration's offensive to stop the spread of communism in Central America. Soon, the CANF would play a key role in helping push Reagan's Nicaraguan Contra aid packages through Congress.

Whether CANF was born as an effort by Cuban exiles to influence Washington or vice versa is an open question. Claims by Cuba's vice-minister of foreign relations Ramón Sanchez Parodi—the Castro regime's senior expert on U.S. affairs—that CANF was a creation of the Reagan Administration may be accurate. Constantine Menges, the top Latin American adviser on the Reagan Administration's National Security Council, would later concede that in 1980 he had proposed a plan to President-elect Reagan to curb Cuban adventurism abroad, bolster Cuban-exile efforts to discredit the Castro regime, and ultimately create a Cuban government in exile. The first part of his program—fighting Cuban-backed regimes in Nicaragua, Angola and other countries, and providing moral support to the Cuban exiles—was enthusiastically adopted by the new administration.*

To convince a skeptical American public opinion about the need to support Nicaragua's Contra rebels, the Reagan Administration needed to underscore the danger that Nicaragua—and all of Central America—could become another Cuba. The CANF's aggressive propaganda campaigns about Cuba's expansionism in the Western Hemisphere and its effective lobbying in Congress would provide much-needed support for Reagan's policies.†

In addition to public relations, Cuban exile leaders provided key practical assistance to U.S. officials involved in the Nicaraguan Contra war effort. Through Mas Canosa and other prominent Cuban exiles, National Security Adviser Col. Oliver North recruited anti-Communist exiles to set in motion his secret Nicaraguan Contra supply network. Felix Rodriguez, a former CIA agent who was a key figure in North's Contra arms supply program at a time when such shipments were prohibited by Congress, was introduced to U.S. officials by Mas Canosa himself, according to a State Department official's testimony in the Iran-Contra hearings. Mas Canosa's name would appear repeatedly in North's 1985 diaries, often in connection with Rodriguez.

By the mid-eighties, Mas Canosa had powerful friends in key Washington D.C. offices. Congressman Dante Fascell (D-Fl.), the head of the House Foreign Affairs Committee, was one of several politicians who had seen their Miami congressional districts turn into Cuban-exile-dominated areas over the years. As a Democrat in a district where the Cuban majority was solidly behind the Reagan Republicans, Fascell needed the CANF to vouch for his hard-line anti-Castro stand. The CANF soon became an essential endorsement for any politician—Democrat or Republican—courting votes in southern Florida.

Within the Reagan Administration, the CANF had the enthusiastic support of Vice-President George Bush, whose son Jeb lived in

---

* *Moral support for the Cuban-exile cause would soon turn into massive material support when the CANF-backed Radio Martí broadcasts to Cuba were passed by Congress in 1983 with an initial budget of $14 million. Although the CANF didn't run Radio Martí, Mas Canosa soon became its behind-the-scenes chief, according to Radio Martí executives at the time.*

† *In addition to fighting Communism, many of the CANF directors were also protecting their vast business interests in Honduras, Guatemala, and other Central American countries at the time threatened by Nicaragua's Sandinista regime. At least half a dozen CANF directors had land or business interests in Central America.*

Miami and was CANF director Armando Codina's business partner. U.S. ambassador to the United Nations Jeane Kirkpatrick, who also had a son living in Miami, was an enthusiastic backer and frequent speaker at CANF fund-raisers. Several Cuban exiles close to the CANF had also been appointed by Reagan to influential jobs in the American foreign policy apparatus, including former CANF president José Sorzano as the main deputy to U.N. Ambassador Kirkpatrick and later as senior Latin American expert for the National Security Council, Nestor Sanchez as deputy assistant secretary of defense for inter-American affairs, and Otto Juan Reich as head of a high-profile State Department office to rally support for U.S. policies in Central America.

Over the years, Bush's Miami-based son Jeb would become a darling of the CANF's Cuban-exile businessmen. A fluent Spanish-speaker with a Mexican wife—Columba Garnica Gallo—and a degree in Latin American studies from the University of Texas, Jeb Bush had arrived in Miami in 1981, at age twenty-eight, to take a job with Codina's IntrAmerica real estate investment management firm. Jeb had quickly established his credentials as a warm supporter of the Cuban exile cause, appearing in a white guayabera at the Miami Airport to welcome a just-released Cuban political prisoner or luring top-name Republicans—including his own father and Reagan's daughter Maureen—to attend Republican Party fund-raisers in town and make sure they would not forget to speak out against Castro. By 1984, Jeb Bush was the Dade County Republican Party's chairman.

The romance between the Reagan Administration and Miami's Cuban exiles grew progressively. In mid-1987, when Vice-President George Bush arrived in downtown Miami's Little Havana section to preside over a ceremony in which a section of Southwest Twelfth Avenue was renamed "Avenida Ronald W. Reagan," he received a roaring welcome from Cuban exiles. After the ceremony, Bush sipped a *café cubano* on the sidewalk in front of the Cuban restaurant where Reagan had dined during a presidential visit five years earlier, and strolled down the street to the cheers of hundreds of Cuban-Americans. Walking at his side were his wife, Barbara, and their son Jeb, by then Florida secretary of commerce.

That day, as he had done in several previous visits to Miami, the vice president underscored the Reagan Administration's commitment to freeing Cuba and its unwavering support for the Nicaraguan Contras. A moved Miami Mayor Xavier Suarez, a Cuban exile himself, told Bush that "it is not an exaggeration to suggest that there will never be a vice-president who cares more for Miami, who feels more at home among our people, who carries closer to himself our foreign and domestic concerns." A year later, with Jeb working full-time as chairman of his father's 1988 election campaign in Florida, Bush would sweep the state with near-blanket support from south Florida's Cuban-Americans.*

In 1990, when the CANF held its mass rally at Miami's Orange Bowl to honor Reagan, it chose Jeb Bush to act as master of ceremonies. The presidential son got a standing ovation from the crowd, and shared a first-row seat on the podium with Reagan, then Florida governor Bob Martinez, Mas Canosa and Valladares.

Jeb's role as an informal liaison between Miami's Cuban community and the White House grew substantially since his father's move to the Oval Office. Cuban exiles would soon credit Jeb, among other things, with helping coordinate the greatest U.S. propaganda victory over Cuba in years: the 1991 U.N. Human Rights Commission's vote in Geneva that appointed a human rights monitor for Cuba, placing the Castro regime under the same scrutiny that had been reserved for rightist governments such as that in El Salvador.

On Sunday, March 3, 1991, former Reagan State Department appointee Otto Reich, by then on a special mission to Geneva to help win the case against Castro at the United Nations, placed a call to his friend Jeb in Miami. It was three days before the U.N. vote, and it didn't look like the U.S. would be able to break the traditional reluctance of Latin American countries to vote against Cuba. Reich had sent a fax to the White House that same weekend, asking for an urgent lobbying effort with Latin American presidents, but wanted to make sure that his message would reach the right ears.

"Jeb, we need help. You've got to call your friend," Reich said. He would later confide, "We refer to the president as 'friend.' These are international calls."

Jeb Bush called the White House and would later tell Reich, "I hope it helps." Hours later, with the nation focussed on the Persian Gulf war, Bush was calling Argentina's President Carlos Menem; Vice-President Dan Quayle was calling Venezuelan President Carlos

---

* Jeb Bush's ties with Miami's Cuban exiles would sometimes spell trouble for his father. In 1987, it was disclosed that Jeb had forwarded to his father a letter by pro-Contra Guatemalan politician Mario Castejon, in which the Guatemalan offered to help the Contra war effort. Bush responded to the letter, putting Castejon in contact with Lt. Col. Oliver North and his secret Contra supply network, at a time when American aid to the Contras was banned by the U.S. Congress. Bush would later say he routinely referred Contra-related letters to North, often without reading them.

Andres Perez, and U.S. diplomats around the world were visiting foreign ministers urging a tougher stand on Cuba at the U.N. commission.

When the vote came on March 6, twenty-two countries supported the anti-Castro resolution, six voted against, and fifteen abstained. Argentina became the first Latin American commission member to vote against Cuba. Mexico and Brazil—longtime supporters of the Cuban position—abstained for the first time when it became clear that their pro-Castro motion would lose. A proud Jeb Bush would comment of his father later, "If I weren't around, he would have done it anyway."

Among CANF's many coups in Washington were its help to win U.S. military aid for the rebels fighting the Cuban-backed Marxist regime in Angola, and its proposal for and the subsequent congressional blessing of the creation of Radio Martí. The bill was approved in 1983, and Mas Canosa was soon appointed to the Radio Martí Presidential Advisory Board. He immediately started a successful lobbying campaign to launch TV Martí, which would begin operating—although its signal was jammed in Cuba—in 1990.*

The CANF also entered an agreement with the U.S. State Department to manage a resettlement program for Cuban refugees who wanted to enter the United States from third countries. More than three thousand Cuban refugees had benefited from the program by 1990. By the early nineties, Mas Canosa was all over Miami and New Jersey Cuban-exile radio stations. He could rightly claim to his staunchly anti-Communist audience that he was the one Cuban exile who was getting things done. He had become a president-in-waiting, or Castro's U.S.-based nemesis.

To skeptics, Mas Canosa's aggressive broadcast-to-Cuba campaign was mainly aimed at provoking an escalation of U.S.-Cuban tensions. According to this school of thought, Mas Canosa hoped that such a confrontation would eventually lead to an American invasion—and to his own appointment to a leading role in a U.S.-installed regime. Mas Canosa denied he favored an American invasion—sort of.

---

* In order to get more than $32 million from Congress for TV Martí's first two years on the air, the CANF somehow managed to convince Congress that the station's broadcasts could be seen in Cuba despite the fact that Castro's regime was regularly jamming its signal. Unlike Radio Martí, which had a big audience in Cuba, TV Martí was hardly seen or heard on the island: I never ran into a single Cuban who had seen or heard TV Martí.

"We're totally opposed to a U.S. military intervention," he told me at his CANF offices in Miami. "If an intervention in Cuba is necessary, not to get rid of Castro but because Cubans are being subjected to a bloodbath, it must be under a multinational agreement of the Organization of American States with Panamanians, Hondurans, Brazilians, etc., as well as with an American group, which would create a peacekeeping force."

But while he was an artful politician in Washington and could be charming in private meetings, Mas Canosa often came across on the south Florida Spanish-radio talk shows as a neighborhood bully. A hot-blooded man, he seemed to be constantly rolling up his sleeves for a fight.

In 1986, he challenged then Miami city commissioner Joe Carollo to a duel with firearms after the city official nixed a $130 million real estate development Mas Canosa and former U.S. ambassador Kirkpatrick were involved in.

"I'm going to prove to the Cubans that you are a clown and a coward," Mas Canosa told Carollo in a Spanish-language radio program. "Your bullying in Miami has ended because you have encountered a man, with a capital M."

The duel didn't take place, but Mas Canosa would soon make headlines with a new brawl—this time with his brother. Mas punched his younger brother Ricardo in the nose and chest, threw him against glass, had his company car stolen, and then tried to ruin him financially, Ricardo Mas said in a 1986 lawsuit. In October 1990, a Miami jury ruled in favor of Ricardo Mas's civil suit. Mas Canosa was sentenced to pay $900,000 in compensation and punitive damages.

But the CANF chairman had a hard time keeping his business affairs out of the headlines. Mas Canosa's legal fight with his brother was not yet over when the exile leader was hit with a new lawsuit: former CANF vice-president José Luis Rodriguez was charging that Mas Canosa and three other CANF directors had illegally split up among themselves money from a Kentucky real estate corporation in which all four were partners. Although Mas Canosa and his partners denied any wrongdoing, press reports about the lawsuit unearthed new tales of alleged vendettas and blackmail among CANF leaders.

Did Mas Canosa stand any chance of becoming Cuba's president in the absence of a U.S. intervention? Contrary to conventional wisdom in Cuba, the island was fertile ground for a rightist *caudillo*. In addition to his drive and reputation as a doer, Mas Canosa had a big thing going for him: Castro's intransigence. The Miami Cuban-exile

leader knew that the longer Castro stuck to his now-discredited orthodox Marxism, the more of a chance Mas Canosa had of becoming
Cuba's post-Communist savior.

The events in Eastern Europe and the Soviet Union had shown
him that most people coming out of Communist systems were not
eager to follow moderate Socialist reformers—they wanted a radical
departure from the past. Mas Canosa was confident that, in the long
run, Castro's ironclad communism—and the rapid economic down-
turn that went with it—would pave the way for a major turnabout in
Cuban politics. He hoped that time—and Castro's stubbornness—
would work in his favor.

<>

In the short run, however, Cuba's state security was more worried
about the small groups of dissidents on the island who wanted a
peaceful transition to democracy through political negotiations with
the government. It was these people, who vowed to preserve the
revolution's key social gains, that posed the most immediate security
risk to the Castro regime. Some considered themselves Socialists,
others Social Democrats. Their thinking was far more popular among
the Cuban population than that of Mas Canosa's hard-line exile group.

In addition to Arcos's Human Rights Committee, and Sanchez's
National Commission for Human Rights and National Reconciliation,
there was poet Cruz Varela's Alternative Criterion group of dissident
intellectuals, journalist Yndamiro Restano's Harmony Movement, the
Tercera Opción (Third Option) coalition of Communist Party defectors and half a dozen other small organizations. Virtually all at some
point had supported the revolution.

Their members were often arrested or harassed by state security
forces, which periodically organized "repudiation rallies" in front of
their homes by MININT agents trying to play the part of spontaneous
demonstrators. In most cases, the moderate dissident groups had
fewer than a dozen active members each. But their revolutionary
backgrounds and nonaggressive pleas for political change were gaining them growing support among listeners of The Voice of CID,
another Miami-exile short-wave radio program that did not follow the
CANF's hard-line rhetoric.

Increasingly, the moderate groups were finding articulate spokes-
persons to represent them in the United States, Spain and Latin
America. The moderate human rights groups' representatives abroad,
led by journalist Carlos Alberto Montaner in Spain and businessman

Ramón Cernuda in Miami, were beginning to gain political credibility—and to challenge CANF's right to speak for all Cuban exiles. By helping move exile politics toward the center, Montaner's Democratic Platform and Cernuda's Coordinator for Human Rights Organizations in Cuba (CODEHU) were beginning to dispel the notion in Cuba and in international liberal circles that Cuban exile activists were nostalgic Batista followers. The moderate groups were beginning to corrode the Cuban regime's main propaganda claim: that exiles—all of them—wanted to turn the country into a U.S. colony, and that Fidel Castro represented Cuba's only hope to retain its national sovereignty.

The regime was aware that groups like these had been the ones to precipitate the downfall of communism in several Eastern European countries, and it was determined to nip their expansionary efforts in the bud. The trouble was, Castro could not afford to use force indiscriminately against moderate dissidents whose demands sounded increasingly reasonable amid the worldwide collapse of communism. He could arrest some and harass others, but he could not allow any to be killed and made into martyrs.

For all its human rights violations, the regime had always been careful not to appear as another Latin American military dictatorship. The Cuban military had come to believe after years of revolutionary indoctrination that it was a "people's army" which would never be asked to shoot at its fellow citizens. And as popular discontent over food shortages rose, there were growing questions over whether the new Rapid Response militias would respond aggressively. What would Castro do if, as had happened throughout the Soviet bloc, the small dissident groups evolved into a major political force?

"We're in a bind," a Communist Party academician with links to the military told me as we walked on a Havana street. "This is a country with little tolerance for bloody dictatorships. The two openly repressive regimes we had, Machado and Batista, were quickly overthrown by the people.

"If we crack down too hard, the revolution's mystique would be shaken in its very foundations," he said. "The day we have to shoot at a massive opposition demonstration, it will be all over."

By mid-1991, Cuba lay in a kind of torpor. Neither the regime, nor the dissidents, nor the silent majority between them wanted to make a radical move that could have devastating consequences for any of them. Public employees holding make-work jobs and the large numbers of Cubans who had gained access to housing and education with the revolution were fearful that drastic political change might threaten these social gains.

Even if many were increasingly disenchanted with the revolution, they knew of no opposition leader with enough charisma to seriously challenge Fidel. And the exiles in Miami were perceived to be too power-hungry—and remote—to be followed in their short-wave radio calls for anti-Castro riots. There was no magnet to draw a sizable part of the population out of its state of zombiehood, and into the streets. Most Cubans would rather wait for Fidel himself, or the people around him, to make a drastic political turnabout in light of the country's economic collapse—perhaps at the forthcoming Fourth Congress of the Communist Party.

"Algo tiene que pasar," people said. "Something is bound to happen."

12

Courting the Babalaos

◄◄◄◄◄ **A**t 9 A.M. on the morning of January 1, 1991, when the streets of Havana were finally quiet after a long night of New Year's parties, small groups of solemn-looking black men in white clothes approached a house in the suburb of Diezmero. About 110 of them were gathering at the home of Angel "Bebo" Padrón for a meeting that millions of Cubans considered crucial for the country's future. Fidel Castro was not present, nor were any of Cuba's top Communist Party leaders. There were no television cameras, nor reporters. In fact, the secret gathering was never reported, either in Cuba or abroad.

Yet a sizable part of the Cuban population spent that day—as they did every New Year's day, San Manuel day—waiting for news from the symposium of Cuba's senior Babalaos, the Santería priests. They would issue their Oddun of the Year—their prediction for the future of Cuba. Large numbers of Cubans held a deep-rooted belief that nobody could escape the fate the Orishas—or Gods—had laid out for them. Within hours of the end of the daylong meeting, the Gods' verdict would spread from one end of the island to another, by word of mouth.

Top government officials were among those waiting for the Babalaos' word with unusual interest: Santería religion played an important role in Castro's political survival strategy. The Cuban leader had called for a major government effort to muster the support of the large masses of Santería followers—mostly dark-skinned, working-class Cubans who had benefited from the revolution but were becoming increasingly impatient over growing economic hardships. Since late 1990, the regime had launched an unprecedented propaganda campaign to warm up to practitioners of Afro-Cuban religions.

These cults had been deeply entrenched in Cuba since the eighteenth century, when large numbers of African slaves had begun to practice them openly on Cuba's sugar plantations. Three major Afro-Cuban cults—the Yoruba tribes' Santería, the Bantu tribes' Palo Monte and the Abakuá secret societies—had since mushroomed on the island. It became an official priority to insure that the cults did not turn against the revolution—and that their Gods' predictions did not stir the population's rising anxiety.

This year in particular, amid growing speculation that Fidel Castro's regime would soon fall, Cubans across the political spectrum were anxious to know what the Orishas had forecast. Since 1989, the Gods had been pessimistic about the island's future. Santería priests had warned of terrible calamities following the government execution of one of the De La Guardia twins. In Santería, there is no greater sin than separating twin brothers: *Jimaguas*—twins—are considered messengers of the Gods, and ultimate carriers of good luck. Killing Col. Tony De La Guardia had been an affront to the Gods, the priests had warned.

Most of the Babalaos who showed up at the Diezmero house on the first day of 1991 were black men in their fifties or sixties. They dressed in white from top to toe, except for their necklaces and wristbands, which displayed the colors of the deities they worshipped. The followers of Changó—the God of fire, lightning and war—wore collars decorated with red and white plastic beads. Worshipers of Ochún—the Goddess of the rivers, love and female sensuality—sported yellow and white beads.

Padrón, sixty-two, the highest priest of the Yoruba house of Cuba's Santería religion, welcomed his fellow Babalaos and escorted them to a back room in his two-story house. He had sacrificed two goats, five cocks and dozens of doves for the ceremony. Their blood was now being offered to the Orishas in soup plates lying all over the house. When everything was ready to start the ceremony, Padrón sat on a stool surrounded by candles, the blood-filled soup plates, plastic dolls, wood-sculptured ships, statuettes of Catholic saints and a vari-

ety of other small items. He opened the proceedings by asking the
Gods if enough coffee, alcohol and blood had been offered to satisfy
their celestial appetites. To get their answer, he threw four square
coconut chips on the floor: if two or more fell white side up, the
answer was yes. After a few tries it turned out the Gods wanted more
coffee and brandy, and the Orishas were ready.

"*Ñangaré, Ñangaré, Ñangaré,*" Bebo intoned.

"*Ñangoreo, Ñangoreo, Ñangoreo, Olorum Mafoiu,*" the Babalaos
chanted, telling the Gods that the food and drink was in their honor.
The men then passed around cups of water, honey, egg yolk—and
blood. Each participant took the blood-filled cup to his mouth and
soaked his lips.

For the next eight hours, Bebo ritually questioned the Orishas.
The answers would emerge as he dropped sixteen palm tree seeds in
a powder-covered tray and studied the prints they made. Late in the
afternoon, after hundreds of minor predictions, the seeds falling from
Padrón's hand issued a forecast that sent shock waves through the
room.

The marks on the tray indicated that 1991's Oddun would be
marked by Baba Eyogbe's sign—treason. The Babalaos looked at one
another in awe. It was a devastating prediction. Under Baba Eyogbe's
reign, the year would be dominated by Changó, the indomitable God
of war, and Yemayá, the Goddess of the sea, known for her terrifying
rage and ruthless punishment.

"This Oddun is marked by rivalry, discord, defections and treason," said the written summary of the Oddun that later circulated
secretly among the Babalaos who had participated in the ceremony.
"It talks of splits in the family, in races, in tribes, and political
groups."

<><>

Afro-Cuban religions were experiencing an unprecedented boom in
Cuba. Since the growth of the black and mulatto population after the
flight of Cuba's upper classes in the early sixties, Afro-Cuban cults
had spread from the black-populated towns in Oriente to white neighborhoods in Havana.

They had mushroomed despite repeated government efforts in
the early sixties to discourage any religious expression, and to turn
Marxist atheism into Cuba's new national credo. Although there were
no official estimates, Santería insiders calculated that there were as
many as four thousand Babalaos in Cuba. In comparison, there were
only two hundred fifty Roman Catholic priests in Cuba.

The Santería religious fervor was a product of economic hard times, the growing social weight of blacks in Cuba, and the war in Angola. The estimated half million Cuban soldiers who had served in Africa in the seventies and eighties—a disproportionate number of whom were black—had brought home a renewed interest in Afro-Cuban religions. In Cuba, the desperation brought about by worsening food shortages had already driven millions to visit their neighborhood Babalaos in search of advice and comfort.

The Santería priests offered quick relief without moralizing sermons. Unlike those of their counterparts in the Catholic Church, their recommendations for physical or spiritual ailments were eminently practical—there was always a concoction to help you fight an illness, a prescribed ritual to correct a problem. No matter that you had cheated on your wife, drunk too much or stolen goods from your workplace. The Babalaos were not too interested in the moral issues.

By 1991, you could see growing numbers of white-clad men and women on the streets. They were people who had just made their Santo, had gone through Santería's initiation rites. Some of them were white, and every day you could see more Communist Party members wearing Santería necklaces or wristbands. Huge crowds of Santeros were showing up at Roman Catholic churches, carrying black dolls and other amulets they held high as they prayed before the altar.

Similar scenes repeated themselves with growing regularity in the street processions for Catholic saints who were also venerated by the Afro-Cuban religions. Once-small annual church celebrations became huge affairs. In 1990, more than two hundred thousand people turned out for one of Havana's December 17 processions for San Lázaro—the Catholic equivalent of the Santería deity of Babalú Ayé, the God of epidemics and venereal diseases. At least two hundred fifty thousand people, many of them carrying Santería amulets, participated in the annual procession for the Caridad del Cobre Virgin in the eastern city of Santiago in September 1991.

To Santería believers, San Lázaro, Santa Barbara or the Caridad del Cobre Virgin were simply corresponding images of their ancient African Gods. In the days of the colony, when African religions were prohibited by the Spanish, the slaves had adopted Catholic saints as a way to cover their worship of African Gods. The tradition had survived untouched. Many Cubans would now pray in front of a Santa Barbara statuette during the day, and worship the same figurine as Changó, Santería's male God of war, after dark. In Cuba, the Gods changed their sex at midnight.

<>

Monsignor Carlos Manuel de Céspedes, the Catholic Church's Vicar of Havana, kept a big poster of Santería's God of war behind his office door in the archbishopric. It wasn't meant as a joke.

De Céspedes, a descendant of independence hero Carlos Manuel de Céspedes, readily conceded that Santería had become a formidable social force. He had been an avid student of Santería for many years. Cuba's Church hierarchy had long tolerated its practitioners in the Church. He had made it a point to talk regularly with the Babalaos. As a Catholic priest in Cuba, he explained, he had to follow Santería closely—or risk being completely out of touch with his flock.

In early 1991, for instance, De Céspedes found strange packages scattered all over his Old Havana parish. A dead goat wrapped in red cloth was found by the church's front door; dozens of red flowers were laid in front of the altar, and scores of red objects were strewn on the pews or at the building's entrance.

The vicar understood the meaning of the packages, because he had heard the Oddun prophecy for the year. Frightened about the future, his parishioners were trying to placate Changó and Yemayá, the irate deities of war and sea. They believed that the goat sacrifices and red objects would mollify the ferocious Orishas.

"To understand Cuba, one has to understand Santería," De Céspedes told me. "Cubans are very superstitious, magical people. Unless you know what they believe the Orishas have told them, you won't understand their behavior."

<>

The Castro regime could not afford to ignore the spreading influence of Santería. In late 1990, the Central Committee had launched an all-out campaign to coopt the island's three major Afro-Cuban religions. By far the most important one was Santería, the Yorubas' Catholic Church-influenced cult. Next in popularity was Palo Monte, a Bantu cult that relied heavily on magic. The third-largest cult was that of the Abakuás, which consisted of small mutual-protection secret societies that practiced ancient African warriors' rituals.

The Central Committee had instructed its Religious Affairs Department to substantially increase its economic and political support for the Afro-Cuban religions' priests as a way to win them over. The Party's Propaganda Department was ordered to plan a media campaign portraying all three cults in a favorable light.

The Interior Ministry's Counterintelligence Religious Affairs Office—known within Cuba's state security as Department III-4—was stepping up covert operations to penetrate the Afro-Cuban cults' underworld. The various Communist Party and government offices would try to befriend the Santeros and try to steer them to support the regime—or at the very least to stay away from criticizing it.

Cuba was soon flooded with government-sanctioned Santería propaganda. Hardly a week went by without a major feature on Santería in the otherwise grim pages of *Granma*, *Juventud Rebelde* or the weekly magazine *Bohemia*. Most of these were interviews with progovernment Babalaos, who described their Santería rites and their African roots. They were the only stories dealing with religion allowed to appear in the Cuban press.

Documentaries on Afro-Cuban cults began to appear regularly on prime-time television. A new album by folk singer Celina Gonzalez featuring the song "Que Viva Changó" ("Long Live Changó") was distributed and heavily promoted by the regime. In 1991, the Union of Cuban Writers and Artists (UNEAC) published *The Orishas in Cuba*, a book by Natalia Bolivar de Arostegui, a one-time revolutionary who had been semi-ostracized for her liberal views in recent years. Written as a reference book, it was a compendium of the Santería deities, their stories, their favorite colors, and the sacrifices they liked best. The book sold out in a matter of hours. In a rare case of political tolerance, the regime also allowed publication of the Santería classic *El Monte*, by exiled writer Lydia Cabrera, who had long ago defected and was living in Miami. Most Cuban writers in exile were never even mentioned in Cuban media.

The Ethnographic Museum of Guanabacoa on the outskirts of Havana was expanded to include several new rooms devoted to Santería. The Museum of Havana's House of Africa was opened in Old Havana to offer exhibits and lectures on Afro-Cuban cults. A government-sanctioned Afro-Cuban Association began to hold regular meetings in Guanabacoa. The Cuban Institute of Friendship with the Peoples (ICAP) invited foreign delegations of Santería followers to visit the island and attend Afro-Cuban ceremonies.

Even more surprisingly, the Communist Party—long used to putting its members through exhaustive courses on Marxism—started sponsoring crash Santería courses for its cadres. Among them was a Santería seminar at the Afro-Cuban Association in Guanabacoa for dozens of Havana librarians, university professors and journalists. The once-a-week course taught party members the basics of Afro-Cuban religions.

"We were told we needed to take these courses to stay in closer touch with the people," said one Havana librarian at the seminar. "We were given time off from our jobs to come here."

The Santeros had provided crucial support for Fidel in the early days of the revolution. Cuban blacks and mulattos had been attracted by the new leader's promises to end racial discrimination and share the white elite's wealth among the poor. But there was more than that. There were several seemingly innocuous events involving Fidel at the time that went largely unnoticed by the rest of the world, but that were interpreted by millions of Santería believers as signs from the Orishas that Castro was an *elegido*—a man chosen by the Gods.

Among them: The revolution had triumphed on January 1st, the day of San Manuel, a holy day for the Orishas. It was highly significant that the guerrilla leader who was promising major changes in Cuba's history had overthrown the government on the very day that Orishas set the course of history.

When Castro and his fellow guerrillas arrived in Havana from their outpost in Oriente—a largely black-populated area in the mountains where Afro-Cuban religions were strongest—many of the rebels wore Santería collars and bracelets they had received from supportive peasants. The detail did not escape the attention of Santería believers. Although Castro himself was not among the guerrilleros influenced by the religion, his small rebel army was rapidly seen as friends of Santería.

Furthermore, the red-and-black flag of the young guerrillas' 26th of July Movement had a key meaning for the Cuban masses: they were the colors of Elleguá, the God of destiny. According to Santería, Elleguá opens and closes the doors to happiness and disgrace. Most Cuban homes, even those of nonbelievers, keep an Elleguá vase as a good-luck talisman behind the front door. When the red-and-black flags made their triumphant entry into Havana, it seemed to many as if Elleguá would from now on give protection to Cuba and its people.

But what Babalaos had long cited as the best evidence of Fidel's heavenly protection was what happened at his first speech after his arrival in Havana. Castro was addressing the nation from Camp Columbia on January 8, 1959, when, all of a sudden, two doves flew over the audience and started circling the brightly illuminated podium. The crowd followed the birds with fascination. Then, one of the doves descended, sat on Fidel's left shoulder, and remained there for a few seconds. The scene touched off an explosion of "Fee-del! Fee-del! Fee-del!" among the ecstatic onlookers.

The Gods couldn't have sent a clearer signal, the Santeros said: doves are symbols of Obatalá, the Son of God. In Santería, Obatalá is the God who shaped the human body, and rules his mind, thoughts and dreams. The dove on Fidel's shoulder was a message from the Gods that Fidel was their chosen one to guide Cuba for years to come, they said.

But the Santeros' love affair with Castro would be short-lived. In the early sixties, as Castro sought to impose the dogma of Scientific Communism in Cuba, the regime restricted drum ceremonies in public places and sought to convert Afro-Cuban rituals into "folkloric" ballets. By the end of the sixties, followers of Afro-Cuban religions were often characterized by government officials as a potentially criminal element. A truce between the regime and the Babalaos evolved over the next two decades, during which the Santeros were allowed to practice their religion in private under the vigilant—and condescending—eye of the state.

In the late eighties, as Marxism was rapidly losing its appeal to the Cuban people, Castro decided to extend an olive branch to the rapidly growing Santería movement. In 1987, he invited Nigerian religious leader Alaiyeluwa Oba Okunade Sijuwade Olobuse II—the Oni of Ife, or the Pope of the Yoruba religion—for a five-day visit to Cuba. The Yoruba Pope, clad in a majestic white robe with a pearl-covered fez, showed up with several of his wives, a dozen Obas—or tribal leaders—and a large delegation of businessmen. The Cuban media, which until then had ignored or derided Afro-Cuban cults, portrayed his presence in Cuba as a major international event.

Although officially a guest of the ICAP, the visiting religious leader was given a statesman's welcome. He was declared "illustrious guest" of Havana, and was received several times by Fidel and other top government officials. (One of them was Angel Gómez Trueba, then head of Cuba's Foreign Construction Enterprises Union [UNECA], with whom the Yoruba Pope reportedly discussed starting joint business ventures.)

The regime's Santería propaganda offensive, which had begun as a way to broaden the social base of the revolution, intensified after the pessimistic Oddun prophecies for 1989, 1990, and 1991. The regime decided its public relations campaign was not enough. Officials were worried. Were the Babalaos' prophecies planting thoughts of civil war in people's minds? Were the Gods promoting political instability? Were the Orishas—and their representatives on earth—turning against Fidel?

It wasn't a trivial issue. Prophecies of political unrest attacked the core of the regime's political propaganda strategy: that the Castro revolution was invincible and, thus, safe from any domestic challenge. Officials feared that the bleak Oddun forecast could become a self-fulfilling prophecy. Something had to be done. A comprehensive Santería policy was urgently needed.

At the request of the Central Committee, the Academy of Sciences' Department of Socio-Religious Studies drafted a new policy. In an internal report to the Party leadership, the academy recommended a shift in government policy. Rather than ignoring Afro-Cuban cults, the Party should begin actively supporting them, the report said.

Santería was not only the most popular religion in Cuba, but it offered the most fertile ground for expanding grass-roots support for the revolution, the report said. It was the religion of the blacks and the poor—the people in whose name Castro had taken power. The regime could recover part of its support from the black majority by casting Cuba's political split in racial terms. The government should portray itself as an ally of the blacks and their culture.

The Santeros could be brought around to actively supporting the revolution, and to help fill the void left by the demise of global Marxism, the Academy researchers said. At the very least, the Santeros could be asked to stay away from issuing gloomy and demoralizing prophecies. With proper planning, the Babalaos could even be manipulated to help pursue the revolution's propaganda goals.

"These religious expressions lack institutional or doctrinal development, if you compare them with the centralized nature of Roman Catholicism," said the academy report, which later became the new official guideline on Santería. "Therefore, there is no theoretical or social reason to hinder the inclusion of believers in the creation of the new [Socialist] society."

Enrique Lopez Oliva, an independent-minded professor of history at the University of Havana who specialized in religious affairs, summed up the new government policy this way: "The revolutionary leadership is desperate to rebuild its social base, which has been deteriorating gradually for the past thirty-two years. The leadership is trying to restore the revolution's social base by luring the same sectors that provided the core of its support in 1959: the blacks and the poor."

"In today's Cuba, if you want to regain the backing of the blacks and the poor, you have to accept their culture," he said. "And their culture revolves around Santería."

There was another major reason why the regime was so eager to coopt the Santería religion: it would help weaken the Roman Catholic Church. Relations between Castro and the church had hit a new low in early 1990, when Cuba's Catholic bishops enraged the Cuban leader by sending him a private letter demanding a political opening.

The dispute followed a dinner on February 19, 1990, at the Vatican embassy in Havana, where the Comandante met with Cuba's bishops and Cardinal Bernard Law of Boston in an effort to improve relations with the church. Castro was fishing for the church's condemnation of the U.S.-financed Radio Martí, which was one of Cuba's top foreign policy concerns at the time.

Instead, he received the private letter signed by Cuba's seven bishops, demanding among other things that he start democratic reforms and a process of reconciliation with Cuban exiles. The letter was never publicized, but a furious Castro soon lashed out against the Cuban church, saying its hierarchy "never identified with the revolution and has remained somewhat hidden, waiting to act against the revolution." Relations deteriorated steadily from there. Havana archbishop Msgr. Jaime Ortega would soon, among other things, turn down Castro's much-trumpeted invitation to Catholics to join the Communist Party, and criticize the regime's pro-Santería propaganda campaign.*

As Castro's relations with the bishops worsened, the regime became increasingly worried about the church's expanding popularity. Growing numbers of young people were attending mass at Havana's churches, and many old Communists shaken by the fall of Marxist regimes abroad were returning to the church. In the year 1990, the Archdiocese of Havana had performed 33,000 baptisms, up from 7,000 a year in the late seventies.

It made good political sense for the regime to support pro-Castro Santeros, if for no other reason than to help lure people away from the

---

* *In his monthly "La Voz del Obispo" bulletin of November 1990, Bishop Ortega criticized the avalanche of Santería stories in government media. He said the regime was "artificially creating a cultural phenomenon" to drive a wedge between Catholics and Santería followers. He asserted that most followers of Afro-Cuban religions in Cuba were Catholics who practiced "a kind of grass roots Catholicism not unlike others that can be found in countries of ancient Catholic traditions, such as Spain and Italy."*

church. Many government-supported Babalaos soon started to echo the official description of the church as an institution responding to Cuba's ousted oligarchy.

"The Catholic Church is the white man's church," said Enrique "Enriquito" Hernandez Armenteros, Cuba's most prominent government-backed Babalao. "We are a religion for black people, for the destitute, for the descendants of the slaves who were brought here by force."

<>

I realized how blatantly the government was using Santería to undermine the Catholic Church the day I visited the Church of the Virgin of Regla. It was on a September 8, the Virgin's day, which Santería devotees in the predominantly black area on the bay facing the Port of Havana had long celebrated as the day of Yemayá—the Goddess of the sea.

The eighteenth-century church was packed with Santería followers. Many were wearing blue and white—the colors of Yemayá. Many carried black dolls with white kerchiefs on their heads. They were holding the dolls in front of the Virgin, hoping they would be thus blessed for the rest of the year. Others had brought candy, cookies and small toy presents to Yemayá, which they laid in front of the Virgin's altar.

Suddenly, the sound of African drumbeats coming from outside captured everybody's attention. I walked out, with many others, and followed the music. It was coming from next door. City authorities had opened a "Santería Exhibit" as an addition to the Regla Museum located a few blocks away. On display were life-size images of the Orishas and dozens of Santería cult objects, with explanatory texts. The music came from two brand new loudspeakers inside the two-room museum.

"This used to be part of the church's property," one of the nuns at the church explained to me later. "Two years ago, the government asked the two families that were renting the rooms to relocate across town. Then, a few months ago, we saw government people moving in with big packages. Next thing we knew, the Santería Museum opened its doors."

But hadn't she said it was on church property? Yes, she continued. They had even built a bathroom cutting into the Church's patio. But the priest had decided not to make a big fuss about it. Why not? I asked. She shrugged, smiling, without answering my question. I could only assume the priest had decided to save his limited clout for more important battles.

As we walked toward the dock where I was to take the ferry back to the Port of Havana, I couldn't help making a sarcastic remark about the scene I was leaving behind: the Church was sandwiched between the government's Santería exhibit and a big sign showing an image of Fidel with the legend, "Commander in Chief, Awaiting Your Orders!"

The nun shrugged and smiled, once again. "What can we do?" she said. "That's the way things are."

<>

Government agencies such as the ICAP and the Museum of Guanabacoa actively promoted pro-Castro Babalaos—and helped them make small fortunes. These agencies referred to the Babalaos growing numbers of Latin American visitors—mainly from Venezuela, Puerto Rico and the Dominican Republic—who were willing to pay exorbitant sums to go through Santería initiation rites. The Babalaos' average fee for such a ceremony: four thousand dollars.

There was widespread speculation among foreign diplomats and Catholic Church officials that at least part of that money went back to the state. One dissident Santería priest told me he knew of several cases where the government had collected the entire sum. The Babalao performing the ceremony had been allowed to accept only an electric fan or a television set from the visitors. Whatever the agreement, there was no question that the government-associated Babalaos were getting a sweet deal.

<>

Enriquito Hernandez Armenteros was a case in point. When I asked at the government's Ethnographic Museum of Guanabacoa where I could meet a real-life Santería Babalao, I was told to see Enriquito in the La Hata neighborhood. It was at his Children of San Lázaro Afro-Cuban Religious Association that the Communist Party's Santería courses were being held. He was one of Cuba's best-known Santería priests, I was assured.

Enriquito was a seventy-four-year-old retired shoemaker. He was the founder and president of the Children of San Lázaro association. I had no trouble finding his house: it was the only two-story residence in the neighborhood, and the only one with a ten-foot-high statue of San Lázaro in its front yard.

Its opulence stood out amid the general decay that surrounded it, not the least because it had a fresh coat of pink paint. In the waiting room inside, there were two television sets and a stereo. Down the block, there were two other big properties belonging to the Santería priest, which housed at least half a dozen of his children and their families. Enriquito was doing so well that his eleven children had quit their respective jobs to become his assistants. In the fifty-yard-long backyards of their homes, barbed wire fences enclosed dozens of goats, cocks, chickens and doves—a treasure in a country where you could go to jail for privately raising a single chicken.

Enriquito even had a business card—the only nonofficial one I ever saw in Castro's Cuba. It had his name engraved on the left side, a picture of San Lázaro on the right side. In his living room was a guest book, with the names of the Canadian, German and Colombian visitors the museum was referring to him. If there was any government-sanctioned private enterprise in Cuba, I was looking at it. Enriquito had obviously learned from the regime's profitable Diplotiendas and Diplo-restaurants. He had become a Diplo-Babalao.

When he finally emerged from a back room, Enriquito excused himself for the delay. He was a short, plump man, dressed in a white undershirt and wearing a brand new pair of U.S.-made sunglasses with their brand sticker still glued to one of the lenses. He was very busy these days, he said. A Japanese delegation was scheduled to arrive later that afternoon.

How had the Japanese come to know him?

"When people from abroad want to learn about Afro-Cuban religions, state entities send them to me," he said. "I take good care of them."

How much did he charge for consultations? How much did he keep for himself?

"We, the priests, get only small donations from the people who come to see us. People give whatever they can give. If they can't give anything, they don't," he claimed. "For initiation rites, however, we have to charge, because animals have to be sacrificed. Animals cost a lot of money."

I asked Enriquito about the Orishas' prophecy for 1991. Was Cuba on the verge of civil war? No, he said. He and a small group of Babalaos from the Bantu tribe had held their own Oddun ceremony on January 1, and had come to a slightly different conclusion.

"Our prophecy foresaw violence, bloodshed, war and devastation, but it didn't say where it would take place," Enriquito said. "Our interpretation is that it wasn't referring to Cuba. It was referring to the world. Months later, we were proved right: a major war erupted in the Persian Gulf."

So were the Gods still protecting Fidel?

"Of course they are. Fidel is an *elegido*, chosen by the Orishas. He's the Gods' envoy to guide the Cuban people along the right path. Don't you know that white doves once sat on his shoulders? Fidel has a mandate from God."

But the chosen one wasn't relying solely on Babalaos who were willing to support the revolution out of political conviction or personal convenience. An entire Interior Ministry office—the MININT Counterintelligence Department III-4—was making sure that others would be "motivated" to cooperate as well. Much as Papa Doc Duvalier had done with voodoo priests in neighboring Haiti decades earlier, the MININT recruited hundreds of Santería priests as collaborators, according to Cuban officials familiar with the procedures. Cuba's Babalaos would become key assets of the regime's internal security apparatus.

Department III-4 operated from a high-rise building on the corner of Havana's 19th and O streets, opposite the Hotel Nacional. Department III, which held the characteristically pompous title of "Ideological Sphere," was in charge of spying into Cuba's intellectual groups, the media, universities and churches. Each of these areas had its own office and staff, which were designated with Roman numerals that followed the department's overall designation.

At Department III-4, the office dealing with the churches, the number of desk officers was about sixty, while another six hundred worked on the street infiltrating religious groups throughout the island. The MININT's Intelligence Department had a separate office—known as Q-23—to penetrate Church organizations in other countries and influence them to support the revolution.

Each priest, whatever his religion, had a dossier at Department III-4. They were divided into four major categories: "Agents" were those who consciously and systematically carried out clandestine missions for the counterintelligence service; "subjects of confidence" were those who openly worked for the services; "useful associates" were those who helped the service without being aware of it; and "uncooperative subjects" were desirables who systematically refused to associate themselves with government agents.

Department III-4 had made great inroads into Cuba's Protestant churches, and had been somewhat less successful in penetrating the Catholic Church. Now, it was focusing its resources on Santería.

The plan was to neutralize possible challenges to the revolution from within the Santería movement, and to try to turn the religion—as several Protestant churches already had been turned—into an active source of support for the regime. In addition, infiltration of the Santería cults was to provide a wealth of intelligence on people's state of mind and political beliefs.

Nobody knew people's secrets better than the Babalaos, and few could be more helpful to uncover antirevolutionary activities in their neighborhoods. There was hardly a family in Cuba, including those of generals, ministers and members of the Central Committee, that didn't have one or more members who consulted regularly with their neighborhood Babalao. If there was an antigovernment conspiracy in the making, or if dissidents had recruited large numbers of supporters in a certain part of town, chances were that the Babalaos would hear it soon from relatives or friends worried about the fates of their loved ones.

<>

It was relatively easy for Cuba's counterintelligence service to recruit Babalaos. Department III-4 only needed to visit the Santería priest—or have his neighborhood committee's representative knock on his door—and let him know that they were aware of his various illegal activities. In fact, Babalaos regularly broke every rule in the book: they charged fees for consultations as if they were private businesses, held meetings without state authorization, and raised animals without government permits. Often, the state security visitor only needed to offer to turn a blind eye on these transgressions in order to win the priest's unconditional loyalty.

"About half of Cuba's Babalaos have been recruited by the counterintelligence service," said Enrique García Diaz, a former captain with the MININT's intelligence service who specialized in religious affairs. "I've personally seen thousands of dossiers of Babalaos and Santeros who were collaborators."

Whether they consistently provided juicy information to their minders is unclear, however. While some Babalaos probably helped identify dissidents or potential defectors, most would volunteer little more than neighborhood gossip—just enough to keep the MININT off their backs. Only a few would become the highly motivated revolutionary vigilantes the regime wanted them to be.

◄►

One Afro-Cuban cult that Department III-4 was especially concerned about was the Abakuá secret society. Unlike the Santeros, the Abakuás—also known as Ñañigos—had never supported the revolution. What was even more worrisome for the secret police, the Abakuás were the single most violence-prone group in Cuba. There were dozens of Abakuá secret societies left in Cuba, down from more than four hundred at the beginning of the century.

The Abakuás were a centuries-old mutual aid society originally brought to Cuba by black slaves from Africa. They had settled in the Havana suburbs of Regla, Guanabacoa and Marianao, and developed a reputation for their ruthless behavior. The *ekobios*—as members of these societies referred to one another—were known as Cuba's most ruthless killers.

In fact, the Abakuás only killed to avenge the murder of one of their society, members said. The all-male societies were based on a collective promise to protect each *ekobio*, offer him refuge if he was being persecuted by the authorities, or economic help if he was in deep financial trouble.

"They are very industrious and avaricious, also choleric and hasty in temper," a European traveler had written during colonial times. "Most of the free negroes in the island who are rich belong to this tribe."

To be accepted by the society, a candidate had to go through a nasty initiation rite. He would be stripped naked from the waist up, his eyes covered with a kerchief, then the *ekobios* would perform various ceremonies to the sound of drums. One member of the group would rub a dead chicken on the initiate's body until the animal blood covered his back. Another would make him drink various concoctions from a human skull, while several *irines*—*ekobios* clad in straw garments symbolizing little devils—would dance around.

Over the years, the Abakuás had attracted numerous white members, and the society became a formidable force at Port of Havana and the nearby section of Guanabacoa. Despite the revolution's efforts to control the stevedores' unions, it was an open secret that the docks belonged to the Abakuás.

As times were getting tougher in the early nineties, growing numbers of young men joined the society. Becoming an Abakuá member could get you a well-paid job in the docks or, what was more important, access to the wide black-market smuggling business port workers had access to. There was no greater *socio*, or buddy, than a fellow *ekobio*.

Others joined the society in search of personal protection, or out of fascination for the group's macho reputation. Among the newly initiated *ekobios* were many policemen, members of the territorial troops and other low-ranking armed forces personnel. It was a group to which they were proud to belong.

As Cuba's economic crisis worsened, Department III-4 of the MININT counterintelligence felt increasingly uneasy about the Abakuás. There had been reports of clashes at the Port of Havana between dock workers—many of them members of Abakuá groups— and Communist Party bosses. In one such incident, port workers had gone on strike to protest shipments of rice to Iraq at a time when Cubans' own rice rations were being drastically cut.

The *ekobios* were not as easy to manipulate as their fellow Santeros. And they could become a formidable enemy. Infiltrating the Abakuás became a major priority for the MININT, according to one source familiar with the state security covert operations. It was also one of the most dreaded assignments for counterintelligence agents: not even the most committed secret agent relished the prospect of enduring the dead-chicken-rubbing ceremony.

Would the regime succeed in its crusade to coopt Santería? Only up to a point. Although many Santería priests had been recruited with promises of economic reward or through blunt intimidation, Castro could not prevent the leading Babalaos like "Bebo" from independently issuing their gloomy Oddun prophecies.

For every Babalao recruited by the MININT's Department III-4, there was another who was just becoming initiated in the Santería religion and wanted to prove his independence. Some, like Lázaro Corp Lleras, a white *palero*—black magic practitioner—had even joined Cuba's fledgling dissident movement.

Corp Lleras, an athletic man in his late thirties, was one of the leaders of the opposition Harmony Movement. A former port of Havana worker who had been fired for attempting to start a strike, he now worked at the bar of a brothel, and lived in a run-down tenement near the port. He was one of the few whites in his building, where dozens of families lived crammed in small rooms, some of them only separated by an improvised curtain. During our conversation at his tiny apartment, he offered a surprising explanation for the reason why many Afro-Cuban religious leaders were shunning the regime's overtures.

In addition to disliking the government, many saw it as bad business, he said. A silent Babalao rebellion against the Castro regime had been brewing, and it was over money matters. The revolt had taken place after growing numbers of Venezuelans and other Latin Americans had begun visiting Cuba to become initiated in Santería—paying an average of four thousand dollars each for their *santo* initiation ceremonies. The Castro regime had directed the tourists to Enriquito and other sympathetic Babalaos—and had kept most of the money for itself.

"Many Babalaos don't like this at all," Corp Lleras explained. "They want to get their clients on their own, and keep the money for themselves."

So large numbers of Babalaos had come to prefer as little truck with the government as possible; they wanted to rely on referrals from Santería practitioners exiled in Miami, Caracas and Santo Domingo. As arrivals of Santería-attracted tourists soared, the competition between the regime and the Babalaos had grown nastier.

By late 1991, some Santería priests who had begun collaborating with the government were changing their minds. They were not only reluctant to share their honorariums with the government, but felt increasingly uneasy about the regime's interference in their religious affairs. How could they tell their people that the Castro regime would have a bright future when everything around them was crumbling? Despite Castro's efforts to win them over, a sizable number of Babalaos remained stubbornly uncommitted. The religious part of Castro's survival strategy was not significantly more successful than the plan's economic and political faces.

IV

COLLAPSE OF A REVOLUTION (1991–1992)

<<<<<<<<<<<<<<<<<<<<<<<<<<<<<<<<<<<<<<<<

13
The Soviet Coup

⊏⊏⊏⊏⊏ It could have been one of the happiest days in Fidel Castro's
life. Not even the most optimistic of his aides had expected the series
of extraordinary events that unfolded on Sunday evening, August 18,
1991.

It was the closing day of Castro's much-trumpeted XIth Pan
American Games in Havana. The thirty-nine-country sports event
had kept Cuba transfixed for three weeks, and was coming to a glorious grand finale. Just before 4 P.M., Cuban heavyweight boxer Felix
Savon whipped a U.S. challenger with a demolishing right-hand hook
before an audience of Fidel Castro and ten thousand cheering fans,
and minutes later the loudspeakers at the Havana Sports City Arena
announced that Cuba had won the games with an unprecedented 140
gold medals.*

It was the first time in forty years that a Latin American country
had defeated the United States in the Pan American Games. An
overjoyed Castro, moved to the brink of tears, threw up his hands.
The band kicked in. The crowd exploded in cheers. "Cuba! Cuba!
Cuba!" Then, "Fee-del! Fee-del! Fee-del!"

---

* The U.S. team had won in the total count of gold, silver and bronze medals, but Cuba claimed overall
victory based on its gold medal supremacy.

The sports fiesta had been a major public relations coup for Castro. A record thirteen hundred foreign journalists had come to the island for the event. At first, the Comandante appeared only to make a one-minute speech opening the games. But as days went by and Cuban teams began winning one competition after another, a delighted Castro placed himself at the center of an ongoing national celebration. Suddenly, the Comandante was everywhere: giving medals, kissing spectators, joking with foreign journalists and posing for photographers with Cuban and visiting athletes. He had not been seen in such a good mood in years.

The Cuban victory gave the island a much-needed morale boost. Government press releases emphasized that Cuba could only have achieved more gold medals than the United States because the revolution had done so much to improve the country's health standards. Foreign sportswriters were flooded with Cuban government statistics about the island's growing life expectancy, declining child mortality rates and important scientific discoveries. Latin American reporters were given computerized charts comparing Cuba's health statistics with those of their own countries. It was a vindication of Cuba's age-old claim: the island nation could vie with any world power in terms of medical care and education.

Castro's big gamble in opening Cuba's doors to foreign journalists had also paid off in a big way. Not only had there been no demonstrations by dissidents—the regime had organized the civilian Rapid Response Brigades and placed them in the sports stadiums to deter any possible protests—but the visiting journalists had generally written positive stories.

ABC Sports carried images of Cuban beaches and luxury hotels to millions of American homes, and CNN—whose owner Ted Turner attended the games with Jane Fonda—was unusually kind to the regime in its coverage. Most U.S. reporters seemed genuinely impressed by the crowds cheering Fidel in the stadiums. At the American office of Cuba's Foreign Relations Ministry, whose staff monitored the American press coverage, the consensus was that Cuba had scored big.

Latin American leaders sent congratulations to Castro for Cuba's victory in the games. The warm messages were coming on the heels of July's twenty-three-country summit of Latin American, Spanish and Portuguese leaders in Guadalajara, Mexico, where Castro had been received with respect, and where two countries—Colombia and Chile—had announced they would resume consular and trade relations with Cuba. At long last, in its darkest hour, the Castro revolution seemed to have spotted a ray of sunshine.

Then, at about 11:30 P.M., as Castro was celebrating the end of the games at the Siboney suburb protocol house of Mario Vazquez Raña, the Mexican businessman who presided over the Pan American Sports Organization, the Comandante would get even more heartening news.

It was a small dinner party for about twenty international sports officials and a few diplomats involved in the games' organization. Vazquez Raña had just made a toast "to the best games in history," when an agitated Castro aide walked to the head table and notified the Comandante that he had an important telephone call. Castro left to take it in a room nearby.

It was Communist Party ideology chief and top Castro aide Carlos Aldana, calling with critical news: a coup had been attempted in the Soviet Union. An emergency committee of eight hard-line Kremlin officials had ousted Soviet President Mikhail Gorbachev. The Committee had been led by Vice President Gennady Yanayev, and included KGB Chairman Vladimir Kryuchkov, Defense Minister Dmitri Yazov, and Defense Council Deputy Chairman Oleg Baklanov.

It was a miracle. Castro knew the new Soviet rulers well: they were Cuba's best friends in the Kremlin, old-guard Communists who had serious qualms about Gorbachev's reforms. Like Castro, they had long feared that Gorbachev's Perestroika would inevitably lead to the collapse of communism, and to the disintegration of the Soviet Union.

Yanayev, an old Communist Party bureaucrat, had last been in Havana in 1990 as president of the Soviet Workers' Federation (VESPS), and had been a strong Cuba supporter since ascending to the vice-presidency in December that year. KGB Chairman Kryuchkov had just visited in June 1991 on a mission to strengthen Soviet intelligence ties with Cuba. Defense Council Deputy Chairman Oleg Baklanov had last come to Havana in 1990, and was Raúl Castro's top contact man with the Soviet weapons and military supplies industries; Defense Minister Yazov had been based in Cuba as a young officer in the early sixties, and his name was prominently displayed on a commemorative plaque at the site of a former Soviet SAM missile base in Cuba's eastern province of Holguín.

Only a few weeks earlier, Castro had sent Aldana to Moscow to meet with Gorbachev and other top Soviet Communist Party leaders to discuss the Cuban situation. The exchange with Yanayev had been the most encouraging for the Cuban leader. Aldana had complained to him that the Soviets had failed to live up to their trade commitments during the first half of 1991. Soviet grain shipments to Cuba were far behind schedule, and the shortages were creating havoc on the island. Yanayev could hardly have been more sympathetic. He told Castro's envoy that Cuba would get "total support from Moscow" during the second half of the year.*

A week before the Soviet coup, *Pravda* had quoted Yanayev as strongly supporting continued Soviet subsidies to Cuba. He had called U.S. pressure on the Kremlin to reduce aid to Cuba "absolutely unacceptable." When Fidel heard of the coup, and that Yanayev had been appointed a leader of the eight-member ruling junta, it was clear to him that with his friends taking power in Moscow, Cuba would emerge from its quandary. But he also knew that if they failed, the backlash could be brutal.

Castro returned to Vazquez Raña's dinner table. He asked his aide Jesús Montané, who was sitting near him, to get hold of the international news agencies' cables from Moscow. As the first wire stories were brought to him minutes later, Castro shared the news with the other guests, matter-of-factly. The dinner went on, as Fidel waited for more news.

Meantime, Cuban officials at more than a dozen parties throughout Havana celebrating the end of the Pan American Games were ecstatic. "They toasted the return of the old guard," a Western diplomat who attended one of the parties recalls. "I had never seen them so happy."

For Cuba, the coup couldn't have come at a better moment: a day later, Gorbachev was to sign a crucial treaty that would have given virtual economic autonomy to Russia and eight other Soviet republics. The Russian Federation—source of virtually all the Soviet oil shipped

---

* Weeks later, after the coup was foiled, Soviet Foreign Ministry officials wondered about Yanayev's assurances to Aldana. Had it been a subtle hint to Cuba that the hard-liners would soon take power? Or a simple Soviet commitment to carry out their obligations under existing agreements? Some Soviet officials speculated that Castro might have been informed in advance of the coup, but there was no hard evidence of that at the time of this writing. Most likely, Castro only speculated that the hard-liners would soon make a comeback—in all likelihood at the behest of Gorbachev himself—to prevent the disintegration of the Soviet Union. During the Guadalajara summit of Ibero-American heads of state in late July 1991, three weeks after the Aldana-Yanayev meeting, Castro told at least two presidents in private conversations that he was expecting a normalization of Soviet exports to Cuba, based on the assumption that Gorbachev would have to take a harder line to prevent the collapse of the Soviet Union.

When I asked Aldana whether he had received any hints of the upcoming coup attempt, he said, "Absolutely none." Referring to the hard-line Soviet officials he had met with, he added, "On the contrary, I found widespread pessimism about the Soviet Union's future." But of course, if Cuba had received a hint of the upcoming coup, Aldana would hardly have admitted it to a foreign journalist after the plot's failure.

to Cuba—was to gain control of its natural resources and foreign trade. Russian Federation President Boris Yeltsin had already expressed opposition to continued subsidized oil shipments to Cuba. Now, the new hard-line regime would straighten things out. A conservative Soviet-Chinese axis could re-emerge, since the Chinese had already reverted to hard-line Marxism with their 1989 Tiananmen Square crackdown on prodemocracy forces. Cuba would once again have a strong Communist bloc on which it could rely.

But Castro looked anxious as he read the cables. He stood, sat, stood again, walked to a nearby room, then came back, the cables still in his hand. The coup leaders' claims that Gorbachev had fallen ill at his vacation house in Crimea didn't sound credible. Two hours later, as Vazquez Raña and his guests were finishing dessert and the reports continued, it was evident that the plotters had failed to take control of the country.

Despite the junta's harsh-sounding state of emergency decrees, Yeltsin hadn't yet been arrested, and his top aides were even talking to CNN. The story was far from over. Castro turned to a sports official sitting next to him and pointed out that the news could spell trouble for Cuba: chaos in the Soviet Union was potentially more harmful to Cuban trade—at least in the short run—than an orderly transition to a federation of autonomous Soviet states. With anarchy came the danger that oil shipments to Cuba could come to a complete stop, Fidel said.

"He looked confused," the sports official recalled later. "He shared the news with us in a casual way, but he was clearly concerned about the situation. He wasn't celebrating."

For the next twenty-four hours, the Cuban regime remained silent on the Soviet coup attempt. The West had thrown its weight behind Yeltsin's immediate call for Gorbachev's return to the Kremlin. Libya and Iraq had promptly stated their support for the new junta.

Castro issued an official statement on the evening of August 20, 1991, after virtually all countries had taken sides on the coup attempt, and only twelve hours before the putsch collapsed. The carefully worded document had been painstakingly crafted not to burn Castro's bridges with either side.

The communique indicated that it was "not the task of the Cuban government to judge events in the USSR," and expressed Cuba's hopes that the Soviet Union could "overcome its difficulties peacefully, and that that great country stay united." In a slip that Castro would regret later, however, it referred to the coup leaders as "the Soviet authorities."

"We had been led to error," Aldana told me later, reflecting on the embarrassing delay and the neutral tone of Cuba's reaction. "We had received an official note (from the Soviet embassy) stating that Gorbachev was ill. . . . We then saw Yanayev on television, saying that Gorbachev would be reinstated in a few days. In those first hours, one could not exclude the possibility that . . . it hadn't been a coup attempt. I would like people to put themselves in our shoes in those first hours, and say whether they would have acted differently." In fact, except for China, Iraq and Libya, everyone else in the world had acted differently, although few had as much to lose as Cuba.

When the junta disbanded itself sixty hours after it had taken power and a humbled Gorbachev returned to Moscow late August 22, Castro could only take solace in the fact that he had not rushed to publicly embrace the coup leaders. His friends Yanayev, Kryuchkov, Yazov and four others were quickly arrested and prosecuted on charges of high treason. Interior Minister Boris Pugo committed suicide as police were arriving at his house to arrest him.

After the Soviet Union's three-day-long political roller coaster, the Cuban regime was in deeper trouble than ever before. Yeltsin had become the undisputed leader of the Soviet post-Communist era.

The morning after Gorbachev's return to Moscow, Yeltsin announced before a crowd of more than one hundred thousand Muscovites that the Communist era's red flag with its hammer-and-sickle would be replaced by old Russia's red-white-and-blue. Thousands of jubilant Russians swarmed to tear down the statue of KGB founder Felix Dzerzhinsky outside the Soviet secret police headquarters. Lenin's statues in the Baltics met with the same fate.

But what disturbed the Cuban regime most was the dismantling of the Soviet Communist Party; its cells in the army, factories and foreign embassies were outlawed, and its 5,000 buildings seized. When Cuban officials tried to call their old Party comrades in Moscow a few days later, they were shocked to discover that they had been evicted from the Soviet Communist Party Central Committee headquarters. A new crowd was answering the phones: the building had been taken over by the Foreign Affairs Ministry of Yeltsin's Russian Federation.

Yeltsin, at once Gorbachev's savior and nemesis, was cashing in on his new standing by signing decrees right and left, acting as the de facto leader of the entire union. Gorbachev would have little choice but to go along and put his signature where Yeltsin wanted it.

<>

The new Russian leader was Castro's worst nightmare. Yeltsin was a hard-drinking populist who advocated a swift move to a free-market economy, and strongly opposed continued Soviet aid to Cuba. His meetings with Miami's Cuban exiles over the previous two years— and the smiling pictures showing him with Mas Canosa in Miami— had infuriated Havana.*

Yeltsin's policy toward Cuba had made a 180-degree turn after his first meeting with Cuban exiles in Miami in September 1989, at the end of an eleven-city U.S. tour. A Czech-born Soviet specialist at the University of Miami, Jiri Valenta, had collected thirty-four thousand dollars—largely from Mas Canosa's CANF and independent Cuban exile business people—to sponsor the Russian politician's visit to Miami. From the moment of Yeltsin's arrival at the Miami airport, local Cuban-American journalists bombarded him with questions about Castro. The Russian leader looked lost.

On his way to a Miami Beach hotel aboard a white stretch limousine, Yeltsin was warned by Professor Valenta about the intensity of anti-Castro feelings in Miami. The Russian was surprised and somewhat confused. He had read only positive stories about Cuba in the official Soviet press, stating that Castro was conducting his own reforms at home, at his own pace.

He did not hold a personal grudge against Fidel at the time. On the contrary, he remembered Fidel as one of the few people who had embraced him publicly at a 1987 Soviet Communist Party Congress where he had suffered his humiliating demotion as the most powerful politician in Moscow. Castro had embraced him three times, in the Russian fashion, in front of the party leaders who had voted against him.

"But isn't Castro doing his own version of Perestroika?" Yeltsin asked Valenta as their limousine crossed over the scenic Miami Beach bridges.

---

* At the time of Yeltsin's meetings with the Miami Cuban exiles, Soviet Foreign Ministry officials were forbidden from establishing such contacts. The Foreign Ministry's Latin American Department chief Yuri Pavlov had met with Cuban exiles at an academic conference in Miami that was partly sponsored by Mas Canosa's CANF in October 1990. But after Cuba protested to the Soviet ambassador in Havana, the Kremlin issued a statement saying Pavlov had met with the exiles in their capacity as U.S. citizens, and "not because they are Cuban emigres."

No, said Valenta. Speaking in Russian, the professor told his guest about the Ochoa affair, about recent incidents of repression against dissidents in Cuba, and of Castro's refusal to accept any meaningful political or economic reforms. Then, Valenta informed Yeltsin about the nearly seven hundred thousand Cuban exiles in Miami, and how they had helped transform the city from a sleepy southern town into a prosperous international trade center.

Yeltsin, in the heat of his own political battles back home, obviously had not been briefed about Miami, or Cuba. He raised his eyebrows and looked out the window at the Miami Bay waters. He had had no idea.

On the next morning, Valenta held a small meeting in his home and introduced Yeltsin to Mas Canosa, the CANF chairman. The three talked for more than one hour about Cuba and continued their conversation through a five-hour boating trip in the bay.

"There was an immediate affinity among us, from the moment we made eye-to-eye contact," Mas Canosa recalls. "We shared a visceral repudiation of the Communist system."

The CANF decided to pursue the relationship. Over the next two years, Valenta made half a dozen trips to Moscow—several of them funded by Mas Canosa's CANF—to cement the Miami exiles' ties with Yeltsin. The two sides could help one another. The exiles wanted Yeltsin to get the Kremlin to cut Soviet aid to Cuba. Yeltsin wanted the influential CANF lobby in Washington to improve his image in the United States—he had been recently portrayed in American media as an ineffectual boor, an alcoholic, and a womanizer. In addition, Yeltsin hoped the CANF could help him obtain direct U.S. economic aid for the Russian Federation.

On one of his trips to Moscow, at an October 1989 dinner party in Yeltsin's home, Valenta proposed an "official" visit by CANF's leaders to the Soviet Union. The visit by a four-member CANF delegation took place nearly a year later, in September 1990. It resulted in an informal agreement of mutual cooperation between the Miami exiles and the Russian Federation.

Yeltsin asked the CANF leaders for help in getting an official invitation from President Bush to visit Washington. He needed the exposure at home for his upcoming presidential campaign, but Bush had been reluctant to invite him because he feared offending Gorbachev. The Russian leader asked the exiles to use their good contacts—especially with Bush's Miami-based son Jeb, House Foreign Affairs Committee chairman Dante Fascell (D-Fla.) and Florida's senators—to get him an official invitation to the United States.

CANF leaders, in turn, asked Yeltsin whether he would maintain subsidies to Cuba if elected Russian president. They got the answer they were hoping for: a resounding *"Nyet!"* With that assurance in hand, CANF went to work on behalf of Yeltsin.*

<>

After the failed coup attempt, reformers at the Kremlin came back with a vengeance, just as Castro had feared. Newly promoted foreign policy officials—many of them former Yeltsin aides—set out immediately to revise economic ties with Cuba, Vietnam and other countries that they considered to be drains on already meager Soviet resources.

Shortly after the foiled coup, the Soviet Foreign Ministry's Latin American Department produced an internal document suggesting a "drastic reduction of Soviet-Cuban cooperation." Havana "is not ready to understand Soviet Perestroika, and still has its own dogmas," the document said. It said that while Moscow wanted to "de-ideologize" its foreign relations, Havana "persists in its anti-imperialistic policies."

Fidel Castro was rapidly becoming an obstacle to the Kremlin's renewed efforts to improve ties with the West. "Cuba sometimes engages in a hyperactivity in international affairs that does not match the real possibilities of the country," the Soviet Foreign Ministry paper said. "Cuba is starting to contradict Soviet policy, especially on the issues of human rights, on reduction of the armaments race . . . and in its views on regional conflicts." It was time for the Kremlin to sever its three-decade-old bond with Castro.

Meanwhile, the Russian Federation's Foreign Ministry had produced its own new policy guidelines regarding Cuba. A three-point in-house memorandum declared that Cuba would no longer be a foreign policy priority; that the Russian Federation would no longer provide political or military assistance to the Cuban regime, and that the Russian Federation would only continue trading with Cuba on a hard-currency basis, at world market prices.

Buoyed by the latest events, Cuban exile leaders rushed to Moscow to cash in on their relationship with Yeltsin. A CANF delegation led by Mas Canosa landed in Moscow a few days after Gorbachev's return to the Kremlin, met with top Yeltsin aides, and opened a public relations office four blocks away from the Kremlin. CANF's

---

* *CANF lobbied for Yeltsin's trip to Washington, but the Bush Administration did not extend the official invitation until after Yeltsin was elected Russian Federation president.*

Moscow office hired three Soviet journalists to help in the anti-Castro lobbying crusade, including Alexander Machov, a former columnist of the liberal *Moscow News* who had been based in Havana in the mid-eighties. Machov had been one of the first Soviet journalists to criticize the Castro regime in the Soviet press—and one of the first to be invited to Miami by Professor Valenta's University of Miami Institute of Soviet and East European Studies. In addition to his new CANF job, Machov was soon hired as a stringer for Radio Martí. His reports from Moscow would soon begin to be broadcast daily to Cuba on the U.S. government-financed radio.

As dollar-paid CANF employees in a country where the local currency plummeted and newspapers were laying off hundreds of reporters, Machov and his coworkers were the envy of Moscow journalists. Frequent travel came with the job: in late 1991, Machov escorted five key members of the Russian Parliament to Florida on a CANF-paid visit to Disneyworld, with a two-day stop in Miami for a press conference in which they announced new moves to cut aid to Cuba.* Among their other tasks, the CANF's Russian journalists were to get former Kremlin officials to sell them documents that would prove embarrassing to the Castro regime.

Gorbachev's public statements during his first day back at the Kremlin were not as ominous for the Castro regime as many Cubans feared. At his first post-coup press conference, the Soviet president abstained from criticizing Cuba's bland response to the coup attempt. He denounced the Libyans and Iraqis for their support of the putsch, but did not mention—as President Bush had done hours earlier—Castro's belated and ambiguous reaction.

A secret cable the Soviets sent to Havana in late August gave Castro new hope that the post-coup Kremlin leadership was still interested in maintaining a good working relationship with Havana. In the cable, the Soviets asked for an emergency shipment of Cuban sugar to help alleviate rapidly growing food shortages.

Cuba responded in less than twenty-four hours, saying it was ready to advance shipments that were originally scheduled to be delivered months later. Castro ordered a massive effort to put the ship-

---

* *Among the visiting Russian legislators were Alexei Surkhov, vice-president of the Russian Parliament's committee of foreign relations, Victor Shohkin and Valeri Skripchenko, of the banking and finances committee.*

ments together. Cuban officials worked around the clock to have them ready. But the work was for naught.

"You know what happened? They didn't come to pick up the shipments!" recalls Carlos Aldana, the Cuban Central Committee's ideology and foreign affairs chief. "They had already reached a point where the Soviet leadership was unable to enforce its own directives."

Gorbachev had lost much of his power, and was increasingly resigned to relying on Yeltsin's forces as he discovered more details of how his former hard-line aides had betrayed him. Soon, Gorbachev caved in to Yeltsin's demands that he fire virtually every senior official who had not immediately stood against the coup plotters. "After that, all his steps were marked by that experience," Aldana reflected.

Evidence of Gorbachev's personal change came with a big bang on September 11, 1991. In a move to symbolize the end of the super-power tensions that had lingered since the 1962 Cuban missile crisis, Gorbachev announced the withdrawal of the 2,800-man-strong Soviet combat brigade in Cuba. He made the dramatic announcement at a joint press conference with U.S. Secretary of State James Baker shortly after the two emerged from the first high-level American-Soviet talks after the foiled coup attempt.

When Castro heard of it, he exploded in anger. Gorbachev had not even gone through the formalities of apprising the Cuban leader in advance. In what the Cuban leader saw as an even greater humiliation, Gorbachev had made the announcement with Baker at his side. Newspapers throughout the world would carry the news alongside a smiling picture of Gorbachev and Baker, making image-obsessed Castro look as if he were a peon adrift in the new world order.

"Our reaction was one of colossal indignation," recalls Aldana, who had watched the Gorbachev press conference on CNN in Castro's office. "It was something unthinkable, clumsy, completely unnecessary, outside the most basic [diplomatic] rules."

Adding insult to injury, the Soviet Foreign Ministry documents criticizing Cuba's dogmatism were leaked in Moscow shortly thereafter to the *Miami Herald*, which—like anything with the name Miami on it—was anathema to Castro.

There was no use in continuing to pretend that Cuban-Soviet relations remained marked by the "unbreakable friendship" between the two countries, as the Castro regime had stated sanctimoniously in its official communiques for the previous three decades. The gloves were off.

In a response issued through Cuba's Foreign Ministry hours after Gorbachev's announcement, Castro complained that "these public declarations by President Gorbachev were not preceded by consultations or any previous advice, which constitutes inappropriate behavior both from the point of view of international norms and of the agreements which exist between the two countries."

It wasn't just a question of diplomatic etiquette. Castro, who for three decades had flexed his military muscle around the world, couldn't bear the thought of suddenly becoming a paper tiger—or of being perceived as such. The public relations embarrassment brought about by the Soviet pullout announcement was more worrying to the Cubans than the reality of how the withdrawal would actually affect the Cuban armed forces, which were almost entirely reliant on Soviet equipment and spare parts. A furious Castro set out to make it as hard as possible on the Soviets to execute their withdrawal plans.

On September 14, 1991, three days after the Gorbachev announcement, Cuba's Foreign Ministry issued a statement saying that the Soviet pullback "would amount to giving a green light to the United States to carry out its plans of aggression against Cuba."

Castro was effectively asking the Soviets to reconsider, or at least to save Cuba's face by negotiating a United Nations resolution that would demand a simultaneous American withdrawal from Guantánamo, the U.S. naval base in southern Cuba. An estimated six thousand U.S. military and civilian personnel were based in Guantánamo under a 1903 treaty, which had long been denounced by Castro and other Cuban nationalists before him.*

When Gorbachev sent Soviet Vice-Minister of Foreign Affairs Valery Nikolayenko to Havana on September 21, 1991, to discuss the Soviet brigade pullout, the Cubans gave him an icy welcome. Nikolayenko, a fluent Spanish-speaker who was on a first-name basis with most senior Cuban officials, was received at Havana's José Martí airport by a Cuban vice-minister of foreign relations, who would officially represent the Cuban government in the talks with the visiting official.

---

* *"After the Soviet statement, the only proper procedure is to negotiate the withdrawal of the Soviet brigade and of the naval base of Guantánamo," the new Foreign Ministry statement went on to say. "Cuba is ready to be part, to that effect, of an international agreement guaranteed by the United Nations."*

It was a major indignity for Nikolayenko: only four months earlier, he had visited Havana as a lower-ranked director of the Latin American Department of the Soviet Foreign Ministry, and had been received by the Comandante himself. His earlier mission had been to discuss the war in El Salvador—a minor issue compared with his present assignment.

The Cubans told Nikolayenko that they wanted to discuss the Soviet brigade issue with a higher-ranking official, and suggested Gorbachev's close adviser Alexander Yakovlev. The meetings ended after three days without a joint statement.

When Nikolayenko prepared to give an airport press conference minutes before his departure, he was cordially told he could not use the VIP conference room. The VIP section was occupied that morning by a top Chinese Communist Party official who was also about to leave Cuba. The irony was not lost on members of the Soviet delegation.

But Castro miscalculated the depth of the changes in the Soviet Union. His tantrums were no longer drawing sympathy—or even concern—at the Kremlin. The Soviets, struggling to keep their fragile union from falling apart, were interested only in improved ties with the United States. Accordingly, Nikolayenko left directly for Washington from Havana.

At a meeting with U.S. Assistant Secretary of State for Inter-American Affairs Bernard Aronson, he offered assurances that Moscow would not make the announced withdrawal of its combat brigade contingent on a U.S. exit from Guantánamo. Two months later, Gorbachev sent a new envoy to Havana to discuss the Soviet brigade withdrawal—it was Special Ambassador Vyacheslav Ustinov, a specialist in African affairs whose rank was significantly lower than Nikolayenko's.

<><

When I arrived in Cuba a few days after the foiled Soviet coup attempt, the country was in a state of consternation. Cuban television, facing competition from U.S.-based exile radio stations, had little choice but to show the images of red flags and statues of Lenin coming down across the Soviet Union. Cubans watched, dumbfounded. It was as if the Vatican had suddenly renounced Catholicism, and a devout congregation in a faraway parish was watching the rest of the world rejoice.

Torrential summer rains were paralyzing Havana every afternoon. The lines in front of gasoline stations stretched for three blocks—

there were rumors that Soviet oil shipments would come to a complete halt. People went about their daily business, scurrying for pieces of cardboard to protect themselves from the rain, lining up for bread, or waiting at jammed bus lines. But their minds seemed to be elsewhere.

Anxious Cubans asked visitors what would happen next. Was it true that the Soviets were turning against Cuba? Would they use their Lourdes intelligence-gathering facilities to spy on Cuba? Would the newly appointed KGB chiefs engineer a coup to topple Fidel?

Predictably, the Castro regime responded to the growing public anxieties by flexing its muscles. A strongly worded *Granma* editorial lamenting the "tragedy" in the Soviet Union vowed that neither Lenin's statues nor Marxism-Leninism would ever be toppled in Cuba.

"Our most sacred duty is to save the nation, the revolution and socialism," the front-page banner headline read. But, despite the emotional appeal to Cubans' patriotism, Castro looked more vulnerable than ever in his role as lone keeper of the Communist faith.

I dropped in unannounced late one afternoon at the office of Union of Cuban Writers and Artists (UNEAC) president Abel Prieto, just after a brutal downpour had subsided. The receptionist in the lobby of the magnificent UNEAC mansion was gone. Upstairs, I found Prieto alone in his office, his feet on the round conference table that dominated the room.

The usual coterie of intellectuals lining up in front of his office to plead for cars, houses or travel permits was not there. The phones were not ringing. There was an eerie silence in UNEAC's usually frantic office. I could only wonder whether everybody had gone home because of bad weather, or because of the general shock that had followed the events in Moscow.

Prieto, the long-haired writer who was one of the regime's rising stars, bit his lips and shook his head when we talked about the news from the Soviet Union. He could not believe that U.S. Ambassador to the Soviet Union Robert Strauss had spoken at the funeral of the three Russians who had died defending Yeltsin's headquarters. He had just read in that morning's *Granma* that the Soviet Federation of Artists and Writers, with which his group had various cultural agreements, had been outlawed.

"I am sick to my soul," he said. "These people throwing down statues of Lenin . . . the closing of the Federation of Writers. . . . It's all so sick . . . ! I drank a whole bottle of rum yesterday, just to try to get it out of my mind."

Without waiting for my response, he talked on, a deep sadness in his eyes.

"Obviously, for people to react so angrily against communism, everything over there must have been artificial. There must have been a great many lies holding that system together."

<>

A few days later, I held a similar conversation with Cuban Vice-President Carlos Rafael Rodriguez, the seventy-seven-year-old Marxist politician who had been in charge of Cuba's relations with the Kremlin for nearly four decades. A Communist leader long before Fidel had publicly embraced socialism, Rodriguez—now a ranking member of the Politburo and the most respected brain within Castro's inner circle—was watching his life's devotion crumble throughout the world.

Aren't you devastated? I asked. "Believe it or not, I'm less shocked than others," the veteran Party leader told me, his eyes assertive behind his thick glasses. "I've known that system better than most. I had become disenchanted with it many years ago, but couldn't say it publicly. When it finally collapsed, I was not among the surprised."

Like others, Rodriguez insisted that he was only referring to *that* system. Cuba was a totally different case—a young revolution that had not lost touch with its people, he claimed.

Could he really believe that? Hardly. He was too smart for that. He was known to have used his political stature to try to convince the Comandante to save the revolution by adopting economic and political reforms. He was not only influenced by pro-Perestroika friends in Moscow, but had often talked with Castro critics abroad, especially at the home of his exiled daughter in Spain. But the veteran politician had invested his life in pursuing the Marxist dream. At seventy-seven, he was not about to give it up.

Younger, less prominent government officials were venting their anxiety more openly. A Cuban Foreign Ministry official whom I had known for a long time, and who until then had never even wanted to discuss the possibility of political change in Cuba, asked me two astounding questions over a cup of coffee.

"What do you think will happen? Is this going to fall?" he asked.

At first I thought he was just doing his job and hunting for clues on where I stood, but there was only candor in his eyes.

The Cuban revolution was beginning to lose its aura of invincibility—the very foundation of its long-effective psychological program to discourage an active political opposition.

On the streets, Cuba was descending rapidly into its Zero Option mode. The regime had just reduced once again the goods citizens received under the ration-card system. Clothing supplies were cut in half: instead of one pair of slacks a year, you were now only entitled to one pair every two years.

A drastic drop in Soviet feed for poultry production had added chicken to the list of foodstuffs in short supply. There had been no soap, detergent or cooking oil for more than three months. Writing paper was no longer available in stationery stores and many government offices. Television programming was cut to save energy.

As part of the regime's preparations for survival in a zero fuel scenario, the Communist Youth (UJC) had just announced contingency plans to replace Cuba's domestic airmail system with courier pigeons. It was dead serious.

The first pigeon-mail station was to be erected in late August 1991, in Central Havana's Thirteenth of March Park, across the street from the Museum of the Revolution. And sure enough, three huge wooden poles with pigeonholes at their tops were there when I visited the park shortly after the announcement. Another twenty-five places in Havana had been picked for similar pigeon mail stations. They were scheduled to house at least a hundred pigeons each.

Corruption and black marketeering had reached all-time highs. Often, when I stopped at a gasoline station, attendants would offer to fill my Nissan's tank for cash—at half price—instead of taking my government-issued gas coupons. Their scheme was simple: instead of passing on my dollars to the state, they would exchange them in the black market, pay for the gasoline in pesos at a fraction of the dollars they had received, and forget to mention that a tourist had dropped by. Under the law, tourists had to buy gasoline coupons worth $1.75 a liter at the government's Havanautos agencies.

Once, while stopping for gas in Havana's Miramar section, an attendant bowed over my window. He was a man in his mid-thirties. A thick golden crucifix was hanging from his neck.

"Amigo, can you buy my gold chain?" he asked. "It's eighteen-carat gold, excellent quality."

"I'm sorry, I'm not into gold," I answered with a polite smile. "Why are you selling it?"

"I need the money to move to a better house," he said. "I have a wife and three children."

When I pressed for details, he conceded there was no move in his plans.

"Things are tough, brother," he said. "The ration card is good for about a week of food. Without cash, you don't eat the rest of the month."

<>

Roberto, a middle-aged Health Ministry translator, had just gone through the agony of organizing a birthday party for his three-year-old daughter. The preparations had kept him busy for nearly a month.

Long before the birthday, he had signed up at a toy store to buy a present. His ration card entitled him to three non-specified toys every two years. This year, the only available toys were rubber balls, dolls, and miniature cars. He had chosen a Chinese doll. After signing up and getting his number—he was number 73—he had to show up every day at noon for the roll call. If he failed to show up, he would lose his place. He had gotten the doll after making regular appearances in the line for five days in a row.

To buy a birthday cake, he had signed up two weeks earlier at the bakery, and got number 60 on the waiting list. He was supposed to be in line every day for the 6 P.M. roll call to keep his place. He would go himself whenever he could, or send his mother-in-law, a senior citizen, to replace him when he was tied up at his job.

The same procedure was necessary to purchase soft drinks, which one could get once a year for each family member's birthday. Roberto was number 32 on the list, and had to be in line every day at 7:30 P.M. to avoid losing his place. It took four days of roll call to get the drinks.

Then, there was the problem of candy. There had not been candy for several months at supermarkets or grocery stores. After much scouting around, he finally heard that candy was being sold at the Havana zoo. Once there, he found out that each person was only allowed to buy two small bags. He queued up three times, for a total wait of six hours. The small confections looked cheap and weren't wrapped, but they were better than nothing.

After a long search for cellophane paper to wrap up the candy, Roberto and his wife found it at a funeral home. They got a sheet from the establishment's florist, cut it up, and wrapped the candy piece by piece. The couple didn't even try to find birthday balloons—nobody had seen any in years. Instead, they used what had become the standard birthday ornament in recent times—condoms.

"It's not very chic, but everybody uses them as birthday balloons," Roberto explained. "After a while, you forget what they are."

Carlos Cabrera, the head of the recently renamed University of Havana Scientific Socialism Department, was sitting at his desk under the forty-six-volume complete works of Lenin. He was the stern-looking Marxist studies professor I had last visited in May 1991, when his department had just dropped its previous label of "Scientific Communism."

Now that the Soviet Union had outlawed communism, he looked more confused than ever.

"What can I say?" he shrugged. "We're once again revising all our academic programs."

His department's cooperation agreements with the University of Moscow were now abrogated, and he was trying to start academic exchanges with Latin American schools. But, to his chagrin, he was finding that most universities in the region didn't want to deal with a school that sported "Scientific Socialism" in its letterhead.

"They are scared to be accused of being subversives in their home countries," he said. "And Latin American students fear they won't get a job at home if the word 'socialism' appears in their academic records."

In an effort to dispel fears abroad, Cuba's Education Ministry's Superior Direction of Marxist-Leninist Studies was once again considering changing the name of Scientific Socialism university programs.

"There are proposals to change it to Political Sociology, or Politology," Cabrera said. "Some are even talking about calling it Political Science. . . ."

A more transcendental debate was heating up within Fidel Castro's inner circle as the Soviet pullout from Cuba seemed imminent. The revolution was at a crossroads, and there were only six weeks to go before the Fourth Congress of Cuba's Communist Party.

The October 10, 1991, Party Congress was seen by many Cubans as Castro's last chance to reform the system, pave the way for a peaceful transition to democracy, and avoid a bloody civil war. Castro himself had raised hopes about the Congress when he had convoked it more than a year earlier, calling on all Cubans to come up with new ideas to reform the Party.

The Communist Party was Cuba's supergovernment. It was recognized in Article 5 of the Cuban Constitution as "the highest leading force of the society and the state." Each Secretary of the Party's various departments was a superminister—much more powerful than his or her counterpart in the Cuban government.

Communist Party ideology and foreign affairs chief Carlos Aldana, for instance, was immensely more powerful than Cuba's foreign minister Isidoro Malmierca. It was the same at the provincial and municipal levels. It was the Communist Party bosses—not government officials—who wielded real power.

Since 1975, the Party had met three times to set Cuba's economic and political guidelines for the next five years. Each Congress had brought about significant changes. Now, the Party's 611,627 militants and applicants were to have their Congress in a climate of general realization that the Soviet-model Communist experiment—which officials after three decades continued to call *el proyecto* (the project)— had failed, and that Cuba could no longer expect to be rescued by its former ideological partners. There was widespread expectation that Castro would launch sweeping reforms, and that the Fourth Congress would set a new course.

<><

Cuba's human rights leaders were hoping the Fourth Congress would see a revolt from within the Party ranks that would lead to radical reforms, including the acceptance of a multiparty system. After the collapse of the Soviet bloc, Cuba's Communist Party could only assure itself a spot in Cuba's political future if it paved the way for a transition to a Western-style democracy, opposition leaders said.

Some human rights groups, emboldened by Gorbachev's brigade pullout announcement, decided to test the regime's tolerance by staging their first public anti-Castro demonstrations. On September 6, 1991, a newly formed group named Cuban Democratic Coalition staged a protest in front of the state security headquarters in the Havana section of Villa Marista.

The group, made up of six small center-right parties linked to Miami's CANF, used telephone communications with Radio Martí and the Voice of the Foundation to call for a mass participation at their rally. Only about a dozen people attended and were quickly dispersed by the state security, and coalition leader Daniel Azpillaga Lombard was arrested on the spot, but organizers could claim to have set a precedent of active opposition to the regime.

That same week, leaders of eight better-known opposition groups met at the house of human rights leader Elizardo Sanchez Santa Cruz to sign a document forming the center-left Cuban Democratic Concertation. The groups were mostly human rights organizations that were now crossing the line into political activism. Their leaders were well aware that they were making themselves liable to state charges of "illicit association" just by signing the new organizations' declaration of principles.

I arrived at Sanchez's house in the Havana suburb of Marianao late that evening, when most of the signatories of the Concertation's charter had already left. Sanchez and Maria Elena Cruz Varela, the poet who headed the Alternative Criterion group of dissident intellectuals, were the only ones left. They spoke enthusiastically—and somewhat nervously—about the "historic step" they had just taken.

Puzzled by a small overnight bag Cruz Varela kept next to her— you didn't see many people carrying bags, folders or anything else in Cuba—I asked her if she was about to leave town.

"No, it's not that," she said. "I'm pretty sure I'll get arrested tonight. I brought my toothbrush, toothpaste, a towel and a change of underwear. One must be prepared. . . ."

She was not arrested until two months later, in November 1991, when a government-sanctioned mob staged a "repudiation act" in front of her house for three consecutive days. Then, the mob stormed into the house, dragged her down the stairs, and forced her to eat an Alternative Criterion propaganda leaflet she had distributed on the streets. After the incident, a court sentenced her to two years in prison on charges of spreading antigovernment propaganda, and she was sent to jail.*

A few weeks after the Concertation was formed at the Sanchez house, the group took another bold step. Knowing that a number of

---

* *In January 1992, Cuban television news program Cubavision interviewed a woman named Mirta Isidron, who said she had been one of the people who had forced the leaflets into Cruz Varela's mouth. "It was a normal reaction that could be expected of any revolutionary who receives enemy propaganda," Isidron said in the broadcast, which was picked up and shown on January 3 by Miami's Spanish-language Channel 51. "When she opened the door, we took the propaganda she had handed out to us and stuck it in her mouth."*

foreign journalists had sneaked into the country on tourist visas to cover the Fourth Communist Party Congress, it called a massive press conference—the first ever given by an opposition group in Cuba. More than fifty reporters crammed into Sanchez's dining room.

The group issued a seven-point "proposal" to the delegates to the Party Congress, calling for among other things a general amnesty for political prisoners, state recognition of political and human rights groups, and free national elections. Concertation leaders said copies of the manifesto had been placed on every seat of the train that would carry the Havana Communist Party delegates to the city of Santiago a day later.

"If the Fourth Congress of Cuba's Communist Party were to dismiss the essence and goals of this proposal, it would reject one of the last opportunities to prevent economic and social chaos, and bloodshed the likes of which Cuba has never seen in its history," the statement concluded.

The Communist Party Central Committee was deeply divided over what the Fourth Congress should accomplish. Reformers—led by young Party leaders such as forty-year-old economic czar Carlos Lage, thirty-five-year-old Communist Youth leader Roberto Robaina and thirty-nine-year-old Union of Cuban Writers and Artists president Abel Prieto—pressed for a political and economic opening that would inject new energy into the regime. They were mostly Party leaders in their thirties and forties, who worried about their own future, among other things, if the regime collapsed.

"We want the revolution to survive Fidel," one young Party leader told me privately. "To achieve that, we need to democratize the Party and the government's elective bodies, so we can have stronger institutions. We need a National Assembly with legislators who truly represent their constituents, and who have a real say on domestic and foreign policy issues. Unless we do this, the revolution will collapse in less than twenty-four hours after Fidel's disappearance."

Leaders of the Party's old guard, led by Communist Party administrative chief José Ramón Machado Ventura, sixty-one, argued that, at a time when the revolution was facing its worst crisis ever, any reforms—whether free legislative elections or greater autonomy for state enterprises—could spin out of control and destroy the revolution.

The old guard were mostly middle-aged to older functionaries of the Party's administrative apparatus, including provincial and municipal Party bosses such as Havana City's powerful Communist Party Secretary Jorge Lezcano. By merely issuing their *orientaciones*, or guidelines, these local Party bosses had long exerted a heavy influence over key aspects of political and economic life in their respective jurisdictions.

They cited the Soviet Union and Nicaragua as ominous reminders of what would happen if Cuba opened the doors to political and economic reforms. They recommended sitting tight, and facing the hard times by activating a wave of "revolutionary enthusiasm" through the Party's propaganda machinery.

"We must learn from the Soviet experience," said Julio García Luis, president of the influential Cuban Union of Journalists, when asked whether the Fourth Congress should allow greater press freedoms. "We cannot change horses midstream, when the whirlpools are dragging us down. We must wait until we're closer to the shore."

The Cuban revolutionary elite was in turmoil. The sacred principle of democratic socialism—the Party rule whereby Communists could hold different opinions in closed-door meetings, but had to maintain the party line to the outside world once a decision was adopted—was crumbling. Increasingly, Cuban officials were conceding to me in private that a battle between hawks and doves was raging within the Party.

Castro, meantime, left little doubt on where he stood.

"Nobody should harbor any illusions that Cuba's socialism will make concessions, that the Cuban Revolution will make concessions, because we have one party, one single party!" he said. "And there won't be a market economy, or whatever they call that concoction that doesn't have anything to do with socialism. Our economy will be a programmed economy, a planned economy. We will not fall into the craziness of believing that our country can profit from spontaneous mechanisms."

But Castro had proven to be a realist before. Perhaps, his hardline rhetoric was mere posturing. Proreform Party members were disturbed but not paralyzed by the Comandante's words.

Reformers were encouraged by some hopeful signs. The grass-roots meetings of the Llamamiento—or call for people's proposals—for the Fourth Congress over the past year had resulted in an outpouring of criticism of the regime's policies.

The 1.1 million opinions collected by the Party at the meetings had been compiled into 76 reports totalling 9,063 pages. The confidential reports had been distributed to top Politburo leaders, with a statistical abstract showing that 87 percent of all the opinions garnered had been of a critical nature. Although most did not go beyond criticizing problems of daily life such as the deterioration of the mass transit system, the general message was one of discontent, and the Party hierarchy would find it hard to ignore that.

Even though meetings had been held at workplaces under the vigilant eyes of Communist Party cell leaders, some Cubans had been so bold as to criticize the holiest tenets of the revolution: the one-party system, the centrally planned economy, even Fidel's one-person rule.

A classified Central Committee report on the nationwide polling said 3,300 people had demanded free farmers markets, nearly 100 people had spoken out for a multiparty system, and another 50 had called for a full-fledged market economy. The numbers might seem inconsequential to outsiders, but the fact that anybody would have dared speak out in favor of such drastic reforms at the government-monitored Llamamiento meetings could only mean that there was a strong undercurrent of dissatisfaction in the country.

The bulk of the other opinions expressed at the meetings had criticized Cuba's inefficient service industries, the huge government bureaucracy, and the lack of democratic elections within the Party and the National Assembly of the People's Power. But these were hardly frivolous gripes. Hard-liners would have to seriously consider adopting some reforms to placate an increasingly restive population.

The reformers hoped to persuade the Fourth Congress to change the Party's statutes, and to replace the regime's Marxist-Leninist rhetoric with a more nationalist one that would also appeal to non-Communist Cubans. Carlos Aldana, a middle-of-the-road politician who most often sided with reformers, for example, had begun to refer to the Communist Party in recent months as the "Party of the Cuban Nation." Others, like Armando Hart, the culture minister who was terrified at being labeled a progressive, were talking about "a radical return to the ideas of Martí."

Without explicitly saying so, most wanted Fidel to drop his "Socialism or Death" slogan. Communist Youth Union leader Roberto Robaina had even engaged in a public—if subtle—clash with Castro over the issue. The youth leader had tested the waters by ending an important speech without the customary "Socialism or Death" salute.

It had happened in front of hundreds of thousands of people in April 1991 during a Communist Youth rally at Havana's Plaza de La Revolución. Like most foreign observers at the scene, I hadn't noticed anything out of the ordinary until I was alerted to it later.

Robaina, a boyish-looking former University Student Federation leader and Angola veteran, was the most visible young member of Castro's inner circle. "Robertico," as Fidel called him affectionately, had won some support from the youth for his casual style and his preference for T-shirts, a look that differentiated him from the stuffy guayabera-clad Party leaders. He had recently pumped new life into the six-hundred-thousand-strong Communist Youth by sponsoring rock concerts and opening discotheques. His success in gathering big crowds of youths for Fidel's speeches had given him a special status within Castro's inner circle.

That night, "Robertico" was making a rousing speech exhorting young people to join the Communist Youth. After speaking for more than half an hour, standing in the podium next to Fidel, he closed his speech by raising his hand, clasping his fist, and saluting with the slogan: "We will be like Che—followers of Fidel! Until Victory, forever!"

The crowd at the Plaza applauded with some enthusiasm. Fidel stepped forward and embraced Robaina at the center of the podium. The Cuban leader then made a two-hour speech filled with revolutionary rhetoric and gringo-bashing. It was vintage Fidel—nothing new. It was only when Castro ended his speech that many in the public raised their eyebrows. "We congratulate comrade Robertico for the excellent work he has done at the helm of the [Communist] youth, for his brilliant speech, for his concepts and his ideas, and for the firmness and optimism of his words," he said.

"And in case he forgot to say it because he wanted to finish with that beautiful slogan of Che, I'm saying it for him and for me: Socialism or Death!"

Robaina's omission had not been an oversight: every senior Cuban official had ended his speeches with that motto since the Comandante had come up with it a year earlier. Robaina had made a pitch to phase out the Marxist rhetoric, or the apocalyptic death references linked to it, and he had earned a public slap on the wrist for his transgression. He went out of sight for several weeks thereafter. Like other reformers, he was asked to hold his gripes for discussion at the Fourth Party Congress.

<>

Reformers had drafted elaborate plans—later covered up by the regime—to use the Fourth Congress to convince Fidel Castro that he should relinquish some of his power. It would be a unique opportunity to launch a controlled political opening that could give the revolution a second wind.

The never-publicized project, spelled out to me several months before the Congress by among others National Assembly President and former Justice Minister Juan Escalona, sought a radical change in the course of the Cuban revolution. By transferring some of Castro's powers to the new generation of leaders, the Cuban revolution would prepare the way for a smooth succession when the Comandante died, and lay the ground for a process of transition to a more democratic system. Latin American and European governments would certainly applaud the move, and Cuba would start preparing the ground for the long-term survival of the revolution.

Under the plan, Castro would remain as president, head of the Council of State, and Communist Party leader, and would be in charge of making Cuba's long-term strategic decisions. Meanwhile, a prime minister would be appointed to head the Council of Ministers and run the government's day-to-day affairs. The prime minister's job was scheduled to go to Carlos Lage, the young reformer who was already running the country's economic affairs.

There was no such thing as a prime minister in the current government structure. Castro held absolute powers as President of the Republic, President of the Council of State, President of the Council of Ministers, Secretary General of the Communist Party, and Commander in Chief of the Armed Forces.

Reformers hoped to convince Fidel that the proposed structure would allow a young leader and his aides to gain experience in running the government's daily affairs, and would allow Fidel more time to chart the long-term future of his revolution. Besides, with the harder times ahead, it would not be a bad idea to have somebody else take the blame for worsening economic conditions.

"Nobody is talking about making Fidel become something like the Queen of England," I was told by a supporter of the plan within Castro's inner circle. "He would still get involved in everything, but he would have more time to spend on the state's strategic decisions."

Fidel had given a green light to Escalona in early 1991 to look into the plan, and to analyze its pros and cons within closed doors at the regime's upper levels. At times, Castro would even show some enthusiasm for the project in private conversations with selected foreign friends.*

Escalona was one of the most fervent believers in the prime-minister plan. As National Assembly president and head of a forty-eight-member subcommittee in charge of proposing constitutional changes to the Castro-led Fourth Congress organizing committee, he was in a key position to push the concept. On the other side of the argument were Machado Ventura followers, who feared the proposed prime minister's office would give more powers to the government, at the expense of the Party.

But Escalona, backed by Robaina and most other young Party leaders, pressed on. A man haunted by his image as the unyielding attorney general who had sent Div. Gen. Arnaldo Ochoa and Col. Tony De La Guardia to their deaths—a decision he had described to me as "justified" but "extremely traumatic"—he seemed eager to project a moderate image. In various interviews at his office, he struck me as one of the most friendly—and outspoken—members of Castro's inner circle.

"If we had a prime minister, he would take care of the daily struggle, and the president would be the chief of state," Escalona told me in April 1991. "We will take to the Fourth Congress the discussion of all major structural changes, including this one."

The prime-minister idea had wider implications—it could mark the start of a gradual political opening. Because article 141 of the Cuban Constitution required a national referendum to make major changes in the Constitution, the regime would have to call a plebiscite to legalize the new government post. The referendum would be Cuba's first in more than a decade and would most likely encourage dissidents to defy the system in the polls. Even if they were outlawed under Cuba's one-party system, small dissident groups would be able to campaign as de-facto opposition parties.

In the eyes of the reformers, the state still had enough leverage over the Cuban people to win the referendum, and the voices of dissent would only help legitimize the Cuban regime internationally.

---

* *At a January 1992 closed-door meeting with former U.S. Defense Secretary Robert McNamara and a group of former U.S. and Soviet officials to discuss the 1962 Cuban missile crisis, Castro conceded that he had considered a transition plan. "It's crossed my mind to resign, to find a substitute for me in this changing world," Castro told participants. But he went on to say that he couldn't do that, because "It still has to be proven that we can resist," according to an unidentified participant at the meeting quoted by the* Miami Herald *on January 18, 1992.*

Many governments would step up political and economic ties to the island if they saw the beginning of a political opening, their argument went.

In addition to seeking an office of prime minister, reformers such as Carlos Rafael Rodriguez, Robaina and Prieto pushed for the possible adoption at the Fourth Congress of many of the proposals that had surfaced during the nationwide Llamamiento assemblies.

At the closed-door meetings of the Fourth Congress seventy-member organizing committee, the reformers suggested that the agenda of the Congress include discussion of free and direct elections to the National Assembly, in which candidates would be nominated by the people rather than by the Communist Party or its mass organizations; free farmers markets; legalization of craftsmen such as plumbers and carpenters; and a greater openness in the media.

At the Congress's organizing committee, made up of Fidel Castro and the elite of his regime, reformers found an unexpected ally—Raúl Castro.

Sitting at the presiding table next to Castro and five top Communist Party leaders—Aldana, Lage, Machado Ventura, Robaina and Juan Almeida—Fidel's younger brother took an active role in support of reforms, especially on economic issues.

"Raúl was the person who spoke the second most," recalls one Politburo member who was part of the Fourth Congress organizing committee. Only Fidel had spent more time in front of the microphone during the debates.

Many participants were surprised to see the defense minister playing the role of reformer. Only two years earlier, Raúl had helped crack down on Div. Gen. Arnaldo Ochoa, and had cleaned the Interior Ministry from Perestroika-influenced officials. Now, in his scornful, folksy style, Raúl—like his former military aide Escalona—was sounding like a lifelong moderate. What was going on in Raúl's mind was a big question mark for diplomats based in Havana who had heard rumors about his interventions at the meetings. Some speculated that Raúl, a more pragmatic man than his older brother, was simply more aware than Fidel of the growing popular discontent, and of the need to do something about it.

At one of the Fourth Congress organizing committee meetings, Raúl Castro engaged in an argument with a provincial Party functionary who had warned against embarking on a path of reforms. The official had argued that this had brought about the collapse of the Communist Party in the Soviet Union.

Raúl rejected the argument. "What worries me more is what will happen if we don't make much-needed changes now, and if we don't make them under Fidel," Raúl said.

Journalists Union president Julio García Luis, a member of the organizing committee who witnessed the exchange, says Raúl argued for deregulation of key sectors of the centrally planned economy, drawing from the armed forces' experience in allowing its companies a greater managerial autonomy. "He kept stressing the need to overcome dogmatic barriers," García Luis recalls.

Shortly before the October 10, 1991, opening of the Fourth Congress, the Central Committee announced that the meeting in Santiago de Cuba would be strictly closed. In contrast to the practice at previous Party congresses, foreign journalists would not be allowed in, and there would be no visiting delegations from abroad.

It wasn't necessarily a bad sign. Previous Party meetings that had been open to the press had turned out to be carefully staged events, where no serious debate had taken place. The Party had now vowed the Fourth Congress would be the most democratic ever. Considering the new global politics, there was a real chance that the Party would embark on a process of rigorous self-examination. Hopes were high.

14
The Congress

◄◄◄◄◄At 1 A.M. Wednesday, October 9, 1991, two special trains carrying hundreds of Communist Party delegates to the Fourth Communist Party Congress left Havana for the sixteen-hour trip to the eastern city of Santiago. On its various stops along the 560-mile journey across the island, the convoy was greeted with cheers by thousands of schoolchildren and workers who had been bused to the train stations for the occasion. They chanted, "Awaiting your command, Fidel!" Their banners read, "Socialism or Death!"

Inside the trains, nearly seventeen hundred red-eyed delegates waved to the crowds, slept, or tried to read. Each had received a set of four white-covered booklets marked "Fourth Congress, Draft Resolution." The confidential documents dealt, respectively, with the economy, the Communist Party charter, the Communist Party program, and the National Assembly. They had been prepared by the seventy-member Fourth Congress Organizing Committee.

But as they leafed through the documents, the delegates would not see a word about the plan to relieve Castro of any of his powers. The draft resolutions made no mention of the proposal to create a new post of prime minister. There was no reference to a possible referendum to introduce major reforms in the Constitution. The proposal

to re-establish free farmers markets, one of the most widespread public demands at the grass-roots meetings preceding the Fourth Congress, had vanished from the text.

Even worse for reformers, the delegates to the Congress had been
chosen from the Communist Party's most conservative quarters. Most
passengers on the trains were middle-aged men in military uniforms,
or in the conventional guayaberas and black leather shoes. Nearly
seven hundred were full-time Party officials; about two hundred forty
were members of the military, including thirty-five generals and fifty-
three colonels; the remaining hundreds were government ministers
(Cuba had nearly fifty officials with the rank of minister, and two
hundred vice-ministers), heads of government agencies and diplomats.

Relatively few blue-collar workers were on board, and fewer than
150 intellectuals, academics and students—the Party's most avant-
garde sectors. Essentially, the Castro-headed delegate screening committee had chosen a docile crowd of Party apparatchiks from the
forty-six thousand candidates submitted by grass-roots Party organizations.

Badly outnumbered, the reformers would face an uphill battle to
reintroduce their proposals into the hard-line draft resolutions. They
had participated in the earlier stages of the preparations for the Congress and felt they had paved the way, but the Castro-led organizing
committee had wiped out most of their suggestions.

The Fourth Congress of Cuba's Communist Party opened Thursday,
October 10, 1991, with a big surprise. At nine o'clock that morning,
Fidel Castro and the rest of the members of the Politburo took their
places on the stage of the 2,500-seat Heredia theater, but there was a
conspicuous absence in the assembly. Armed Forces Minister Gen.
Raúl Castro was not among them.

The delegates in the audience looked at one another, perplexed.
Castro's brother was the Communist Party's Second Secretary General, its highest-ranking official after Fidel. He had presided over one
of the Fourth Congress's three organizing committees and had been
in charge of drafting the agenda for changes in the Party's structure,
content and working style. He had been at center stage during the
previous three Party congresses, and had been second only to Fidel as
the most active speaker in the closed-door preparatory meetings for
this one. What was going on?

Esteban Lazo, the Politburo member and Santiago Party boss who made the opening speech, tackled the irregularity head on. Standing before the microphone, under the giant portraits of José Martí and Karl Marx affixed to the theater's dark blue curtains, Lazo read from a prepared text and extended his welcome to all participants.

"A large number of delegates who represent the Communists within our glorious revolutionary armed forces and the Interior Ministry, including the army chiefs . . . are not present because they are in their respective units protecting our country's skies, coastline and soil," Lazo said. "Among those who are absent from this opening session, absences we greatly regret but at the same time understand because they are necessary for the defense of our country, are our beloved comrade Raúl Castro, and our beloved interior minister, comrade Abelardo Colomé Ibarra."

The explanation wasn't very convincing. Raúl had disappeared from the public scene before, fueling widespread speculation that he was seriously ill. "Where is Raúl Castro?" the *Washington Post* had asked in August, after Cuba's first brother had successively missed Fidel Castro's July 26 address to the nation and the opening ceremony of the XIth Pan American Games.

Raúl had surfaced hours after news agencies carried the *Post* story, at a ceremony honoring two retired Portuguese army officers. He was shown on Cuban television's evening news that day and appeared in two photographs on the front page of *Granma* on the following day. In the weeks that followed, he had taken an active role in the closed-door preparations for the Congress, but failed to appear once again at public events.

At the Fourth Congress, delegates would be told privately that the general's absence was due to a military emergency. U.S. troops had just landed at the U.S. Naval Base on Guantánamo, ostensibly to help evacuate American residents from neighboring Haiti following the September 30 military coup that had ousted President Jean-Bertrand Aristide.

The U.S. State Department was saying that the troops sent to Guantánamo were exclusively related to the Haiti crisis, but Cuba could not rule out a Yankee provocation during the Fourth Congress, delegates were told.

Raúl would finally show up toward the end of the four-day Congress, and would corroborate the official explanation that he had remained at his command post due to the unusual U.S. activities in Guantánamo. He would preside over the Congress's session to elect a new Central Committee and Politburo, and showed up at the closing ceremony.

Still, his absence during the Congress's opening sessions continued to be a mystery. Raúl had been increasingly linked to Cuba's
reformists in recent years. He had approved new management practices in armed forces enterprises, allowing them to operate with growing autonomy from the centrally planned economy. He was known to
be more down-to-earth, folksy and candid than his older brother, and
stories of his caustic jokes at Politburo meetings about Cuba's economic situation had long circulated in Communist Party circles.

On the other hand, Raúl—even at age sixty—expressed total loyalty to his older brother in public. Under Fidel's wing since their days
at the Sierra Maestra, Raúl still seemed cowed in his presence—more
an underling than a brother. When Fidel showed up, Raúl clicked his
heels.

Delegates could not help but review the same questions that had
churned through the general population's rumor mill in previous
months. Was Raúl really suffering from ischemia, or lack of blood
supply to the brain, as had been long suspected? Was he recovering
from an alcohol detoxification cure? Was Raúl, the street-smart
orthodox-turned-reformer, trying to put some distance between himself and his dogmatic older brother? Or had he had to quell a growing
restlessness among the armed forces?

Fidel Castro's five-hour speech opening the Fourth Congress dumped
a bucket of cold water on whatever hopes remained that the Fourth
Congress would effect a change from within the Communist Party.

After accommodating the microphones and accepting a standing
ovation from the delegates—many in the crowd chanting, "Awaiting
your command, Fidel!"—Castro began his nationally televised speech
in a slow, halting voice. Sitting at the center of the dais—it was the
first time many Cubans would see Fidel making a speech from a
seat—he spent three hours describing Cuba's dire economic situation
following the collapse of the Soviet bloc. As usual, his rhetoric rose in
a crescendo.

Did Cubans know how much rice had arrived from the Soviet
Union during the first half of 1991? "None!" And how much grain?
"None!" And how much butter? "None!" And how many spare parts
for Soviet television sets, refrigerators, fans and bicycles? "Not one
single piece!"

And did Cubans know what had happened with shipments from
Eastern Europe? The new unified Germany had revoked all of East
Germany's cooperation contracts with Cuba! Czechoslovakia had done

the same! Hungary, and all the other former Eastern European nations, had done the same! Only Soviet oil shipments were coming in at a rate more or less according to what had been accorded in the December 1990 Soviet-Cuban agreement.

"As for the rest of the essential products, nothing!" Castro told the Congress. "I'm not saying all this as a reproach or as criticism. I'm simply explaining why things are as they are. I can attest to the efforts that the Soviets have made to meet these commitments . . . but, with the chaos and disorganization that have taken over that country, it's a very difficult task."

How could the Soviet Union have ended that way? Fidel had a ready answer: the Soviet leadership had not listened to what he— Fidel Castro—had told it as early as 1987. He had warned the Soviet bloc at a COMECON meeting that year about the dangers of Gorbachev's reforms. The Fourth Congress delegates nodded, as if it were only natural that Fidel had been the only one to foresee the disintegration of the Soviet bloc long before the fall of the Berlin wall.

"I fulfilled my historic duty by warning them that, at least, they shouldn't support those trends—that is, that they shouldn't give in to the temptation to copy capitalism. . . . When I saw that the authority of the Soviet Communist Party was being destroyed, when I saw that the authority of the government was being destroyed, and when I saw that the history of the USSR was being reduced to dust . . . I immediately understood that it would have terrible consequences in that great government, in that great nation."

Cuba would not make the same mistake, he assured. How could anybody even think that Cuba would be better off without communism? How could he betray the "millions" of revolutionaries, hundreds of thousands of Communist Party members, the Communist Youth, the Cuban Workers' Union? No, he could not betray the Cuban people the way the Kremlin leadership had let down the Soviet people. Cuba's Communist Party would continue to guarantee Cuba's independence from Yankee imperialism.

"If imperialism could get Cuba on its knees and impose capitalism in our country again, what would remain of what we have done in the past one hundred twenty-three years?" he asked, setting the beginning of his revolution ninety-one years before its time, at the beginning of Cuba's 1868 independence war.

"Will we let ourselves become another Puerto Rico?"

"Nooo!" the audience shouted back.

"Will we let ourselves become another Miami, with all the repugnant rottenness of that society?"

"Nooo!" the delegates shouted once again, even though, deep down, many of them knew full well that the reaction from large numbers of Cubans watching television in the privacy of their living rooms would be a resounding *Sííí!*

<><>

In his lengthy interventions over the next three days, Castro promoted a quasi-mystical brand of Socialist fundamentalism. With the zest of a television evangelist, he appealed to his guiding light as "La Revolución." Delivered under a banner that read, "Our most sacred duty is to save the fatherland, the revolution and socialism," Castro's speeches were dominated by words such as "sacred," "moral" and "miracle."

La Revolución was much more than the Castro regime, he would stress repeatedly. It was a historic process that had begun with Martí, De Céspedes, Maceo, Marx, Engels and Lenin. Countless people had shed their blood for it, and no one had the right to renounce it.

Fidel described himself as "a slave" of power. La Revolución had placed on him the sacred responsibility to uphold its principles in an increasingly hostile world. Like Martí before him, he emphasized, Castro had been called upon to save La Revolución not just for the Cuban people, but for all mankind. That's why he could not step down, nor would he consider relinquishing any of his powers.

"Never did we intend to transform everything: history and life imposed that duty on us," he said. "That is why the world is looking at Cuba with great hope. The world admires this small country. The world admires this small island of dignity. . . . The world admires Cuba, and it will admire it even more for our abilities to fight on and win." He would later sum it up saying, "Destiny has turned us into the standard-bearers of the world revolutionary, progressive and democratic movement."

That's why La Revolución was demanding greater and greater sacrifices from the Cuban people. How could anybody dare to go against La Revolución or against its representative on earth, the Communist Party?

"The question of the Party's influential role is a sacred, essential thing," he explained. One had only to look at the disasters that had befallen the Soviet Union when the authority of the Communist Party had been undermined. "It was a horrible, terrible, inconceivable thing," Castro said of Soviet President Mikhail Gorbachev's decree outlawing the Soviet Communist Party. "Now just imagine if it occurred to me here to issue a decree dissolving the Party. . . . What man can be given such power? Nobody has the right to abolish the Communist Party!"

"It's good that we talk about democracy, once and for all," Castro told the Congress at another session. "And let's forget about the world's criteria. So-called Western democracy has nothing to do with [real] democracy. It's complete garbage."

La Revolución would never accept a multiparty system in Cuba, he said. "Multiparty systems are 'multitrash' systems," he said. Cuba already had "the most complete democracy there is." That's the way La Revolución wanted it, and that's the way it had to be.

The Congress that Fidel had described as "the most democratic political congress ever held anywhere in the world" turned out to be a sham. Instead of a serious debate on major issues, it was a four-day celebration of Castro's power.

With Fidel acting as master of ceremonies, moderator, judge and reviewer, delegates dutifully took the microphone to recite the accomplishments of their respective workplaces—and to state that none of their achievements would have been possible without the Comandante's visionary recommendations.

Much of the time was taken up by participants who said production at their respective factories had been disastrous until Fidel had paid a visit and had recommended key changes in production methods that had eventually resulted in major production gains. Several recited poems in the Comandante's honor, or walked across to the stage to offer him presents.

One delegate from Havana, Nilo Otero, presented the Comandante with a box full of jewels inherited from his grandparents so that the government could buy spare parts or medicines. Caibarién factory worker Hector León gave Castro a Cuban flag, which he said was sent by his town's university students as a testimony of their love for the Comandante. Another delegate presented Fidel with a just-published atlas of Santiago de Cuba. A delegation from Matanzas province presented a sheepskin carved with the symbols of Cuba's independence war. A group of filmmakers offered Fidel a copy of the new documentary about Ernesto "Che" Guevara and Camilo Cienfuegos, and took the stage to tell stories about their experiences shooting the film in the Sierra Maestra.

Then came a procession of scientists who explained in detail what they described as watershed scientific discoveries that would soon boost the Cuban economy. Their dissertations took up much of the Congress's working hours.

Carlos Gutierrez, head of Cuba's National Center of Scientific Research, took the seat next to the Comandante to announce the discovery of a wonder drug named PPG that reduced cholesterol levels, helped prevent heart attacks and improved the quality of sex. PPG had proven to increase "the number of orgasms and erections," he said. Fidel cheerfully welcomed "the sexual functions" of the new drug, and all the delegates felt allowed to laugh, jeer and applaud the Comandante's naughty remark.

Manuel Limonta, head of Cuba's Biotechnology Center, reminded the audience that none of Cuba's scientific achievements would have been possible had not the Comandante taken an interest in the subject following his fateful meeting with American scientist Randolph Lee Clark in 1980. Now, thanks to Fidel, Cuba had become Latin America's leading country in scientific development.

"Neither Venezuela, nor Colombia, nor any other country can compare with, let's not even mention Havana, but Camagüey," Limonta trumpeted proudly.

Another speaker concluded, "All of us workers in the scientific sphere feel committed to the fatherland, to the revolution, to our brand of socialism, and to the best of all Cuban scientists: our Commander in Chief, Fidel Castro." Castro applauded, along with everybody else.

<>

In one of the few exchanges that resembled an open discussion, the journalist delegates demanded a greater openness in Cuba's media. The Cuban press, in its zeal to meet its duty to the revolution, was offering a rosy picture that was in sharp contrast with Cuba's reality, they said. They demanded more news, and less political propaganda.

Pedro Martinez Pirez, a respected, professorial news executive of Cuba's short-wave Radio Havana Cuba broadcast, made a concrete proposal to add a sentence to the draft resolution on the Cuban press. His proposed text specified that the press should continue exercising its propaganda role "without neglecting the systematic and profound criticism of everything that obstructs the betterment of society." Caridad Diego, of the Communist Youth's Editorial Abril publishing house, took the microphone to support the motion.

The suggestion didn't go anywhere. Journalists Union President García Luis made a lengthy speech in which he partly blamed the journalists for not doing a better job under existing press guidelines. Then, Party ideology chief Aldana muddied the waters further by saying the issue of the press was too complex, and perhaps should be discussed at greater length sometime in the future. The motion was dismissed entirely.

The only other exchange that approximated a discussion came when Manuel Alvarez, a delegate from Pinar del Río province, told the Congress that he had been asked by his grass-roots organization to bring up the issue of free farmers markets. His two-minute statement was followed by a three-hour invective by Castro against free markets.

It was good that the delegate from Pinar del Río had brought up the issue, Fidel began, because many Cubans were asking themselves whether farmers markets wouldn't be a solution to food shortages. That's why he was happy to debate the issue, he said.

"Although many arguments have been raised, there is still a lack of convincing arguments," Castro said. Free farmers markets "would truly complicate the situation. It would disrupt everything we're doing, it would sow corruption and demoralization."

Fidel ended his speech expressing "great respect for the delegate from Pinar del Río, because he had things to say and he said them with all honesty, integrity and courage." Castro added, "We thank him because he has given us the opportunity to demonstrate the respect, liberty and democracy with which we discuss these issues." Motion dismissed.

<><>

The four-day-long Fourth Congress of Cuba's Communist Party ended on October 14, 1991. Cubans watching the edited versions of the proceedings on state television saw a sea of delegates mechanically approve the Congress's resolutions with the distinctive horizontal applause that Cuban Communists had copied from their Soviet mentors.

Before closing, the Congress approved the changes Castro had suggested for the Politburo and the Party Central Committee. The new Politburo was to be made up of twenty-five members—eleven more than the previous one. Some old-time Politburo members were retired, including Culture Minister Armando Hart, Cuban Women's Federation leader and Raúl Castro's wife Vilma Espin, former Education Minister José Ramón Fernandez, and old-guard revolutionary leaders Pedro Miret and Jorge Risquet.

Among the new Politburo members were Party ideology and foreign affairs chief Carlos Aldana, Communist Youth leader Roberto Robaina and Union of Cuban Writers and Artists (UNEAC) president Abel Prieto.

While the newly expanded Politburo incorporated several reformers, they would never be able to prevail on a vote. The new Politburo included sixteen Party functionaries, four generals, one construction worker, one intellectual, one union leader, one scientist and one Castro personal aide. Reformers held only about half a dozen seats.*

Surprisingly, when the results of the Fourth Congress's secret vote for the Party's top authorities were read aloud in the closing session (which was not televised or otherwise released to the media), it was learned that three delegates had voted against Fidel Castro's re-election, and four had cast their ballots against Raúl Castro.

Although the Castro brothers were re-elected as first and second secretary respectively with an overwhelming majority of the votes, the show of dissent was a first. No delegate to a Cuban Communist Party Congress had ever cast a vote against Fidel. Both Raúl Castro and Carlos Rafael Rodriguez took the microphone to criticize the anonymous delegates who had voted against the Party leadership. Fidel, once again playing the good cop, calmed them down. "This is what democracy is all about," he said, reassuringly.

"They were baffled that anybody would vote against them," a senior government official who witnessed the scene as a delegate to the Congress told me later. "If there had been votes against Fidel in a congress attended by the general population, nobody would have been surprised. But these votes had come from among the seventeen hundred most trusted government supporters in the country! It made a big impact on all of us."

The resolutions approved by the Congress contained few surprises.

On internal affairs, it reaffirmed the status of the Communist Party "as the single Party of this Cuban nation based on the principles of Marxism, Leninism and Martí's ideas." It also approved elections to the National Assembly and provincial legislatures "by direct vote of the people," leaving the details of the new electoral laws to be discussed at a later time.

---

* *The new twenty-five-member Politburo elected by the Fourth Congress of Cuba's Communist Party was as follows: Fidel Castro Ruz, Raúl Castro Ruz, Juan Almeida Bosque, Osmany Cienfuegos Gorriaran, Abelardo Colomé Ibarra, Esteban Lazo Hernandez, José Ramón Machado Ventura, Carlos Rafael Rodriguez, Julian Rizo Alvarez, Ulises Rosales del Toro, Roberto Robaina Gonzalez, Pedro Ross Leal, Carlos Lage Davila, Carlos Aldana Escalante, Jorge Lezcano Perez, Alfredo Hondal Gonzalez, Alfredo Jordan Morales, Nelson Torres Perez, Concepción Campa Huergo, Yadira Garcia Vera, Maria de los Angeles Garcia, Candido Palmero Hernandez, Abel Prieto Jimenez, Julio Casas Regueiro and Leopoldo Cintra Frias.*

On economic issues, it authorized independent work by trades-men "under the limits and parameters imposed by the special period and the construction of socialism." On foreign affairs, it called for stronger ties with Latin America, China, Vietnam and North Korea.

The only major news at the Congress—and perhaps the most important resolution to come out of it—was a new rule giving the Central Committee "exceptional powers" to overrule any other gov-ernment body in "unpredictable situations." The new resolution made it virtually impossible for any branch of government to single-handedly challenge the Castro leadership. If the new legislators elected by direct vote of the people ever tried to force Castro out of power, the Central Committee would be empowered to invalidate their decision immediately.

But the fact is, none of these resolutions were a result of any debate during the four-day Congress. Unbeknownst to the Cuban people, the fix had been in from the beginning.

A few weeks after the Congress, I obtained copies of several of the secret draft resolutions prepared by the Fourth Congress Orga-nizing Committee—the booklets the delegates had been given before the meeting. Except for a word here and there, they were carbon copies of the texts that were later published in *Granma* as final reso-lutions. The meeting had been little more than a big circus, whose function was to rubber-stamp a text that had already been approved.

In the twenty-one-page draft resolution about the economy, not one single article was changed from the original text, except for the inclusion of a short sentence stating that the sugar industry also played a vital role in Cuba's economic development (the original text hadn't mentioned the sugar industry, which still accounted for more than 70 percent of the country's foreign income).

In the fifteen-page resolution on the National Assembly, I only found a two-word change from the original text. The draft clause calling for direct elections stated that the planned study on the nom-ination process would "also take into account the experience of uni-versal practice." The phrase was changed at the Congress to read "other experiences," so that nobody would get the wrong idea that Cuba necessarily would embrace Western democracy practices.

Other than that small change, the Congress did not add or delete one single comma from the draft text. So much for Castro's promise of accepting new ideas in what had been billed as the most democratic Congress ever.

◄►

What had happened to the plan to appoint a prime minister and call a referendum to write a separation of powers into the Constitution? National Assembly President Juan Escalona Reguera, who had been so enthusiastic about the proposal six months earlier, was all smiles when he received me in his office a few weeks after the Congress.

"Are you among those who are saying that the Fourth Congress was a disaster?" he joked, slapping me affectionately on the shoulders. Then he tackled the prime minister question head on.

"The plan died from scratch," he said. "We began to study Latin American constitutions, and concluded that [a separation of powers] was not suitable for this country's leadership in the present circumstances. We arrived at the conclusion that our current government structure is best, if we improve it."

Escalona claimed his constitutional reforms commission had nixed the plan on its own initiative, but other officials with access to the closed-door debates said that Escalona had withdrawn the motion after Castro had ordered him to shelve it. The Cuban leader had decided the plan was too risky, if nothing else because it would have required a referendum to change the Constitution.

"We would have had to hold a referendum," Escalona conceded. "The time is not ripe for that. We would have had to paralyze the country, agriculture, everything. We're not living under such normal circumstances that we can do something like that."

In later conversations with top Politburo members, it became apparent to me that Castro had decided not to allow significant reforms at the Fourth Congress partly because of economic considerations. Many emphasized that Cuba would not make the mistake Daniel Ortega and the Sandinistas had made in Nicaragua, and call a referendum—or any other democratic exercise—amid a major economic crisis.

The regime's projections showed Cuba would only start emerging from its "worst moment in history" in the mid-nineties. According to Carlos Aldana, Cuba's economic crash would bottom out in 1992 or early 1993. According to these estimates, Cuba's economy would begin expanding in 1994, when its huge investments in tourism and biotechnology would start rendering significant profits.

Judging from the words of Aldana, Escalona and other top government officials, Castro had decided to put off any plans for major political reforms until the economy picked up in 1994.

"I think our first duty is to resist," Aldana told me shortly after the

Fourth Congress. "For the revolution to be perfected, it first has to close ranks. For us to develop new democratic processes and apply economic recipes . . . that lead to an improvement in our standard of living, for all of that to happen in 1994, we have to resist now."

Aldana, a serious-looking man, was cordial to me but tense as he delivered the new Cuban Party line at his Central Committee office. He chose his words with extreme care, as if Castro's ghost were in the room watching. Two aides sat with him through the nearly three-hour interview.

He had a big tape recorder turned on the minute I stepped into the room, so that even our small introductory talk was recorded. It was an advanced case of the Armando Hart syndrome: the higher you got in the Cuban hierarchy, the greater your fear of stepping out of line, no matter how slightly.

The powerful Communist Party ideology chief continued explaining the rationale behind the regime's decisions at the Fourth Congress:

"Our challenge today is to find out which elements of change contribute to resistance, and which—even though they are desirable—would be counterproductive. That's the key issue we faced at the Fourth Congress." He added, "I think that any serious and unbiased observer of Cuba's reality will agree that, considering the country's situation, the Fourth Congress has taken important steps."

Most Cuban people didn't think so. The much-awaited Fourth Congress had been a total fiasco. The people's cries for free farmers markets, legalization of small businesses and democratic reforms had been postponed for better times. The hard-liners had won.

<>

So where did that leave Cuba? Possibly the most chilling answer to that came from Castro himself at the closing ceremony of the Congress. His address to the nation had sounded like an impassioned call to collective suicide.

Standing beneath a huge metal monument to independence fighter Maj. Gen. Antonio Maceo at Santiago's newly dedicated Antonio Maceo Square, and speaking as a tropical shower drenched his audience of more than one hundred thousand people, Castro called on the Cuban people to prepare themselves for economic catastrophe, war and martyrdom.

The words "death" and "blood" permeated his rhetoric, as if he had already resigned himself to the inevitability of a tragic ending. Like a cornered animal, his eyes spilling rancor, he vowed to die—

taking the Cuban people with him—rather than allow La Revolución to be sullied by Yankee imperialists. Cubans would redeem themselves only by dying in battle against their enemies.

In a dramatic gesture, Castro turned to the gigantic statue of Maceo above him, and began a strange conversation with the black independence hero as heavy raindrops began to cover the open-air stage.

"Thank you, Maceo, for giving us this opportunity! We are all pygmies beside you, all of us who grew up hearing about and honoring your name. Thank you, thank you for your example, thanks to the people that you and those like you forged! . . . We, who are pygmies beside you, we feel like giants, because with the blood of those like you who showed this country its path, a people of giants emerged.

"We never had pretensions of receiving such extraordinary honors. We never had such great expectations, but history and life imposed them on us, and we will know how to fulfill them."

Turning again to the crowd under him, his face now wet with the intensifying shower, he raised his arms, pointed his index fingers downward, and recited what Cubans on the street would soon refer to as "Fidel's ode to death":

"We're invincible!" he shouted. "Because if all members of the Politburo have to die, we will die, and we will not be weaker for it! If all members of the Central Committee have to die, we will die, and we will not be weaker for it! If all the delegates to the Congress have to die, all the delegates to the Congress will die, and we will not be weaker for it! . . . If all the members of the Party have to die, all the members of the Party will die, and we will not weaken! If all members of the Young Communist Union have to die, all the members of the Young Communist Union will die!

"And if, in order to crush the revolution, they have to kill all the people, the people, behind its leaders and its Party, will be willing to die! And even then we will not be weaker, because after us they would have to kill billions of people in the world who are not willing to be slaves, who are not willing to continue being exploited, who are not willing to keep going hungry!"

Turning again to the Maceo statue, he concluded, "People die, but examples never die! People die, but ideas never die! And here we are ready to water our ideas with our blood!"

15

Requiem for a Revolution

I was eating a sandwich at the bar of the Havana Libre Hotel a few weeks after the conclusion of the Fourth Congress of the Communist Party when a slender man in his mid-thirties nervously approached my table. Kneeling before me, he introduced himself as Raúl.

He asked if I could do him a big favor. He was feeling terribly awkward about asking a favor from a foreigner, but he was dying for a cigarette. He had acquired the vice many years ago, and for the first time in his life he had been unable to get a pack. The government had begun rationing cigarettes a few weeks earlier. Could I buy a pack of cigarettes for him at the hotel's dollar store? He would pay for it, he assured me.

Sure, no problem. I purchased a pack of Cuban-made Montecristo cigarettes for ninety-five U.S. cents, and took it to the lobby where he was waiting. We began to talk about what had long become the single most important topic of conversation—the shortages. The situation was terrible, he said, as virtually every other Cuban was saying at the time. He had always been a good revolutionary—and had never thought he would have to beg for cigarettes—even less from a foreigner. I thought it was a fairly ordinary conversation, until Raúl told me what he did for a living: he was a *jefe de cuadros*—a political commissar—at a well-known government institution.

Are you serious? I asked. He was. Raúl's job was to look into the ideological purity of every party cadre applying for a job or a promotion. He was the official in charge of reviewing the Biographical Data of the Cadre forms such as the one I had been shown by a midlevel Party official several months earlier. Upon receiving the forms, Raúl went to each applicant's neighborhood-watch committee to ask about his or her participation in government mass rallies and voluntary work. He would then go to each of the applicant's previous work centers, and talk with the local Communist Party boss about the person's professional qualifications and ideological commitment.

I immediately suspected Raúl was an agent for state security, and had been sent to spy on me. After two years of research, I was accustomed to almost daily questioning about the nature of my work. Almost no social occasion went by without a government official asking me about what I would write about specific issues—and without veiled threats that I wouldn't get to see top functionaries if I proved hostile to the revolution.

Raúl didn't ask me anything, however. Instinctively, we began walking toward the street to avoid being listened to by the Havana Libre lobby's hidden cameras. What he told me after a long conversation left me startled.

"Brother, this can't go on like this," he told me. "There's no food. There's no hope. There's no nothing. We've reached a point where I don't care who takes over, as long as he puts bread on our table. Even if it's the Miami exiles . . ."

It was the first time I had heard such a radical statement from a Communist Party member—quite apart from the fact that I was hearing it from a political commissar. It had to be a ruse to gain my trust—and to make me talk. But to my surprise Raúl didn't ask questions and made no move to meet again.

I decided to put him to a test. I told him I would love to continue our conversation at another time. Would he call me? I gave him my hotel and room number. If he was a spy, he would surely get in touch with me. He never did. I could only conclude that Raúl, the wavering political commissar, had been a spontaneous acquaintance—a random measure of Cuba's economic and ideological disarray.

Fidel Castro was doing the unthinkable—delivering Cuba to the right. His veto of meaningful economic and political reforms at the Fourth Congress had begun moving a sizable number of his former followers to the opposite side of the political spectrum. To many Cubans, the Congress had marked the end of illusions that the system would reform itself from within.

Until then, the Comandante's stubbornness was still celebrated by many Cubans as the eccentricity of a political genius. Whenever Fidel would assume new bravado, as he had when he came up with his slogan "Socialism or Death!" when the rest of the world was shunning socialism, many Cubans would shake their heads admiringly and say, "There he goes again." His Machismo-Leninismo had its charm. But by early 1992, as world communism was crumbling and the economic vise gripped Cuba, Fidel's intransigence was no longer amusing.

Much to the despair of liberals within the Communist Party, Castro was doing nothing to begin a transition that would ensure the survival of the revolution's hard-won social gains. It was becoming increasingly clear that his decision at the Fourth Congress to postpone significant reforms until the economy improved in the mid-nineties had been a major miscalculation—the Cuban people were not likely to passively accept the growing food shortages for that long, nor was the economy likely to bounce back strongly so soon. Every minute that Castro remained in power now without enacting sweeping reforms, he was doing a little more to sabotage his revolution and deliver his country to his historic adversaries.

Did the new generation of Communist Party leaders—Yummies such as Carlos Lage, Roberto Robaina and Abel Prieto—sense the danger that the Comandante's intransigence would ruin the revolution? They most probably did. In private conversations with several of them, I got the distinct impression that they were smart, observant people who were constantly reminded by friends and relatives about growing discontent in Cuba.

While receiving many privileges, their families were not immune to the hardships of daily life. Politburo member Carlos Lage's mother was often seen standing in line for hours at her neighborhood bakery in Havana's Nuevo Vedado section. Lage himself was seen at least once after his appointment to the Politburo riding his bike without escorts on 26th Street. "It's good exercise," he said, smilingly, to a friend who greeted him from a car.

The young Party leaders had developed a biting sense of political humor. When I told newly appointed Politburo member Abel Prieto that I had accidentally forgotten my wallet at a cafeteria and a man had come running after me with it, he raised his eyebrows in a gesture of surprise.

"Wow, you must have stumbled onto *el* Hombre Nuevo (*the* New Man)," he said, as if the Cuban revolution had only produced one.

Why were these young political leaders sticking to an increasingly hopeless political process? Part of it was their continued admiration for Fidel. Fidel had proven to be right many times before, when everybody around him had disagreed, they said. Perhaps his political instinct would prove right again.

In the mid-eighties, when almost everybody around Fidel had rushed to embrace Soviet Perestroika, Fidel had warned of the Soviet Union's coming disintegration. In Nicaragua, when Cuban reformists had applauded the Sandinistas' 1989 elections, Fidel predicted their defeat. In August 1991, while most Cuban officials celebrated the Soviet putsch, a worried Fidel had taken the news with prudent skepticism.

"Fidel has long headlights," a member of the Politburo's new generation told me. "He makes mistakes, but fewer than the rest of us. You can't dismiss his political genius."

Certainly, the young Communist Party leaders were not so naive as to think they could make the Comandante change his mind on major issues. They knew better. Their strategy was largely one of damage control—trying to talk the Comandante out of his most utopian plans, such as his constant desire to ask Cubans for more nonpaid "voluntary" work. Ultimately, their goal was to position themselves to be there the day Fidel disappeared from center stage.

They were "betting on the life expectancy sweepstakes," as a close aide to one of them explained to me. Fidel was about to turn sixty-six, and there was a good chance he would die within a decade. The new generation of Communist Party bosses wanted to be there, with solid experience behind them, for when that moment came.

It wasn't just a matter of personal ambition. The new generation of Party leaders shared the general fear that Fidel's death would bring about a bloodbath. They believed that if they quit the government, the revolution's hierarchy would be dominated by hard-line *históricos* of Fidel's generation, and by the Machado Ventura–led Party apparatus. The transition would be more traumatic—and bloodier.

Some of the Yummies I had known for years would tell me privately they wanted to work for a political opening that would turn Cuba into a Mexican-style system of a strong leftist party, but one that would respect civil liberties and give way to private initiative. They felt Castro's health care and education programs, as well as his heroic defense of nationalist values, had generated enough support for the revolution to make it a viable political party in a free society.

They felt they would be more useful inside the Party than outside it. As the regime began drafting new laws for the National Assembly elections scheduled for the end of 1992, the young reformers wanted to have a say in the process. The Fourth Congress had left key questions of the electoral rules open, including who would nominate candidates and to what extent non-Party candidates would be given a chance to win. They felt there was still a chance that Fidel would make a 180-degree flip and allow a political opening before the elections.

If anti-Castro forces were given a political space—no matter how small—in the new National Assembly, Cuba could begin an orderly process of transition, they said. There would be a strong revolutionary party and a small minority of dissident legislators, who would operate as a de-facto opposition party even if they were not legally recognized as such. Making the system more democratic would help "institutionalize" the revolution—and ensure the long-term survival of its philosophical principles.

The Yummies' plans had sounded feasible in the late eighties, when the revolution still commanded a sizable—if rapidly diminishing—portion of public support, and Soviet bloc supplies were still flowing into the island. But by the early nineties, the population's disaffection was rapidly outpacing Castro's aging process. Patience was running out. Barring a U.S. intervention that would move Cubans to rally behind their flag, only a bold, eleventh-hour political opening launched by Castro himself would save the revolution. The young Party leaders were hanging on, waiting for it to happen.

As the situation deteriorated, so did Castro's ego. In the absence of a new international credo to replace communism, he blatantly encouraged a personality cult. More than ever before, Fidelismo was put forth as the new state religion.

The new Communist Party slogan, *"Te Seré Siempre Fiel"* (I will be always faithful to you), was a not-so-subliminal play on words with the name Fidel. By the end of 1991, Castro was making almost daily speeches on television, often for hours at a time. His image was constantly on the screen—visiting farms or welcoming foreign business delegations. Cubans began to call him the "television test pattern," like those after-hours still pictures. Whenever you turned on the box, Fidel's face was there.

Yet Castro looked increasingly isolated, as if he were the only one not grasping the growing public unhappiness. Whatever impact his personality cult was having on the Cuban people, one thing was clear—it was working on him.

<>

On November 2, 1991, as he addressed Cuba's First Congress of Pioneers, he sounded as if he had lost total touch with reality, or at the very least with his audience.

It was a sunny Saturday afternoon, and Fidel was to make the keynote address at the Communist children's meeting. More than a thousand children aged six to fourteen packed the auditorium of Havana's Convention Palace. Before Fidel rose to speak, a succession of boys and girls came to the podium to recite poems in his honor, sing songs in praise of his heroic deeds, and bestow medals on him for his unswerving service to Cuba's children.

Their teachers had been preparing them for several months. They had been bused to the convention center early in the morning. When the much-awaited encounter with Fidel came, the youngsters were visibly moved.

One girl cried at the sheer emotion of being so close to Fidel. Another girl took the microphone to tell Fidel that Cuba's children were ready to "replace our pencils with rifles" to defend the revolution and socialism. A third girl, aged twelve, called for the creation of children's brigades to crack down on fellow students who were being influenced by foreign ideas. "We, the pioneers, want to be allowed to form Rapid Response Brigades in our schools," she said, as Fidel nodded approvingly.

When Fidel took the stage and started his nationally televised speech, he began by smiling at the children—and commiserating with them.

"Dear Pioneers and happy guests: After so many moving moments we have been through, I don't want to run the risk of boring you too much from this stage," he began. The kids were quick to respond in a chorus, "Noooo!" Fidel was clearly off to a charming start.

Two and a half hours later, Fidel was still addressing the Communist children's gathering. But the atmosphere had changed completely. Now, a stern-looking Castro was delivering sugar-production statistics, shouting war threats, banging the podium with his fist and lecturing about Che Guevara. He was speaking in terms that were clearly incomprehensible to the young audience in front of him.

"We must look at Che from a dialectical point of view," Castro said, as the children stared back with blank eyes. "Because when we talk of Che, we talk of a human prototype. . . . He can't be, he's not a mystical idea, he's a rational idea . . . he's a prototype, a figure that represents our socialist, communist, internationalist era."

A few kids were still managing to look intrigued, but the cameras had a hard time dodging images of other children poking their noses, playing with their pencils, or building paper airplanes while the old man finished his talk. It was no surprise that Fidel had talked beyond what anybody expected: this was, after all, the man who had once made a fourteen-hour speech, and who was listed in the Guinness Book of Records for making the longest speech ever at the United Nations (four hours and thirty minutes).

But three hours to an audience with six-year-olds in the front row? Talking about the dialectics of Che? Fidel had obviously forgotten who was out there. He was talking to himself. Even in his longest speeches, Fidel had always established a quasi-magical connection with his listeners, often by engaging in casual dialogue with acquaintances sitting in the audience or by open-heartedly admitting that a decision made by his government had been wrong. The connection was no longer there.

Existing guidelines on Fidel's treatment by the media were updated with directives to make the Comandante look better. Shortly after the Fourth Congress, newspaper editors were reminded to be especially careful with the Castro pictures they picked for publication.

The problem had arisen when a member of the newly elected Politburo—UNEAC president Abel Prieto—happened to be taller than the Comandante. Editors were reminded that no picture should ever be used showing the imposing, six-foot-one-inch-tall Castro with someone taller next to him.

Pictures showing Castro eating were also prohibited. A reminder to the government-run media emphasized existing guidelines whereby no details of Castro's personal life should ever be released.

Juventud Rebelde, the mass-circulation Communist Youth newspaper, had recently saved itself from great embarrassment by a last-minute decision to ban a picture showing Castro at a tourist hotel's dedication ceremony. The picture showed Fidel with his hand holding a shrimp over his open mouth. All pictures of Castro eating were thenceforward banned—just in case.

"We can't show him eating, we can't show him resting, we can't show his family," one journalist familiar with the *Juventud Rebelde* shrimp-picture incident told me. "He has to be larger than life."

<>

The traditional November 7 reception at the Soviet embassy for the anniversary of the Russian revolution had long been the most-awaited diplomatic event of the year. Everybody who was somebody in the upper echelons of the Cuban government would be among the fifteen hundred guests. It was the only regular diplomatic reception Fidel Castro never missed. It was also one of the few that was attended by Raúl Castro, all members of the Politburo, and the Cuban armed forces' top generals. For diplomats and foreign journalists in Havana, it was a rare chance to rub elbows with Cuba's elusive power elite.

But in 1991, following the dissolution of the Soviet Communist Party, Soviet and Russian authorities had decided to cancel all celebrations, and to make the traditional November 7 holiday an ordinary workday. Soviet diplomats in Havana could only speculate that Fidel Castro would follow their lead—after all, it had been a Soviet holiday.

He didn't. A week before the anniversary date, stories about Cuba's plans to celebrate the new anniversary of the Russian revolution began to appear daily in the Cuban press. There would be a formal ceremony at the main auditorium of the Armed Forces building, a lecture on Lenin's contributions to mankind at the Soviet-Cuban Friendship Association, a solemn ceremony in front of the Mausoleum to the Soviet Internationalist Soldier and thousands of smaller ceremonies in front of Lenin statues throughout the country.

Granma's lead story November 5 announced that "the great Socialist Revolution of October's seventy-fourth anniversary and especially the figure of Vladimir I. Lenin will be commemorated in all corners of our country. . . ." A few pages later in that same issue, *Granma* carried a short story entitled "Russia will not celebrate anniversary."

Fidel planned to attend a few of the ceremonies, and made sure that all of them were prominently announced in the state media.

Fewer than one hundred people attended the Lenin lecture in the Soviet-Cuban Association's magnificent mansion on Linea Street, which had once belonged to a wealthy sugar-mill owner. Only three Soviets were in the audience—the recently demoted former head of the Soviet Communist Party cell at the Soviet embassy in Havana, a representative of the Soviet school, and a Soviet television journalist.

In the front row stood Cuban Col. Arnaldo Tamayo Mendez, who had made it into the Cuban revolution's history books by becoming the first Cuban cosmonaut. In a much-celebrated gesture of Soviet-Cuban friendship, he had participated as a crew member in a 1980 Soviet space flight. He had been decorated with the Lenin Order, the Gold Star of the Soviet Union, the Hero of the Soviet Union medal, and dozens of other Soviet and Cuban awards. Now, Tamayo Mendez presided over the Soviet-Cuban Friendship Association in Havana. A young-looking fifty-year-old with a Boy Scout personality, he displayed his dozens of medals on his light-brown uniform.

"This is surrealistic," the Soviet journalist muttered, shaking his head as we watched the scene together from the back row. "Back home, they're selling those Kremlin medals to antique shops. Fidel has gone nuts."

<>

Could a leader surrounded by yes-men who saw his picture wherever he looked and heard his voice on radio and television around the clock maintain a proper sense of reality? Hardly, most Cubans said.

His closest aides were certainly not contradicting him, especially in those matters about which he felt strongly. When Fidel entered the room, members of the Politburo not only stood up, but stood firm. Even his brother Raúl Castro paid his respects with a military bearing when Fidel showed up.

Foreign visitors getting to see Castro were carefully screened: the Comandante was too busy to try to convince enemies of the revolution. Press interviews were strictly limited to friendly reporters, mostly young women from Latin American newspapers who were dazzled by the Cuban leader's legend, or European leftists who found the Cuban drama exotic.

It hadn't always been like that. During his first two decades in power, Castro had been kept fully alert of the talk in the streets by his devout secretary and fellow Sierra Maestra veteran Celia Sanchez. She had been his closest personal aide—and main tie to reality—until her death of cancer in 1980. That same year, Haydee Santamaria, another dear friend who had accompanied him since the days of the Moncada attack and dared to contradict him when they disagreed, committed suicide.

Having lost the two women friends he respected the most, Fidel turned progressively remote, consumed in his own thoughts, unaware of much that was going on in Cuba's daily life. Only Carlos Rafael Rodriguez, the nearly octogenarian Communist Party founder, occasionally contradicted Fidel—politely—in closed-door meetings. But Carlos Rafael was old and his health was deteriorating rapidly. He was not up to fight.

Reformers in Fidel's inner circle would occasionally lobby for their ideas when the Comandante gave them a green light to explore certain questions. Virtually all of them, especially Robaina and Prieto, were known to support the short-lived notions of instituting a separation of powers in government, the free farmers markets, and a greater diversity in the media. But they would not dare to argue with Castro once he had made up his mind on a hotly debated problem, or on a pet issue.

The newly appointed Yummies in the Politburo Lage, Robaina and Prieto were even less likely to confront the Comandante than the outgoing *históricos*. It was a general assumption in Havana that disillusioned old-timers would always be more willing to put their jobs on the line than ambitious newcomers.

"There's nobody who will dare contradict him anymore," I was told by a well-connected Cuban who knew Castro since his school days. "Whoever dares criticize him too much is out within twenty-four hours. Fidel is living in a different world."

If one was to believe Castro's personal pollster, there was solid ground to conclude that the Comandante had little idea of the depth of public discontent in Cuba. Darío Machado, head of La Opinión del Pueblo (The People's Opinion), a little-known Central Committee polling group that carried out confidential weekly public-opinion surveys for the Politburo, had little but good news to report to his boss.

Machado, forty-five, a white-haired but boyish-looking political scientist who was a member of the Central Committee, had a huge polling machine at his disposal. La Opinión del Pueblo had a staff of forty-five professionals, most of them statisticians, sociologists, psychologists and computer programmers, who prepared and conducted the polls. They had a network of twenty thousand Communist Party militants throughout the country, who collected what they called "spontaneous opinions"—notes they took while standing anonymously at bus stops or breadlines in every city and neighborhood.

Thousands of these "spontaneous opinion" reports were sent up each week from municipal offices to the Communist Party's city authorities. They were then sorted out, and those dealing with national issues were sent to La Opinión del Pueblo's headquarters in Havana. The unidentified white house sat on C Street, looking like any other house in that residential neighborhood. But in the rear, more than a dozen young women worked in a computer room, feeding data into computer terminals.

What kind of figures was the Comandante getting? I asked. Machado said he would show me some of the confidential polls he had recently submitted to the Politburo. I couldn't wait to see them.

The first was a nationwide poll of 2,500 people on whether Cuba's problems should continue to be solved through a one-party system. The results: 95 percent said yes, 3 percent marked no, and 2 percent abstained.

Another poll dealt with the renewal of Politburo seats at the Fourth Communist Party Congress. Out of 1,037 people, 98 percent had said they were happy with the new appointments, while 1 percent had agreed with the assertion that more members should have been replaced, and the remaining 1 percent had agreed with the statement that renewing Politburo seats would not necessarily lead to a better government.

Was there a poll on Fidel's leadership? I asked. Yes, Machado said. He cited a 1989 poll where Cubans were asked "who is the most important political personality of the world today?" An estimated 89 percent had responded Fidel Castro. Soviet leader Mikhail Gorbachev was a distant second with 6 percent, he said.

Wasn't there any bad news? Was the Comandante being led to believe that everybody loved him and his policies?

Not at all, Machado said. He showed me a poll of Havana residents, conducted shortly before the Fourth Congress, showing that 85 percent of all people wanted the state to allow farmers to sell excess products in free markets. That was clearly against Party policy at the time—and to a lesser degree still was.

After more than two hours of glancing through computer printouts marked "confidential," I told Machado that—quite frankly—I did not believe that this was all that the Comandante got to see. Either there was a second set of secret polls he wasn't showing me, or there was a second secret pollster whose existence was unknown to me.

"No," he responded. "We're the only ones to do political polling.

There is also the 'spontaneous opinions' mechanism, through which they get a sampling of what average citizens say on the street. But that's it."

As for secret polls that only the Comandante got to see, sure, there were some, Machado said. La Opinión del Pueblo did some, as well as the Interior Ministry and the armed forces.

"But they're not what you think," he said. "They deal with specific problems we don't want our enemies aware of, because they would exploit them to their advantage. On the big political issues, this is what the Politburo gets to see."

Why didn't Fidel's pollster pose his questions in a more daring way, such as asking people if they didn't want a multiparty system?

"We're not interested in that," Machado said. "You have to start from your own reality, not from what others would like your reality to be. The only purpose of asking that question would be to satisfy the curiosity of people abroad. It wouldn't help solve any problems in Cuba."

So what are you telling the Comandante? I asked. Are you asserting that a regime that has been in power for more than three decades does not suffer from political erosion?

"I'm saying that there is some erosion in support for the idea of a centrally planned economy, like the one we copied from the Soviets. But there is no erosion in the people's determination to save the fatherland and to save the revolution."

La Opinión del Pueblo's figures weren't made up, judging from the stacks of computer charts I was allowed to see at Machado's office. But the whole polling mechanism had been designed to produce figures that would please the Comandante. It operated just as Cuba's factories did, which were geared to achieve production quotas—to meet projected numbers no matter how defective their products would be.

A polling form Machado allowed me to keep explained it all. It was a poll on Cubans' reaction to the tourism industry that had been distributed at work centers throughout the country. It started, "Compañero: The Opinión del Pueblo Research Center wants to know our population's opinion regarding tourism. That's why we seek your help, expressing your most sincere opinion when answering this questionnaire, on which it is not necessary to write your name. Thank You."

In Cuba's big-brother-is-watching-you atmosphere, every Cuban would have been well aware that the poll was conducted by a Communist Party entity. To begin with, nobody but a Party agent would be permitted to enter a workplace and distribute a survey. And even for those who had never heard of La Opinión del Pueblo, the *compañero*—comrade—reference left little doubt about its affiliation. Any dissident would know that he could easily be identified, by his handwriting, if nothing else. Little wonder that the overwhelming majority of the people polled claimed to support Castro's policies.

But did Fidel believe these clearly biased surveys? I posed the question to dozens of Cuban officials, foreign diplomats and other political analysts in Havana. To my surprise, virtually all agreed that he probably did. Some said the Interior Ministry and armed forces' polls were probably more realistic, but doubted whether anybody would dare confront Castro with figures that showed his popularity plunging.

Making the Comandante face the reality would destroy the one thing that was keeping the Cuban revolution—and the officials' jobs—alive: Castro's messianic conviction in the virtue of what he was doing. The men surrounding Fidel did not want to cripple Fidel's boundless self-confidence. They assumed, correctly, that Fidel didn't want it either. It was essential to keep the Comandante's psychological defenses strong; the fire in his eyes alive. La Revolución was too important a concept to toy with its wellspring and driving force.*

One well-placed Communist Party militant suggested that Castro—a political fox—may have been aware that the polls' questions were biased, but felt that it didn't really matter. The surveys' results proved the important thing: that the Cuban people were still under his control, as long as they continued to respond positively under the right mix of propaganda and pressure. In Castro's mind, the polls—whether they were accurate or not—proved the system was still working.

Alina, Castro's daughter, felt Castro was genuinely convinced that his hard-line socialism-or-death policy was still supported by a majority of Cubans.

* Contributing to the Castro aides' reluctance to deliver the bad news to Fidel were the Comandante's own calls for mutual moral support. "We cannot become demoralized," Castro told the National Assembly of the People's Power December 29, 1991. "We are doing what must be done. Among the things that must be done is keeping up morale. We must not forget that. We must keep up morale of the party members and the youth, in the first place. We must keep up the morale of the revolutionaries. Nothing that may occur should harm us . . ."

"Nobody will dare deliver the bad news to him, nobody," Alina said. "He's God."

"Have *you* had political arguments with him in your adult life?" I asked her.

"Yes."

"Does he listen to you?"

"He's not used to listening. He explains things to you."

"As if you didn't understand . . ."

"No, not as if I didn't understand—as if I wasn't there."

<><>

As Fidel stuck to his hard-line stand in early 1992, the lights were gradually going off in Cuba, literally. Growing sections of Havana looked like dark holes. Traffic lights in most of Havana's main intersections were disconnected, and policemen were put to work in their place. The Soviet Union had just informed Cuba that it would have to cut its oil supplies to about half its previous levels, and perhaps even more. Castro warned the Cuban population that the country might have to do with 4 million tons of oil a year, about a third of Cuba's average consumption in the late eighties.

"This is the most difficult period in Cuba's history," Castro told the National Assembly December 29, 1991, referring to the coming years. "It is not just the most difficult period of the revolution."

The Castro regime had ordered factories around the country to cut back and retain skeleton staffs only. Many had closed down altogether for lack of raw materials. Bus routes in Havana had been reduced from 169 to 88. Hundreds of thousands of workers had been sent home. They would continue receiving 70 percent of their pay—for as long as the government could afford it.

To help alleviate food shortages, the regime had begun distributing one two-day-old live chicken per family. Cubans were being told by the government-run media to grow the animals, and eat them after 120 to 180 days, "when it reaches its optimum weight for consumption." Instructions in the Communist Youth newspaper *Juventud Rebelde* explained how to build a small chicken box in a front yard or apartment balcony.

"I can't see myself killing that chicken after it has become part of the household," a Havana father of two said. "Can you imagine telling your kids, We're going to eat our pet tonight?"

<><>

Not even the Santería Gods had words of hope for the coming year. In a new failure by the Cuban counterintelligence services to influence their predictions, Cuba's senior Santería priests had come up on January 1, 1992, with their most ominous forecast in recent memory—and their fourth gloom-and-doom prophecy in as many years.

After their daylong ceremony where they repeatedly threw palm tree seeds on the powder-covered tray to question the Orishas about Cuba's future, the white-clad Babalaos had forecast that 1992 would be marked by Eyogbe Iwori—a sign of disaster, epidemics, and violence. Under Eyogbe Iwori's sign, the year would be dominated by Obatalá, the son of God and ruler of the planet, who carved the human body and rules its mind; and Ochun, the Goddess of the rivers and symbol of female sensuality, known to provoke fights between Gods and men bewitched by her enchantments. As the word of the new prophecy got out, many Cubans began to look for white kerchiefs and clothes to wear during the coming year: it was Obatalá's color, and wearing it was believed to help have the son of God on one's side.

"This Oddun is marked by disaster, epidemics, physical and psychological crisis," said a summary of the 1992 prophecy. "It is also marked by bloody internal fights and hunger."

It is 11 P.M. on Havana's crowded Malecón promenade. Thousands of young people sit on the seawall, which they jokingly call "the sofa." It is Havana's version of a town square—the place to see and be seen. It is one of the few places that look alive in a Cuba that has slowly come to a halt.

Everybody is there, pacing up and down the street, or sitting with a close eye on their bicycles parked at the curb. Some have brought Soviet-made transistor radios, which blast salsa music. Small groups of *roqueros*, with their long hair and ripped jeans, exchange gossip about the latest black-market prices for rock group T-shirts. Young lovers sit at a prudent distance, kissing, or facing the caress of sea breezes.

Middle-aged men in guayaberas sit with their backs to the sea and hold bottles of rum—often homemade out of cooking alcohol—which they offer to passersby. Prostitutes, usually in groups of two or three, stand curbside in their tight pant suits, waving and throwing kisses to the men swooping by in Havanauto tourist cars. Foreigners are everybody's focus, everybody's prize.

"Tío! Tío!" people at the Malecón shout at anybody who looks like an *extranjero*. They have taken the expression—literally meaning "uncle"—from Spanish movies shown on Cuban television, and use it under the statistically correct assumption that most foreign visitors to Cuba come from Spain. "Amigo! Amigo!"

Eight-year-old kids run after a couple of German tourists walking along the Malecón in their leather sandals. "A dollar, a dollar to buy chewing gum!" they beg. "Come on, amigo, give me a dollar, please!"

"Tío, you want to exchange some dollars?" one teenager following me shouts. I decline his offer. What else do you sell? I ask out of curiosity. He offers Cohiba cigars, probably stolen from state warehouses. No thanks. Black coral, great for jewelry. Sorry, not interested. Medicinal mud, very good for backaches or muscular pain. No thanks.

"You need a girl?" He grins, running out of patience. "I can get you a good one!"

The Malecón has become Cuba's marketplace. Some call it "Wall Street." Others call it "Calle 8," after the commercial street in Miami's Little Havana. There are no goods visible on the street other than bottles of rum, but that's where a buyer or a seller makes his contacts.

The Malecón is just a metaphor for the business fever that reaches all corners of society in Cuba. A joke making the rounds in Havana asks, What is the definition of socialism? The answer: the longest road between capitalism and capitalism.

<>

The quest for tourism is Cuba's only visible pocket of economic life. Four giant construction cranes stand out in Havana's skyline. The twenty-one-story seaside Cohiba Hotel, scheduled to be Cuba's finest, is near completion. Its top stories are lit at night, to allow construction crews to work around the clock.

But people walking along the Malecón across the street are skeptical of the regime's claim that tourism will save the revolution. Some have heard such assertions before. Dictator Fulgencio Batista had also begun a massive hotel construction drive shortly before he was toppled. The giant Havana Libre and Riviera hotels, Cuba's biggest until now, were opened in the two years before the 1959 revolution.

"In Cuba, commercial real estate booms have always been a prelude to political change," one intellectual theorizes, dropping a few examples starting late in the last century. "These new hotels can only mean that Fidel's days are numbered."

I try to pay for a tankful of gasoline with the special coupons the government's Havanautos rental company sells to its foreign clientele. It is the same gas station where I was once timidly approached by an attendant and asked if I didn't want to pay him cash at half the going price.

Now, a few months later, two attendants walk over to my Nissan and offer the same deal openly. They know that stealing gasoline from the state is a crime punishable by imprisonment. They don't care. They are fairly confident that none of the half dozen people watching the scene will report them. The attendants have probably already struck a deal with their supervisor, and he with his boss.

I tell them that I would like to do business with them, but I fear I will get caught. When foreign visitors return their rental car at the Havanautos agency, employees usually check the vehicle's mileage and calculate if it corresponds to the amount of gasoline purchased by the driver. If they find out I have driven thousands of miles and have only purchased gasoline with my coupons for a few hundred miles, I will be in trouble.

"No problem," one of the attendants says, quite naturally. "Go to the back street of the Havana Libre, and you'll find a lot of guys standing there who can fix your car's odometer. Don't let them charge you more than five dollars. Everybody does it."

Corruption is so pervasive in Cuba that few are arrested for stealing from the state. If the government was serious about cracking down on corruption, it would have to put the whole island behind bars, the current explanation goes.

A South American visitor staying at the Victoria Hotel is shaken. He is a long-time sympathizer of the Cuban revolution, and has visited the island on many occasions. He is heartbroken by what has happened to him on this trip. He tells his story:

On the first night after his arrival, as he was in his bed fast asleep, he was awakened by a telephone call. It was a girl. In a sensual voice, she said her name was Laura. She told him she felt very lonely, and would love to spend some time with him. She could meet him in ten minutes around the corner, on M Street. He declined, thinking she had dialed the wrong number.

A few nights later, he was awakened again at 1 A.M. It was another girl. She sounded very young, certainly in her teens. She said her name was Carla, and asked if he was alone. With this second call, he realized that the women were just ringing up hotel rooms at random, hoping to catch a lonely *extranjero*.

It is a shocking reality in a revolution that had once caught the imagination of Latin America with its proud claims of having transformed Cuba from a prostitution center for wealthy Americans into a showcase of social justice and human dignity.

The eradication of prostitution had been one of Castro's greatest claims to fame since the early days of the revolution. Despite the obvious resurgence of prostitution, he could still be heard using the same propaganda line: "What future would there be for us if we became slaves, if we became a colony?" he said in a speech December 8, 1991. "They [the United States] imposed capitalism on us for almost sixty years. And what did we inherit from Yanqui neocolonialism after sixty years? We inherited a hundred thousand prostitutes. . . . The daughters of the aristocracy and the bourgeoisie were only educated for marriage. The rest of the women, the daughters of the proletariat and the peasants, were prepared for prostitution, or to work in bars and cabarets, or to do domestic work."

The South American visitor is shaking his head. Doesn't Fidel realize that nothing has changed?

<><

Apartheid is now official at Havana's four-star Comodoro Hotel—management has memorialized it on paper. A one-page letter placed in each guest room warns tourists against letting Cubans into the hotel. The natives are not to be trusted.

The letter states proudly that the Comodoro Hotel has remained immune to the wave of crime affecting other Havana establishments. This is largely because of the hotel's strict security measures, it claims. The general manager therefore wants to share a series of guidelines the distinguished guests should be so kind as to follow.

First, foreign tourists should not invite into the hotel anybody they meet on the street, and should not take any local acquaintances to their rooms. ("Tourists are not allowed to invite Cuban citizens to stay with them at the hotel, unless it is their spouses.") Second, if the guest needs to invite a Cuban to the hotel bar for a business meeting, the Cuban should first be taken to the front desk to register his or her name and his or her ID number. This way, the Comodoro Hotel will be able to continue assuring its guests the high standards of safety for which it has always been recognized.*

◄►

The Cuban revolution has been turned on its head. Free access to hotels and beaches—the very places that were off-limits to certain Cubans during the Batista days—had once symbolized everything the Castro revolution stood for.

It was no coincidence that the first thing exhilarated Cubans did in the early hours after Batista's flight on January 1, 1959, was to storm into the hotels and casinos. To the *revolucionarios*, the tourism apartheid, prostitution and begging in the streets were the most visible symptoms of Batista's oppression of the poor.

The Castro regime started to build its egalitarian image by abolishing privileges for foreign tourists. A Cuban's right to have free access to any public place had been elevated to such a tenet of the revolution that it was written into the regime's 1976 Constitution. Article 42 establishes the right of "all citizens" to "be served at all restaurants and other public service establishments," and to "enjoy the same resorts, beaches, parks" and other recreational facilities.

The revolution's most celebrated poet, the late Nicolás Guillen, dedicated one of his most famous works to the end of the Batista era's tourism apartheid. His 1964 poem "Tengo" (I Have), learned in school by generations of Cuban revolutionaries, summed up all the good things the Cuban revolution had brought about for a black, working-class man like himself.

Its key verses read, *"Tengo, vamos a ver / que tengo el gusto de andar por mi país / dueño de cuanto hay en él . . . / tengo, vamos a ver / que siendo un negro / nadie me puede detener / a la puerta de un dancing, de un bar / o bien en la puerta de un hotel."* (I have, let's see / I have the pleasure of going around my country / owning whatever there is in it . . . / I have, let's see / that being a black, / nobody can stop me / at the door of a dancehall, of a bar / or at the front desk of a hotel . . .)

Today, Guillen's verses, and even Cuba's Constitution, sound subversive—a mocking portrait of what Cuba has turned into. In his

---

* *Tourism apartheid was creating such resentment among the population that the Politburo ordered the takeover of the Comodoro Hotel's "Havana Club" discotheque in December 1991. The Spanish firm that managed the nightclub was promised reimbursement of its $1 million investment, and the Communist Youth Union took over the place. The takeover was also intended to crack down on prostitution, since the front door of the discotheque had become the mecca of Havana prostitutes looking for foreign tourists, according to a* Juventud Rebelde *story on January 10, 1992.*

desperate quest for dollars to maintain a bankrupt regime, Castro has recreated the very inequalities he sought to destroy. The revolution has come full circle.

<>

It is showtime at La Divina Pastora, an elegant foreigners-only restaurant overlooking the Havana bay on the outskirts of the city. Spanish, German and Italian tourists sitting at the tables are asked to move to the patio, where a waiter is offering Mojitos and rum. The Omo Olorum—Children of the Sun—troupe is to shortly begin its performance of Afro-Cuban dances.

The tourists take their seats on the patio and ready their cameras. At the rumble of African drums, the first dancer bursts onto the scene. She is a beautiful mulatto—naked from the waist up. A minuscule G-string bikini is her only garment, and much of her body is painted in white and red stripes.

The woman takes catlike steps toward where we sit and begins to move her breasts frantically to the music. Her hard nipples stand out as one of the few unpainted parts of her body. Soon, there are six women dancers on the stage. They perform erotic contortions around a gigantic black man in an Abakuá costume.

A chubby, middle-aged Spanish tourist with two lovely mulatto companions applauds enthusiastically. He is soon invited to the dance floor, while his friends take pictures of him with the sculptured dancers. *Obaaa, Obaaa*, the band sings, in the language of the ancient Yoruba tribes.

Julio Perez Medina, an artist who paints the women's bodies three nights a week for the show, watches the performance from a corner. He tells me the dancers make the minimum wage—140 pesos a month, or a meager seven U.S. dollars at the black market rate. They don't get to eat at the restaurant, but at the *comedor obrero*, the workers' cafeteria.

He doesn't provide more details, but it is hard to believe that the dancers can live on that. If they are like most Cubans, they make most of their income through other means. Their job provides them with access to the most precious commodity in today's Cuba—the chance to meet an *extranjero*.

I go back to my seat. The dancers are now shaking their bodies center stage; one of them carries a bottle and pours a circle of kerosene around the others. In seconds, the fuel is ignited, and flames shoot up around the wriggling group.

The show is tasteful and the dancers are quite good, but the

Spanish tourist with the two mulatto women next to me is reading my mind. Bending over my table, he asks me, "How long do you think it will be before the government opens the peep shows?"

<>

Castro's attempt to save communism with a dose of capitalism was a losing proposition. There was no way to keep his isolated enclaves of free enterprise from spilling over to the rest of the economy. As growing numbers of Cubans flocked to tourism-related industries and added to a soaring black market of goods and services, the capitalist way was spreading like wildfire in Cuba.

The population's political thinking was rapidly following economic realities. If Cubans working in the capitalist enclaves were the only Cubans doing well, why not make the whole economy capitalist? The people were becoming convinced that socialism with a dollop of capitalism would never be as effective as capitalism full strength.

Castro was on a road to nowhere. If he dropped his centrally planned economy, the economy would improve, but his regime would lose its political control over the workers. If he stuck to his centrally planned economy, he could look forward to economic collapse, famine, and a likely popular rebellion.

Even in the unlikely event that his pockets-of-capitalism plan managed to net more profits than expected, there was another potentially insurmountable problem. For the economy to start growing without Soviet subsidies, the government had to drastically reduce its budget for social programs.

The regime's guarantees that all Cuban citizens would always receive a decent diet, free medical care, a good education and a good pension were already eroding fast. Free lunch at the workplace was a thing of the past. Hundreds of thousands were working on reduced schedules, or had been laid off altogether.

If necessary evils had to be brought in to defend the revolution's social programs, and still the programs were disappearing one by one, why dally? Why not embrace full-fledged capitalism at once? In the minds of growing numbers of Cubans, cold-blooded capitalism would make more sense than well-meaning socialism with dwindling social programs.

<>

At what point would Cubans take to the streets? The consensus was, when they no longer had anything to lose. The overwhelming majority of the Cuban population had long depended on the government for their pay, including those who had been sent home with 70 percent of their salary.

It was only a matter of time before massive layoffs, further reductions of unemployment benefits, and a workers' exodus to the growing pockets of capitalism would create a critical mass of Cubans with nothing to fear from openly defying the regime.

Only a serious threat of U.S. intervention, or a new wave of Cuban-exile terrorist attacks such as those that had placed the island on a war footing in the sixties, could give the Castro regime a second wind. Cubans had no sympathy left for communism, but most still felt strongly nationalistic. If Washington stepped up its interventionist rhetoric, or if extremist Cuban exiles launched new armed raids on the island, enough Cubans might rally around the flag, even if they would do so without the enthusiasm of earlier days. Castro, who had recently imposed a war economy on a country at peace, would finally be able to invoke a real war to justify his regime's draconian economic and political measures.*

Could the Cuban revolution survive Fidel? Not unless Castro implemented sweeping reforms—and soon. The Cuban leader could still resort to his reform-minded aides and Cuba's moderate human rights leaders—people like Gustavo Arcos and Elizardo Sanchez—to work out a peaceful transition to democratic socialism. But time was running out—fast. The Fourth Congress of the Communist Party had marked a turning point for large numbers of Cubans who had hoped for economic and political reforms. Cuba's socialist experiment had long been in bad health. Now, it was under intensive care. Barring a major American or Cuban-exile initiative that would revive nationalistic fervor on the island, its death was near. The Comandante would be able to muddle through and stretch his final hour for a few months, perhaps even a few years, but his socialist dream was doomed.

---

* *In January 1992, the arrest of three armed Miami Cuban exiles who had sneaked into Cuba to carry out terrorist actions played right into Castro's hand. The three—Daniel Santovenia, thirty-seven, Pedro de la Caridad Alvarez, twenty-six, and Eduardo Diaz Betancourt, thirty-six, had been arrested with explosives, rifles and pistols after their landing near the western city of Cárdenas. After the exiles confessed they were part of radical Miami exile leader Tony Cuesta's "Commandos L" paramilitary group, Castro had them sentenced to death, and summoned the country to a maximum state of alert to defend the revolution. He was further helped by Miami Cuban exile radio station WAQI-AM's January 1992 campaign for one hundred thousand signatures to demand that the U.S. government allow the renewal of exile military operations against the Cuban regime. The new exile terrorist expedition and the Miami radio station's campaign gave ammunition to the Cuban regime's claims that the CIA was mounting a new armed offensive against Cuba using both Miami exiles and dissidents on the island. The Cuban regime cited the new events to justify an escalating crackdown on dissidents in early 1992.*

Fidel Castro had closed the doors to a transition that would have kept the achievements of his revolution alive—Cuba's health care, its education and sense of national dignity. Instead, he was setting the stage for a radical reaction against all he had stood for. As time went by, whatever reforms he planned to adopt later were likely to be too little, too late.

Castro's failure to respond imaginatively—and boldly—to the extraordinary events that shook Cuba in the early nineties marked the demise of a revolution that had once seemed firmly entrenched in the Cuban soul. Surely the principles at the core of Fidel's "sacred" revolution had been quashed, along with the lives of his executed military aides. The Cuban leader's rejection of plans for a political opening at the Fourth Congress would bury most Cubans' hopes of resurrecting them.

Cuba's tragedy in the aftermath of the Fourth Congress was that the longer Castro stuck to his "Socialism or Death," the more difficult a peaceful transition to democracy would be, and the less inconceivable it was that a right-wing *caudillo* would take office with the backing of the Cuban people in a not-so-distant future. As months went by and Fidel clung to his old dogmas, what had been highly unlikely only a few years earlier became increasingly possible—that Castro would go down in history not as the idealist who started Cuba's social revolution, but as the man who destroyed it.

"Esto ya se cayó; estamos en el papeleo," a man on the street told me toward the end of my last trip to Cuba. "This has already gone under; we're just going through the paperwork."

Epilogue

New developments have shaken Cuba—and U.S.–Cuban relations—since this book's first edition was published in mid–1992. A Democratic Administration took office in the United States and faced the challenge of deciding whether to change three decades of hardline U.S. policies on Cuba. Its dilemma was greater than that of its predecessors: it realized that thirty-four years of hawkish U.S. policies on Cuba had failed to unseat Fidel Castro, yet it feared that, at a time when Cuba went through its worst crisis ever, easing U.S. sanctions posed the risk of rescuing Castro from imminent political death.

In the closing pages of *Castro's Final Hour*, I wrote that the Cuban revolution's mystique was gone, and that Castro's economic survival program to save communism with a small dose of capitalism was doomed. My conclusions stand.

In fact, the Cuban economy has deteriorated at a faster pace than I anticipated. Cuba's foreign income collapsed from $8.1 billion in 1989 to $2.2 billion in 1992, according to Cuban government figures, and was likely to fall even further in 1993. Trade with Latin America and China, which officials had hoped would replace part of Cuba's former commerce with the Soviet bloc, remained marginal, with little chance of growing.

Cuba's global social product, the regime's version of the gross domestic product, fell by 24 percent in 1991 and by another 15 percent in 1992, and was projected to continue falling in 1993, according to the Communist Party's Centro de Estudios Sobre America (CEA) in Havana. Despite efforts to diversify the country's income, traditional exports such as sugar and tobacco continued accounting for 90 percent of Cuba's foreign income.

Sugar, which accounted for more than 65 percent of Cuba's foreign income, faced a disastrous year in 1993. "The sugar industry cannot remember a more troubled crop since the beginning of the revolution," said Pedro Ross Leal, head of the Cuban Workers' Union (CTC), in a speech broadcast by Radio Rebelde in early 1993. "Today, tens of sugar mills have their machines idle because of shortages of oil, tires, lubricants and other raw materials." A few months later, Cuba announced it would be unable to fulfill its commitments to foreign clients, citing torrential rains that had severely damaged the harvest. Cuban officials conceded that sugar production had fallen from 7 million tons in 1992 to 4.2 million tons in 1993—the worst harvest in thirty years.

Tourism, the only bright spot in Cuba's economy, was far from making up for even a slight portion of the Soviet bloc subsidies Cuba had lost since 1989. Foreign investments, while making headlines overseas—the Italian clothing firm Benetton opened several only-for-tourists shops in Havana with great fanfare in 1993—were few and relatively small. Havana's CEA projections indicated that tourism and foreign investments would account, at best, for 30 percent of Cuba's foreign income by 1995. This, according to the Communist Party think tank, would be "nearly 40 percent below a minimum level of imports necessary for a normal functioning of the economy."

The regime's attempt to save communism with islands of capitalism offered no hope of resurrecting the country's economy. Living conditions, already dreadful in my last trips to the island in late 1991, continued to deteriorate. Government rations of milk and meat were in shorter supply than ever. A chicken on the black market cost 120 pesos—a month's salary for an office worker. The Havana office of the United Nations Children's Fund (UNICEF) was reporting in early 1993 that 50 percent of children between six months and a year suffered from anemia due to lack of vitamins. An epidemic of a progressive eye disease, linked to Vitamin B complex deficiencies, swept through the island. Thousands lost their ability to perceive color, and many victims face the possibility of losing their sight completely.

Daily blackouts left Havana in the dark on most nights. Prostitution in the streets reached record highs.

Only a drastic acceleration of market-oriented reforms could save the Cuban economy. But Castro kept delaying radical reforms, fearing that if the government ceased to be the only employer in town, it would lose political control over the population. If the regime allowed people to work privately, how could it coerce them to attend Castro's speeches or to spend months in the countryside performing "voluntary work"? Workers who no longer depended on the state for their livelihood were likely to be increasingly independent minded. Castro had watched it happen in Eastern Europe and did not want it to happen in Cuba.

In mid-1993, there were indications that the Cuban economy would soon hit rock bottom and that Castro might have no choice but to allow Cubans to hold U.S. dollars in hopes that Miami exiles would send up to $1 billion a year in remittances to their relatives on the island. The move, if adopted, was likely to stop temporarily the Cuban economy's free-fall, but at a tremendous political cost.

A rapidly growing private sector—who would stay at a government job paying the equivalent of $3 a month, if one could get much more than that from a relative in Miami without breaking the law?—was likely to undermine the regime's political control. Also, the "dollarization" threatened to reward Cubans with relatives abroad—who happened to be the most "disaffected" part of Cuba's population—and to punish revoluntionary families who did not have relatives abroad or had broken ties with them, and would now find themselves working for the state for worthless Cuban pesos. If Castro stuck to his Socialism-or-Death strategy, he faced economic collapse; if he further opened the doors to capitalism, he faced political turbulence.

In an effort to stop Cuba's economic collapse, Castro extended several olive branches to the Clinton Administration in early 1993. In an ABC network interview aired March 4, 1993, Castro said: "I am under the impression that Clinton is a man of peace. I also have the impression that he is a man with an ethic." Days earlier, the sixty-six-year-old Cuban leader suggested he may resign when his upcoming five-year term as president of the Council of State expires in 1998. He told a press conference with foreign reporters in Santiago de Cuba that "even marathon runners get tired" and that he would like to step down in five years' time. It was the first time Castro had put a time frame on his possible retirement.

"Although I consider myself a slave of duty, a slave of the revolution, I hope that conditions in five years' time will be different from now," Castro said at the February 24 press conference. "But even if there still existed a special period (in five years' time) I hope that my compatriots will understand that others can do the same, or better, or much better than I can."

At the time of this writing, the Clinton Administration had its hands full trying to pass its domestic economic package through Congress and had not given serious thought to Cuba. Short of striking a massive oil deposit, Castro could not count on any quick way out of his predicament. Time did not work in his favor: the more the Clinton Administration delayed a review of U.S. policy on Cuba that could lead to a partial lifting of the trade embargo, the closer it came to the U.S. 1994 congressional election—when the Cuban issue would once again be influenced by domestic political considerations and subject to pressure from Cuban exiles.

<>

The Castro regime could only take some solace from isolated propaganda victories—some of them courtesy of the U.S. government. In October 1992, in the closing days of the Bush Administration, Congress approved the Cuban Democracy Act championed by the Cuban American National Foundation (CANF). Also known as the Torricelli Law, it tightened the U.S. embargo on Cuba. It also gave the Castro regime a much-needed excuse to mount a new propaganda offensive in Europe and Latin America against what it termed a new act of "U.S. aggression."

Among the key provisions of the law, which was sponsored by Congressman Robert Torricelli (D-N.J.), was a prohibition on foreign subsidiaries of U.S. companies from undertaking new trade with Cuba. The law also prohibited vessels that trade with Cuba from loading or unloading cargo in the United States within 180 days after calling on Cuban ports, unless granted a special exemption by the U.S. secretary of the treasury.

In a section that reminded many Cubans of the worst days of U.S. meddling in the island's internal affairs, the law establishes specific measures a post-Castro regime will have to follow before becoming eligible for a resumption of U.S. trade and aid. It prohibits lifting the U.S. trade embargo until *after* Cuba holds free and fair elections (a provision that would hurt rather than help any Castro successor in his critical first weeks in power) and until the new government moves "toward establishing a free market economic system." In Cuba, where most people still wanted a democratic socialism that would preserve free health and education systems, this language fell like a cold shower. Even Cuba's Roman Catholic bishops, who had become increasingly outspoken in their criticism of the Castro regime, signed a statement October 3, 1992, declaring their opposition to the new law.

Sponsors of the Torricelli Law said the new legislation would cost Cuba up to $700 million a year in lost business, although skeptics noted that the Castro regime could circumvent the new restrictions with relative ease through third-country shell corporations.

"I'm very, very happy," an exultant CANF president Jorge Mas Canosa said hours after the signing. "It's a historic day for Cuba. I think the countdown for the end of Castro's days in power has really begun."

As soon as the Torricelli Law was passed, Latin American and European countries rallied behind Cuba. On November 24, 1992, the United Nations General Assembly voted overwhelmingly for a Cuban resolution criticizing the Torricelli Law. By a vote of fifty-nine to three, with seventy-one abstentions, the U.N. called on all countries to repeal laws that interfere with "the freedom of trade and naviga- tion" between sovereign nations. Only the United States, Israel and Romania voted against the resolution.

In Cuba, the regime mounted one of its biggest propaganda cam- paigns in years, encouraging street protests against the new law and railing against it in front-page editorials and broadcasts. European and Latin American media that in recent months had begun to focus on Cuba's human rights abuses were once again shifting their attention to Cuba's David-versus-Goliath struggle with the United States. For a few months, Cuba succeeded in shifting the focus of the debate onto the U.S.–Cuba confrontation, away from Cuba's failure to re- spect fundamental freedoms.

In the United States, Republican and Democratic politicians backed the Torricelli Law—as most previous U.S. initiatives dealing with Cuba—with an eye to pleasing conservative Cuban exile leaders. Clinton had backed the Torricelli bill throughout his presidential campaign. In fact, in an effort to woo Miami's Cuban exile leaders away from the Republican Party, he endorsed it even before Presi- dent Bush did.

At an April 1992 fund-raiser in Miami's Cuban-exile Victor's Cafe restaurant, at which he netted $125,000 for his campaign, Clinton said: "I think this administration has missed a big opportunity to put the hammer down on Fidel Castro and Cuba." He added, "I have read the Torricelli-Graham bill, and I like it"—the bill's cosponsor was Senator Bob Graham (D-Fl.). Bush, who in the closing days of the campaign faced the possibility of losing Florida's twenty-five electoral votes, dropped his initial reservations to the bill and signed it at a partisan party in Miami October 23.

Cubans on the island reacted with characteristic black humor to what they saw as the twin evils of tighter U.S. sanctions and Castro's refusal to allow democratic reforms. A joke making the rounds in Havana went like this: Two planes, one carrying Castro and one carrying Clinton, crash in midair. Who is saved? The answer: eleven million Cubans.

<><>

An additional domestic propaganda boost for the Cuban regime came from stepped-up exile paramilitary attacks on Cuban territory. The Miami-based group Comandos L—whose December 1991 raid into Cuba resulted in the arrest of three of its members and the execution of one of them—approached the Cuban coast October 7, 1992, and strafed the Spanish-owned Melia Varadero Hotel with automatic gunfire. Alpha 66, another Miami-based paramilitary group, claimed similar incursions into Cuban territory and attacks on military targets. The incidents heightened tensions between Washington, D.C., and Havana, and fed the fears among many Cubans on the island about what would happen to them if hard-line anticommunist exiles took power.

Some of these attacks were known in advance—if not supported—by the Cuban regime. In November 1992, only a few weeks after the most-publicized exile raids on the island, it was revealed that one of the exile groups' leaders had met regularly with a Cuban official to discuss plans for exile commando raids on Cuba. The admission by Francisco Avila, of Alpha 66, confirmed what many already suspected—that the Cuban regime condoned, and perhaps even promoted, raids on the island to maintain the credibility of its claim that Cuba could not embark on a political opening as long as it faced outside aggression.

It all started when Avila turned up one day at Miami's WSCV Channel 51 with a seemingly fabulous tale: he had long been a double agent working for Alpha 66 and the Cuban government, and he wanted to come out in the open before the Castro regime's fall. Reporters challenged Avila to prove his story. A few days later, Avila walked into a Queens, New York, restaurant with a hidden microphone for a meeting with his Cuban contact, Carlos Manuel Collazo, who was the third secretary at Cuba's mission to the United Nations. Channel 51 also smuggled a hidden camera into the restaurant.

During the conversation, the two men discussed an upcoming raid on a hotel in Varadero. After the tape was put on the air, Avila said Cuba had given him money and weapons to organize Alpha 66 raids on Cuba, including $12,000 to buy a boat for the attacks. Collazo, the Cuban diplomat, was expelled from the United States by the Bush Administration hours after the tape was aired.

On February 24, 1993, Castro held his long-promised elections for the National Assembly of the People's Power. It was largely aimed at pacifying Cuba's anxious Latin American allies. In recent months, Castro's closest friends in Latin America—Mexico, Venezuela and Colombia—had sent strong signals of impatience over lack of democratic change in Cuba. Salinas, in an unprecedented move for a Mexican president, had received the CANF's Mas Canosa and the more moderate Cuban exile leader Carlos Alberto Montaner. Castro needed something to show his last Latin American supporters before the July 1993 summit of Ibero-American states in Brazil, where the Cuban issue was sure to come up.

In what the Cuban government billed as Cuba's first secret election in three decades, Cubans elected a new 589-member National Assembly. According to official figures, 95.2 percent of the Cuban people voted for the government ticket—and 99 percent for Castro's candidacy as deputy for Santiago de Cuba.

In fact, the election involved no real choice: candidates were nominated by party-controlled mass organizations, thus making it impossible for dissidents to run. The regime had backed off from its earlier promises during the Fourth Congress to hold open legislative elections where Castro critics would be allowed to run, and to keep the party out of the nomination process. Many voters were intimidated by rumors that antigovernment votes would be tracked to those who had cast them through ballots marked with invisible ink. Some voters told foreign reporters that, since the elections' final result was a foregone conclusion, it wasn't worth the risk to cast a blank protest vote.

The legislative elections did not help Castro prove he still enjoyed the support of the Cuban people, but they helped show that he could still coerce Cubans into doing his will. In interviews with U.S. reporters, Cuban officials stressed this was a clear sign that Castro was not going to fall—and that the United States should therefore change its Cuban policy. It was realpolitik at its worst: Cuba was no longer emphasizing the legitimacy of the Castro regime but the need of others to accommodate to the reality of a still-effective police state.

<><>

Predictably, the new National Assembly elected Castro on March 15, 1993, to a new five-year term as president of the Council of State by unanimous vote. Raúl Castro was again elected first vice-president of the Council of State, also by 100 percent of the vote.

In a shuffle of his inner circle, Castro promoted Lage to vice-president of the Council of State (replacing the octogenarian Carlos Rafael Rodriguez) and Ricardo Alarcón to president of the National Assembly (replacing Brig. Gen. Juan Escalona, the former chief prosecutor in the Ochoa–De La Guardia case). By now, Lage and Alarcón were the indisputable rising stars within Castro's inner circle.

The two took over much of the power held by Carlos Aldana, the former No. 3 man in the Castro regime. Aldana was abruptly fired from his key jobs as Communist Party ideology and foreign relations chief in September 1992 and expelled from the Party shortly thereafter. The official reason for his ouster was "major personal errors" and alleged illegal enrichment in his business deals with Eberto Lopez Morales, the Cuban representative for Sony, in the purchase of audiovisual equipment.

The near-unanimous interpretation in Havana diplomatic circles was that Aldana was fired because he had accumulated too much power. As in the case of Gen. Arnaldo Ochoa three years earlier, Aldana's ouster was turned into an exemplary lesson for other Cuban officials. In his only public appearance after his ouster—in a controlled interview with pro-Castro Mexican publisher and Olympic official Mario Vazquez Raña—Aldana stated that "in my work as director I fell into errors, into carelessness."

Unlike Ochoa, Aldana was not formally charged with any crime. He was allowed to go home and live under virtual house arrest as a non-person, ostracized from all centers of power. He was replaced in his Communist Party jobs by José Ramón Balaguer, a former ambassador to Moscow known for his absolute subservience.

Among other big-name departures from the Cuban hierarchy was that of Castro's son Fidel Castro Diaz-Balart, better known as Fidelito. He was fired as executive secretary of nuclear affairs at Cuba's Atomic Energy Commission for what his father described as "incompetence." Friends in Havana said Fidelito had first tendered his resignation to his father after heated discussions over Cuba's energy program and economic policies. Fidelito has since vanished from public view.

<>

Since I finished writing *Castro's Final Hour*, the Cuban leader also stepped up repression of government critics. Several of the dissidents I interviewed during my travels to Cuba were arrested in late 1992 and early 1993.

Yndamiro Restano, the journalist and founder of the opposition Harmony Movement, was arrested on charges of illicit association and instigating rebellion and sentenced to ten years in prison. His crime: delivering anti-government pamphlets. Sebastian Arcos Bergnes, brother of human rights leader Gustavo Arcos Bergnes and fellow member of the Cuba's Human Rights Committee (CCDH), was sentenced to four years and eight months in prison on charges of spreading enemy propaganda. Filmmakers Jorge Crespo Diaz and Marco A. Abad, whose film *An Average Day* had poked fun at the Castro regime, were sentenced to two years in prison each for their government criticism.

Elizardo Sanchez Santa Cruz, the leader of Cuba's Commission for Human Rights and National Reconciliation (CCDHRN), was attacked by a government-assembled mob and suffered cracked ribs and several bruises. He was detained for several days and released under an avalanche of international protests. His trial is pending at the time of this writing.

Former Gen. Patricio De La Guardia continued serving his thirty-year prison sentence, under harsher security conditions. Shortly after publication of my book, a handwritten letter by De La Guardia was published by the French daily *Le Monde*; in it he said his executed twin brother Tony De La Guardia's drug-trafficking activities had been authorized "at the highest levels."

In the letter, which was authenticated by Patricio De La Guardia's son Hector in the United States, the ousted general also reveals that former interior minister José Abrantes confessed to him that he had kept five hundred kilos of cocaine at the Cimeq Hospital in Havana for their sale on the international market. De La Guardia said he himself had not participated in the MININT drug-trafficking operation, and asked for a revision of his sentence.

The plea, directed at two Politburo members and obtained by *Le Monde*, was not taken into account, and De La Guardia's prison privileges—a television set, a fan and daily breathers at the prison's patio—were immediately withdrawn.

But as Castro put some of Cuba's top human rights leaders in jail, others—growing numbers of them with an impeccable revolutionary history—took their places. Vladimiro Roca, the son of Cuba's Communist Party founder Blas Roca and a former Soviet-trained Cuban air force fighter pilot, became a powerful spokesman for Elizardo Sanchez' CCDHRN. His 1992 break with the Castro regime became the talk of the town in Cuba. Like other democratic socialists, he presented disillusioned Communists on the island with a new alternative: demanding radical changes in Cuba without siding with those outside the island who favored a tighter U.S. embargo and continued U.S. possession of the Guantánamo Base.

Col. (Ret.) Alvaro Prendes, a war hero of the Cuban Revolution, joined Roca and Sanchez' Democratic Socialist Project on December 3, 1992, when he released an open letter to Castro in Havana calling for a national dialogue and an "economic opening." Prendes thus became the highest-ranking former military man to join active dissidence on the island. Born in 1926, he first became known when, as an air force pilot under late strongman Fulgencio Batista, he refused orders to bomb Castro rebel positions near Cienfuegos in 1957 and instead dropped his bombs in the sea. He was sentenced to fifteen years in prison. Two years later, he was released and made an instant hero by the Castro revolution. In 1961, he would become a revolutionary war hero for his combat role in the failed Bay of Pigs invasion. In early 1993, he was defying government-run Repudiation Acts in front of his Havana home and calling for a national dialogue between Cubans from all political factions—in Cuba and in exile—to end Cuba's drama.

Military defections rose substantially in 1992 and 1993, along with daring escapes by growing numbers of Cubans. In a major public relations embarrassment for the Cuban government, former Cuban air force major Orestes Lorenzo Perez, who had defected in a MiG combat plane in 1991, returned to Cuba December 19, 1992, in a small, two-engine Cessna without being detected by Cuba's radar system, and picked up his wife and two sons in a highway near Varadero.

Lorenzo's Hollywood-style landing and takeoff, his good looks and articulate speech, turned him into an instant talk-show personality in the United States—and into a hero for large numbers of Cubans on the island. Miami radio stations and Radio Martí filled the airwaves with Lorenzo interviews, which were followed with glee by Cubans on the island. In a country that venerates courage, many said about the thirty-six-year-old Lorenzo what they had once said about Castro: "Tiene cojones" (He's got guts).

<>

As this edition went to press, the pace of Cuba's economic and social demise was accelerating. Popular discontent was spreading, and the economy was deteriorating at growing speed. Only fear of the unknown—alarm that Miami exiles would descend on Cuba to reclaim their properties and take revenge against former *revolucionarios*, or that a capitalist Cuba would leave millions of unemployed, as was happening in Eastern Europe—prevented a popular rebellion. Only the failure of U.S policy makers and Cuban exile leaders to allay these fears and perhaps even to recognize some of the early social gains of the revolution kept the Cuban people from turning their discontent into active defiance.

More than ever, Castro's failure to renew his revolution made it more likely that it would not survive his time in power. Without communism to motivate people into sticking to *el proyecto*—the revolutionary project—Castro sounded increasingly like the head of a law-and-order military regime. By moving toward capitalism while refusing to adopt democratic reforms, he faced going down in history as just another Caribbean president for life.

As time went by, an increasingly disaffected Cuban population, including many who until recently had supported his revolution, was likely to seek a radical departure from the past. Whatever time Castro had left in power—whether it was a few months or the five years he was now suggesting for his possible retirement—his failure to change with the times seemed almost sure to condemn his once-acclaimed revolution to a lonely death.

Acknowledgments

Thanks to Lindsey Gruson, of the *New York Times*, who started it all by insisting that I write a book; Douglas C. Clifton and Pete Weitzel, the two top editors of the *Miami Herald*, who gave me the time to write it; Tom Shroder, editor of the *Miami Herald*'s Sunday "Tropic" magazine, who made excellent suggestions to liven up the manuscript, and Mark Seibel, the former *Miami Herald* foreign editor and the best content editor a foreign affairs writer could find.

Two people without whom this book wouldn't have been possible are Marie Arana-Ward, senior editor and vice president at Simon & Schuster, and Russell Galen, my agent at the Scott Meredith Literary Agency in New York. I want to thank both for believing in this project from the very start; and especially Marie Arana-Ward for her sharp questions and great editing—she helped me say what I wanted to say in a fraction of my original words.

For their help in my research, I wish to thank Mimi Whitefield of the *Miami Herald* and Pablo Alfonso of *El Nuevo Herald*, who have done the most consistent coverage of Cuba in any American newspaper, and French journalist Jean-François Fogel, one of the best-informed reporters on Cuban affairs. I am also grateful to José de Cordoba of the *Wall Street Journal*, Ramón Mestre of the *Miami Her-*

ald, Bertrand De La Grange of *Le Monde*, Rita Neubauer of the *Stuttgarter Zeitung*, Tomás Regalado of *Radio Mambí*, and Jorge Davila of *El Nuevo Herald* for their ideas and help in contacting people in Cuba and Miami.

Ambler H. Moss Jr., dean of the University of Miami's Graduate School of International Studies, and Jaime Suchlicki, executive director of the University of Miami's North-South Center, gave me access to the University's Cuban Affairs Library; Anthony Maingot, of Florida International University, added depth and historic perspective to the sections on José Martí in Chapter 4 and Cuba's racial relations in Chapter 11; Maria Cristina Herrera, of Miami-Dade Community College and the Institute of Cuban Studies, offered good advice throughout my research; and Ramón Cernuda, the Miami representative for Cuba's Commission for Human Rights and National Reconciliation, provided key contacts.

In Cuba, I am grateful to Alfredo "Chango" Muñoz-Unsain, the veteran Agence France Presse reporter, who outshines us all in knowledge about the Castro revolution. He guided me through the political minefield of the Cuban government bureaucracy. I also received precious collaboration from Bertrand Rosenthal, the Agence France Presse bureau chief in Havana; Pascal Fletcher, Reuters' bureau chief in Havana, and Andrei Kamorin, the correspondent of *Izvestia*, who are doing a first-class job under difficult circumstances. Luis Baez of *Prensa Latina* helped me in the early stages of my research, and Argentine journalist and rock musician Abel Gilbert was of great assistance in my last two trips to Cuba. Natalia Bolivar de Arostegui, Cuba's top expert on Afro-Cuban cults, provided key background on the Santería Gods discussed in Chapter 12.

Finally, I wish to thank more than a dozen Cuban government officials who opened doors to me, knowing I would write a critical book about Cuba's reality. For their own safety, I will not name them. They know who they are. Many of them are well-meaning, honest individuals, who I hope will play a role in a post-Castro era. They will probably feel compelled to criticize this book as long as Castro remains in power, but I am sure that—deep down—they will agree with most of my conclusions. I look forward to the day when we can again share a drink and compare notes.

Notes

CHAPTER 1

Description of the execution: Partly based on author's interviews in Havana (April 12, 1991, and November 8, 1991) with former chief prosecutor Div. Gen. Juan Escalona Reguera, who was present at the scene. Other details were provided by Ochoa's wife, Maida Gonzalez, Ochoa's friend Norberto Fuentes, and more than half a dozen relatives of the executed officers, who obtained the information from the military doctors and other witnesses.

Fidel's statement, "Murió como un hombre": from author's interviews with two senior Cuban officials in Havana, and with a Western European ambassador to Cuba, who said he heard it directly from Fidel.

Reinaldo Ruiz background, financial schemes, visa business in Panama, feelings toward Cuba, first meetings with cousin Miguel Ruiz Poo: from more than a dozen interviews and three letter exchanges between the author and Reinaldo Ruiz between January 1990 and Ruiz's death on December 31, 1990.

"Switching from computers to drugs wasn't that big a leap": from author's telephone interview with Reinaldo Ruiz on April 24, 1990, and Miguel Ruiz Poo's statements during trial, in trial transcripts reproduced in *Causa No. 1: Fin de la Conexión Cubana*, Havana: Editorial José Martí, 1989, page 238. Ruiz Poo said in his trial that the suggestion came first from his cousin Reinaldo Ruiz; Reinaldo Ruiz hinted to me that it came from his cousin Ruiz Poo.

Reinaldo Ruiz's trip to Cuba, first meeting with Tony De La Guardia, conversation during boating trip: from author's interviews with Reinaldo Ruiz on April 24 and May 16, 1990. Also, from trial transcripts *Causa No.1: Fin de la Conexión Cubana*.

Rubén Ruiz's visit to Santa Clara airstrip, meeting with Interior Ministry officials, promises that "you have the Revolutionary Air Force at your disposal": from DEA's secret videotapes of Rubén Ruiz's conversations with pilot Hu Chang, copies of which were given to me in 1990 by the U.S. District Court, Southern District of Florida.

Tony De La Guardia's lifestyle, visit to the United States, childhood stories, arrest for gunrunning: from author's interviews with Bernardo Benes in Miami, March 9, 1990; Max Lesnik in Miami, April 17, 1990; Ignacio Elso in Miami, April 17, 1990 and January 9, 1991; Franz Arango in Miami, April 17, 1990; and Nestor Suarez in Fort Lauderdale, Florida, April 25, 1990.

De La Guardia brothers' first meeting with Fidel Castro at Varadero regatta, lunch at Castro's house in Varadero: from author's interview with Rolando Cubela in Madrid, Spain, April 24, 1990, and Cubela tape recalling the incident.

Tony De La Guardia's assignment to bomb the United Nations: *Proa a la Libertad*, Rafael del Pino, Mexico: Editorial Planeta, page 428. Also, author's interview with De La Guardia's friend and well-known novelist Norberto Fuentes, April 3, 1991, in Havana.

Tony De La Guardia's covert operations in Chile, Switzerland, Batista kidnapping plan, Jamaica and Nicaragua: from a De La Guardia family member with personal knowledge of De La Guardia's involvement in these operations. Argentina's Montonero guerrilla leader Mario Firmenich has said the ransom money was later deposited at the Banco Nacional de Cuba in Havana ("The Curious Case of the Guerrilla Gold," Guy Gugliotta, *Miami Herald*, November 11, 1989).

Raúl Castro's meeting with Carlos Lehder, Cuba's involvement with Medellín cartel to fly weapons for M-19 guerrillas: "Lehder: Cuba Cleared Drug Flights," *Miami Herald*, November 21, 1991.

The 1984 Noriega-Castro meeting in Havana: this has been described at length by, among others, former Noriega aides José Blandón and Felipe Camargo, as well as by convicted Colombian drug trafficker Carlos Lehder. Author's account of the meeting is largely based on interviews with José Blandón in New York, December 1987, and Felipe Camargo, at the El Renacer prison in Panama, May 23, 1990.

Ruiz's first cocaine shipment through Cuba, trouble with U.S. Coast Guard, landing in Fort Lauderdale: from author's interviews with Reinaldo

Ruiz, April 24 and May 16, 1990, DEA agent Gene Francar in Miami, May 7 and 17, 1990, and U.S. Customs agent in Miami, July 1990.

Reinaldo Ruiz contact with Hu Chang, Chang's background, airport-misunderstanding anecdote: from author's interviews with DEA agent Gene Francar in Miami, May 7 and 17, 1990, author's interview with Reinaldo Ruiz, May 16, 1990, and U.S. District Court, Southern District of Florida, indictment against Reinaldo Ruiz, Case No. 88-127-CR.

Quotes from DEA's videotapes of Reinaldo Ruiz and Rubén Ruiz's conversations at Chang's office: from the DEA's secret videotapes, copies of which were given to me in 1990 by the U.S. District Court, Southern District of Florida.

Reinaldo Ruiz's detention, efforts to contact Cuba: from author's interviews with Reinaldo Ruiz, April 24, 1990, Colette Ruiz, June 8, 1990, and DEA agent Gene Francar, May 7, 1990.

CHAPTER 2

Colette Ruiz's telephone calls to Havana and to the Cuban Interests Section at the Czechoslovakian embassy in Washington, loneliness in Miami, etc.: from author's interviews with Colette Ruiz, June 8 and July 11, 1990; Southern Bell Telephone records of February 23, 1990; and Reinaldo Ruiz letter to the author, June 6, 1990.

Colette's phone threats, quote, "You're a bunch of bastards": from author's interview with Colette Ruiz, June 8, 1990. Also, interviews with Reinaldo Ruiz and Gene Francar of DEA, May 17, 1990.

Felix's trips to Cuba, messages from Reinaldo Ruiz and Miguel Ruiz Poo: from author's interviews with Reinaldo Ruiz in 1989 and 1990, Reinaldo Ruiz's letter to the author, June 6, 1990, and telephone interview with Felix, August 9, 1990.

José Luis Llovio Menéndez call to the FBI: author's interview with Llovio Menéndez, March 17, 1990 in Miami, and July 18, 1990, telephone interview from New York.

Felix, Colette Ruiz meeting, Colette's phone calls, etc.: from author's interviews with Colette Ruiz, June 8 and July 11, 1990, and author's interview with Felix, August 1990.

Miguel Ruiz Poo and Tony De La Guardia's plans to defect: from author's interviews with Reinaldo Ruiz, Colette Ruiz, DEA agent Gene Francar, all of whom said, in separate interviews, they had been told by Felix of Ruiz's plans to defect. Felix confirmed the story in interview with author, December 23, 1991.

Tension between MINFAR and MININT: author's interview with Gen. Rafael del Pino, and *El Nuevo Herald*, July 12, 1987. Troop figures, from *Cuban Leadership After Castro, Biographies of Cuba's Top Generals*, Rafael Fermoselle, Miami: Ediciones Universal, 1987.

Division General Abrantes's purchase of 1,300 Lada cars from Panama: Havana television, August 29, 1989, reproduced in U.S. State Department Foreign Broadcast Information Service—Latin America, August 31, 1989, page 2. Raúl Castro's complaint to Fidel about it, author's interview with a top Raúl Castro aide familiar with the case, Havana, April 15, 1990.

Division General Abrantes speech to the Union of Cuban Writers and Artists (UNEAC): *Granma*, March 24, 1989.

Raúl and Fidel Castro's investigations, radio counterintelligence reports, dossier received by Abrantes: from Fidel Castro's speech to the Council of State, July 9, 1989, U.S. State Department Foreign Broadcast Information Service—Latin America, July 13, 1989.

Miguel Ruiz Poo begged his boss, "Tony, please, turn in everything, down to the last cent": from trial transcripts as quoted in *Causa No. 1: Fin de la Conexión Cubana*, Havana: Editorial José Martí, 1989, pages 247 and 253.

Raúl Castro's orders to wiretap party at Torralba's house: from sources close to Cuba's Interior Ministry, and handwritten letter from one of the alleged agents who placed the wiretaps. Party description based on account of two people who attended it.

Operation Greyhound: Based on author's interviews with DEA agent Gene Francar, May 7 and 17, 1990; U.S. Customs Special Agent in Charge Leon Guinn, June 21, 1990; U.S. Customs Special Agent Patrick O'Brien, June 19, 1991; former U.S. Customs Commissioner William Von Raab, June 18, 1991; former U.S. Customs Agent David Urso, July 25, 1991; U.S. Assistant District Attorney Thomas Mulvihill, August 20, 1991, and others. Also, see Carl Hiaasen, the *Miami Herald*, citing Lucy Morgan of the *St. Petersburg Times*, July 19, 1989.

David Urso indictment: the *Miami Herald*, August 23, 1989.

Classified report on Operation Greyhound: it was dated in early June 1989, four months after the original draft from Urso in Miami. The report reached the desk of the special U.S. agent in charge of the Miami office on June 13, 1990, but was written a few days earlier, according to customs officials.

Ochoa's childhood, military campaigns, car anecdote, exchange of cars with Sandinista army major Joaquin Cuadra: author's interview with Ochoa's widow, Maida Gonzalez de Ochoa, in Havana, October 12, 1990. Also, author's interviews with Ochoa's best friend, writer Norberto Fuentes, in Havana, April 30 and November 3, 1991, and an Ochoa relative in Miami.

Ochoa's business deals, Nicaraguan arms purchase, Angolan radio, black market Candonga operations in Angola: from trial transcripts as appeared in *Causa No. 1: Fin de la Conexión Cubana*, Havana: Editorial José Martí, 1989, pages 89–138; and U.S. State Department Foreign Broadcast Information Service—Latin America, June 29, 1989, pages 17 and

19; and Captain Martinez Valdes testimony, U.S. State Department Foreign Broadcast Information Service—Latin America, July 6, 1989, page 16.

Ochoa's predecessors had been shipping diamonds, ivory, etc., to Europe for ten years: Gen. Rafael del Pino, "Cuba Situation Report," Office of Research for Radio Martí, May–August 1989, page 86.

De La Guardia's meeting with Llicas in Havana, machine description, Captain Llicas testimony: U.S. State Department Foreign Broadcast Information Service—Latin America, June 29, 1989, page 19.

$200,000 in Panama bank account: from trial transcripts as appeared in *Causa No. 1: Fin de la Conexión Cubana*, Havana: Editorial José Martí, 1989, page 92.

Martinez Valdes meetings with Colombian drug traffickers in Havana: from Martinez Valdes testimony, U.S. State Department Foreign Broadcast Information Service—Latin America, July 6, 1989, pages 21–23.

Padrón quote, "That's unthinkable": U.S. State Department Foreign Broadcast Information Service—Latin America, July 6, 1989, pages 21–23.

Fidel Castro spent 80 percent of his time on Angola: Castro speech before Council of State, July 9, 1989, U.S. State Department Foreign Broadcast Information Service—Latin America, July 13, 1989, page 9.

Castro's quotes, "The fate of the revolution . . ." and "For the soldiers, even candy . . .": from Castro's speech to the Council of State, July 9, 1989, as quoted in *Causa No. 1: Fin de la Conexión Cubana*, Havana: Editorial José Martí, 1989, page 443, and U.S. State Department Foreign Broadcast Information Service—Latin America, July 13, 1989, page 9.

Fidel's secret cables to Ochoa in Angola, December 2 and 20, 1987; January 26 and February 15, 1988: from Fidel Castro's address to the Council of State, July 9, 1989, as quoted in *Causa No. 1: Fin de la Conexión Cubana*, Havana: Editorial José Martí, pages 430, 431; also, see U.S. State Department Foreign Broadcast Information Service—Latin America, July 13, 1989, pages 4–6.

Ochoa remarks at dinner party in Luanda, "Fidel has gone crazy": author's interview with Maria Isabel "Cucusa" De La Guardia in Havana, September 6, 1991.

Granma on nine Cuban generals signing Namibia agreement at United Nations: *Granma*, December 21, 1988.

Ochoa's return to Havana, disappointment with future life in Cuba, sympathy for unhappy Angola veterans, etc.: author's interview with Ochoa's widow, Maida Gonzalez de Ochoa, in Havana, October 12, 1990.

Ochoa's nomination had been approved by the Central Commission of Cadres, the Central Committee and Fidel Castro: see Raúl Castro speech to the Western Army, June 14, 1989, U.S. State Department Foreign Broadcast Information Service—Latin America, June 20, 1989, page 6.

Discovery of alleged sex scandal involving Ochoa and Patricio De La

Guardia, claims of young woman returning from Angola, letter from angry mother, etc.: from Fidel Castro's address to the Council of State, July 9, 1989 ("We found . . . irrefutable and unquestionable evidence of the immoralities in which Ochoa and one of the De La Guardia brothers were involved . . . We found out that one girl who had attended one of the parties was disguised as an internationalist combatant . . . In February 1989, the girl began talking about certain things"). U.S. State Department Foreign Broadcast Information Service—Latin America, July 13, 1989, page 19. Also, author's interview with Maida Gonzalez de Ochoa, Maria Isabel De La Guardia and four other sources familiar with the incident in Havana in 1990 and 1991.

Raúl Castro summoned Ochoa to his office on May 29, 1989: from Raúl Castro's address to the military tribunal, June 24, 1989, U.S. State Department Foreign Broadcast Information Service—Latin America, June 27, 1989, page 3; Raúl Castro's address to the Western Army, June 20, 1989; and author's interview with Ochoa's widow, Maida Gonzalez de Ochoa, who talked with her husband after the meeting, in Havana, October 12, 1990.

Raúl Castro's quotes, "I calmed down. I drank a cup of tea" and "Look, Fidel is our father": Raúl Castro speech to Western army, June 14, 1989, U.S. State Department Foreign Broadcast Information Service—Latin America, June 20, 1989, pages 17–18.

Raúl Castro feared a possible defection: from Raúl Castro's address to the military tribunal June 26, 1989 (". . . which led us to fear that he may desert"), U.S. State Department Foreign Broadcast Information Service—Latin America, June 27, 1989, page 4.

Raúl Castro had ordered surveillance of Ochoa earlier: see "Cuba Situation Report," Office of Research for Radio Martí, May–August 1989, page 72; also *Granma*, July 8, 1989.

Raúl Castro's quote, "No matter what happens, today, tomorrow . . .": Raúl Castro speech to Western Army, June 14, 1989, U.S. State Department Foreign Broadcast Information Service—Latin America, June 20, 1989.

Ochoa's arrest, June 9 meeting with Raúl Castro: from Fidel Castro's speech to the Council of State, July 9, 1989, Raúl Castro's speech to the Western Army, June 14, 1989, U.S. State Department Foreign Broadcast Information Service—Latin America, June 20, 1989, and author's interview with Ochoa's widow, Maida Gonzalez de Ochoa, who saw her husband after the meeting, in Havana, October 12, 1990.

Fidel Castro's plan to consolidate the Ochoa and De La Guardia cases: from more than half a dozen sources with access to the Cuban military and Interior Ministry investigations into the Ochoa–De La Guardia affair, in Havana, 1990–1991. Also, see passages of Fidel Castro's July 9, 1989, address to Council of State, in footnote on page 94.

Division General Ochoa's first days in custody were marked by confusion: from author's interviews with Ochoa's widow, Maida Gonzalez de Ochoa, October 12, 1990, and Maria Isabel "Cucusa" De La Guardia, April 3 and September 6, 1991, both of whom talked to Ochoa before his second, definitive arrest.

Ochoa and the De La Guardia brothers near-escape on June 12, 1989: from author's interviews with Maria Isabel "Cucusa" De La Guardia, April 3 and September 6, 1991, who was told the story by her husband, Patricio. Also, interview with two other close relatives of Tony De La Guardia, who visited with him in prison before his death.

The De La Guardias' birthday party, Patricio's quote, "Don't worry, Cucusa . .": author's interview with Maria Isabel "Cucusa" De La Guardia, April 3, 1991, in Havana.

Granma's report on arrests of Ochoa, Tony and Patricio De La Guardia: *Granma*, June 22. *Granma* quote on the inexorable weight of justice: *Granma*, June 16, 1989.

Fidel Castro's public letter to the prosecutor in Rolando Cubela's trial: quoted in *Insider: My Hidden Life as a Revolutionary in Cuba*, José Luis Llovio Menéndez, New York: Bantam Books, 1988, page 139.

CHAPTER 3

Gabriel García Márquez getting the news of Ochoa–De La Guardia arrests, preparing trip to Cuba, relationship with Fidel Castro, discussion with Castro on Perestroika: from author's interviews with García Márquez in Bogotá, Colombia, April 4 and 5, 1990.

García Márquez's Mercedes-Benz, four maids, driver, etc.: from author's interview with former García Márquez secretary Antonio Valle Vallejo, December 15, 1990, and two sources close to the novelist in Havana.

Raúl Castro's address to the Western Army: U.S. State Department Foreign Broadcast Information Service—Latin America, June 20, 1989, pages 5–21.

General Del Pino's statement that an "uprising" had taken place: "Narcotrafico o Purga Politica?" *El Nuevo Herald*, June 25, 1989. Barnett bank, 15 percent drop in real estate, Alpha 66 training in Everglades, etc.: Sandra Dibble, *El Nuevo Herald*, March 12, 1990.

Fidel and Raúl Castro spent nearly seven days at MINFAR building since the moment of Ochoa's arrest, reports from Cuba's counterintelligence, raids of homes: from Fidel Castro's speech to the Council of State, U.S. State Department Foreign Broadcast Information Service—Latin America, July 13, 1989.

Visit by Major Pino to Villa Marista on eve of trial, promises of leniency: from author's interview with Maria Isabel "Cucusa" De La Guardia in Havana on September 6, 1991, and Tony's daughter, Ileana De La Guardia, on October 5, 1991, in telephone interview from Paris. Both women saw Patricio and Tony De La Guardia in prison several times after the visit by Major Pino.

Ochoa's quotes before military tribunal: *Granma*, June 28, 1989, and trial transcripts as appeared in *Causa No. 1: Fin de la Conexión Cubana*, Havana: Editorial José Martí, 1989, pages 56–61; and U.S. State Department Foreign Broadcast Information Service—Latin America, July 3, 1989, pages 3–16.

Fidel Castro's visit to Tony De La Guardia's cell, promise of leniency: from author's interview with Tony De La Guardia's daughter, Ileana, from Paris, October 5, 1991. Ileana De La Guardia says she was told the story by her father in one of her visits to his jail before the execution. The story was confirmed by Patricio De La Guardia through his wife, Maria Isabel, in interviews with author in Havana, April 2 and September 6, 1991.

Captain Ruiz Poo's statement that operations had been approved "at the highest levels," and his subsequent disclaimer: from trial transcripts as appeared in *Causa No. 1: Fin de la Conexión Cubana*, Havana: Editorial José Martí, 1989, pages 244–255.

Marilena and Maria Isabel "Cucusa" De La Guardia interrupting proceedings with shouts, insults: author's interview with Maria Isabel "Cucusa" De La Guardia, in Havana, April 3, 1991, and one other source who witnessed the incident.

Ruben D'Toste defense attorney statements: Joint Publications Research Service—Latin America, July 25, 1989, page 162, quoted in *Proa a la Libertad*, Gen. Rafael del Pino, Mexico: Editorial Planeta, page 392.

Prosecutor Escalona's closing remarks, final verdict: *Causa No. 1: Fin de la Conexión Cubana*, Havana: Editorial José Martí, 1989, pages 325–343; and U.S. State Department Foreign Broadcast Information Service—Latin America, July 11, 1989, pages 3–10.

Ileana De La Guardia on visit to García Márquez house: "Asi Fusiló Fidel a mi padre," Ileana De La Guardia interview with Spanish daily *El Mundo*, September 29, 1991, confirmed by Ileana De La Guardia in interview with author, October 5, 1991.

Fidel Castro's visit to García Márquez House after the death sentences were handed down, dialogue between novelist and Castro: from author's interviews with García Márquez in Bogotá, Colombia, April 4 and 5, 1990.

Council of State meeting, statements, Raúl Castro and Fidel Castro speeches: *Causa No. 1, Fin de la Conexión Cubana*, Havana: Editorial José Martí, 1989, pages 370–481; and U.S. State Department Foreign Broadcast Information Service—Latin America, July 13, 1989, pages 1–26.

García Márquez returns to Havana, painting anecdote: author's interviews with Gabriel García Márquez in Bogotá, Colombia, April 4 and 5, 1990.

Maida Ochoa's statements on conspiracy theory, Ochoa's political thinking: author's interview with Maida Gonzalez de Ochoa in Havana, October 12, 1990.

Ochoa's death certificate, as told by Maida Ochoa to the Spanish daily *El Mundo*; see "Quiero que Castro me devuelva el cadaver de mi esposo," October 11, 1991.

Div. Gen. José Abrantes's death in prison: from author's interviews with friends of the Abrantes family in Havana, 1990 and 1991, and author's interview with Maria Isabel "Cucusa" De La Guardia, whose husband Patricio was in the same prison with Abrantes, in Havana, September 6 and November 3, 1991.

Abrantes's statement that he had authorized Tony De La Guardia's first drug shipments: author's interview with Maria Isabel "Cucusa" De La Guardia, September 6 and November 3, 1991.

Escalona's quote, "We had to do it . . . ": author's interview with Juan Escalona in Havana, April 12, 1991.

CHAPTER 4

Raúl Castro's statements, "even the smallest signs . . ." and "We need . . . a continuous and systematic national purge": from Raúl Castro speech to the Council of State, July 9, 1991, in *Causa No. 1: Fin de la Conexión Cubana*, Havana: Editorial José Martí, 1989, page 422; and U.S. State Department Foreign Broadcast Information Service—Latin America, July 19, 1989, page 22.

Fidel Castro's quote, "Now that capitalists and imperialists . . .": from Castro's November 7, 1989, speech at the dedication of the construction materials factory Juan Roberto Milian, as quoted in *Rectificación*, Havana: Editora Politica, 1990, page 109.

Fidel Castro's statement that Cuba "will carry out the role that history has assigned to us": from December 7, 1989, speech to internationalist troops, as quoted in *Rectificación*, Havana: Editora Politica, 1990, page 115.

José Martí statement, "A mistake in Cuba . . .": Martí speech published in *Patria*, April 17, 1894, reprinted in *Letras Fieras*, José Martí, Havana: Editorial Letras Cubanas, 1985, page 117. Martí's assertion that Cuba's freedom would help preserve "the equilibrium of the world": from *José Martí: Obras Completas*, Havana: Editorial Nacional de Cuba, 1963–1973, volume IV, page 111.

Chibás suicide: from *Fidel: A Critical Portrait*, Tad Szulc, New York: Avon Books, 1986, pages 209–211; and *Guerrilla Prince*, Georgie Anne Geyer, Boston: Little, Brown and Company, 1991, pages 86–88.

Anecdote of Fidel Castro in cane field: from *Fidel: A Critical Portrait*, Tad Szulc, New York: Avon Books, 1986, pages 13–14.

There were about 22,000 African, Asian and Latin American students in

Cuba on fellowships: Fidel Castro in interview with Italian journalist Gianni Mina, in *Habla Fidel*, Buenos Aires: Editorial Sudamericana, 1988, page 106.

Fidel Castro himself had admitted to holding about 800 political prisoners: from *Habla Fidel*, Gianni Mina, Buenos Aires: Editorial Sudamericana, 1988, page 84. Mina's interview with Castro was held June 28, 1987.

Sixty-one percent of babies born out of wedlock: from *Bohemia*, "Marriages without papers," May 31, 1991, page 7. Chart shows 61.2 percent of all newborns were born out of wedlock, while 37.2 were born of married couples and the remainder from "Other" sources, presumably single mothers.

Figure of 160,000 abortions a year: from *Juventud Rebelde*, quoted in *El Nuevo Herald*, story by Pablo Alfonso, March 4, 1991.

"Sculptured object" exhibit and incident that led to its closing: author's interview with artist Angel Delgado in Havana, October 27, 1991.

Cuba's Roman Catholic Church, figures of Cubans attending church, estimate of 250 priests and their situation: from author's interviews with Vicar of Havana and former Secretary General of Cuba's Council of Bishops, Msgr. Carlos Manuel de Céspedes, in Havana, April 5, 1991.

Cuba's infant mortality rate of 11 per 1,000 births, Cuba's literacy rate of 98 percent, low school dropout rates, 40,000 physicians, 300,000 teachers: from Fidel Castro, in meeting with Brazilian intellectuals, quoted in *Fidel en Brasil*, Havana: Editora Politica, 1990, pages 127–129.

CHAPTER 5

Description of U.S. invasion of Panama: based on author's reporting in Panama during the 1989 U.S. military intervention and interviews in Havana with former Cuban ambassador to Panama, Lázaro Mora (May 28 and November 4, 1991). Also, *Panama: The Whole Story*, Kevin Buckley, New York: Simon & Schuster, 1991.

Telephone dialogue between Cuban ambassador Lázaro Mora and Noriega's secretary Marcela Tasón, meeting at Cuban embassy on eve of invasion: from author's interview with Mora in Havana, November 4, 1991.

Panama's official exports to Cuba: "Panama Lets U.S. Forces Sidestep Trade Blockade," Christopher Marquis, the *Miami Herald*, January 14, 1990.

Noriega–CIA cooperation, copy machine at Omar Torrijos airport: from author's interview with Maj. Felipe Camargo, former officer of Panama's G-2, at El Renacer prison, Panama, May 23, 1990; and former Noriega intelligence aide José Blandón in New York, December 5, 1987.

Size and timing of first Cuban covert military aid to Noriega: from classified documents from the Joint Debriefing Center, 470th Military Intelligence Brigade, U.S. Southern Command, Panama. In secret reports No. 9 and 84, Noriega's liaison with Castro, Maj. Felipe Camargo, places his trip to request Cuban military aid in early 1988. Camargo's story is by all accounts accurate, but misplaced in time. According to the Panamanian air force travel logs and Maj. Augusto Villalaz, who piloted the aircraft that took Camargo to Cuba, the first trip to pick up Cuban weapons took place on December 7, 1987, three months before Noriega's drug indictment.

Capt. Felipe Camargo's conversation with Castro requesting weapons, Castro's Panamanian resistance plan and suggestions to form Dignity Battalions: from classified reports No. 9 and 38 of the Joint Debriefing Center, 470th Military Intelligence Brigade, U.S. Southern Command, Panama, and author's interview with Camargo at El Renacer prison, Panama, on May 23, 1990.

Villalaz-Camargo flights to Havana to pick up weapons, meeting in Havana, second flight to pick up $50 million: from author's interview with Maj. Augusto Villalaz in Miami on January 31, 1991; and interview with Maj. Felipe Camargo at El Renacer prison, Panama, May 23, 1990.

Cuban training by Tío Pepe, Rogelio and Eladio in Panama, Cuba's help to set up new Panamanian intelligence service: from classified documents of the Joint Debriefing Center, 470th Military Intelligence Brigade, U.S. Southern Command, Panama, and author's interviews with senior Panamanian and Cuban officials.

Noriega seeks SA-7 missiles from Cuba, Libya, the Soviet Union and the PLO: from classified documents of the Joint Debriefing Center, 470th Military Intelligence Brigade, U.S. Southern Command, Panama; and author's interviews with former Panamanian intelligence major Felipe Camargo at El Renacer prison, Panama, on May 23, 1990, and former Noriega aide Luis Gómez in Havana, September 6, 1991.

Cuban Politburo ideology and foreign relations chief Carlos Aldana's quote on missiles: from author's interview with Aldana in Havana, November 8, 1991.

CHAPTER 6

Fidel Castro preached moderation to Sandinista leaders, recommended multiparty system, respect for Roman Catholic Church: author's interview with former Nicaraguan president Daniel Ortega, in Managua, Nicaragua, March 6, 1991.

Cuban military presence in Nicaragua, at least 3,000 of the 9,000 Cubans in Nicaragua were assigned to military: from U.S. State Department and U.S. Department of Defense background paper, "Nicaragua's Military Build-up and Support for Central American Subversion," July 18, 1984, page 11. Cubans at Nicaraguan Interior Ministry: from U.S. Department of State, "Inside the Sandinista Regime: A Special Investigator's Perspective," February 1986, page 16.

Early Sandinista war tactic, Gen. Humberto Ortega's trip to Havana in late 1983 in search for help, seeking Cuban brigade: author's interviews with former Humberto Ortega aide Maj. Roger Miranda Bengoechea in Miami, June 17, 1990, and May 20, 1991; and former Sandinista air force chief Col. Javier Pichardo Ramírez, in Managua, Nicaragua, March 1, 1991.

Cuban-Nicaragua plan to invade Central America: from author's interviews with former Humberto Ortega aide Maj. Roger Miranda Bengoechea in Miami on June 17, 1990, and May 20, 1991, and with Cuban defector Brig. Gen. Rafael del Pino, who also describes the story in his book *Proa a la Libertad*, Mexico: Editorial Planeta, 1990, page 260.

Cuban economic support for Nicaragua: from author's interview with former Sandinista *comandante* and Economic Cooperation Minister Henry Ruiz, in Managua, Nicaragua, March 7, 1991, and other Sandinista and Cuban officials.

Cuban-Nicaraguan differences over Esquipulas agreement: from author's interviews with four Sandinista *comandantes*, top Cuban Foreign Ministry officials and Julio Carranza, of Cuba's Centro de Estudios de America, in Havana. For a complete analysis of Cuba's opposition to the 1987 Esquipulas Agreement, see "La Politica Cubana hacia Centroamerica," Juan Valdez Paz and Julio Carranza Valdes, *Cuadernos de Nuestra America, Centro de Estudios sobre America*, vol. VII, July–December 1990, page 201.

Nicaraguan-Cuban quarrel over Cuban ambassador Julián Lopez: from author's interviews with two former Sandinista *comandantes* in Nicaragua in March 1991. Appointment of new Cuban ambassador Norberto Hernandez: from Nicaraguan daily *Barricada*, November 25, 1987.

Sandinistas' decision to call elections, meeting with Latin American presidents in Caracas: from author's interview with former Nicaraguan president Daniel Ortega in Nicaragua, March 6, 1991, and former Ortega adviser Paul Reichler, in Washington, February 14, 1991.

Castro-Ortega meeting after Central American summit, anecdote about Castro's warning that Sandinistas may lose elections: from author's interview with former Nicaraguan president Daniel Ortega in Nicaragua, March 6, 1991, and author's interview with former Nicaraguan foreign minister Miguel D'Escoto, May 21, 1991.

Lunch at Cuban foreign minister Isidoro Malmierca's house, Mora's suggestion that Sandinistas would lose: from author's interviews with Cuban Foreign Ministry Latin American director Lázaro Mora in Havana, May 28 and November 4, 1991, and former Sandinista foreign minister Miguel D'Escoto, in telephone interview from Nicaragua, May 21, 1991.

Castro's statement about Nicaragua's "right-wing" economic policy: this was made to the ambassador of a major Western European country, who recalled the remark in a July 1991 interview with the author.

Cubans' efforts to persuade the Soviet Union against Nicaraguan elections:

from author's interviews with former Soviet Foreign Ministry Latin American Affairs director Yuri Pavlov, in Miami, November 27 and December 2, 1991.

Carlos Aldana's admission that Cuba opposed Nicaraguan elections: from author's interview with Aldana in Havana, November 8, 1991.

Pavlov's quote, "They wanted money to put consumer goods in the stores . . .": from *Time* magazine, June 4, 1991. The June 4, 1991, *Time* magazine story about the Aronson-Pavlov talks on Nicaragua is the best and most detailed report on the U.S.-Soviet talks on Central America at the time.

Pavlov's quote, "The Sandinistas also knew . . .": from author's interview with Pavlov in Miami, November 27, 1991.

Secret mid-1989 talks in which Castro informed Sandinistas he would have to stop food, medicine and oil shipments: from author's interview with former Sandinista *comandante* and Economic Cooperation Minister Henry Ruiz, in Managua, Nicaragua, March 7, 1991.

Castro-Ruiz argument over Cuban oil shipments: from author's interview with former Sandinista *comandante* Henry Ruiz in Managua, March 7, 1991. Castro had obliquely referred to the cutbacks in a speech on March 7, 1990, U.S. State Department Foreign Broadcast Information Service—Latin America, March 8, 1990, page 7.

Dispute over military honors to Div. Gen. Arnaldo Ochoa: from "Cuba Loses Allure for Nicaraguans," Mark Uhlig, the *New York Times*, January 18, 1990. Additional information from *La Prensa*, Nicaragua, March 12, 1986, and Nicaragua's army press office.

Cuban-Nicaraguan split over Salvadoran guerrillas, Cuba's Piñeiro visit to Managua: from author's interview with a top Sandinista *comandante* who was directly involved in relations with Cuba, in Nicaragua, March 1991.

Chilly atmosphere at New Year's Eve party, from "Cuba Loses Allure for Nicaraguans," Mark Uhlig, the *New York Times*, January 18, 1990, and author's interview with former Sandinista vice-minister Victor Hugo Tinoco, in Managua, Nicaragua, March 5, 1991.

Daniel Ortega's quote, "The time has come to put away the olive green," and Bayardo Arce's reference to Sweden: from "Nicaragua Picks Future," Christopher Marquis, the *Miami Herald*, February 25, 1990.

Castro's conversation with García Márquez about Nicaraguan elections: from author's interview with García Márquez, in Bogotá, Colombia, April 4, 1990.

Sandinista *comandante* Bayardo Arce's statements about Castro's misgivings: from author's interview with Arce in Managua, Nicaragua, March 7, 1991.

Castro's speech to the Confederation of Cuban Workers: U.S. State Department Foreign Broadcast Information Service—Latin America, January 30, 1990, page 10.

Cuban military advisers' departure without formal ceremony: from author's
interview with former Sandinista air force chief Col. Javier Pichardo
Ramírez, in Managua, Nicaragua, March 1, 1991.

Vote at United Nations Human Rights Commission in Geneva: *El Nuevo
Herald*, March 7 and 8, 1990.

Castro's speech to the Federation of Cuban Women: U.S. State Department
Foreign Broadcast Information Service—Latin America, March 8, 1990,
page 4.

CHAPTER 7

Estimate of 5,000 Soviet technicians in Cuba before 1990 pullout: from
Soviet embassy sources in Havana. Estimate of 7,700 Soviet military in
Cuba: from testimony by U.S. Deputy Assistant Secretary of State for
Inter-American Affairs Michael Kozak before House Committee on For-
eign Affairs hearing, "Cuba and the United States: Thirty Years of
Hostility and Beyond," August 2, 1989.

Estimates of Soviet subsidies to Cuba: Testimony of U.S. Assistant Secretary of State Bernard Aronson, June 20, 1991, before the House subcommittee on Western Hemisphere affairs. He said that Soviet military
aid to Cuba in the late 1980s was worth $1.3 billion a year.

Cuba's dependence on Soviet raw materials, Soviet-sponsored public works,
figure of more than 70 percent of Cuba's worldwide foreign trade in
1989 was with the Soviet Union, while another 17 percent was with
other Soviet bloc countries: from Cuba's Foreign Trade Ministry, given
to the author by Cuba's Vice-Minister of Foreign Trade Miguel Castillo
in Havana in April 1991.

Cuban government's administrative bureaucracy grew from 2 percent in 1973
to 7 percent in 1985: from author's interview with economist José Luis
Rodriguez, head of Cuba's Center of World Economy Research (CIEM)
in Havana, April 19, 1991.

Gorbachev, Castro, García Márquez conversation at reception: from author's
interview with García Márquez in Bogotá, Colombia, July 4, 1991.

Castro's contacts with Gorbachev before 1985: from Castro's interview with
Italian journalist Gianni Mina in *Habla Fidel*, Argentina: Editorial Sudamericana, 1988, page 141.

Castro scolding Spanish reporter, admonishing Peter Jennings, Dan Rather
and Tom Brokaw: from "Split Unhealed by Soviet-Cuban Unity Show,"
Alfonso Chardy, the *Miami Herald*, April 6, 1989; and "Activists in Cuba
Seek Franqueza," Alfonso Chardy, the *Miami Herald*, April 9, 1989.

Yuri Pavlov's quote on Castro press conference: from author's interview with
Pavlov in Miami, November 27, 1991.

Cuba's troubles buying refrigerators and washing machines in Soviet
Union: from author's interview with Ramón Gonzalez Vergara, Cuba's
former ambassador to the Soviet-Cuban Council for Mutual Economic

Assistance, in Miami, December 19, 1990, shortly after Gonzalez Vergara defected to the United States. Also, from Soviet Trade Office in Havana, where officials confirmed the stories and offered additional data.

Castro's speech to COMECON meeting, "It used to be customary in COMECON . . .": from Castro's January 29, 1990, speech before the Sixteenth Workers Federation Congress, in U.S. State Department Foreign Broadcast Information Service—Latin America, January 30, 1990, page 1.

Visits by Leonid Abalkin and Konstantin Katushev to Cuba, trade talks in Moscow: from author's interviews with Cuba's Vice-Minister of Foreign Trade Miguel Castillo in Havana, April 12, 1991, former Soviet Foreign Ministry Latin American Affairs director Yuri Pavlov in Miami, November 17, 1991, and Soviet trade sources in Havana.

Cuban Foreign Trade Minister Ricardo Cabrisas's statement about 25,000 Soviet organizations: from *Granma*, January 21, 1991, reproduced in U.S. State Department Foreign Broadcast Information Service—Latin America, February 25, 1991, page 6.

Carlos Rafael Rodriguez's remark about growing uncertainty: from "Cuba Will Endure Changing Relationship with Soviets," Carlos Rafael Rodriguez, *New Perspectives Quarterly*, December 1990.

CHAPTER 8

Plan to mobilize 200,000 Havana residents to the countryside: from Fidel Castro statements published in *Granma*, September 25, 1990.

Fidel Castro's proclamation of the "era of the bicycle," from *Bohemia*, April 26, 1991.

Bohemia editorial on bicycles: from *Bohemia*, April 26, 1991.

Soviets were supposed to ship 120,000 tons of animal fat a year: from Radio Rebelde, quoted in "Cuba por dentro," Pablo Alfonso, *El Nuevo Herald*, June 7, 1991.

Bohemia deodorant recipe: from *Bohemia*, March 1991.

Cuba's health system deterioration: from author's interviews in Havana. Dr. Rubén Pineda's quote from "La Medicina en Cuba," *El Nuevo Herald*, June 23, 1991.

More than 1,000 rafters arrived in Florida in the first half of 1991: from "In Search of a Fresh Start," Lizette Alvarez, the *Miami Herald*, July 27, 1991.

Balsero farewell parties in Jaimanitas: from "Voyage of Desperation for Cubans," Mimi Whitefield, the *Miami Herald*, June 2, 1991.

Queen Elizabeth's yacht picking up rafter: from "Cuban Rescued by Queen's Yacht," the *Miami Herald*, May 29, 1991. Surfer story: from the *Miami Herald*, March 3, 1990.

Reuters reporter stumbling onto rafter: from "Snorkeling Correspondent

Finds Lone Rafter after Aborted Escape," Pascal Fletcher, Reuters, published by the *Miami Herald* on October 8, 1991.

Youth statistics, from *Granma*, quoted by *El Nuevo Herald*, December 24, 1990; and "La Juventud en la Revolución Cubana," Juan Luis Martin, *Cuadernos de Nuestra America*, Havana, July–December 1990, page 139.

CHAPTER 9

Interviews with Canek Sanchez Guevara: on October 29 and November 1, 1991, at his home in Havana.

Texts from elementary school reading book: from *Lectura I*, Ministerio de Educación, Havana: Editorial Pueblo y Educación, 1975. The book was reprinted several times; its 1986 edition had the same text.

Pablo Guevara's statements: from author's interview with Pablo Guevara in Havana on October 28, 1991.

Che Guevara's letter to daughter Hilda: from *Ernesto Che Guevara: Obras 1957-1967*, Havana: Casa de las Americas, page 694.

Hilda Guevara statements: from author's interviews with Hilda Guevara in Havana on October 29, and November 1 and 6, 1991.

"Nati" Revuelta's story, Fidel Castro's statement, "Nati missed the boat . . .": from *Guerrilla Prince*, Georgie Anne Geyer, Boston: Little, Brown and Company, 1991, pages 147 and 151.

Spanish magazine story about Alina: "Alina Castro, La hija discola de Fidel," in *Tiempo*, Madrid, September 30, 1991.

Alina Fernandez Revuelta's statements: from author's interviews with Fernandez Revuelta in Havana, November 10, 11 and 12, 1991.

CHAPTER 10

Castro's caviar quote: *Fidel*, Gianni Mina, Mexico: Compania Editorial Edivision, 1991, page 198.

Tourism figures: from author's interview with Cubanacan president Abraham Maciques, in Havana, April 28, 1991.

Carlos Pereda quote to *Bohemia*, "Business with Cuba: Better, Impossible": *Bohemia*, May 10, 1991.

36,000 enrolled in hospitality courses: "All Questions Have Answers," *Juventud Rebelde*, May 12, 1991.

Castro's quote about Cuban scientists: Fidel's year-end address to the National Assembly, quoted by AP, February 25, 1991.

Castro's Option Zero quote: "Castro comenta crisis Sovietica," Pablo Alfonso, *El Nuevo Herald*, December 22, 1990.

Cuba's exports to Latin America and the Caribbean, 3.5 percent for 1989: from Comité Estatal de Estadisticas, Anuario Estadistico de Cuba, 1989.

Cuba's trade figures: from Pedro Monreal of Center of American Studies, Havana, and Sergio Roca, "Cuba y la nueva economia internacional," July 1990.

CHAPTER 11

Statistic of nonproductive jobs: from *Censo de Población y Viviendas de 1981*, Comité Estatal de Estadisticas; vol. XVI, book I, July 1983, table 14, page CCIX.

Figure of 304,000 in "other intellectual work occupations," Ibid, page CCXII.

Llamamiento document by Central Committee: "El Futuro de nuestra patria será un eterno Baraguá," *Editora Politica*, Havana, March 15, 1990.

Carlos Rafael Rodriguez, "five difficult years": interview by Arturo Alape, *Cuadernos de Nuestra America*, vol. VIII, no. 16, January–June 1991, page 161.

Castro's hopes that hard-liners in Soviet Union would prevail: from author's interviews with two senior Cuban officials in separate interviews before the August 1991 Soviet coup attempt. The two officials said Castro hoped Gorbachev would adopt more "realistic"—hard-line—policies.

Fidel's quote on opposition organizing itself: *Fidel*, Gianni Mina, Mexico: Compania Editorial Edivision, 1991, page 141.

Attorney General's prison estimates: "Cuba says it has less than 200 political prisoners," Reuters, August 17, 1990.

Elizardo Sanchez's prisoner figures: interview with author in Havana, September 4, 1991.

More than half of all Cubans had been born after the revolution: *Censo de Población y Viviendas de 1981*, Comité Estatal de Estadisticas, Oficina Nacional del Censo, vol. XVI.

Race statistics: Cuba's 1981 Census had put the island's nonwhite population at 34 percent, but government officials admit that the figure is unreliable: the Census Bureau had asked Cubans whether they were black, white or mulatto, and an overwhelming majority of mulattos—living in a country with a history of endemic racial discrimination—had classified themselves as white. I based my estimate on unofficial government estimates and those of Carlos Moore, in *Castro, the Blacks and Africa* (Los Angeles: Center for African-American Studies, UCLA, 1988), who calculated Cuba's nonwhite population at 58 percent in 1990, up from 45 percent in 1959. See also "Exiles Plans Out of Touch with Cuba's Blacks," David Hancock, the *Miami Herald*, February 22, 1990.

Figure of nonwhites in Communist Party Politburo: from "Radio Martí Program, Cuba-Quarterly Situation Report," Washington, D.C., USIA, May 1986, appendixes II and III.

CANF, Mas Canosa on properties: "Divining Cuba's Future," the *Miami Herald*, September 29, 1991.

Paid ad by National Association of Ranchers: from *El Nuevo Herald*, October 18, 1991.

Castro quote on Miami exiles seeking properties: Castro's address, October

10, 1991, to the inaugural session of the Fourth Congress of the Communist Party, *Granma International*, November 3, 1991, page 26. Other quote is from Castro's December 27, 1991 address to the National Assembly, quoted by Spanish agency EFE, Havana, December 29, 1991.

Orlando Bosch rally, the *Miami Herald*: "Send Guns, Cash to Cuba, Bosch Urges Exiles at Rally," October 12, 1991.

Orlando Bosch's statements on airliner bombing, killing of Olympic fencing team members, justification of violence: from author's interview with Orlando Bosch in Miami, October 19, 1991.

Gov. Bob Martinez defending Bosch: "Martinez Attends Meeting on Bosch," the *Miami Herald*, July 15, 1988.

Mas Canosa quote "Americans and Cubans . . .": from the *Wall Street Journal*, May 11, 1990.

Mas Canosa quote, "because 10 to 15 percent of our people have been living . . .": "Divining Cuba's Future," the *Miami Herald*, September 29, 1991.

Mas Canosa May 20 speech, reprinted from CANF's *Fundación* magazine, July 1991, and tape of speech provided by CANF to author.

CANF President Francisco "Pepe" Hernandez's statement about private conversation with Ronald Reagan: from "*Ronald Reagan en Miami*," an article written by Hernandez for the CANF's *Fundación* magazine, July 1991.

Mas Canosa's Mercedes-Benz car: "U.S. Customs Seizing of Cuban Art as Contraband Stirs Miami Furor," José de Cordoba, the *Wall Street Journal*, August 7, 1989. Mas Canosa did not return more than half a dozen phone calls to confirm this report.

Cuban Vice-Minister Ramón Sanchez Parodi's claim that CANF was created by Reagan Administration: from author's interview with Sanchez Parodi in Havana, April 29, 1991. Constantine Menges's plan: from author's interview with Menges in Miami, January 7, 1992, and "Regime in Exile Proposed for Cuba," the *Miami Herald*, January 8, 1992.

Mas Canosa's appearance in Oliver North's diaries: diary entry, in "The Iran-Contra Connection," Celia Dugger, the *Miami Herald*, July 21, 1988.

George Bush's visit to Miami, dedication of Avenida Ronald Reagan, and Miami mayor Xavier Suarez's comments: from "Bush Arrives to Dedicate Ronald Reagan Ave.," Tom Fiedler, the *Miami Herald*, June 18, 1987.

Jeb Bush's call to President Bush, voting at U.N. Commission for Human Rights, and comments by Otto Reich and Jeb Bush: from "Clout of 'Bright Shining Star' Delights Some, Angers Others," Christopher Marquis, the *Miami Herald*, March 25, 1991.

Mas Canosa's quote, "We're totally opposed to a U.S. military intervention": from author's interview with Mas Canosa in Miami, September

20, 1991. Mas Canosa did not respond to more than half a dozen subsequent phone calls from the author to clarify other points referred to in this chapter.

Mas Canosa's duel incident, quote, "I'm going to prove to the Cubans . . .": from "Leader's Zeal Powers Exile Lobby," Celia W. Dugger, the *Miami Herald*, April 10, 1988.

Mas Canosa fight with brother, court decision: "Mas Ordered to Pay Brother $1.2 Million," Donma Gehrke, the *Miami Herald*, October 27, 1990, and author's interview in Miami.

Lawsuit by José Luis Rodriguez against Mas Canosa: from "Exile's Suit Exposes Rift in Anti-Castro Group," Gerardo Reyes, the *Miami Herald*, November 24, 1991.

CHAPTER 12

Estimates on number of Santería Babalaos in Cuba: from author's interview with Claudia Mola, director of the museum of Havana's House of Africa, in Havana, September 4, 1991.

Figure of Roman Catholic priests in Cuba: author's interview with Havana vicar Msgr. Carlos Manuel de Céspedes, July 2, 1991.

Examples of Babalaos' contention that Fidel was blessed by the Gods: from author's separate interviews in Havana with Santería experts Natalia Bolivar and Miguel Barnet on April 4, 1991, and from "Revolution, Charisma and Santería: The Cuban Case," a paper by University of Mexico professor Nelson P. Valdes.

Dove scene on Fidel's shoulder: from *Fidel: A Critical Portrait*, Tad Szulc, New York: Avon Books, 1986, page 516.

Followers of Afro-Cuban religions described as potential criminals in the sixties: from *Castro, the Blacks and Africa*, Carlos Moore, Los Angeles: Center for Afro-American Studies, UCLA, 1988, page 102.

Yoruba Pope's visit to Cuba: EFE Spanish news agency story published by *El Nuevo Herald*, June 28, 1987, and *Granma Weekly Review*, June 29, 1987.

"These religious expressions . . .": Academy of Sciences Social-Religious Studies' Department booklet, *The Revolution in Culture*, chapter V, "Thoughts about the Religious Influence of Africa in Cuba," Havana: Editorial Academia, 1990, page 121.

Fidel's quote on church hierarchy: from "Cuban Church Cancels Plans for Pope's Visit Until Date Set," the *Miami Herald*, May 16, 1990.

By 1990, there were 33,000 baptisms at the Archdiocese of Havana: Msgr. Carlos Manuel de Céspedes, from Interpress Service story published by *El Excelsior*, Mexico, July 3, 1991.

Enrique "Enriquito" Hernandez Armenteros's quotes about Catholic Church, Fidel Castro, etc.: from author's interview with "Enriquito," in Havana, April 9, 1991.

Former MININT captain Enrique García Diaz's estimate that about half of Cuba's Babalaos work for the state security: from author's interview with Enrique García Diaz in August 1991. García Diaz defected to the United States in 1989.

Dozens of Abakuá secret societies, down from 400 at the beginning of the century: from author's interviews in Havana with researchers from the Ethnographic Museum of Guanabacoa.

CHAPTER 13

"Total support from Moscow": from Soviet Foreign Ministry source familiar with the meeting, in September 1991.

Carlos Aldana quote, "Absolutely none" (in footnote): from author's interview with Carlos Aldana in Havana, November 8, 1991.

Yanayev quote, "absolutely unacceptable": the *Miami Herald*, August 20, 1991.

The Cuban communique indicating that it was "not the task of the Cuban government to judge events in the USSR," reference to "the Soviet authorities": from Reuters News Service, August 22, 1991.

"We had been led to error": from author's interview with Carlos Aldana in Havana, November 8, 1991.

Footnote on Pavlov's meetings with exiles: from "Exiles Plan Talks on Cuba in Moscow," the *Miami Herald*, October 15, 1990, and author's interview with Yuri Pavlov in Miami, December 3, 1991.

Kremlin's post-coup internal document on Cuba, recommending "drastic reduction of Soviet-Cuban cooperation": from "Soviets See Drastic Cuts in Cuba Aid," Juan Tamayo, the *Miami Herald*, September 26, 1991.

Alexander Machov's visit to Miami: from Machov's letter to the *Miami Herald*, September 19, 1990.

Visit by Russian Parliament members: the *Miami Herald*, December 10, 1991, and author's interview with Alexander Machov in Miami, December 9, 1991.

Sugar shipment incident: from author's interview with Carlos Aldana in Havana, November 8, 1991.

Carlos Aldana quote on Castro's reaction to Soviet Brigade pullout: author's interview with Carlos Aldana in Havana, November 8, 1991.

Cuban Foreign Ministry statement on Gorbachev's Soviet Brigade announcement: *Granma Weekly Review*, September 22, 1991, and "Cuba Reacts Angrily," the *Miami Herald*, September 12, 1991.

Nikolayenko incident: from author's interviews with Soviet diplomatic sources in Havana, November 1991, and author's telephone interview with U.S. Assistant Secretary of State for Inter-American Affairs Bernard Aronson, November 21, 1991.

Carlos Rafael Rodriguez quote on socialism: *Cuadernos de Nuestra America*, vol. VIII, no. 16, page 178, January–June 1991.

Maria Elena Cruz Varela statement on her bag: author's interview with Cruz Varela in Havana, September 5, 1991.

Concertation statement: "Oposición en Cuba exige democracia," *El Nuevo Herald*, October 8, 1991.

Julio García Luis quote, "We must learn from the Soviet experience . . .": from García Luis lecture at Seminar for Cuban Journalists, in Machurrucutu, Cuba, September 1, 1991.

Fidel Castro quote on concessions: from Castro's speech at the 30th anniversary of the Girón Victory, on April 19, 1991, published days later by *Juventud Rebelde* as an undated supplement.

Roberto Robaina quote at April 4 speech: from *Granma*, April 5, 1991.

Fidel Castro quote from April 4 speech, "We congratulate comrade Robertico Robaina . . .": from *Granma*, April 5, 1991.

Fidel Castro had given a green light to the plan: from author's separate interviews with three members of Castro's inner circle in Havana, April 1991.

Escalona quotes on prime minister, referendum: from author's interview with Escalona on April 12, 1991, at Escalona's office. In a second, shorter conversation with the author in early September 1991, Escalona reiterated that the plan was "alive and well."

Raúl quote, "What worries me more . . .": quoted by UPEC president Julio García Luis, a member of the organizing committee. Author's interview with García Luis, September 5, 1991.

CHAPTER 14

Esteban Lazo's opening speech at the Fourth Congress: from Radio Havana Cuba broadcast transcripts and U.S. State Department Foreign Broadcast Information Service—Latin America, October 11, 1991.

Raúl's disappearance: "Rumors Rife after Raúl Castro Misses Brother's Speech," Lee Hockstader, *Washington Post*, August 8, 1991.

Castro's quote, "I fulfilled my historic duty . . ." and other quotes at inaugural speech at the Fourth Congress of the Communist Party: from Cuba's weekly *Bohemia* magazine, October 23, 1991.

Castro's quote about being a "slave" of the revolution: from Reuters News Service, September 25, 1991, reprinted in the *Miami Herald*, September 26, 1991; also, in Spanish magazine *Tiempo*, October 7, 1991. Castro said, "For me, power is like a form of slavery, I feel like a slave."

Castro's quote, "Destiny has turned us . . .": from Castro's closing speech to the Fourth Congress of the Communist Party: official translation appearing in *Granma International*, November 3, 1991.

"The question of the party's influential role . . .": from "Castro Attacks Removal from Power of Soviet Communist Party," Reuters News Service, October 11, 1991.

Castro's quote about Western democracy being "complete garbage": from

Cuban television, October 14, 1991; picked up by Spanish news agency EFE in "Fidel Castro: La democracia burguesa es una basura completa," October 14, 1991, and partially quoted by Reuters News Service, October 14, 1991.

Castro's quote, "The most democratic political congress ever held anywhere in the world," from Castro's speech at the end of the Fourth Congress at the Antonio Maceo square in Santiago: published by *Granma International*, November 3, 1991, page 28.

Scientists speaking at Fourth Congress: in *Granma*, Sunday, October 13, 1991, and Radio Rebelde broadcast, Saturday, October 12, 1991.

Pedro Martinez Pirez proposal on press resolution: *Granma*, October 13, 1991, page 6, and author's interviews with Martinez Pirez in Havana, November 1991.

Fidel's exchange with Pinar del Río delegate and speech on farmers markets, Castro's October 13, 1991, speech to the Fourth Congress: published by *Granma* on October 29, 1991, page 3; U.S. State Department Foreign Broadcast Information Service—Latin America, October 13, 1991

Three votes against Fidel Castro, four votes against Raúl Castro: from author's separate interviews with two participants at the Fourth Congress of the Communist Party, in Havana, November 1991.

Resolutions on the Communist Party Platform: from *Granma International*, October 20, 1991.

Resolutions on the National Assembly: from *Granma International*, October 20, 1991.

Resolution on the economy: from *Granma International*, October 20, 1991.

Resolution on foreign policy: from *Granma International*, October 20, 1991.

Resolution giving exceptional powers to the Central Committee: from *Granma International*, October 20, 1991.

Carlos Aldana's estimate on Cuba's economic recovery, quotes about "duty to resist": from author's interview with Carlos Aldana in Havana, November 8, 1991.

Castro's closing speech at the Fourth Congress: from *Granma International*, October 20, 1991.

CHAPTER 15

Fidel Castro's speech to the Pioneers Congress: from Cuban television broadcast and *Granma*, November 5, 1991.

Cuban celebrations for the November 7 Russian revolution anniversary: from *Granma*, November 5, 1991, and author's reporting at the Soviet-Cuban Friendship Association meeting November 7, 1991.

Footnote on Castro's speech to the National Assembly: from U.S. State Department Foreign Broadcast Information Service—Latin America, January 2, 1992.

Castro's quote, "This is the most difficult period . . .": from Fidel Castro's address to the National Assembly, U.S. State Department Foreign Broadcast Information Service—Latin America, January 2, 1992, page 13.

Santería forecast for 1992: from author's telephone interview with a top Cuban Santería expert familiar with the ceremony, January 12, 1992.

Fidel Castro's quotes about prostitution: from Castro's December 9, 1991 speech to the Federation of Secondary Students, published in a report of U.S. State Department Foreign Broadcast Information Service—Latin America, December 13, 1991, page 9.

Comodoro Hotel manager's letter: Dated Havana, December 10, 1990, but continued to be placed in guest rooms in late 1991. It was signed by Armando Añel Puig, general manager.

Footnote on armed incursion by Miami Cuban exiles, Miami Spanish-language radio collecting 100,000 signatures: from "Cuba Orders Firing Squad for Three Miami Exile Raiders," the *Miami Herald*, January 12, 1992.

Bibliography

Bolivar de Arostegui, Natalia. *Los Orishas en Cuba*. Havana: Ediciones Union de Artistas y Escritores de Cuba, 1990.

Buckley, Kevin. *Panama: The Whole Story*. New York: Simon & Schuster, 1991.

Bosch, Adriana. *Orlando Bosch: El Hombre Que Yo Conozco*. Miami: Editorial Sibi, 1988.

Castro, Fidel. *Fidel en Brasil*. Havana: Editora Politica, 1990.

Castro, Fidel. *Rectificación, Selección Tematica*. Havana: Editora Politica, 1990.

Causa No. 1: Fin de la Conexión Cubana. Havana: Ediciones Plus, Editorial José Martí, 1989.

Del Aguila, Juan M. *Cuba: Dilemmas of a Revolution*. Boulder, Colorado, and London: Westview Press, 1988.

Del Pino, Rafael. *Proa a la Libertad*. Mexico: Editorial Planeta, 1990.

Dominguez, Jorge. *Cuba: Order and Revolution*. Cambridge: The Belknap Press, Harvard University Press, 1978.

Falk, Pamela S. *Cuban Foreign Policy: Caribbean Tempest*. Lexington, Mass.: Lexington Books, 1986.

Fermoselle, Rafael. *Cuban Leadership After Castro: Biographies of Cuba's Top Generals*. Miami: Ediciones Universal, 1987.

———. *The Evolution of the Cuban Military: 1492-1986*. Miami: Ediciones Universal, 1987.

Franqui, Carlos. *Diary of the Cuban Revolution*. New York: Viking Penguin, 1980.

Geyer, Georgie Anne. *Guerrilla Prince: The Untold Story of Fidel Castro*. Boston: Little, Brown and Company, 1991.

Horowitz, Irving Louis. *Cuban Communism*. New Brunswick: Transaction Publishers, 1989.

Hudson, Rex A. *Castro's Americas Department*. The Cuban American National Foundation, 1988.

Kirk, John M. *José Martí: Mentor of the Cuban Nation*. Tampa: University Presses of Florida, 1983.

La Religion en la Cultura. Havana: Editorial Academia, 1990.

Llovio Menéndez, José Luis. *Insider: My Hidden Life as a Revolutionary in Cuba*. New York: Bantam Books, 1988.

Loory, Stuart H., and Ann Imse. *Seven Days that Shook the World*. Atlanta: CNN Reports, Turner Publishing Inc., 1991.

Luque Escalona, Roberto. *Fidel: El Juicio de la Historia*. Mexico: Producción Editorial Dante, 1990.

Mañon, Melvin, and Juan Benemelis. *Juicio a Fidel*. Santo Domingo, Dominican Republic: Editora Taller, 1990.

Martí, José. *Letras Fieras*. Havana: Editorial Letras Cubanas, 1985.

Mina, Gianni. *Fidel*. Mexico: Compania Editorial Edivision, 1991.

———. *Habla Fidel*. Buenos Aires: Editorial Sudamericana, 1988.

Moore, Carlos. *Castro, the Blacks and Africa*. Los Angeles: Center for Afro-American Studies, University of California, 1988.

Nolan, David. *FSLN: The Ideology of the Sandinistas and the Nicaraguan Revolution*. Miami: University of Miami, 1984.

Preston, Julia. "The trial that shook Cuba," *The New York Review of Books*, December 7, 1989.

Riefe, Robert H. *Moscow, Havana, and National Liberation in Latin America*. Miami: University of Miami North-South Center, 1991.

Sanchez Perez, Manuel. *Quien Manda en Cuba: Las Estructuras del Poder*. Miami: Ediciones Universal, 1989.

Smith, Wayne S. *Portrait of Cuba*. Atlanta: Turner Publishing, Inc., 1991.

Suchlicky, Jaime, and others. *The Cuban Military under Castro*. Miami: University of Miami Institute of Interamerican Studies, 1989.

Szulc, Tad. *Fidel: A Critical Portrait*. New York: Avon, 1986.

Thomas, Hugh S., Georges Fauriol, and Juan Carlos Weiss. *The Cuban Revolution 25 Years Later*. Boulder, Colorado: Westview Press, 1984.

Timerman, Jacobo. *Cuba: A Journey*. New York: Alfred A. Knopf, 1990.

Index

Picture Credits

Lesbia Jorge 2, 20
Courtesy of *La Semana*, Bogotá 7
Andres Oppenheimer 7, 9, 10, 11, 14, 15, 16
Courtesy of the *Miami Herald*/Marice Cohn Band 8, 13, 17, 18, 19, 21,
    26, 31, 32.
Courtesy of Center of Genetic Engineering and Biotechnology 12
Courtesy of *Granma* 22 (all)
Courtesy of CANF (Cuban American National Foundation) 23
Courtesy of the *Miami Herald*/Albert Coya 24
Courtesy of the *Miami Herald* 25
Courtesy of Panama Defense Forces' Press Office 27
AP LaserPhoto 28
Courtesy of the *Miami Herald*/David Walters 29, 30